THE TRANSFORMATION OF THE ENGLISH NOVEL, 1890–1930

The Transformation of the English Novel, 1890–1930

Daniel R. Schwarz

Professor of English
Cornell University

MACMILLAN
PRESS

First published 1989

Published by
THE MACMILLAN PRESS LTD
Houndmills, Basingstoke, Hampshire RG21 2XS
and London
Companies and representatives
throughout the world

Printed in Hong Kong

British Library Cataloguing in Publication Data
Schwarz, Daniel R.
The transformation of the English novel,
1890–1930.
1. English fiction–20th century–
History and criticism
I. Title
823'.912'09   PR881
ISBN 0-333-44707-7

4|4|89

For My Sons, David and Jeffrey, and for My Brother, Robert

Contents

vii

Acknowledgements

As always, I am indebted to my Cornell students and colleagues. The opportunity in 1984 and 1986 to direct National Endowment for the Humanities Summer Seminars for College Teachers entitled 'Critical Perspectives on the early Twentieth Century British Novel' gave me two intellectual communities to test many of my ideas; I owe a great debt to the participants. I am also grateful to the participants in my two National Endowment for the Humanities Seminars for Secondary School teachers on Joyce's *Ulysses*.

I should like to acknowledge the friendship and encouragement of Mike Abrams, Mike Colacurcio, Ian Gregor, Tom Hill, and Phillip Marcus. Joanne Frye provided helpful advice on several chapters, and Steve Ferebee read my Woolf chapter with judiciousness and care. Some of the ideas in Chapters 7 and 8 evolved in an informal colloquium of my graduate students; I am especially indebted for conversations with my former students, Beth Newman and Caroline Webb.

Chapter 1 first appeared in *The University of Toronto Quarterly* (1982). Chapter 2 appeared in *Modern Fiction Studies* in 1972 and Chapter 6 appeared in 1983; Chapter 4 appeared in *Studies in the Novel* (1976); Chapter 5 in *Ariel* (1980), Chapter 3 was originally an essay in *Critical Approaches to Thomas Hardy* (1979), ed. Dale Kramer (Macmillan). A shorter version of chapter Seven, 'The Case for Humanistic Formalism' appeared in *Novel* (1987–88), while a version of Chapter Ten appeared in *The Journal of Narrative Technique* (1987). Parts of Chapter 8 appeared in reviews in *Modern Fiction Studies, English Literature in Transition*, and *JEGP*. I am grateful to the various editors and publishers who have let me reprint this material. The Hogarth Press and Harcourt, Brace and Jovanovich have given me permission to quote from *Mrs. Dalloway* and *To the Lighthouse*.

I am especially grateful to Jonathan Hall who has been an immense help with the proofreading and indexing; Chris Miller also played an important role in these tasks. For the past five years, I have enjoyed the secretarial support of the exceptionally able, good-natured and loyal Phillip Molock.

Introduction

The Transformation of the English Novel, 1890–1930 is part of a larger critical project that I began with *The Humanistic Heritage: Critical Theories of the English Novel from James to Hillis Miller* (1986), in which I defined the theory and method of Anglo-American novel criticism. In my next book, *Reading Joyce's 'Ulysses'* (1987), I used the principles of what I call humanistic formalism to create a dialogue between traditional and more recent theory and, most importantly, between theory and Joyce's great epic novel. My purpose is to reinvigorate the humanistic study of fiction by creating a dialogue between traditional and recent theory as well as between theory and texts. I have been called a progressive traditionalist and a pluralist, both of which terms I welcome. For me theory is important only when it enables us to think conceptually about how works behave and cohere and what they mean and signify.

The Transformation of the English Novel, 1890–1930 is divided into two major parts. Originally published as essays from 1972 to 1983, Part One shows how historical and contextual material is essential for humanistic formalism. Thus the first chapter, entitled ' "I Was the World in Which I Walked": The Transformation of the English Novel', calls into question such New Critical shibboleths as 'exit author' and the 'biographical fallacy' and discusses how the author becomes a formal presence within the text. I argue that the novels of Hardy, Lawrence, Conrad, Joyce, Forster, and Woolf represent a radical break from the past and require different critical programmes for discussing them than their predecessors. The changes in the novel reflect the authors' realization that the relative stability of the Victorian era give way to the anxiety and dubiety of the modern era. In the remaining five chapters of Part One, I discuss Hardy, Forster, and Lawrence in terms which show how these authors' struggles with their personal crises and social concerns determine their narrative techniques and modes of representation.

Changes in the novel's form and modes of representation relate to changing historical circumstances. But changes in our perception of the form of the novel also relate to changes in the way we read. Written recently, Part Two speaks of the transformation in the way we read and think about authors, readers, characters, and

1

form in the light of recent theory. In two polemical chapters – 'The Case for Humanistic Formalism' and 'Modes of Literary Inquiry: a Primer for Humanistic Formalism' – I offer an alternative to the way that the deconstructive and Marxist ethos have sought to transform literary studies. I discuss the following basic questions: How can we talk about the author as a formal presence in the work? How can thinking about a group of novels enable us to reach an understanding of literary culture? How does one speak of a period? Can one think about the 'development' or 'evolution' of the British novel and, if so, in what terms? How can one speak of the novels of this period in terms of cultural and literary history? My goal is to provide a map for the study of the English novel from Hardy through Woolf, a map that integrates critical theory, historical background, and powerful, close reading. But I also wish to demonstrate the theoretical and practical validity of a criticism that focuses on human authors, imagined worlds, and readers who think and feel.

The final three chapters of Part Two focus on the transformation of the role of the reader. I demonstrate how a pluralistic reader who is familiar with the various approaches on the critical mindscape responds to complex novels by Conrad (*Lord Jim*), Woolf (*Mrs. Dalloway, To the Lighthouse*), and Joyce (*Ulysses*). I imagine a reader whose knowledge of recent theory and awareness of traditional theory enables him to understand the theoretical implications of his reading experience. For reading the novel in a university setting has been transformed by new ways of reading and the surge of interest in 'Theory'. Yet even while acknowledging that novels contain the seeds of linguistic and deconstructive readings that deflect the reader from his efforts to discover one alternate meaning or significance, I shall contend that the transformed reader – the reader alert to new modes of reading – finally depends on what Stevens calls 'our rage for order' to make coherent patterns. Moreover, I shall be implicitly arguing that 'progressive' traditional criticism, too, has fresh stories of reading to tell.

Literary works, particularly novels, depend on readers who care about human characters and who respond to the human narrative voice which lived in the imagined world created by the author. The modern British novelists depend upon a reader who must create some of the patterns that were once provided by the omniscient narrator. Like the author and the major characters, the reader must undergo his own quest for meaning. As he or she experiences a complex novel's tentative form and its putative values, does not the reader negotiate an odyssean journey? For example, as I have argued in my *Reading Joyce's 'Ulysses'* (1987), the odyssean reader of Joyce's *Ulysses* is often tempted by the novel's stylistic experimentation to abandon the quest for meaning, but the focus of *Ulysses* usually returns to its interest in character and plot. I will use the figure of the odyssean reader to focus on the process of reading as a journey with many adventures, including ones that treacherously challenge our understanding. The odyssean reader not only has to work his way through the difficulties provided by texts, but also those provided by recent critical approaches to literature. The reader must avoid temptations that deflect him from focusing on representation without ignoring the claims of recent theory that language does not signify absolutely. Without overlooking form and style, he needs to be attentive to theme. He should not lose sight of the historical reality implied by the imagined world of the literary and historical conditions that produced a work. He must be willing to allow the novel to change its emphasis as he reads.

The complex process by which works create readers needs to be more accurately described. Our stories of reading must include a self-conscious awareness of what makes each of us unique readers bringing something of her or his own experience to a text. But it must also include an awareness of how the novel's structure of effects and its rhetoric – conscious and unconscious – shapes an ideal reader both now and when it was written. When authors respond to other works, we need to assume that the author had in mind a reader with an intertextual perspective. Even as we engage in sophisticated discussions of narrators and narratees and of implied authors and implied readers, we should recall that the one figure that authors rarely forget is the actual reader; usually, the author conceives the reader as an historically grounded figure who exists in the community at large. While he is imported into the imagined ontology of the novel as a figure who will listen with sympathy to the telling and might undergo change, his values represent that of a large putative audience. Put another way, the reader is a metaphor for one aspect of a larger community.

The word 'transformation' in my title also refers to my conceiving that the form of a novel is not a static third-dimensional object, but an evolving process in which novels undergo metamorphoses as they are experienced by readers. For form, like language, is always constituted and constituting. While Victorian novels transform their shape and meaning as we read, the transformation of the modern novel is more radical, open, inconclusive, contradictory, and paradoxical. I conceive the process of reading as a temporal event in which things happen to the reader. I stress how readers of novels – especially modern novels – must respond to the way a novel's narrative process proposes, tests, modifies, transforms, and discards interpretations of characters and events. My frequent focus on beginnings and on endings shows how major modern British novels simultaneously formally *urge* and *claim* a transformation of values, even while these novels fail to resolve the issues raised in the episodes prior to the conclusion.

The novelists of this period oscillate between what I call sacred and profane readings of the world. By a sacred reading of the world, I mean one in which most perceptions fit into *a priori* categories. A sacred reading implies a reading that mimes the unity and totality that man in earlier eras attributed to God's creation. While in this sense Lawrence's *The Rainbow* and *Jude the Obscure* are sacred texts, so are, for the most part, *Lord Jim* and *A Passage to India*. By contrast, one kind of profane reading of the world stresses momentary immersion in life and the nominalistic, disparate details of experience. Such a reading stresses the gratuitous, serendipitious, incongruous nature of life. (Do not Lawrence in *Sons and Lovers* and Forster in *Where Angels Fear to Tread* and *A Room With A View* do this?) A very different kind of profane reading is interested in the free play of language as signifier rather than in its mimetic or signified potential. Joyce and, to a lesser extent, Woolf propose and test both kinds of profane reading before embracing their own version of sacred reading. The oscillation within complex novels between sacred and profane readings of the world urges similar responses in readers making their way through these novels.

Part One

1

'I Was the World in Which I Walked': the Transformation of the British Novel

In the Sculpture Garden of the Museum of Modern Art stands Rodin's large 1897 statue, *Monument to Balzac*. The imposing figure of Balzac is 10 feet tall, and it rests on a 5 foot-high slab. At first, the observer may wonder what this seemingly realistic piece is doing in the citadel of modernism. But gradually he realizes that the work is a crystallizing image of modernism, for it depicts the artist as outcast and hero. Towering above onlookers, Balzac is wearing the expression of scornful magisterial dignity. With back stiffly yet regally arched past a 90° angle, Balzac looks into the distance and the future as if oblivious and indifferent to the opinions of the Lilliputians observing him from below. The large moustache, massive brows, flowing hair, and enormous ears and nose all emphasize the immense physical stature of the figure. As observers we crane our necks to see the features of this commanding figure whose gigantic head is disproportionate to his body. His features are boldly outlined but not precisely modelled. His huge head dominates the massive form; the body enwrapped in a cloak is a taut cylinder; the only visible feature is the feet, which are in motion as if they were going to walk off the slab. Indeed, one foot actually overhangs the slab as if it were about to depart. In the geometric shape of an isosceles triangle, the intimidating figure asserts the dependence of content upon form.

In a number of ways this sculpture, I think, helps us to understand literary modernism. Rodin has presented the artist as an *Übermensch*, as a physical and moral giant who is indifferent to the opinions of his audience. He depicts Balzac the way Rodin would have liked to see himself. 'I think of [Balzac's] intense labor,' he wrote, 'of the difficulty of his life, of his incessant battles and of his great courage. I would express all that.'[1] As Albert E. Elsen remarks, 'Rodin has transformed the embattled writer into a godlike visionary who belongs on a pedestal aloof from the crowd.'[2] Rodin's presence in the sculpture of Balzac speaks for art as self-expression and thus declares a new aesthetic that questions the impersonality and objectivity which Balzac sought in his role of moral and social historian of the human comedy. Rodin's Balzac is not someone who serves the community but someone who answers to the demands of his imagination and psyche; he does not imitate reality, but transforms what he sees into something original. He is more a visionary than a realist. His integrity derives from his genius and his independence. The sculpture shows, too, the inseparable relationship between subject and object – the poised tension between content (Balzac) and form (the original stone) – that is central to modernism. Finally, Rodin understands that art requires an audience to complete the hermeneutical circle, for he declared that the suggestiveness of his *Balzac* required the viewer to use 'the imagination to recompose the work when it is seen from close up'.[3]

I would like to take the Rodin statue as a point of departure for speaking of the great change in major British fiction from the realistic to the expressionist novel, a change that begins roughly in 1895, the year of Hardy's last novel, *Jude the Obscure*,[4] and reaches a climax with Woolf's major novels, *Mrs. Dalloway* (1925) and *To the Lighthouse* (1927). That some or all of the great British modernists – Conrad, Joyce, Lawrence, Forster, and Woolf – withdraw from their work, eliminate the intrusive author, and move to objectivity and impersonality is still one of the shibboleths of literary history. In this chapter I shall argue that by making themselves their subject they have, in fact, created a more subjective, self-expressive novel than their predecessors, and that they *are* present in their works.

Influenced by English romanticism, developments in modern art, and a changing intellectual milieu that questioned the possibilities of universal values or objective truth, these novelists erased the boundaries between art and life. They no longer believed that they could or should recreate the real world in their art and they questioned the assumption that verisimilitude was the most important aesthetic value. They realized that each man perceived a different reality and lived in what F. H. Bradley has called a 'closed circle'.[5] Thus, while mid-Victorian novelists believed in the efficacy of their art, twentieth-century writers have often despaired at the possibility of communication. They wrote not only to urge their perspectives upon their audience but to create their own identities and values. On the one hand, the artist doubts that he can change the world but, on the other, he tries to convince himself and his audience that he can.

Twentieth-century British writers invent ways of seeing the human psyche in a more subtle and complex manner. While the Victorian novel focused upon man in his social aspect, Conrad, Lawrence, Joyce, and Woolf isolate their characters from the social community by focusing on the perceiving psyche. As J. Hillis Miller has noted, there is little self-consciousness in most Victorian novels: 'the protagonist comes to know himself and to fulfill himself by way of other people'.[6] But the English novel from 1890 to 1930 made self-consciousness and self-awareness its subject, and the streams of consciousness within the soliloquy and interior monologue – both direct and indirect – became more prominent. Since characters are often versions of the author who either does not or cannot achieve the traditional distance between author and characters, the experience and self-consciousness of the characters reflect those of the authors.

In traditional novels we are more conscious of the characters, actions, themes, and rhetoric and less conscious of what I shall call the author's presence. Patricia Meyer Spacks notes: 'Writers before the nineteenth century ... often insisted by implication on their *lack* of psychology, defining themselves in relation to their audiences or in terms of a historical tradition rather than by personal reactions or feelings.'[7] The conventions of editor or omniscient narrator deserve such a description. In *Moll Flanders* and *Clarissa* the presence of the author is often felt as an editor; in *Tom Jones* the author depicts himself as the reader's host. In Victorian fiction he becomes an omniscient voice. Yet because modern writers have written first for themselves, they have been more insistent on affirming their living presence in their works than on using rhetorical tools to shape their readers.

II

Twentieth-century novels are often songs of myself, and anxious self-doubting ones at that. In varying degrees the later Hardy in *Jude*, Conrad, Forster, Woolf, and Joyce take their own imaginations as a major subject. In a sense their novels are about the process of transforming life into art. While reading *Emma* is the discovery of a finished three-dimensional imagined world, reading the major British novelists in the period 1890–1930 involves participating in their process of struggling to define their values and their concepts of the novel. It is the difference between a Constable or a Gainsborough and a Matisse or a Picasso. The novel depends on a continuing dialogue between the author's avowed subject and his efforts to discover the appropriate form and values for that subject. Writing of how the artist finally must discover the world in himself, Stevens defines in 'Tea at the Palaz of Hoon' (1921) the relationship between text and author that informs the writers under discussion:

> I was the world in which I walked, and what I saw
> Or heard or felt came not but from myself;
> And there I found myself more truly and more strange.

The author's struggle with his subject becomes a major determinant of novel form. In the 1898–1900 Marlow tales, *The Rainbow* (1915), *Ulysses* (1922), and *Mrs. Dalloway* (1925), each author writes to define himself or herself. The writer does not strive for the rhetorical finish of prior novels but, rather like Rodin in his sculpture, instead invites the reader to perceive a relationship between the creator and the artistic work, and to experience the dialogue between the creative process and the raw material. While the Victorian novelist believed that he had a coherent self and that his characters could achieve coherence, the modernist is conscious of disunity in his own life and the world in which lives. The novelist becomes a divided self. He is both the creator and seeker, the prophet who would convert others and the agonizing doubter who would convince himself while engaging in introspective self-examination. Even while the writer stands detached, creating characters, we experience his or her urgent effort to create a self. Thus the reader must maintain a double vision. He must apprehend the narrative and the process of creating that narrative. In such diverse works as the Marlow tales, *The Rainbow* and *To the Lighthouse* (1927), the process of writing, of defining the subject, of evaluating character, of searching for truth, becomes part of the novel. Yet, as Woolf writes in 'Mr. Bennett and Mrs. Brown' (1924), 'where so much strength is spent on finding a way of telling the truth, the truth itself is bound to reach us in rather an exhausted and chaotic condition'.[8] 'Finding a way' – the quest for values and the quest for aesthetic form – becomes the subject. Telling becomes a central action in these novels. The reader experiences the author's engagement in defining his values as he writes. As the search for values often takes precedence over story and as the form of these novels enacts the author's quest, traditional chronology, linear narrative, and ordinary syntax are discarded. Sometimes, as in the Marlow tales, the author's quest for values is transferred to another character whose central activity becomes the search for meaning and for the appropriate language with which to tell the tale. Sometimes a character will become the spokesman for values that the omniscient voice articulates; this is the case in *Jude the Obscure*, *Sons and Lovers* (1913), and *Women in Love* (1920). But this kind of doubling – the protagonist (Jude, Paul, Birkin) and narrative voice saying much the same thing – is a function of the author's need to convince himself of the accuracy of his perceptions as well as of the difficulty of his achieving irony towards a version of himself. The structure of a novel is no longer a preconceived pattern in which characters move towards discovering values held by an omniscient voice who is a surrogate for the author. To read the novel is to participate in a process by which, through his characters, the novelist proposes, tests, examines, and discards moral and aesthetic values.

Thus it becomes increasingly difficult for writers to remove themselves from the text. In fact, the major modern British authors remain in their work in much the same way as some Renaissance painters who placed an image of themselves in a corner of their canvas watching the main spectacle. The stream of consciousness, which has been thought of as a movement towards objectivity, is actually often a disguise for authorial presence rather than a means for the author to absent himself. For example, do we not feel that Joyce is selecting and arranging the stream of consciousness, including mythic parallels and image patterns that help give the stream its meaning and significance? We know a great deal more about Joyce from *A Portrait* (1916) and *Ulysses* than we know about Austen from *Emma* and *Pride and Prejudice*, or about Fielding from *Tom Jones*, notwithstanding his host-narrator. Austen or even Fielding would hardly have asserted, as Conrad did in 1912:

A novelist lives in his work. He stands there, the only reality in an invented world, among imaginary things, happenings, and people. Writing about them, he is only writing about himself. But the disclosure is not complete. He remains, to a certain extent, a figure behind the veil; a suspected rather than a seen presence – a movement and a voice behind the draperies of fiction.[9]

While there was always an autobiographical strain in the English novel (*Tristram Shandy*, *The Mill on the Floss*, *David Copperfield*), this was surely a minor motif in the history of the genre. *Jude the Obscure*, *Sons and Lovers*, and *A Portrait of the Artist* thinly disguise the presence of the author in their work. The quest of Stephen for artistic values, for self-recognition, and for the approval of others is Joyce's quest. The *agon* is the author's quest to understand himself. Hardy becomes a spokesman for *Jude* because he sees Jude as a version of himself – the outsider aspiring to be recognized by a more educated élite society. In *Sons and Lovers* the omniscient narrator of Part I gives way in Part II to a spokesman for Paul's perspective. He strains to justify Paul's (Lawrence's surrogate) role in his relationship with Miriam (Jessie Chambers). Our reading of Lawrence's dramatic scenes often belies the interpretation imposed by his narrative voice. For example, the voice does not recognize that Paul suffers from the very problems of frigidity and repression of which he accuses Miriam. Nor does he understand that he turns away from Miriam at the very time that she begins to respond sexually to Paul or that Paul discards Clara because his relationship with her threatens to succeed.[10] Paul's oedipal relationship with his mother requires that he find fault with Clara as soon as he consummates that relationship.

Once there is no longer agreement about values, an author cannot depend upon the reader to recognize the ironic disjunction between what a character thinks and what the author wants the reader to think. The omniscient narrator may be thorough and careful in establishing his point of view, but he has no special status. The novelist does not believe that any single perspective holds the entire truth. As we read modern novels told by a omniscient speaker, we realize that the novelist's commentary has imposed a perspective upon events, even while implying, through the dramatic actions and sometimes his pluralistic values, the possibility of another perspective. This is true not only for *Jude the*

Obscure and *Sons and Lovers*, in each of which the omniscient narrator becomes more and more an empathetic spokesman and apologist for his major character, but even for *The Rainbow* and *Ulysses*. Thus the technical convention of omniscience survives, but not the concept of a shared value system which originally gave rise to the convention.

The recognition that self-expression and subjectivity are at the heart of the transformation of the British novel was long inhibited by the acceptance in fiction criticism of the New Critical credo that the best literature depends on the author's separating his personal life from the imagined world of his novels or, at the very least, on his repressing those aspects of his experience that do not have 'universal' interest. If we are to come to terms with the expressive aspect of fiction, we must develop an appropriate aesthetic. For example, can we separate the prophetic voice of *The Rainbow* from Lawrence's personal quest for self-realization or his quest for the appropriate grammar of passion with which to render sexual relationships, if we recall his writing, 'Now you will find [Frieda] and me in the novel, I think, and the work is of both of us'?[11] Nor can we ignore the parallels between Marlow's search for values and Conrad's.

Wayne Booth's *The Rhetoric of Fiction* (1961) still stands as the indispensable study of rhetoric and voice in fiction. Booth's reluctance to appreciate the ambiguous rhetoric of modern literature has often been criticized. But has anyone gone beyond his work and developed a rhetoric to describe the authorial presence within a novel that may be either narrator or character or both? Yet Booth's concept of implied author, while valuable, does not seem quite satisfactory to define the mask that the author wears within his works. In each of an author's novels this presence is somewhat different for each novel because its personality and character are functions of the words chosen and the events and characters described. Booth's implied author may be somewhat workable for a Fielding or Austen novel, where the narrative voice is an artifice controlled and manipulated by an objective author in full command of his rhetorical devices. But it does not do justice to the strong subjective authorial presence within much modern fiction. To approach the modern writers under discussion, we must reconcile fiction as rhetoric and as self-contained ontology with fiction as self-expression. For there are frequent moments in twentieth-century fiction when the subject is the author's quest to define himself. In much of the work of Conrad, Joyce, Woolf, Forster, and Lawrence, the speaker is a thinly disguised version of the writer's actual self who is actively seeking moral and aesthetic values; this self, or presence, of the author is a dynamic evolving identity which is an intrinsic – not an implied – part of the novel's form. The presence that the novelist projects reflects the particular circumstances of the novelist's life when he wrote the novel and the *Zeitgeist* in which the novel was written. While we should begin with what a book is and what a book does, we should not ignore what the author does, particularly in novels where the subject is the author's self. The best way to locate the presence within the text is to know beforehand something about the historical figure. In other words, the text more readily yields its presence to those who know about the author's other works, his life, and his historical context.

As readers we respond to an *imitation* of the real creator of the text. The actual author is in the imagined world as a distortion – at times, a simplification, an obfuscation, an idealization, a clarification – of the creating psyche. In early periods the words of a novel signify a human presence within the text; that presence may be urging the reader to a particular attitude, but in modern fiction the presence is also usually involved in affirming his identity and values. The reader, knowing that the presence mimes a historical figure who wrote the book, imagines that figure as a reality. As Spacks notes, 'if poets create themselves as figures in their poems, readers choose, consciously or unconsciously, to accept such figures as more or less appropriate to reality'.[12]

Since novels are written by people, it seems the antithesis of a humanistic approach to settle for a formalism – whether it be New Criticism or more recent varieties – that excludes authors from the text. The process of locating a human being within the text recognizes that reading is not merely a verbal game but a shared experience between writer and reader. It is another way of saying that we wish words to signify something beyond themselves. Because we desire coherence and meaning, we seek a tangible identity within the imagined world and respond to the energy of the author's creative imagination. We demand of words that they form connections to human experience, even though we make fewer demands of lines and shapes or musical notes. (Painting and sculpture, of course, have had a tradition of mimesis while music has not.)

The author's presence in the text usually serves the rhetorical purpose of reinforcing the meaning conveyed by the other elements: structure, narrator, language, characterization, and setting. But at times the presence is subversive in that it undermines the meaning that the author intended. In many modern novels that voice is divided into two or more aspects, each of which projects a different identity. Sometimes we can speak of a dominant and a secondary voice, or, as in *The Nigger of the 'Narcissus'* (1897), of a tension between competing voices. Conrad's effort to overcome writer's block by means of mastering the raw material of his narrative – the sea experience of his earlier life – is as much the subject of the novel as the journey of the *Narcissus*. For Conrad the sea voyage – with its clearly defined beginning and ending, its movement through time towards a destination, its separation from other experience, and explicit requirements that must be fulfilled by the crewmen and officers – provided the necessary model for completing a work. Since he had actually sailed on a ship named the *Narcissus* in 1884, he could draw upon romantic memories of an ordered and accomplished voyage at a time when his creative impulses were stifled by doubts. Thus the voyage of the *Narcissus* provided Conrad with an imaginative escape from his writing frustrations. *The Nigger of the 'Narcissus'* also reflects a reductive dichotomy within Conrad's psyche between the evil land, where he was terribly frustrated as he launched his new career, and the sea, where, as he remembered it, he had been fairly tested and had ultimately succeeded. This dichotomy explains the schism between the first-person speaker who is a part of the crew and the third-person speaker who strives to play the role of the traditional omniscient speaker.[13]

Ulysses is Joyce's attempt to resolve the Stephen and Bloom within his psyche and that effort is writ large on every page. Among other things, *Ulysses* is a search for values, a dialogue within Joyce's psyche between the intellectualism and abstraction of Stephen, the humanity and empiricism of Bloom, and the sensuality and spontaneity of Molly. The novel works its way through a panorama of values in modern life. It tests and discards patriotism, nationalism, piety, Platonism, and aestheticism, and affirms the family paradigm, affection, consideration, tolerance, and love. Beginning with 'Wandering Rocks', *Ulysses* examines not only ways of living but ways of telling. Joyce parodies romantic fiction in 'Nausicaa', examines whether fiction can be patterned on musical composition in 'The Sirens', explores the possibilities of the scientific temperament in 'Ithaca', and tests the mock epic in 'Cyclops'. 'Eumaeus', narrated by Joyce's omniscient narrator in the style in which Bloom would have told it, is Joyce's love song for Bloom in the form of an affectionate parody and the author's sequel to the end of 'Hades' when Bloom affirms the value of life. In 'Ithaca' not only Bloom's humanity but the possibility of significant action in the form of personal relationships emerges despite the mechanical nature of the scientific catechism, a style that represents the indifference and coldness of the community to individuals. Thus *Ulysses* is Joyce's odyssey for moral values and aesthetic form. It is not only Bloom but Joyce who survives and triumphs over what he calls in 'Aeolus' 'grossbooted draymen' of the modern city. This kind of pastiche of former styles in the service of a quest for personal values is also very much a part of modern painting and sculpture. It is in this sense, in this profoundly humanistic sense, that modern painting is about painting and modern literature is about writing.

III

Virginia Woolf wrote that 'on or about December 10, 1910 human character changed',[14] because the first post-impressionist exhibition organized by Roger Fry and called 'Manet and the Post-Impressionists' ran in London from 8 November 1910 to 15 January 1911. According to Samuel Hynes, she 'chose that occasion as an appropriate symbol of the way European ideas forced themselves upon the insular English consciousness during the Edwardian years and so joined England to the Continent'.[15] The post-impressionists provide an example for the abandonment of realism and the movement of the artist to centre stage. The post-impressionists had discarded representation for form. For example, in his famous 'Card Players' Cézanne is less an observer of peasant life than a composer of formal harmony and disparate pictorial planes, while in his works Signac is concerned with the possibilities of objectively capturing light. These painters demonstrated that the artist could create his own order in a chaotic world. Thus they intentionally neglect some details, while they simplify, distort, exaggerate, and stress others to express their emotions, solve problems of pictorial space, and create effects. In a sense, the artist's temperament and perspective become the subject in the work of Van Gogh, Derain, Matisse, and Picasso. We recall Van Gogh's insistence that 'what is eternally alive is in the first place the painter and in the second place the picture'.[16] It is quite possible that the abrupt cutting of figures, the elimination of traditional perspective, the foreshortening of images influenced the tendency of Woolf, Lawrence, Forster, and Joyce (who, of course, saw similar paintings in Paris) to move beyond realism to more expressive forms of art. Can one read *Ulysses* or *The Secret Agent* without realizing that something has happened to the visual imagination of nineteenth-century novels and that even Dickens did not continually create the kinds of illuminating distortions, cartoons, and grotesques that populate these modern urban novels? Novelists no longer wrote what they saw, but what they knew.

The 1978 London exhibition, *Great Victorian Pictures*, made clear, I think, the revolutionary character of Fry's exhibition. Victorian painting often told a story, either of history or of contemporary life. As Rosemary Treble wrote in the introduction to the catalogue for that exhibit: 'The constant refrain in all the writing of the period and the touchstone of every judgment was whether the work attained "truth" generally to nature and therefore, by implication, to God's creation, whether its sentiment was appropriate and whether it was morally healthy and therefore fit for consumption.'[17] And the values by which Victorian fiction writers were evaluated were not too different. A painting like William Powell Frith's *The Railroad Station* (1862) was considered a national epic because it included every class. William Edward Frost's allegorical women were thought to be uplifting, although to us they seem self-absorbed and repressed. The avant-garde in England, beginning with the Pre-Raphaelite brotherhood and including Burne-Jones's precious symbolism, hardly affected the supremacy of conventional painting. To be sure, the works of Whistler and Walter Sickert were exceptions. But the fact remains that until Fry's exhibit fiction usually conformed to the existing theories of art, and those theories (most notably orthodox realism, often in the service of Victorian pieties) with few exceptions tended to serve conventional morality.

The English novel after Hardy was deeply affected by Russian art in a number of ways.[18] In the Edwardian years the Russian influence challenged British insularity. Dostoevsky, although

patronized by Conrad, now became popular, and the exuberant
and flamboyant Russian Ballet appeared in 1911. In the pre-war
years Russian music and painting made their mark on London.
(Russians were included in the second show of post-
impressionism.) In general, Russian art, more than British art,
depended more upon energy than craft, more upon fantasy than
realism, more upon the artist's vision than subjectivity, more upon
flux than stasis, more upon experimentation than tradition, more
upon mysticism than reason, and more upon the spiritual and
psychological than the moral. As Woolf understood, these qualities
inevitably questioned the conventions of the British novel: 'The
novels of Dostoevsky are seething whirlpools, gyrating sand-
storms, waterspouts which hiss and boil and suck us in. They are
composed purely and wholly of the stuff of the soul.'[19] The
violence of Dostoevsky's emotions influenced not only Conrad in
Under Western Eyes (1911), but, in more subtle ways, Woolf,
Lawrence, and Forster.[20] Indeed, Lawrence consciously imports
this element into his imagined world in the person of the Slavic
Lydia Lensky, who is the mysterious, libidinous, passionate soul-
mate for Tom Brangwen, Lawrence's *Übermensch* of the passions,
and the grandmother of Ursula, the novel's heroine, who, like
Lawrence, must come to terms with twentieth-century life. Indeed,
Lawrence used the Dostoevskian strain – the inchoate, urgent,
uncontrolled 'stuff of the soul' – to fertilize the English novel of
manners.

The novel also changed because artists increasingly felt that the
modern world required different kinds of art. The search for
innovation in form and technique is inseparable from the search
for values in a world where the British empire had lost its sense of
invulnerability, the political leadership had suffered a crisis of
confidence, and industrialization had created worker unrest. We
see the first two in *A Passage to India* (1924) and *Mrs. Dalloway*, and
the effect of the third in the character of Verloc in *The Secret Agent*.
The urbanization of England undermined the sense of continuity
that had prevailed in England since Elizabethan times, a continuity that even the Revolution of 1640 did not entirely disrupt. The
continuity derived from land passed down from generation to
generation, from the rhythms of rural culture, from monarchical
succession, from the strong sense of English family, and from the
relatively stable role played by the clergy, the aristocracy, and
Parliament. George Dangerfield has described how England had

become by 1914 'a liberal democracy whose parliament had practically ceased to function, whose Government was futile, and whose Opposition had said enough to put lesser men in the dock for treason'.[21] Modern writers are conscious of writing in a period of crisis and transition; certainly this sense of crisis gives *Nostromo*, *The Rainbow*, and *Ulysses* much of their intensity. It may be that the boldness and scope of these novels are a response to the ennui, cynicism, and solipsism of the *fin de siècle*, a response all the more violent because their writers felt threatened by these negative attitudes. The great modernists – Joyce, Lawrence, Conrad, Forster, Hardy, Woolf – have a clear and ordered sense of a past from which they felt permanently separated. Conrad realizes that traditional personal values are threatened by compulsive materialism, often in the guise of politics. For Hardy and Lawrence a pastoral vision of agrarian England is an alternative to present mechanism and utilitarianism. *Jude the Obscure* and *Howards End* (1910) are elegies for this rural civilization. For Joyce, like T. S. Eliot, it is European cultural tradition that has been debased by the meanness of the present. Joyce, Conrad, Woolf, and Forster long for a tradition of social customs and personal relationships that has become obsolete under the pressure of urbanization and materialism.

Noel Annan has written of the change in England between 1880 and 1910, a change which affected the subject matter of the novel:

> The restraints of religion and thrift and accepted class distinctions started to crumble and English society to rock under the flood of money. The class war, not merely between labour and owners, but between all social strata of the middle and upper classes began in earnest. . . . A new bitterness entered politics, a new rancour in foreign relations and a materialism of wealthy snobbery and aggressive philistinism arose far exceeding anything hitherto seen in England.[22]

Although often bourgeois in their impulses and unscathed by these factors, novelists began to write more frequently about class struggle (*Jude the Obscure*), the ethics and effects of imperialism (*A Passage to India*), the implications of politics on private lives (*The Secret Agent*), and the corrupting influence of industry and commerce (*Nostromo*).

If we compare *Mrs. Dalloway* with the novels of Austen, we see how the sensibilities of Woolf's major characters have been deeply influenced by wars, empire, and commerce (although these play less of a role in the rather anachronistic life of Mrs Dalloway than in the lives of Peter Walsh and Septimus Smith). The lack of community value is enacted in the fragmented form, in the lack of meaningful purpose in politically influential figures (Richard Dalloway, Lady Bruton), and finally in the crystallizing image of Septimus Smith, who, as he walks the streets of London, seems to epitomize the failure of Londoners to discover purpose or coherence in their city. The confrontation of traditional English values with those of other cultures is central to *A Passage to India*, *Heart of Darkness* (1898), and *Women in Love* (especially in the Bohemian and European sections). Yet even as novelists write about different value systems, they explore the importance of those systems for their own lives. They do not, like eighteenth-century novelists, simply measure the strange cultures against established values. The structure becomes a process, a process that mimes the author's quest for values. Thus even in *A Passage to India* – which we think of as an heir to the Victorian novel – the oscillation among Moslem, Hindu, and English and the shifts in narrative distance between the limited perspective and the geographic perspective reflect Forster's search. As Wilfred Stone has written, Forster's novels are 'dramatic installments in the story of his struggle for selfhood.... They tell of a man coming out in the world, painfully emerging from an encysted state of loneliness, fear, and insecurity'.[23] The same, I am arguing, could be said of Woolf, Joyce, Lawrence, and Conrad.

Comparing Wells, Bennett, and Galsworthy with their major predecessors, Woolf wrote:

> *Tristram Shandy* or *Pride and Prejudice* is complete in itself; it is self-contained; it leaves one with no desire to do anything, except indeed to read the book again, and to understand it better. The difference perhaps is that both Sterne and Jane Austen were interested in things in themselves; in character in itself; in the book in itself. Therefore everything was inside the book, nothing outside. But the Edwardians were never interested in character in itself; or in the book in itself. They were interested in something outside. Their books, then, were incomplete as books, and required that the reader should finish them, actively and practically, for himself.[24]

But I think the major British twentieth-century figures under discussion, including Woolf herself, were interested in both 'something inside' and 'something outside'. For these writers no longer accepted the traditional Christian beliefs that divine providence expresses itself in earthly matters or that this life is a necessary prelude to eternity. And the world outside could no longer be limited and contained by authors whose own moral vision was tentative, incomplete, and lacking in conviction. We should not be surprised that the movement of *Nostromo*, *Women in Love*, or *Ulysses* enacts kinds of uneasiness and turbulence that are absent in, say, an Austen novel. Because the writer is striving to discover his moral and aesthetic values, this uneasiness and turbulence at times reflect unresolved social issues, characters whose motives the novelist does not understand, and inchoate form.

The social and historical milieu in which an artist writes determines the artistic problems that he must solve. Thus Conrad, Lawrence, Joyce, Forster, and Woolf had to discover an appropriate form with which to show (if I may baldly list the striking characteristics of the period) that motives could not be fully understood, that the world was not created and shaped by divine providence, that chance might determine man's destiny, that man's desires and aspirations were not likely to be fulfilled, that social institutions were ineffectual, and that materialism and industrialization were destroying the fabric of life. Consequently, they invented plots that at times reflect disorder, flux, discontinuity, fragmentations, and disruption without themselves having those qualities; they needed to use the *Odyssey*, *Hamlet*, and the Bible, and even in *Ulysses* such Jewish legends as 'The Last of the Just', to give shape to seemingly random events. They had to invent means not only for rendering the inner life but for showing the unacknowledged private self that played such a large role in shaping behaviour. Thus Conrad shows that Jim is the victim of compulsions, obsessions, and fixations that he cannot understand. They needed syntax and language to reveal the secret recesses of each psyche and the impact made upon it by experience, especially the kind of ordinary daily experience that was once thought to be insignificant. The unpunctuated, effervescent stream of consciousness of Molly fertilizes that of both Stephen and Bloom by emphasizing, in form and content, fecundity, sexuality, spontaneity, passion, and indifference to history and morality.

IV

Let us think for a moment of some major Victorian novels – say *Bleak House, Vanity Fair,* or *Middlemarch.* Victorian fiction depends on the mastery of space and time in an unfolding narrative. It seeks to create an imagined world that both mirrors and exaggerates the external world. Its use of a omniscient, ubiquitous narrator implies the pre-eminence of the individual perceiver. Now let us think of *The Secret Agent* (like *Bleak House,* a novel of London), *Ulysses* (like *Vanity Fair,* a satirical examination of relatively recent times), and *The Rainbow* (like *Middlemarch,* a panoramic novel about provincial life). Do not these examples of modern British fiction undermine the idea that space and time can be mastered by anyone, including the author? Like the subject-matter, the setting resists the traditional patterns. The setting itself recoils from idealization, control, and order and expresses the turmoil and anxiety within the author's psyche. (By becoming foreground rather than background, setting plays a similar role in the post-impressionist works of Van Gogh, Matisse, and Picasso.) The setting – the physical conditions under which the imagined world functions – becomes not background but a moral labyrinth which the characters are unable to negotiate and which not only shapes their destiny but often subsumes them. Hardy's Wessex, Forster's India, Joyce's Dublin, and Conrad's London are manifestations of an amoral cosmos that pre-empts the characters' moral choices. By forging a web of social circumstances that encloses and limits characters, these settings displace the traditional role of individual will in shaping the lives of characters. Yet even as these settings often become coterminous with destiny and fate, they may also be a symptom or cause of a bankrupt social system, or a metaphor for the narrator's and his characters' own moral confusion.

In the nineteenth-century novel characters are defined in terms of their moral choices in social situations. Becky Sharp consciously chooses to seek wealth and status, although we do not watch the processes of her mind, and Esther Summerson's loyalty, sympathy, and integrity result mostly from conscious decisions. But Woolf, Joyce, Lawrence, Forster, and, quite frequently, Conrad perceive their characters in terms of the honesty and integrity of perceptions rather than in terms of the moral consequences of their behaviour. What they are is more important than what they do. The integrity and purity of their souls are standards by which they are primarily judged. *Is-ness* (the quality and intensity of the soul and heart) replaces *does-ness* (the effects of behaviour) as norms for characters. Thus we value Bloom and Mrs Ramsay for their uniqueness rather than their effectiveness. And this corresponds to the shift in emphasis in the art of the novel from traditional effects upon audience to self-dramatizing narrators in search of values and feelings.

The writers we are discussing saw that people no longer lived together bound by common values and social purposes. Each man is his own secular sect, and the interaction of these sects creates a social Babel. The order of art becomes a substitute for the disorder of life, and the novel mimes a momentary unity in the novelist's mind rather than in the external world. Thus in Woolf and Joyce, a novel's lack of form may seem to have a coherence that the subject of the novel lacks because the texture is reflexive and self-referential. Indeed, at times they try to replace, as Malcolm Bradbury puts it, 'the linear logic of story, psychological process, or history' with the 'logic of metaphor, form, or symbol'.[25] But do we not see that this effort has a compulsive quality, and that Woolf and Joyce are as much committed to transforming their lives into art as to creating a symbolic alternative to realistic fiction?

The great modernists wrote fiction to define themselves outside the social world and to confirm their special status as artists. They did not want to re-enter the social world but rather to leave it for islands (actual and imaginary) where life was more honest and true to the promptings of their hearts; these islands were often their novels.[26] They could look at a society from which they felt excluded and criticize its values. Woolf's moments of enlightenment, Joyce's epiphanies, and Lawrence's states of passionate intensity emphasize the individual's life as separate from the community. Novels move not to a comprehensive vision of society but to unity within a character's imagination and perception. In *Heart of Darkness* and *Lord Jim* Marlow's experience and insight not only are his own, but leave him, like the Ancient Mariner, separate from his fellows. If in Victorian fiction the narrator is, as in *Our Mutual Friend* or *Vanity Fair*, a detached outsider observing characters who often function successfully within the community, in modern British fiction such as *Ulysses* and *Women in Love* he and the protagonists are both separate from the community, and the community itself is corrupt and morally bankrupt. Woolf saw the problem. On the one hand, she knew that her novels give credence to various kinds of personal Crusoeism and raise the hope of solutions separate from the traditional community. But, on the other hand, she also understood the dangers of her fiction becoming self-indulgent and narcissistic: 'I suppose the danger is the damned egotistical self.... Is one pliant and rich enough to provide a wall for the book from oneself without its becoming ...narrowing and restricting?'[27]

In *To the Lighthouse* the completion of Lily Briscoe's painting might serve as a metaphor for the hermetic nature of one strand of modernism. She has her vision and completes her painting, but she turns her back on the opportunity for community in the form of marriage to Mr Ramsay. Her art is at the expense of social life:

> Here she was again, she thought, stepping back to look at it, drawn out of gossip, out of living, out of community with people into the presence of this formidable ancient enemy of hers – this other thing, this truth, this reality, which suddenly laid hands on her, emerged stark at the back of appearance and commanded her attention.[28]

And Mrs Ramsay's victories are more aesthetic than moral; thinking of Mrs Ramsay, Lily realizes that her friend '[makes] of the moment something permanent (as in another sphere Lily herself tried to make of the moment something permanent) – this was of the nature of revelation. In the midst of chaos there was shape: this eternal passing and flowing (she looked at the clouds going and the leaves shaking) was struck into stability'.[29] Life *struck into stability* is what happens when pattern is imposed on life by art, but it is also a foreshadowing of death. Lily is a version of her creator, and her struggle with her painting mimes that of her author with the subject. We realize that Woolf's quest for values in the 'eternal passing and flowing' continues through the novel.

Even novels with an epic scope – *Ulysses, Nostromo, The Rainbow* – discover meaning in the isolated perceiving consciousness of such characters as Bloom, Mrs Gould, and Ursula. Although these novels present an anatomy of social problems in the tradition of *Tom Jones* and *Bleak House*, they do not propose political and social solutions but personal ones – family ties (*Nostromo*); passion (Lawrence); kindness, tolerance, and affection (*Ulysses*). Indeed, we should understand that the epic and romance strands in Conrad, Lawrence, Joyce, and Forster are part of the search for values of desperate men who seek to find in older traditions a continuity that evades the confusions of modern life. There is a reflexive quality in *Nostromo*, *Ulysses*, and *The Rainbow*, a self-consciousness, a personal urgency, lacking in the eighteenth- and nineteenth-century novel. In *Nostromo* we sense Conrad's awareness that he has very little to offer as an alternative to social and political chaos, an awareness that derives from his feeling that all social systems are 'hollow at the core'. As he searches for values in Costaguana, he proposes every major figure as heroic and every political programme as redemptive only to undermine them systematically and finally to discard them. Furthermore, in *Nostromo* and *Lord Jim* he charts the failure of modern man both by the realistic standards of the nineteenth century and the older standards of romance, epic, and legend. At the very centre of *Lord Jim*, Conrad proposes Stein as an oracular figure before finally revealing him as uncertain and far from articulate in the gloom created by descending night. *Ulysses* and *The Rainbow*, in their reliance on Homer and the Bible for shape and significance, express their authors' nostalgia and enthusiasm for the simpler shapes of human experience and the narratives that rendered that experience. Perhaps this nostalgic enthusiasm is a reaction to their own rather unheroic lives that were punctuated by disappointment and frustration. What they sought was to retrieve their own feelings and attitudes, but, more than that, to convince themselves and their audiences that their feelings and attitudes typified those of others and had the kind of universality which realism had provided for the Victorians. To be sure, Joyce and Lawrence understood the need to invent a syntax and diction to render the flux of perceptual and sensory experience, the life of the subconscious, and the impulses of the unconscious life. But that experience, that life, and those impulses were also their own. When we respond to the presence of the author, when we feel his urgent pulsation within the novel, the focus of fiction is no more 'narrow and restricting' than that of any other kind of mimesis.

The 1980 Picasso exhibit at the Museum of Modern Art makes it clear that, as Hilton Kramer puts it, 'any criticism that refuses to acknowledge the esthetic reality of this autobiographical element in Picasso is doomed to be incomplete'.[30] What distinguishes the movement in modern painting and sculpture from impressionism onward through abstract expressionism, including post-impressionism, cubism, and fauvism, is its expressionist quality, its insistence on the validity of what the artist sees and feels, and this movement has its parallel in literature. The pressures of society had driven the artist from the world to the word. In painting, as the Picasso exhibit reminded us, the shift towards the more abstract, the spatial, and the chromatic was not so much a movement to objectivity but research into the possibilities of art in response to different conditions of life. Could we have *Guernica* without the enormity of modern warfare? Similarly modern fiction's innovations are an effort to breathe new life into a world that seemed to have become inert and superfluous. Or, as Woolf puts it:

> The idea has come to me that what I want now to do is to saturate every atom. I mean to eliminate all waste, deadness, superfluity: to give the moment whole; whatever it includes. Say that the moment is a combination of thought; sensation; the voice of the sea. Waste, deadness, come from the inclusion of things that don't belong to the moment; this appalling narrative business of the realist: getting on from lunch to dinner: it is false, unreal, merely conventional. Why admit anything to literature that is not poetry – by which I mean saturated?[31]

In 'An Ordinary Evening in New Haven' (1949) Stevens (another great modernist who made his life the subject of his art) writes of the relationship between the artist and his art in terms that I have been describing:

> The poem is the cry of its occasion,
> Part of the res itself and not about it,
> The poet speaks the poem as it is,
> Not as it was . . .
>
>   . . . He speaks
> By sight and insight as they are. There is no
> Tomorrow for him . . .
>
> In the end, in the whole psychology, the self
> The town, the weather, in a casual litter,
> Together, said words of the world are the life of the world.

The great British modernists, I think, have said in their fiction that their words are their life; as Lawrence puts it, 'I must write to live',[32] and we respond to those words and the presence behind them because their words are also the life of *our* world. They have transformed the novel from a realistic social document into a 'cry of its occasion' and affirmed that the act of telling is their paramount concern as artists.

Notes

1. Quoted in Albert E. Elsen, *Rodin* (New York: Museum of Modern Art, 1963) p. 93.
2. Elsen, p. 101.
3. Quoted in Elsen, p. 102.
4. See my chapter 2, originally published as 'The Narrator as Character in Hardy's Major Fiction', *Modern Fiction Studies* 18 (Summer 1972) pp. 155–72. Since the scope of my remarks in this chapter leaves less room for evidence than would be the case in a chapter devoted to a reading of an individual novel, I shall on occasion refer readers to subsequent chapters and my other published work for substantiation.
5. F. H. Bradley, *Appearance and Reality: a Metaphysical Essay*, 2nd edn (London, 1908) p. 346.
6. J. Hillis Miller, *The Form of Victorian Fiction* (Notre Dame University Press, 1968) p. 5.
7. Patricia Meyer Spacks, introduction to *The Author in His Work*, eds Louis L. Martz and Aubrey Williams (New Haven: Yale University Press, 1978) p. xv.
8. Virginia Woolf, 'Mr. Bennett and Mrs. Brown' in *The Captain's Death Bed and Other Essays* (New York: Harcourt, Brace, 1950) p. 117.
9. Joseph Conrad, *A Personal Record* [1912] (New York: Doubleday, 1926) p. xv.
10. See my chapter 4, originally published as 'Speaking of Paul Morel: Voice, Unity and Meaning in *Sons and Lovers*', *Studies in the Novel*, 8 (Autumn 1976) pp. 255–77.
11. *The Letters of D. H. Lawrence*, ed. Aldous Huxley (New York: Viking 1932) p. 22 April 1914, p. 191. See my chapter 5, originally published as 'Lawrence's Quest in *The Rainbow*', *Ariel*, 11:3 (1980) pp. 43–66; and chs 4 and 5 in my *Conrad: 'Almayer's Folly' to 'Under Western Eyes'* (London: Macmillan/Ithaca, NY: Cornell University NY: Cornell University Press, 1980) pp. 52–94.
12. Spacks, p. xii.
13. See ch. 3, 'The Necessary Voyage: Voice and Authorial Presence in *The Nigger of the "Narcissus"'*, in my *Conrad*, pp. 35–51.
14. Woolf, 'Mr. Bennett and Mrs. Brown', pp. 96–7.
15. Samuel Hynes, *The Edwardian Turn of Mind* (Princeton University Press, 1968) p. 326.
16. Van Gogh, in an exhibit comment accompanying 'Self-Portrait with Straw Hat' (1887), André Meyer Galleries of Metropolitan Museum of Art, New York.

17. *Great Victorian Paintings* (London: Arts Council Publication, 1968) p. 7.
18. See Hynes, pp. 336–45.
19. Virginia Woolf, 'The Russian Point of View' in *The Common Reader: First Series* (New York: Harcourt, Brace & World, 1925) p. 182. In the essay 'Modern Fiction' in the same volume she wrote: 'If we want understanding of the soul and heart where else [but in Russian fiction] shall we find it of comparable profundity' (p. 157).
20. See E. M. Forster, *Aspects of the Novel* (New York: Harcourt, Brace & World, 1954) pp. 130–5.
21. George Dangerfield, *The Strange Death of Liberal England 1910–14* [1935] (New York: Capricorn Books, 1961) p. 366.
22. Quoted in Wilfred Stone, *The Cave and the Mountain: a Study of E. M. Forster* (Stanford University Press, 1966) p. 250, from Noel Annan, 'The Intellectual Aristocracy', *Studies in Social History: a Tribute to George Trevelyan*, ed. J. H. Plumb (London, 1955) pp. 252–3.
23. Stone, p. 19.
24. Woolf, 'Mr. Bennett and Mrs. Brown', p. 105.
25. Malcolm Bradbury, *Possibilities: Essays on the State of the Novel* (New York: Oxford University Press, 1972) p. 84.
26. In *The Form of Victorian Fiction*, J. Hillis Miller remarks that, for Victorian novelists, 'the writing of fiction was an indirect way for them to reenter the social world from which they had been excluded or which they were afraid to enter directly' (p. 63).
27. Quoted in Quentin Bell, *Virginia Woolf: a Biography* (New York: Harcourt, Brace, Jovanovich, 1972), II, 73.
28. Virginia Woolf, *To the Lighthouse* (New York: Harcourt, Brace & World, 1927) p. 236.
29. Ibid., p. 241.
30. Hilton Kramer, 'The Picasso Show', *New York Times*, 12 Oct. 1980.
31. *The Diary of Virginia Woolf*, III: 1925–30, eds Anne Oliver Bell, with Andrew McNeillie (New York: Harcourt, Brace, Jovanovich, 1980), 28 Nov. 1928, pp. 209–10.
32. *Letters of D. H. Lawrence*, 29 Jan. 1914, p. 180.

2

The Narrator as Character in Hardy's Major Fiction

The very brilliance of J. Hillis Miller's *Thomas Hardy: Distance and Desire* requires that students of the novel examine the assumptions on which it is based. Because Miller's purpose is to discover a 'single design', he assumes that 'works composed over a career spanning almost sixty years can now be thought of as existing simultaneously within a single totality' (*Thomas Hardy*, p. ix).[1] But, we must ask, does a novel have the same relationship to a writer's corpus as an individual chapter does to a novel? I believe each novel has its own unique form which generates values and effects that provide the crucial context for an individual passage or incident.

Each novel has its own consciousness. The formal element for discovering the novel's consciousness is the speaking voice. Yet that is the element of fiction that is often ignored because we have not transformed into critical practice our theoretical understanding that the third person omniscient narrator is a significant character in the fictive world. The narrator's present tense *action* is his telling. His verbal action dramatizes a distinct personality. In a sense, by giving the narrator foreknowledge of the completed pattern and the ability to penetrate the characters' minds and render their thoughts and feelings, an author creates a persona in his own image. But once the act of creation is complete and the final draft is written, the influence of the author's personality ceases and the narrator exists within the fictive universe.

The ontological nature of voice in the novel should never be disregarded because the reader is inevitably involved in the process of responding to the consciousness of a distinct persona. This persona discovers the fictive world for us through his language. The reader's perception of a developing, constantly changing pattern of themes and structures is dependent upon the gradual revelation of the narrator's consciousness. The term omniscient may be misleading because no narrator can really understand the psychology of his own verbal behaviour or all the implications of the novel's evolving structure. In the process of perceiving the world that the narrator's mind contains, we become aware of the distinct personality that gives the world shape and significance. The narrator's verbal behaviour reveals the distinct personality of the teller. Just as with other characters, his verbal behaviour is the function of an interaction between his psychic and moral needs and the world beyond himself.

Ian Gregor has remarked:

> Both Hardy and Lawrence have produced a fiction in which the presence of the author is an important element in our experience, but it is not a presence like that, say, of Fielding or George Eliot, where we feel the author filtering the book through to us, but rather where the author is participant, undergoing the experience of the book with the characters.[2]

It can be questioned whether the narrator is ever a mere filter, completely devoid of personal urgency. Professor Gregor is surely correct that in certain novelists we are more particularly conscious of the narrator's psychic and moral life because of his empathetic involvement in the mental life of his characters. In such novels, the narrator may create a different pattern of meaning than he is aware of. *Sons and Lovers* provides an obvious example. The centre of the narrator's consciousness is usually Paul, and the narrator's intermittent efforts to examine objectively Paul's responses dissolve into complete empathy. The reader, familiar with *Fantasia of the Unconscious*, understands far more clearly than the narrator the full implications of Paul's oedipal love and its shaping effect on his subsequent relationships with Clara and Miriam. But the novel itself generates alternative values because the reader understands that the narrator's interpretation of incident after incident is myopic and wrong-headed. While the narrator stresses the gradual development of Paul's consciousness and thus sees the concluding paragraphs as affirmative, the *narrative* emphasizes the enclosing and limiting nature of Paul's experience. The narrator sees a linear progression from the oedipal love to the possibility of a vital future. But the novel itself suggests that Paul's life is still orbiting around his mother's influence. His walking towards town with fists shut and his mouth set fast – an expression that poignantly recalls Mrs. Morel – is ironic testimony to the continuing deterministic influence of his mother.

The third-person narrator is a distinct personality with his own psychic and moral life, as well as a document of the author's state of mind at the specific time of authorship. Where an author consistently uses the conventional third-person narrator, we can very profitably discuss the progress of an author's career in terms of his dramatized narrators. For Hardy, this approach reveals his commitment to the protagonist and confirms the view of those contextualists who have emphasized how Hardy's deepening involvement in the central social and moral issues of the late nineteenth century shaped his later fiction. What follows is an attempt to show how an analysis of each novel's speaker adds a significant dimension to the reading of Hardy's fiction.

II

Hillis Miller offers an analysis of chapter xxii of *Far from the Madding Crowd* (1874) as an example of Hardy's characteristic method:

> A few pages of *Far from the Madding Crowd* offer an opportunity to watch in detail the advance and retreat of the narrator's consciousness as he identifies himself with his characters or moves so far away in time and space that the story he tells seems only an arbitrary example of laws valid everywhere at all times.
> (*Thomas Hardy*, p. 57)

But he severely distorts the sense of the chapter. He remarks on the chapter's first sentence ('Men thin away to insignificance and oblivion quite as often by not making the most of good spirits when they have them as by lacking good spirits when they are indispensable' [ch. xxii, p. 163])[3] that 'The reader at this point is nowhere and at no specified time, looking at no particular scene in the novel. He is merely listening to the disembodied voice of the narrator' (*Thomas Hardy*, p. 59). But the cited sentence is surely illustrative of the narrator's apparent leisure and detachment which enable him to make generalizations that are not psychically or morally demanded by immediate circumstances. That the narrator takes neither the characters nor himself quite so seriously as the characters take themselves shows that he enjoys nostalgically recapturing the simplicity and innocence of rural life which modern civilization lacks. Yet later events reveal that this is the impression he wishes to create – an impression that is part of a larger effort to recover for himself the innocence of rustic life. The narrator is attempting to idealize the Wessex world into a pastoral version of an agrarian culture that looks away from the hurly-burly of contemporary life to the richer past that is evoked by references to Elizabethan and classical times. He is trying to transform the rural civilization into a Poussin canvas, purging uncomfortable subjects from his vista.

The novel's title implies the essence of the narrator's juxtaposition of the world of Gabriel with the world suggested by the ominous phrase 'madding crowd', a term which hovers over the novel's world as a threat to stability and sanity. Gabriel's world is conceived of as a remote existence where man usually lives in harmonious relationship with nature and his fellow creatures. Even though Weatherbury includes its share of misery and pain, of pride and selfishness, the possibility of a humane civilization remains embodied in Gabriel and in the Wessex folk. Contrasting the permanence of purpose inherent in the barn with the mutability of ecclesiastical and political institutions, the narrator dramatizes an imaginary beholder's response:

> Here at least the spirit of the ancient builders was at one with the spirit of the modern beholder. Standing before this abraded pile, the eye regarded its present usage, the mind dwelt upon its past history, with a satisfied sense of functional continuity throughout – a feeling almost of gratitude, and quite of pride, at the permanence of the idea which had heaped it up. The fact that four centuries had neither proved it to be founded on a mistake, inspired any hatred of its purpose, nor given rise to any reaction that had battered it down, invested this simple grey effort of old minds with a repose, if not a grandeur, which a too curious reflection was apt to disturb in its ecclesiastical and military compeers.
>
> (ch. xxii, p. 165)

Belief in the vitality of the rural civilization pulsates in the narrator's words, for it is clear that the presentation of the beholder's response reflects the narrator's own *gratitude and pride*.

At times, the narrator almost self-consciously adopts a sophisticated style to present the rural world to an audience consisting of 'persons unknown and far away, who will, however, never experience the superlative comfort derivable from the wool as it here exists, new and pure' (ch. xxii, p. 168). Worldliness, loquacity, an aphoristic style, and references to literary and mythological figures emphasize the narrator's distance from the rural perspective. His efforts to place the sheep within a mythic context and his rather clumsy efforts at sophistication remind us simultaneously of the narrator's estrangement from the culture he loves and of the artificiality of transforming the rural culture into a pastoral eclogue: 'The clean, sleek creature arose from its fleece – how perfectly like Aphrodite rising from the foam should have been seen to be realized ...' (ch. xxii, p. 168).

The narrator's consciousness of Gabriel's thoughts and feelings alternates between his consciousness of the larger perspective deriving from his more inclusive knowledge of the world, and his foreknowledge of the developing pattern. He renders Gabriel's response to Bathsheba's rebuke in language which distances the event for him even while it locates it within Gabriel's present perspective: '[His wound] had a sting which the abiding sense of his inferiority to both herself and Boldwood was not calculated to heal. But a manly resolve to recognize boldly that he had no longer a lover's interest in her, helped him occasionally to conceal a feeling' (ch. xxii, p. 170). Style becomes distance; balanced sentences present the narrator's distinct consciousness of the scene. Later, when he returns to rendering Oak's consciousness, he comments: 'Pestilent moods had come, and teased away his quiet. Bathsheba had shown indications of anointing him above his fellows by installing him as the bailiff ...' (ch. xxii, p. 173). A word such as 'anointed' emphasizes the narrator's ironic distance from Oak and the gulf of experience that divides him from a man who exclaims with the fullest sincerity that Henery's tale of Bathsheba's kissing Boldwood is a lie.

What I am saying about the narrator's consciousness in chapter xxii may be clearer if we turn to the voice of *Under the Greenwood Tree* (1872). In the earlier novel, the speaker's perspective is dependent not upon a wider view of life than that of his characters, but rather upon an appreciation and empathy for the social comedy involving near betrayal of a simple rustic by an aspiring woman. The narrator's inflated language and occasionally mythic references are means by which he can laugh good-naturedly at those who share the pastoral world with him. If ever the book seems to transcend the limits of social comedy within a relatively uncorrupted rural world, it is in the comic evocation of the Philomel myth.

To end the novel with the nightingale's song is to affirm the value of the pastoral world where feelings and consciousness have an existence independent of linguistic patterns. When Dick or the members of the Mellstock choir attempt to *verbalize* their feelings, they lapse unintentionally into a parody of civilized discourse. As their interview with Maybold makes clear, conventional speech is one of several ways they communicate and not the one with which they feel most comfortable. Dialogues of gestures and evocatives supplement the role of formal grammar and syntax as a method of communication. The disjointed and disorganized quality of the choir's verbal behaviour mocks rather than imitates usual patterns of discourse. The narrator's reliance upon literary convention, in the form of the nightingale's call, to convey the novel's moral significance seems finally a refusal to take on an interpretive role that would bridge the distance between his position within the pastoral community and the world of the 'madding crowd'. His use of the pastoral calendar to measure time, the prose epithalamium of the closing chapter, and his refusal to intellectualize the greenwood tree into a literary symbol demonstrate that the narrator is a part of the world that he lyricizes.

III

Hardy's novels dramatize the movement of the speaking voice from the perspective of the rural world to one located within the intellectual crosswinds of the nineteenth century's crisis of values. Whereas *The Return of the Native* (1878) illustrates Clym's failure to recapture the 'visionary gleam', the narrator is more successful. At first, after Clym returns to the heath, the narrator's imaginative and emotional responses correspond to Clym's. He is sympathetic to Clym's retraction of worldliness and his rejection of materialistic desires. After Eustacia rebukes him for being satisfied with furze-cutting during his temporary blindness, Clym becomes the spokesman for the dignity of the simple life:

But the more I see of life the more do I perceive that there is nothing particularly great in its greatest walks, and therefore nothing particularly small in mine of furze-cutting. If I feel that the greatest blessings vouchsafed to us are not very valuable, how can I feel it to be any great hardship when they are taken away?

(bk. IV, ch. ii, p. 302)

Later the narrator quite clearly separates his viewpoint from Clym's consciousness because Clym's stress on renunciation and his final position of itinerant preacher are almost a parody of Clym's former vitality and intelligence.

Hillis Miller speaks of the description of Egdon Heath as 'before man or without man', but he neglects the importance to the chapter and to the novel of a particular mode of perception (*Thomas Hardy*, p. 87). The narrator dramatizes how his intuitive and subjective imagination develops the heath into a symbol of awesomeness, timelessness, and the indifference of the physical world to man. The imagined perceiver throughout the first chapter is a receptacle of the narrator's responses and anticipates what Clym's responses will be during his disability. In the first sentences of the first chapter, the heath is imagined as completely inaccessible to man's perception. But by the middle of the second paragraph the narrator posits the furze-cutter in the process of experiencing the impersonal movements of the heath: 'Looking upwards, a furze-cutter would have been inclined to continue work; lokking down, he would have decided to finish his faggot and go home' (bk. I, ch. i, p. 3). Imagining an experiencing perceiver is itself a movement towards control and order, an effort to exorcize the shadow of darkness that the narrator feels hovers over the heath. Similarly, anthropomorphizing the heath is an attempt to contain the frightening energy that the narrator instinctively feels in the heath: 'The face of the heath by its mere complexion added half an hour to evening; it could in like manner retard the dawn, sadden noon, anticipate the frowning of storms scarcely generated, and intensify the opacity of a moonless midnight to a cause of shaking and dread' (bk. I, ch. i, p. 3).

The heath is imagined as a symbolic landscape imbued with the narrator's understanding of Clym's history: 'It was at present a place perfectly accordant with man's nature – neither ghastly, hateful, nor ugly: neither commonplace, unmeaning, nor tame;

but, like man, slighted and enduring; and withal singularly
colossal and mysterious in its swarthy monotony' (bk. I, ch. i, p. 6).
While these hieroglyphs are prophetic for the reader, they are the
distilled residue of the narrator's memory of events. The narrator's
response to the timelessness and invulnerability of the heath
subtly comments upon Clym's final presence on the heath when
he is almost reduced to insignificance. The narrator spiritually
returns to the heath, discovers its myth-making potential, and
brings his outside knowledge to bear by interpreting it for those
living the kind of materialistic life that Clym has forsworn:

> To recline on a stump of thorn in the central valley of Egdon,
> between afternoon and night, as now, where the eye could reach
> nothing of the world outside the summits and shoulders of
> heathland which filled the whole circumference of its glance,
> and to know that everything around and underneath had been
> from prehistoric times as unaltered as the stars overhead, gave
> ballast to the mind adrift on change, and harassed by the
> irrepressible New.... Distilled by the sun, kneaded by the
> moon, it is renewed in a year, in a day, or in an hour. The sea
> changed, yet Egdon remained.
>
> (bk. I, ch. i, pp. 6–7)

The narrator's use of language to contain the chaotic heath is a
kind of victory that eludes Clym. In a crucial passage that
differentiates the narrator's sensibilities from Clym's, the narrator's praise of Promethean rebelliousness contrasts with Clym's
renunciation of Promethean aspirations:

> Moreover to light a fire is the instinctive and resistant act of man
> when, at the winter ingress, the curfew is sounded throughout
> Nature. It indicates a spontaneous, Promethean rebelliousness
> against the fiat that this recurrent season shall bring foul times,
> cold darkness, misery and death. Black chaos comes, and the
> fettered gods of the earth say, Let there be light.
>
> (bk, I, ch. iii, pp. 17–18)

The imposition of linguistic and epistemological patterns upon the
heath is another 'instinctive and resistant act of man', a significant
refusal to submit to the darkness and chaos that threatens men's
efforts to make sense of the cosmos. That the chronological

perspective within the narrator's imagination includes the last geological age and 'the final overthrow' demonstrates language's ability to make sense of a perpetually chaotic portion of the cosmos. To come to terms with the heath, the most radical version of formlessness and resistance to man's strivings, is to demonstrate the possibility of fulfilling the quest for form and meaning that Clym himself valiantly, but not quite successfully, pursues. In a real sense, Clym's pyrrhic victory is juxtaposed to the very real triumph of imagination which the narrator achieves in the first chapter. That chapter is testimony to the potential of language for creating meaning and to the restorative potential of the imagination.

IV

While Hardy dramatized the narrator's ability to wrest order from chaos, to impose stasis upon the not-I world, his triumph was to be an evanescent one. The social and political world could no longer be excluded from his central focus; he felt impelled to move outward from the landscape of his mind to a confrontation with the intellectual issues of the nineteenth century. His narrators become increasingly chroniclers of the patterns of history that Hardy viewed with despair. In *The Mayor of Casterbridge* (1886), the narrator remains outside the consciousness of both Henchard and Farfrae, judging and interpreting their behaviour according to his own moral standards, but consistently sharing the responses and attitudes of neither. Originally, the narrator's *conscience* dominates his presentation of Henchard, and his judgement of the man who had risen from workman to mayor is rather harsh because he never for a moment forgets how Henchard has bartered his wife. But as he gets caught up in the telling and recalls the behaviour of Farfrae, his judgement radically changes. Whether Hardy intended it or not, the telling dramatizes the impossibility of using *a priori* absolutes in regard to human conduct. In the first chapters of Henchard's triumph in Casterbridge the narrator's judgement is still severe, as if Henchard were truly a character of heroic proportions and he were the spokesman of Henchard's nemesis. Assuring the audience that Henchard's past character is very much an ingredient of the present, the narrator comments: 'Those tones showed that, though under a long reign of self-control he had become Mayor and churchwarden and what not, there was still the same unruly volcanic stuff beneath the rind of Michael Henchard as when he had sold his wife at Weydon Fair' (ch. xvii, p. 129). Gradually the narrator gives up his pretensions of presenting a classic tragedy; as he discovers the pettiness and commercialism of the world that is displacing Henchard, he begins to chronicle the disruption of agrarian life in Casterbridge.

The Mayor of Casterbridge is a novel that tests and probes the values that the narrator espouses at the outset. Yet because the narrator develops as a character, it is really a novel that shows the narrator's search for standards that will replace the absolutes that become not so much discredited as irrelevant to the late nineteenth century. Elizabeth-Jane's credo becomes the standard in a world where heroic action is impossible:

> As the lively and sparkling emotions of her early married life cohered into an equable serenity, the finer movements of her nature found scope in discovering to the narrow-lived ones around her the secret (as she had once learnt it) of making limited opportunities endurable; which she deemed to consist in the cunning enlargement, by a species of microscopic treatment, of those minute forms of satisfaction that offer themselves to everybody not in positive pain; which, thus handled, have much of the same inspiriting effect upon life as wider interests cursorily embraced.... Her experience had been of a kind to teach her, rightly or wrongly, that the doubtful honour of a brief transit through a sorry world hardly called for effusiveness, even when the path was suddenly irradiated at some half-way point by daybeams rich as hers.
>
> (ch. xlv, p. 385)

The homiletic consciousness with which the narrator gives linguistic shape to the values that he shares with Elizabeth-Jane is particularly appropriate for a narrator who begins on the side of nemesis and expresses himself throughout as a moral presence. Her conclusions are those to which the narrator has brought the reader by his recapitulation of the story of Henchard and Farfrae:

> And in being forced to class herself among the fortunate she did not cease to wonder at the persistence of the unforeseen, when the one to whom such unbroken tranquility had been accorded in the adult stage was she whose youth had seemed to teach that

happiness was but the occasional episode in a general drama of pain.

(ch. xlv, pp. 385–6)

Yet the reader cannot but feel sadness in the gradual narrowing and limiting of the narrator's perspective, of his movement away from a Sophoclean dimension to the diurnal life of nineteenth-century rural England.

The narrator's conception of his role undergoes several changes. As the narrator recalls Henchard's displacement by Farfrae, he casts himself less as a moralist and more as an historian who records the replacement of an intuitive and spontaneous rural culture by a calculating, self-interested materialism. Later, the narrator's somewhat simplified chronicle of the transformation of values within the Casterbridge community gives way to a more complex view of the influence of the past. He comes to believe that the moral ambiance of a community outlives the specific deeds of its former citizens and to understand that the past has the potential to be activated as part of a living present. At first, he presents Casterbridge as the radial centre of rural life, and enjoys recalling the mutually beneficial relationship between the pastoral city and the way of life that it supports: 'Thus Casterbridge was in most respects but the pole, focus, or nerve-knot of the surrounding country life; differing from the many manufacturing towns which are as foreign bodies set down, like boulders on a plain, in a green world with which they have nothing in common' (ch. ix, p. 70). But as he moves forward in his recollection and becomes increasingly conscious of Casterbridge's grisly past, he realizes the skimming-ton-ride had its antecedents in the Roman games and in the 1705 burning of a woman who had murdered her husband. If the allusions to Cain, Saul, Job, and Oedipus are meant to suggest that Henchard repeats archetypal patterns, these allusions become parodic as Casterbridge repeats its past history of perversity and malice. Rather than a successor to the magnitude of tragic heroes, Henchard, in his inability to understand the compulsions that shape his behaviour, is revealed as a neurotic modern.

V

The confrontation between Giles and Fitzpiers in *The Woodlanders* (1887) may represent a subtle bifurcation in Hardy between the man whose integrity and simple dignity he envied, Giles, and the man he dreaded becoming, Fitzpiers. Nostalgia often dominates the narrator's voice as he chronicles the passing of a way of life indigenous to the rural hamlet. His animus towards Fitzpiers reflects more than a foreknowledge of Fitzpiers' behaviour. The narrator becomes an intruder into the Hintock world because he seems to impose objective and empirical standards on the spontaneous, subjective, and intuitive lives:

> [Hintock] was one of those sequestered spots outside the gates of the world where may usually be found more meditation than action, and more listlessness than meditation; where reasoning proceeds on narrow premises, and results in interferences wildly imaginative; yet where, from time to time, dramas of a grandeur and unity truly Sophoclean are enacted in the real, by virtue of the concentrated passions and closely-knit interdependence of the lives therein.
>
> (ch. i, pp. 4–5)

The urbane and condescending tone towards Hintock inevitably dramatizes his separation from the rural world and places him in a position of *displaying* Hintock's sensibilities for the benefit of those who would be interested in its 'dramas of a grandeur and unity'.

Because Fitzpiers' views often parody those of the narrator, and because Fitzpiers often seems to be impersonating the emotional detachment and intellectual acuity of the narrator, the narrator goes out of his way to express antagonism for the character who most resembles him intellectually. It is Fitzpiers, not the narrator, who articulates the view – held by the narrator and dramatized by the novel's action – that subjective needs transform a person into the object of life: 'Human love is a subjective thing – the essence itself of man... [It] is a joy accompanied by an idea which we project against any suitable object in the line of our vision, just as the rainbow iris is projected against an oak, ash, or elm tree indifferently' (ch. xvi, p. 138). Fitzpiers' amplification of this doctrine tends to be crude, as if the narrator needs to assure us that Fitzpiers' apparent wisdom is merely another version of his hypocrisy: 'So that if any other young lady had appeared instead of the one who did appear, I should have felt just the same interest in her, and have quoted precisely the same lines from Shelley about her, as about this one I saw. Such miserable creatures of circumstance are we all!' (ch. xvi, p. 138). The narrator consistently and relentlessly expresses his hostility towards Fitzpiers. He wants the reader to know, *before* Fitzpiers' behaviour reveals that he is deserving of condemnation, that the doctor is a perfidious character. Commenting upon how the doctor would have felt had he known of Grace's antecedents, the narrator comments: 'Instead of treasuring her image as a rarity he would at most have played with her as a toy. He was that kind of man' (ch. xvii, pp. 146–7).

Giles lives an existence which is far less dependent upon verbal behaviour than the narrator's and Fitzpiers'. Although Fitzpiers chooses isolation when he first arrives at the woodlands, it is soon clear that verbal behaviour is a major part of his life. His verbosity is contrasted with the silence of Giles and, especially, Marty. Concomitantly, the subtlety of Fitzpiers' motives and pleasures is juxtaposed with the ingenuous responses of the Hintock community. Fitzpiers is an epicure of emotions whose professional ability is divorced from dignity and integrity; he is an aberration produced by urban life who threatens the narrator's concept of the humane community. Indeed, Grace, too, is at times separated from Hintock's life because education has transformed her instincts into overly refined sensibilities.

The narrator's role places him closer to Fitzpiers, for whom consciousness is always intellectual and often verbal, than to Giles, the man capable of an inner peace and instinctive communion. To even try to speak of Giles's semiconscious feelings is to transform them into an artificial linguistic pattern:

It has sometimes dimly occurred to [Giles] in his ruminating silences at Little Hintock, that external phenomena – such as the lowness or height or colour of a hat, the fold of a coat, the make of a boot, or the chance attitude of a limb at the instant of view – may have a great influence upon feminine opinion of a man's worth, so frequently founded on non-essentials; but a certain causticity of mental tone towards himself and the world in general had prevented to-day, as always, any enthusiastic action on the strength of that reflection...

(ch. v, p. 41)

Phrases such as 'dimly occurred', 'ruminating silences', and 'mental tone' show how far Giles's mental life is from the narrator's and emphasize how the narrator shares characteristics with

Fitzpiers that he dislikes. In a very revealing passage that occurs immediately after describing Giles's mental life, the narrator for one brief moment despairs at the inevitable oversimplification and distortion of encapsulating the flux of human personality into the stasis of language. With an extremely uncharacteristic glibness that does not begin to disguise the real discomfort the narrator feels at falling into behaviour patterns that Giles's example exposes as superficial, the narrator comments:

> It would have been difficult to describe Grace Melbury with precision, either then or at any time. Nay, from the highest point of view, to precisely describe a human being, the focus of a universe, how impossible! But apart from transcendentalism, there never probably lived a person who was in herself more completely a *reductio ad absurdum* of attempts to appraise a woman, even externally, by items of face and figure.
> Speaking generally, it may be said that she was sometimes beautiful, at other times not beautiful, according to the state of her health and spirits.
>
> (ch. v, pp. 41–2)

VI

In *Tess of the d'Urbervilles* (1891), the narrator faces the significant religious and moral issues of the nineteenth century. His moral consciousness and his attitude towards society develop within the process of narrating Tess's story. As his recollection of the story continues, the narrator's tone becomes more embittered and cynical. Until Tess's seduction by Alec, the narrator's ironic vocabulary and detachment remove him from an empathetic response to her consciousness. At the outset, he conceives her as a representative figure of her age. Born to irresponsible parents unable to care for a family far too large for their resources, she is the victim of an indifferent cosmos which has little concern for her interest or needs. Writing of Tess's reverie before the accident in which Prince is killed, the narrator is often remote, if not anaesthetized: 'The mute procession past her shoulders of trees and hedges became attached to fantastic scenes outside reality, and the occasional heave of the wind became the sigh of some immense sad soul, conterminous with the universe in space, and with history in time' (phase I, ch. iv, p. 34). The vision of 'an immense sad soul' consistently informing chronological time renders time meaningless as it pertains to human events, for time is only meaningful as it pertains to the possibility of change. After Tess's first meeting with Alec, the narrator gives his version of why Tess 'was *doomed* to be seen and coveted that day by the wrong man, and not by some other man, the right and desired one in all respects': 'In the ill-judged execution of the well-judged plan of things the call seldom produces the comer, the man to love rarely coincides with the hour for loving' (phase I, ch. v; emphasis mine, pp. 48–9).

The persona's outrage, bitter irony, and muted passion as he recalls Sorrow's baptism and death dramatize for the reader the developing personal urgency in the narrator's response to the tale he is telling. The incident is a critical one for deepening Tess's intuitive understanding of the irrelevance of conventional moral standards. The narrator would have us understand that by baptizing her child, Tess bravely refuses to have the world impose its own absolute laws upon her. Her enthusiasm had a 'transfiguring effect upon [her] face ... showing it as a thing of immaculate beauty, with a touch of dignity which was almost regal' (phase II, ch. xiv, p. 119).

The very heaviness of the irony and needless repetition gives us an insight into the persona's feelings. The detachment and remoteness dissolve into a thinly controlled rage. When he tells us how her almost regal face of 'immaculate beauty' had been her undoing, we feel that the speaker can barely control his anger towards Alec and the social law that condemns an innocent victim. Rather than indict Hardy for intruding his views, how much more interesting it is to ask what the narrator's rendering of Sorrow's death tells us about him as a personality and his relation to the title character. Tess and the persona become nearly identical for the first time: 'Whether well founded or not she has no uneasiness now, reasoning that if Providence would not ratify such an act of approximation she, for one, did not value the kind of heaven lost by the irregularity – either for herself or for her child' (phase II, ch. xiv. p. 120).

The narrator becomes the spokesman for Tess's emotional and moral consciousness by the end of the second phase. The narrator articulates Tess's instinctive feeling that she retains her vitality, although the social law limits and defines her as a moral exile: 'But for the world's opinion [her] experiences would have been simply a liberal education' (phase II, ch. xv, p. 125). Yet Tess has trouble casting off the moral hobgoblins that seek to intrude themselves upon her primitive consciousness: 'And probably [her] half-conscious rhapsody was a Fetishistic utterance in a Monotheistic setting; women whose chief companions are the forms and forces of outdoor Nature retain in their souls far more of the Pagan fantasy of their remote forefathers than of the systematized religion taught their race at a later date' (phase III, ch. xvi, pp. 134–5). As we see in her first interview with Angel, she is now able ingenuously to articulate her pessimism and gloom. Gradually Tess learns what the narrator now knows: the strong often prey upon the weak; the survival of the fittest often extends into the realm of man; and man has little chance for happiness on this earth. And the narrator is moved by his recollection of Tess to become increasingly more responsive to her poignant dilemma. Finally, when he narrates how Tess killed Alec, in a scene that grotesquely parodies Alec's original assault upon her innocence, the narrator's voice reflects relief from the inexorable pressure of suppressed violence created by his intense empathy.

VII

The focus of the narrator's consciousness in *Jude the Obscure* (1895) is the emotional and psychic responses of the protagonist, Jude. The narrator's early comments on Jude are influenced by fore-knowledge of Jude's destiny. His emotional and intellectual attitudes are approximately those that Jude would have held had he survived to tell the story. The narrator penetrates Jude's mind with none of the tentativeness with which Hardy's previous narrators speculate upon the motives and attitudes of the characters. He renders Jude's interpretation of events without ironic detachment. To a first reader, the narrator's gloom and bitterness in the first chapters seem disproportionate to the events described. But that is because Jude's completed life dominates the narrator's consciousness; he has neither the mood nor the inclination for nostalgic views of former cultures, pastoral settings, or anecdotes about rural folk. The narrator imagines Jude's history as a representative late nineteenth-century drama of a man's abortive effort to improve his socio-economic position. While Jude, upon his arrival at Christminster as on so many other occasions, is lost in dreams of a fulfilling future, the narrator emphasizes how the present is ineluctably weaving a pattern that makes the imaginative future impossible. Commenting on Jude's satisfaction at finally having contact with the students of Christminster, the narrator bitterly recalls:

Yet he was as far from them as if he had been at the antipodes. Of course he was. He was a young workman in a white blouse, and with stone-dust in the creases of his clothes; and in passing him they did not even see him, or hear him, rather saw through him as though a pane of glass at their familiars beyond. Whatever they were to him, he to them was not on the spot at all; and yet he had fancied he would be close to their lives by coming there.

(part II, ch. ii, p. 100)

To those people whose fellowship Jude desperately seeks, he is transparent, a non-person.

Implicit in the attitudes of the narrative voice is that life is barely better than the nullification of life; if death is not to be actively sought, it can be accepted with equanimity in a world inevitably hostile to man's aspirations. The narrator's comments on Jude's weakness of not being able to 'bear to hurt anything' are bitterly ironic: 'This weakness of character, as it may be called, suggested that he was the sort of man who was born to ache a good deal before the fall of the curtain upon his unnecessary life should signify that all was well with him again' (part I, ch. ii, p. 13). When he reflects on his boyhood disgrace, Jude's attitudes are identical to the narrator's:

Events did not rhyme quite as he had thought. Nature's logic was too horrid for him to care for. That mercy towards one set of creatures was cruelty towards another sickened his sense of harmony. As you got older, and felt yourself to be at the centre of your time, and not at a point in its circumference, as you had felt when you were little, you were seized with a sort of shuddering, he perceived. All around you there seemed to be something glaring, garish, rattling, and the noises and glares hit upon the little cell called your life, and shook it, and warped it.

(part I, ch. ii, p. 15)

The shift to the second person conflates Jude's and the narrator's voices and thus implies that the view of life as a hostile force, a mechanistic juggernaut attacking the vitality of a helpless cell, is the narrator's as well as young Jude's.

Father Time is not only an objectification of Jude's present superego and of his earlier despondent understanding of what life offers, but an extension, or at least a reductive version, of the narrator's own attitudes. Like Father Time, the narrator is the victim of his own insight and hyperacuity, and, most of all, of the morbid patterns of human life that his mind contains. To the narrator, the son of Jude and Arabella is an abstraction, a symbolic figure; he is representative of the new generation that is developing as man progresses to greater consciousness of his plight, and as human vitality seems to be increasingly threatened by industrialization.

The narrator ascribes to Father Time a vision that approximates his own: 'A ground swell from ancient years of night seemed now and then to lift the child in this morning-life, when his face took a back view over some great Atlantic of Time, and appeared not to care about what it saw' (part V, ch. iii, p. 332). He imputes the omniscience to Father Time that he claims for himself and implies that Father Time has the ability to hold the entire pattern of the past within his mind as a shaping aspect of his perception of the present. The narrator is conscious of the awesome burden of the child's insight: 'He then seemed to be doubly awake, like an enslaved and dwarfed Divinity, sitting passive and regarding his companions as if he saw their whole rounded lives rather than their immediate figures' (part V, ch. iii, p. 332). Feeling the curse of knowledge that separates himself from those who do not fully understand the plight of mankind, the narrator senses how Father Time's perspicuity corrupts his chances for happiness:

It could have been seen that the boy's ideas of life were different from those of the local boys. Children begin with detail, and learn up to the general; they begin with the contiguous, and gradually comprehend the universal. The boy seemed to have begun with the generals of life, and never to have concerned himself with the particulars. To him the houses, the willows, the obscure fields beyond, were apparently regarded not as brick residences, pollards, meadows; but as human dwellings in the abstract, vegetation, and the wide dark world.

(part V, ch. iii, p. 334)

If Father Time has the vision of doom that Jude was able to partially reject when he was a boy, his instinctive renunciation of life anticipates Jude's final echo of Job: *'Let the day perish wherein I was born, and the night in which it was said, There is a man child conceived'* (part VI, ch. xi, p. 488). For the narrator, Father Time is a pathetic victim, the grotesque result of social law and human frailty:

> On that little shape had converged all the inauspiciousness and shadow which had darkened the first union of Jude, and all the accidents, mistakes, fears, errors of the last. He was their nodal point, their focus, their expression in a single term. For the rashness of those parents he had groaned, for their ill-assortment he had quaked, and for the misfortunes of these he had died.
>
> (part VI, ch. ii, p. 406)

He becomes the symbol of the narrator's morbid wisdom that death alone can make things well for an 'unnecessary life'.

VIII

In his early novels, *Under the Greenwood Tree* and *Far from the Madding Crowd*, Hardy discovered that language provides a means of triumphing over scientific determinism and the discomforting moral and religious issues raised by *The Origin of Species* and *Essays and Reviews*. The early novels dramatize, among other things, the ability of the imagination to recover the lost world of Hardy's childhood. For Hardy, deeply attached to folk beliefs and magic, language became the method of exorcising the ghosts of doubt. The art of fiction replaces disorder with control and provides the kind of hermetic structure in which one can dwell. In the tradition of great Romantic poems of the mind, *The Return of the Native* dramatizes the Promethean capacities of the imagination to impose significant form upon the radical image of a chaotic and indifferent cosmos: Egdon Heath. But Hardy began to become dissatisfied with the kind of imaginative victory that excludes major social and philosophic issues. In *The Mayor of Casterbridge* and *The Woodlanders*, the narrator traces the displacement of the subjective agrarian culture by amoral materialism and focuses upon that something intangible – call it Necessity, Chance, or Fate – which seems to be working to frustrate man's aspirations and human needs.

Near the end of his novel-writing career, Hardy, like Arnold, felt himself caught between two worlds, 'one dead, the other powerless to be born'. But the world not yet born seemed a world of impossible aspirations, while the dying world was the searing actuality. In *Tess of the d'Urbervilles* and *Jude the Obscure*, men are becoming restless, isolated, and frustrated as they lose their physical and moral roots. One of the impressions that remains with us is that of Tess and Jude walking aimlessly through Wessex country, even while they believe they are embarked upon a significant purpose. Arnold could find solace in myths created from the cultural tradition in which he believed; one thinks of the Scholar Gypsy, Thyrsis, Wordsworth, and Goethe functioning as sustaining images within his poetry. But unlike Arnold, Hardy could no longer find the objective correlatives to dramatize the process of discovering values. Because Hardy's narrator is completely empathetic to the plight of Jude, Hardy's most autobiographical character, one might argue that Jude is not transformed from the subjective figure of Hardy's imagination into a representative victim of social and cosmological forces. If Father Time's fate implies Hardy's insight into how painful the burden of knowledge and perspicacity could become, we may have a clue to why Hardy soon abandoned novel writing.

Notes

1. Page numbers in parentheses refer to J. Hillis Miller, *Thomas Hardy: Distance and Desire* (Cambridge, Mass.: The Belknap Press, 1970).
2. Ian Gregor, 'What Kind of Fiction did Hardy Write?', *Essays in Criticism*, 16 (1966) pp. 290–308. See p. 293. See also Mark Schorer, 'Technique as Discovery', *Hudson Review*, 1 (Spring 1948) pp. 67–87.
3. Page references refer to the 1912 Wessex edn (rpt. London: Macmillan, 1920). I have also specified quotations by chapter and, when appropriate, by book, part, or phase because most readers possess one of several paperback reprints of the 1912 edition, and the pagination of these paperbacks varies.

3
Beginnings and Endings in Hardy's Major Fiction

What we call the beginning is often the end.
T. S. Eliot, 'Little Gidding', *Four Quartets.*

Because of the length of a novel, our memory of it is disproportion-
ately related to its opening and ending. In the opening chapters,
the narrator creates for his readers the physical world in which the
novel takes place and the first episodes of the story which begin to
reveal the personalities of the characters. But more significantly,
beginnings introduce the novel's cosmology and the standards and
values by which actions will be judged. (Of course, since the
reading of a novel is an ongoing process, as the reader experiences
subsequent episodes, the moral terms on which the reader makes
his or her judgement will be modified.) Each novel has its own
Genesis and Apocalypse; when we open a novel, our world is
closed off and the genesis of a new ontology begins. The opening
chapters of the novel, that form which more than any other seeks
to have the inclusiveness and specificity of the real world, mimes
the process of Creation as the author's language imposes shape
and form upon silence and emptiness. Imperceptibly, as we read
the first sentences, our sense of time gives way to the internal
imagined time of the novel. The ending is an apocalypse which
reorders the significance of all that precedes; it is the moment
when the imagined world is abruptly sealed off from us and we
return to our diurnal activities.[1]
 If, as I believe is true, on the first reading of a Hardy novel one
has a sense that he has anticipated and almost experienced actions
that occur for the first time, it is because Hardy has created a world
where actions seem inevitable. Hardy's prophetic (and proleptic)
openings in which every detail seems to foreshadow major
themes, in conjunction with conclusions that confirm these
openings, are responsible for this sense of inevitability. The
openings take the reader into a world where man's aspirations are

49

blunted, as external circumstances connive with man's hidden flaws, and where the well-meaning characters rapidly discover that they live in a world in which things are quite likely to turn out badly. By 'fulfilling' the promise of the beginnings, the endings imply that the world in which men live is closed and invulnerable to essential change. The title of *Tess*'s last phase, 'Fulfilment', implies, I think, something about Hardy's world-view and aesthetic. By fulfilment, he means the inevitable bringing to fruition of the pattern that derives from the interaction of the central character's psyche with the world in which he or she is placed. After *Far from the Madding Crowd*, the endings fulfil the prophecies of the opening chapters. The ingredients of the destruction of central characters are implicit in the novels' beginnings. That the language, plot, and narrative comment of the opening are frequently echoed throughout, especially at the ending, enhances this sense of inevitability. When the reader reaches the ending of a Hardy novel, it is as if a prophecy were fulfilled. Hardy's endings perpetuate conditions that have prevailed before his specific narrative has begun and will prevail as given conditions of the imagined world in which these events take place. Turning away from a traditional benevolent resolution, Hardy's endings confirm rather than transfigure what precedes and reject the notion that experience brings wisdom and maturity.

After *Far from the Madding Crowd*, 'fulfilment' of the novel becomes 'fulfilment' of the pattern of a character's demise; this fulfilment is ironically juxtaposed to the narrative that the protagonist tells himself in the form of hopes and aspirations for the future. As Hardy's career progresses, the central character's perspective replicates the narrator's at an earlier and earlier stage in the novels. Hence the ironic distance between the narrator and character disappears and the narrator becomes an empathetic spokesman, an apologist, and an advocate for those central characters whom he envisions to be victims. The gradual movement from innocence to experience that is so characteristic of English fiction before Hardy (except, perhaps, *Wuthering Heights* and *Tristram Shandy*) is, in Hardy, far less noticeable than the intensification of the central character's plight and the narrator's conclusion that the cosmos is antagonistic. The most significant movement is not the development of the central character's moral awareness, but the dwindling of his expectations and the consequent loss of mental and emotional vitality.

Hardy is the first English novelist who wholeheartedly rejects the conventional Christian myth of a benevolent universe. He shows the irrelevance of that myth within his imagined world and shows how his characters are educated by experience to adopt an alternative one. As a self-dramatizing character who is a sceptical, gloomy, fatalistic presence, Hardy's narrator is an immanent presence whose pessimistic philosophical comments and bitterly ironic narration the reader feels on every page.[2] Hardy creates a malevolent world in which characters live not in light which is good, but in moral darkness which is bad. In an 1890 journal entry, he writes, 'I have been looking for God 50 years, and I think that if he had existed I should have discovered him. As an external personality, of course – the only true meaning of the word'.[3] Hardy's creation of a blighted star is his response to the premise that God's creation is a holy plan.[4] It is also his response to those Romantics and Victorians who, as M. H. Abrams remarks, fuse 'history, politics, and philosophy, and religion into one grand design by asserting Providence – or some form of natural teleology – to operate in the seeming chaos of human history so as to effect from present evil a greater good'.[5]

Hardy's novels are in part a response to the Biblical myth of benevolent creation directed by a just and beneficent God. If only to correct the notion that Hardy 'wrote a fiction which presumed a commission to write about the world as he found it',[6] we should think of Hardy in the tradition of Blake and Lawrence, other great mythologizers who create their own world with its own rules and traditions. Hardy goes beyond mimetic narrative and presents a genuine anti-Genesis myth that comments upon the usual nominalistic particularized world of fiction. Hardy's novels question the central postulates of the Christian cosmology by positing an imagined world where man cannot achieve salvation in a benevolent cosmos created under the auspices of a just and merciful God. In the Wessex novels, Hardy's narrator is at times a ubiquitous, omniscient prophet who, anticipating Lawrence in *The Rainbow*, 'Present, Past, & Future, sees'.[7] After *Far from the Madding Crowd*, Hardy's prophecy of disaster contrasts with the biblical prophecy of the second coming of the Messiah, as well as with man's conventional expectation that his fictions will be fulfilled. Fulfilment in the biblical myth depends upon the Messiah, the Last Judgment, and the release of the eternal soul at death. But Hardy, although he liked to think of himself as a meliorist, creates a cosmos where moral improvement is ineffectual and spiritual improvement is impossible.

The opening chapters of the first of the major Wessex novels, *Far from the Madding Crowd* (1874), present a pastoral world and simultaneously invalidate the pastoral myth. These chapters are a kind of prologue in which the traditional pastoral world is demythologized as Gabriel, who had once seemed a 'pastoral king', becomes aware of the indifference of the cosmos to man's aspirations (VI, p. 43). In the early chapters, the narrator is divided between, on the one hand, nostalgically elegizing rural life and comparing it favourably with urban life, and, on the other, somewhat reluctantly acknowledging that the distinctions between town and country often prove apocryphal. But the first chapters illustrate that Bathsheba is as proud, vain, and emotionally self-indulgent as any townswoman might be. After presenting Gabriel's seeming idyllic existence as a shepherd, the narrator shows how the misfortunes of losing his sheep, near-suffocation, and disappointment in love permanently disrupt the illusion that place or profession can imply value. The memorable simile with which the novel opened (in which the 'diverging wrinkles' of his smile extended 'upon his countenance like the rays in a rudimentary sketch of the rising sun' [I, p. 1]) is no longer possible. The narrator registers Gabriel's instinctive non-verbal apprehension that the world is not what he thought it was. Gabriel's perception of the external scene after losing his sheep not only mirrors his internal state, but enables the narrator to provide an alternative to the pastoral myth: 'The pool glittered like a dead man's eye, and as the world awoke a breeze blew, shaking and elongating the reflection of the moon without breaking it, and turning the image of the star to a phosphoric streak upon the water. All this Oak saw and remembered' (V, p. 41).

Gabriel's sense of isolation and his concomitant instinctive movement towards an 'other' that will complete himself show the inadequacy and irrelevance of the pastoral myth to the particular needs of man in the nineteenth century: 'Having for some time known the want of a satisfactory form to fill an increasing void within him, his position moreover affording the widest scope for his fancy, he painted her a beauty' (II, p. 16). In this passage, Hardy identifies the underlying motive and often dimly acknowledged effective cause of every relationship in his Wessex novels. Lacking the sense of an immanent, comprehending God, man seeks a responsive consciousness which he fictionalizes upon the slightest evidence into an omniscient, ubiquitous *alter ego*.

The marriage with which *Far from the Madding Crowd* ends is hardly a fulfilment of what precedes. 'Fulfilment' of the *characters'* aspirations occurs because the ending does not fulfil the pattern of the opening and of subsequent episodes in which the possibility of idyllic life has been evolved, treated, and discarded. As in an Austen or Fielding novel, the central male and female characters marry, presumably conditioned by society and modified by personal experience. Hardy has not defined either an alternative cosmology to the discredited pastoral myth or the traditional novel of manners with its marriage and implied happy future; nor has he invented the formal principles that will mime a new cosmology. In the early chapters, Gabriel had been an unsuccessful fictionalist, unable to impose a form on the recalcitrant material of his life. But ironically, after he passively accepts his isolation, Bathsheba's visit and their subsequent marriage fulfil the narrative that the central character has told himself. This kind of fulfilment will no longer occur after *Far from the Madding Crowd*. While the opening chapters dramatize Bathsheba's repeated intrusion into Gabriel's consciousness and her subsequent rejection of his suit, the ending (especially Chapter LVI) focuses on the intrusion of Gabriel (who had suppressed his hopes in the face of social and economic differences) into Bathsheba's consciousness. Not quite so shy, diffident, and self-effacing, Gabriel has learned how to spar with Bathsheba and how to monitor her solipsistic tendency to create her own reality. Reversing the interview in which he has proposed, it is she who is the petitioner, claiming and believing that it is merely her fear that she has offended him that brings her to his cottage.

What is different from an Austen novel is that after Troy is dead and Boldwood is imprisoned, Bathsheba, like Lydia in *The Rainbow*, responds to a deeper physiological self beneath the conscious self: 'Bathsheba was stirred by emotions which latterly she had assumed to be altogether dead within her' (LVI, p. 448). Bathsheba, who believes herself a person of principle, is, in fact, a chameleonic character whose constancy and stability are still very much in doubt. Bathsheba foreshadows Hardy's mature belief that a man or a woman cannot know his or her own psychosexual needs. Her behaviour discredits the myth of moral education which the ending implies. The marriage takes place within the context of a world where triumphs are evanescent and where external circumstances – fire, storm, death – perpetually threaten to prevent the kind of resolution we find in an Austen or Fielding novel. The resolution of their love in marriage exists side by side with Joseph Poorgrass' closing comment: 'But since 'tis as 'tis, why, it might have been worse, and I feel my thanks accordingly' (LVII, p. 464). Our memory of Fanny Robin's tragedy, Troy's moral idiocy, Boldwood's madness, and Bathsheba's fickleness is stirred by that remark and makes us keenly aware that there is no idyllic life in *Far from the Madding Crowd*. 'Fulfilment' in such a world cannot but be ephemeral.

The opening of *The Return of the Native* (1878) presents the Genesis of the Wessex novels, the refutation of the Christian creation myth, and the proposal of an alternative one. Although in later novels the cosmos will become actively antagonistic, rather than merely indifferent, the heath contains the essential ingredients of the cosmos in which the Wessex novels take place. Its eternality and passivity are juxtaposed to the unrest and temporality of man. Although man has gradually emerged from 'Druidical rites and Saxon ceremonies' into the nineteenth century, the heath remains the same, and its permanence and monotony satirize the vanity of man: 'A person on a heath in raiment of modern cut and colours has more or less an anomalous look. We seem to want the oldest and simplest human clothing where the clothing of the earth is so primitive' (I, I, p. 6). By evoking Genesis in conjunction with the classical myth of Prometheus' rebellion, Hardy creates an alternative vision in which alienation and refusal to submit are plausible and dignified positions: 'Moreover to light a fire is the instinctive and resistant act of man when, at the winter ingress, the curfew is sounded throughout Nature. It indicates a spontaneous, Promethean rebelliousness against the fiat that this recurrent season shall bring foul times, cold darkness, misery and death. Black chaos comes, and the fettered gods of the earth say, Let there be light' (I, III, pp. 17–18). Throughout human history, mankind has organized community rites and rituals as an instinctive response to the world: 'The flames from funeral piles long ago kindled there.... Festival fires to Thor and Woden had followed on the same ground and duly had their day' (I, III, p. 17). As surely as those primitives who first lit a fire, the narrator is struggling with the effort to bring light to what for him threatens to become black chaos. In his effort to comprehend how to impose linguistic form on the illimitable heath, Hardy's narrator describes the heath as if it were alive: 'The place became full of a watchful intentness now; for when other things sank brooding to sleep the heath appeared slowly to awake and listen' (I, I, p. 4).

Paradoxically, the heath is not only a metaphor for the cosmos, but it mirrors mankind's common internal chaos: 'It was found to be the hitherto unrecognized original of those wild regions of obscurity which are vaguely felt to be compassing us about in midnight dreams of flight and disaster, and are never thought of after the dream till revived by scenes like this' (I, I, pp. 5–6). As civilization's enemy, as the scene of primitive rites and ceremonies, as 'the untameable, Ishmaelitish thing that Egdon now was [and] it always had been', the heath corresponds to the atavistic and instinctive darker self which is within each of us (I, I, p. 6). Not unlike Conrad's Congo, something within the heath summons man back to his primordial origins when passions were uncontrolled, when the pace of life was slower, and when the moral distinctions of ordinary life seemed anachronistic if not irrelevant. If the heath is what Auden would think of as a *paysage moralisé* for uncontrolled fantasies and undisciplined passion, then it is a fitting setting for the libidinous energy of Eustacia Vye, whose presence appropriately 'fulfils' the scenes.

The ending fulfils the prophecies of the beginning. Clym duplicates the narrator as a modern consciousness who understands the distinction between man's aspirations and the circumstances of his life. In *The Return of the Native*, unlike *Far from the Madding Crowd*, the plots that circumstances make of men's lives are incongruous with the fictions they tell themselves. Our last views of Clym are not of a man who has triumphed, but of one who has been defeated. Seemingly without passion or vitality after Eustacia's death, he is rather anxious lest Thomasin should propose to him. In an interesting anticipation of Paul Morel in *Sons and Lovers*, he is as dominated by his mother after her death as he had been before it and seems unable to cast off his sense of guilt for not preventing her death. Diggory and Clym change places; he becomes the Ishmaelite of the heath, and Diggory re-enters the community. When, as preacher, Clym takes Eustacia's place on Rainbarrow he is hardly an heroic figure. Clym has learned what the narrator knows: 'That old-fashioned revelling in the general situation grows less and less possible as we uncover the defects of natural laws, and see the quandary that man is in by their operation' (III, I, p. 197). Clym's preaching is limited and self-indulgent. Yet, paradoxically, when Clym, the modern conscious-ness with whom the narrator empathises, acts upon this insight and willingly accepts his fate, he earns Hardy's ire. Hardy has become impatient with Clym's obsession with his mother, his passive and querulous response to vicissitude, and the surrender of his identity to Eustacia, his mother, and the heath. Surely, the emphasis on the penultimate sentence is upon his ineffectuality as a preacher: 'Some believed him, and some believed not; some said that his words were commonplace, others complained of his want of theological doctrine; while others again remarked that it was well enough for a man to take to preaching who could not see to do anything else' (VI, IV, p. 485).

The Mayor of Casterbridge (1886) begins by positing a world where civilization's conventions and moral reason are in a state of suspension and where anything is possible. Before the reader is told anything much about the family that is introduced trudging to Weydon-Priors in an indefinite year 'before the nineteenth century had reached one-third of its span' (I, p. 1), the narrator describes a grotesque bargain: a drunken man sells his wife to the highest bidder. Such characters as the 'haggish' furmity woman and the 'short man, with a nose resembling a copper knob . . . and eyes like button-holes' take us into a nightmare world in which grotesque characters are depicted as cartoons which illuminate as they distort (I, pp. 5, 10). Gradually, the scene becomes transformed into something so strained and charged that a swallow who accidental-ly wanders in desperately wants to escape as if he, too, were shocked by the enormity of the horror. That his wife's misgivings are described as 'bird-like chirpings' equates her with the harmless swallow which escapes the tent and with the innocent bird which sings 'a trite old evening song' at Weydon-Priors 'for centuries untold' (I, pp. 6, 9, 3). In this atavistic scene, Henchard ritualistical-ly casts off his wife as if she were the evil influence that has caused what he regards as his miserable plight.

The second chapter depicts the fetishistic effort of the still anonymous man to reverse his fatal act. Already the fabular ontology gives way to a nominalistic particular world. By Chapter III, Susan is embarked on the hopeless path of trying to reverse the past eighteen years, and the *Walpurgisnacht* atmosphere of the Weydon-Priors fair has entirely vanished. We are back in a world of shame, guilt, and recognizable motive. We begin to perceive that a sado-masochistic husband responds to unconscious psychic stimuli that he cannot even acknowledge, let alone understand. The restraint in Henchard's search for his wife ('a certain shyness of revealing his conduct prevented Michael Henchard from following up the investigation with the loud hue-and-cry such a pursuit demanded to render it effectual' [II, p. 19]) ironically anticipates the practical considerations invoked by Elizabeth-Jane and Farfrae when they plan to abandon their search for Henchard in the last chapter because a very slight financial sacrifice is called for.

In many ways, despite the conclusive ending of the plot of *The Mayor of Casterbridge*, the novel leaves unresolved its moral implications. Henchard's demise and the marriage of Farfrae and Elizabeth-Jane would seem finally to restrain and resolve the concatenation of events set in motion by Henchard's selling of his wife. Set against this consummate act of social anarchy by a man of unrestrained passion is the marriage of two people who have opted for traditional community values. But nevertheless the resolution is equivocal. For one thing, the novel comes full circle and makes Henchard, who had borne throughout the onus of moral opprobrium, the object of considerable compassion. When as a lonely man he reverses his journey of twenty-five years earlier, walking from Casterbridge to Weydon-Priors 'as an act of penance' (XLIV, p. 368), he engages our sympathy. Like Eliot's Bulstrode and Conrad's Jim, who continually experience a harrowing past as if it were the present, Henchard becomes obsessed with his past. His effort to leave the country is thwarted not only by his love for his stepdaughter but by a desire to humiliate himself hardly less strong than his earlier atavistic need to humiliate his wife. He decides to go to the wedding even though the likelihood of rejection is great. When Elizabeth-Jane unforgivingly rebukes him, he lacks the self-esteem to defend himself. As the novel progresses and as the punishment seems more and more disproportionate to Henchard's crime, the novel celebrates the magnitude of Henchard's immoderate and irrational emotions. Elizabeth-Jane's emotional balance and moderation are surely a comment on Henchard's, but his intense feeling in the closing chapters becomes a comment on our last impression of her. When she obeys his will and avoids the 'mournful pleasure' of an elaborate funeral, we cannot forget how easy it is for her to submit passively to social norms or personal idiosyncracies, and to tailor her emotions to fit the circumstances. Her perspective throughout is defined by her emotional limitations; recall how she had immediately felt a kinship with Farfrae, and created him into a fantasy *alter ego* on the flimsiest of evidence.

The closing remarks radically shift our sympathy towards the man that the narrative had discarded and emphasize the ironic nature of the resolution in which Farfrae and Elizabeth-Jane marry:

> As the lively and sparkling emotions of her early married life cohered into an equable serenity, the finer movements of her nature found scope in discovering to the narrow-lived ones around her the secret (as she had once learnt it) of making *limited* opportunities endurable; which she deemed to consist in the cunning enlargement, by a species of microscopic treatment, of those *minute* forms of satisfaction that offer themselves to everybody not in positive pain; which, thus *handled*, have much of the same inspiriting effect upon life as wider interests cursorily embraced.
>
> (XLV, p. 385: emphasis mine).

The circumlocutious syntax, the emphasis on the limited and minute nature of these pleasures, her reliance on *cunning* enlargement of these emotions, and the comparison of her pleasures not to more substantive pleasures but to those pleasures that are *'cursorily* embraced' – all these demonstrate that the means by which she achieves her triumph and her 'unbroken tranquillity' (XLV, p. 386) question the desirability of that tranquillity as an end in itself. But Hardy wants us to see that *her* view is not that of the novel's dramatized experience. The alternative to Henchard's violation of social and moral norms need not be passive submission to whatever life brings and adoption of conventional morality. Elizabeth-Jane's final values are not those of Hardy. While Elizabeth-Jane's perspective parallels the narrator's for a time, she lacks the breadth of feeling, passionate intensity, and imaginative energy that are implied as alternatives to her final position.

Hardy patronizes Elizabeth-Jane's bourgeois upward mobility from her first appearance as a young woman: 'The desire – sober and repressed – of Elizabeth-Jane's heart was indeed to see, to hear, and to understand. How could she become a woman of wider knowledge, higher repute – "better", as she termed it – this was her constant inquiry of her mother' (IV, p. 28). The novel concludes with the narrator presenting the views of someone who has experienced disappointment, and who because of this will accept willingly whatever comes her way since she felt 'happiness was but the occasional episode in a general drama of pain' (XLV, p. 386). But the narrator does not embrace passivity and stoicism. While in the opening chapter he had acknowledged man's potential for 'wilful hostilities' (p. 13) and shown its consequences, he increasingly protests against the nature of the cosmos which arouses man's expectations only to blunt them. If *The Mayor of Casterbridge* begins as Hardy's version of *Paradise Lost* where man is responsible for the evil in which he lives, it ends by affirming that whatever man's shortcomings, the cosmos is unjust to his aspirations.

The Woodlanders (1887) depicts a world in which moral and physical decay is rampant. Hardy posits the possibility that the world will gradually wear itself out. Nature is engaged in a melancholy struggle for survival within the woodlands: 'The trees dripped on the garden plots, where no vegetables would grow for the dripping, though they were planted year after year with that curious mechanical regularity of country people in the face of hopelessness' (XVII, p. 144). The fermenting cider, the 'scene of decay' from the 'perishing leaves', and the moths 'decrepit from late season' convey a sense of nature's disintegration. The struggle for survival intensifies on occasion to a macabre process in which one species seems to devour another: 'Owls that had been catching mice in the outhouses, rabbits that had been eating the winter-greens in the gardens, and stoats that had been sucking the blood of the rabbits ... were seen and heard no more till nightfall' (IV, p. 24). Mrs Charmond and Fitzpiers unconsciously subscribe to a kind of sexual Darwinism by which those with strong sexual drives and few scruples manipulate and prey upon the weak in the interests of their own emotional gratification. Implicit in the narrator's perspective is a Darwinistic view that one creature lives off another. The desperation for human connection derives from each major character's understanding, based on his own experience, that he is involved in a pervasive struggle for physical or emotional survival. In the world of *The Woodlanders*, one person's emotional satisfactions and relationships are at the expense of someone else who is left excluded, suffering, or discarded. Just as Marty suffers from her inability to have Giles, Giles suffers from the loss of Grace, and Grace suffers from Fitzpiers' desertion.

The road to Hintock seems to be a path not simply to a place but to an intensely melancholy and pessimistic state of mind; he notices that 'the bleared white visage of a sunless winter day emerged like a dead-born child' (IV, p. 24). The spot on which the narrator first meditates is marked by 'tomb-like stillness', 'emptiness', and solitude (I, p. 1). The narrator's rhetorical effort to escalate a tale that is more bathetic than sublime to the level of classical Sophoclean tragedy derives from his desire to universalize the events that take place in Hintock.

The nostalgia that informs the narrator's every word is for an agrarian culture that has been displaced by the social pretensions of Grace and her father and the emotional self-indulgence of Fitzpiers and Mrs Charmond. The corruption of an ancient way of life is to be a major motif. The first chapter of *The Woodlanders* dramatizes the intrusion into Little Hintock of the pretensions and superfluities of urban life in the person of the barber who wants Marty South's hair for a wig. His intrusion foreshadows the continuing movement into Hintock of extrinsic social values and emotional and intellectual subtleties. Had Grace not been educated to patronize Giles's manners, she might have been satisfied married to him. Fitzpiers imports Byronic cynicism and worldliness into Hintock, contributing to the destruction of Grace's potential and the unhappiness of Giles and Melbury. Sophistication is anathema to the way of life epitomized by the straight-talking, ingenuous Giles and the faithful, diligent Marty South, both of whom, while often self-conscious about their personal lives, can immerse themselves in their world and seem to have 'intelligent discourse with Nature' (XLIV, p. 399).

Whether it will be the simpler need of Marty or the rococo emotions of Fitzpiers and Mrs Charmond, the narrative gives validity to Fitzpiers' observation: 'Human love is a subjective thing .... it is joy accompanied by an idea which we project against any suitable object in the line of our vision' (XVI, p. 138). With each passing novel, the final marriage becomes a more ironic resolution, and human relationships become more strained. The conclusion shows how people desperately apotheosize those who reject their love. Ironically commenting upon how people will seek in personal relations surrogates for religious certainty, Hardy uses religious language to describe personal commitments at the close of *The Woodlanders*. The very name of Grace enables Hardy to play on the irony of the atheist Fitzpiers' quest for Grace's love: 'He longed for the society of Grace. But to lay offerings on her slighted altar was his first aim, and until her propitiation was complete he would constrain her in no way to return to him' (XLV, p. 407). The dénouement takes place under Timothy Tangs's eye rather than the Divine Eye that Grace hopes is blessing their relationship.[8]

To emphasize the disjunction between human events and the myth of a benevolent God directing events, the iterative plot stresses the impossibility of man's progress. The customs and values introduced by those exposed to urban life and those who have been highly educated demean rather than improve the quality of life among the woodlanders. The process of decay has extended to virtually every human relationship. The return of Grace to Fitzpiers, given Fitzpiers' chameleonic nature and the clear implication that the wooing of Grace is another demonstration that he is an emotional gourmand, is the antithesis to the equilibrium achieved by a healthy marriage. Melbury understands that this marriage is an emotional disease and implies that their rapprochement may be another stage of a macabre cycle: 'It's a forlorn hope for her; and God knows how it will end!' (XLVIII, p. 440). Finally, the narrative returns to Marty living in isolation. However, she is now encapsulated within her own fictive world that is impervious to reality. Not only she, but the rural culture that she represents have become anachronisms. The scene where Marty stands over Giles's grave has perverse, even necrophiliac overtones. There is a touch of fanatical madness in the final words of this 'solitary and silent girl' who seems to have suffered 'continued compression' like the legendary Chinese toys said to have been made from human beings (XLVIII, p. 443; VII, p. 60). 'If ever I forget your name let me forget home and heaven! . . . But no, no, my love, I can never forget 'ee; for you was a good man, and did good things!' (XLVIII, p. 444). She finds her fulfilment in the death of her beloved when she can apotheosize him as her patron saint and finally possess him.

In *Tess of the d'Urbervilles* (1891), Hardy creates a world in which mankind seems to be devolving morally. The focus of the opening chapter is the decline of the d'Urberville family. The chapter introduces the theme of moral and physical decline and stresses how modern life and its social and economic ramifications are affecting the moral fabric of the folk culture. Apparently, man's consciousness (but not his moral intelligence) has evolved to the point where even the ordinary folk recognize the malevolent cosmology in which they live and suffer acutely from that recognition. For Hardy, Tess is immune to conventional moral judgements because her motives are beyond reproach. Finally, the freshness and vitality of her body seem the most natural and instinctive aspect of the world in which she lives. In no prior Hardy novel has the central character discovered the nature of the world's quality before the action begins. The adolescent Tess and her younger brother anticipate Jude in perceiving the disjunction between man's aspirations and the nature of things.

Hardy's blood imagery (of which the characters are unaware) intensifies the reader's sense of a creation where evil and darkness proliferate. That Tess alone of the May Day walkers wears a red ribbon and has a 'pouted-up deep red mouth' and that Prince's 'life blood' spouts from his injured breast and splashes Tess with 'crimson drops' subtly prefigures the breaking of Tess's hymen and her killing Alec (II, p. 13; IV, p. 35). In this world, innocuous details and mildly unsettling events are likely to foreshadow the most dire consequences. The prick on her chin from the rose anticipates the later violation which in turn anticipates the pool of blood created by her stabbing Alec – her desperate subconscious effort to revenge the original rape. No sooner does she consume the strawberries from Alec's hand than the bitterly ironic voice comments: 'Tess Durbeyfield did not divine ... that there behind the blue narcotic haze was potentially the "tragic mischief" of her drama – one who stood fair to be the blood-red ray in the spectrum of her young life' (V, p. 47).

From the first encounter with Alec, Tess's world is a completely closed system where the plots she creates for herself inevitably remain unfulfilled fantasies. The final phase of *Tess of the d'Urbervilles* is entitled 'Fulfilment' to describe Tess's relationship with Angel and to comment ironically on its timing and brevity. The ephemeral nature of that relationship shows that man does indeed live on a blighted star and fulfils the expectations aroused by the novel's opening. We may recall Tess's perception that the wind (and Hardy might have added Nature's plan) is no more morally significant than 'the sigh of some immense sad soul, conterminous with the universe in space, and with history in time' (IV, p. 34). Her adolescent insight has been confirmed by the narrative. Even during their idyllic reunion, Angel does not recognize the quality of Tess's moral being, believing that it resulted from her 'moral sense' being 'extinguished' and from an 'aberration' 'in the d'Urberville blood' (LVII, p. 492). Tess might desperately wish for immortality in Liza-Lu's relationship with Angel. But the reader understands the pathos and desperation of this psychological need, and realizes that Angel and Tess are participating in another futile effort to forestall the inexorable passing away of the d'Urberville family. Since the narrator has sympathetically traced Tess's attempt to be herself despite the accretion of family and personal history that keeps trying to shape her, the notion of Angel's transferring his love to her sister is bathetic. Such a mechanical transference of human affection characterizes the stimulus–response, cause–effect of sociological determinism from which Tess has been trying to escape. Angel and Tess poignantly try to perpetuate her life through Liza because neither believes in the orthodox view that their reborn souls will meet in heaven. If Tess cannot escape the family history, why should we think that Angel and Liza-Lu are unencumbered by the onus of this new d'Urberville ignominy?

The juxtaposition of Angel's and Liza-Lu's final prayers with the previous scene at Stonehenge where Tess had been lying on the pagan altar stresses the impotence of traditional religion to forestall the 'inexorable'. Christianity can no more save Tess than the Druids could prevent their demise by their pagan rites. Since the massacre of the Innocent has social sanction Tess might as well have been a human sacrifice at the Druid altar. Hasn't the blood imagery prefigured her ritualistic death? When the narrator describes Liza-Lu and Angel as resembling 'Giotto's "Two Apostles"' and as 'bent ... as if in prayer' (LIX, pp. 507, 508), he is ironically recalling not only Angel's erratic piety, but their need to embrace the kind of formalism that sentences Tess to death. The experience of the novel has shown that neither Druid pillar nor Christian belief provides the shelter 'from the wind' that Tess seeks before she is caught (LVIII, p. 502). Finally, Hardy's evocation of Aeschylus' 'President of the Immortals' deliberately proposes a pagan myth as an alternative to the discredited myth of the benevolent creator and the equally invalid myths of Apocalypse and human salvation (LIX, p. 508).

The first four chapters of *Jude the Obscure* (1895) are among the great openings in the English novel. In these chapters Hardy dramatizes a young boy's discovery of the moral and metaphysical geography of the hostile world in which he lives. The purpose of the early chapters is to show that Jude's experience is universal rather than particular and idiosyncratic. The world in which Jude and Sue live does not *permit* fulfilment. Virtually every character's foreboding of evil is fulfilled, while hopes, dreams, and emotional and economic needs are not. That there is an inevitable disjunction between what a man would like to be and what he is, is the central philosophic premise of the narrator and the major metaphysical tenet of the novel's world.

Within the major novels, the time comes earlier and earlier when the characters begin to discover that there is a discrepancy between their narrative and the nature of the not-I world. By the age of eleven Jude knows that the world in which he lives is antagonistic. In a rare moment of insight, Jude prematurely discovers the capriciousness of nature's logic when he is humiliatingly spanked for feeding the birds that he is supposed to chase off:

> Events did not rhyme quite as he had thought. Nature's logic was too horrid for him to care for. That mercy towards one set of creatures was cruelty towards another sickened his sense of harmony. As you got older, and felt yourself to be at the centre of your time, and not a point in its circumference, as you had felt when you were little, you were seized with a sort of shuddering, he perceived. All around you there seemed to be something glaring, garish, rattling, and the noises and glares hit upon the little cell called your life, and shook it, and warped it.
>
> (I, I, p. 15)

Jude's melancholy is no mere childish moment, but encapsulates the narrator's mature wisdom, which shapes the entire telling and to which the latter had presumably been brought by adult experience. Jude seems to have prematurely reached an end. Jude anticipates not only his final death-wish, but the vision that caused Father Time to end his own life and that of his siblings. Yet, finally the biological, physiological self beneath Jude's modern consciousness recoils from this insight. Nevertheless, the momentary stasis, the 'fulfilment' reached even before his adolescence begins, remains a position to which the reader reverts. The boy's initial response is validated as Jude's aspirations are continually blunted by a combination of his psychic needs, a hostile social and economic structure, and the remorseless cosmology in which things inevitably turn out badly, While Jude's dreams are filled with scholarship and religion, his instincts respond to the tawdry sensuality of Arabella and his psyche to the sado-masochism of Sue.

Phillotson is as much Jude's double as Sue is. Phillotson anticipates Jude in the way he ambitiously formulates imprecise and ephemeral plans which he has little hope of fulfilling. Phillotson is a prototype of Jude as a hopeful, aspiring man trying to improve himself who, when faced with unanticipated difficulty in mastering a hoped-for skill – such as playing a piano or getting an education – subsequently becomes disillusioned. He shares not only Jude's enthusiasm for learning, but his inconsistency and masochism. In the first chapter, Phillotson is leaving Marygreen, as Jude will years later, for the purpose of getting a university education so that he can be ordained. When Jude subsequently fictionalizes Christminster into the new Jerusalem, it is in part because the one person who treats him like a human being has gone there. His efforts to create Phillotson into a father-figure reflect his isolation and loneliness. But Phillotson, like Jude, cannot fulfil his dreams; rather, he fulfils his intrinsic character and position in Marygreen. The correlative to Jude's desire to be upwardly mobile in professional and educational terms is his bent for travel. Hardy's novels show that when one moves from place to place, one cannot leave one's self behind. They debunk the Protestant myth of self-improvement that pervades English fiction since Defoe. Within a Hardy novel physical movement for a purpose, whether it be Clym's movement to Paris, Tess's in search of her relatives, or Jude's to Christminster, is ironic. The linear movement of the narrative – whether from beginning to end or from episode to episode – confirms that one's character rarely is changed fundamentally by experience.

That Jude remarries Arabella in an alcoholic stupor shows that he has not enlarged himself sufficiently to avoid compulsively repeating the past.[9] While his views remain enlightened and consistently reflect what he has learned, his character and behaviour do not reflect personal growth. Whether he was intoxicated or not, his remarrying Arabella is the manifestation of his own self-destructive and masochistic strains and is hardly less pathological than Sue's conduct. He cannot leave Arabella because he has lost his will to live. Jude intuitively understands the parallelism of their fate and the mutual disintegration of their mental and moral energy. Widow Edlin's remark 'Weddings be funerals' applies to both of them (VI, IX, p. 481). Fanatically and obsessively, they both embrace their own destruction. Jude's quoting Job (who unlike Jude eventually rallied from despair) is an ineffectual exercise in self-pity. His willingness to die and his abandonment of principle are the fulfilment of his boyhood perception of 'nature's logic'.

The iterative structure – the remarriages, the return to Marygreen, the final interview between Gillingham and Phillotson, and the presence of Vilbert at the end – mimes man's fundamental inability to improve himself morally or spiritually. Jude and Sue reiterate the perverse errors of the past in their remarriage to those who are completely wrong for them. These remarriages – just as Father Time's fanatic and psychotic intensification of Jude's perceptions – underline the progressive diminution of man's stature in Hardy's novels. (In *Tess of the d'Urbervilles*, at least the title character retained her moral identity, even if she committed a murder.) Arabella's and Vilbert's survival, while better people are driven to neurotic and compulsive remarriage, madness, and death, reinforces our impression of man's devolution.

If *The Rainbow* is Lawrence's Bible, perhaps we should think of the Wessex novels as Hardy's Bible. Like Kafka and Lawrence, he intensifies some aspects of the world and distorts others to such an extent that he presents an alternative cosmology with its own mode of operation. His cosmos is not a benevolent pattern, moving towards the fulfilment of a divine plan in which the Apocalypse will bring the Heavenly kingdom to deserving souls, but is, to use Conrad's term, 'a remorseless process'.[10] Beginnings and endings 'rhyme' in Hardy's 'plan', but in a way which often makes it seem as if man were the butt of a cosmic joke. The very symmetry of his plots makes a statement about man's inability to progress. Man's condition is inseparable from the process which shapes him; but no moral or spiritual revolution will enable him to affect that process, nor his position within it. In Hardy's later novels, the human psyche becomes the principal means through which the malevolent process works. Increasingly, Hardy wrote about man's psychic needs, compulsions, and obsessions rather than his rational decisions and conscious motives. Anticipating Lawrence, Hardy saw that an unconscious, often libidinous self directs man's conduct, particularly his psychosexual behaviour. Like Conrad, he understood that an atavistic self lurks within each of us. While

Hardy prepares the way for Conrad and Lawrence, he also marks a turning-away from the traditional resolution of Victorian novels. Not only in literary history, but in Hardy's career, what we call the beginning is often the end. For once Hardy completed the groundwork for the modern British novel, he abandoned fiction altogether.

Notes

1. My understanding of endings has been influenced by Frank Kermode, *The Sense of an Ending* (New York: Oxford University Press, 1967) and by Alan Friedman, *The Turn of the Novel* (New York: Oxford University Press, 1966).
2. For further discussion of Hardy's narrators, see my chapter 2.
3. See Florence Emily Hardy, *The Early Life of Thomas Hardy, 1840–1891* (London and New York: Macmillan, 1928) p. 293.
4. As Scott Elledge indicates in his Norton Critical edition of *Tess of the d'Urbervilles* (New York: Norton, 1965) p. 19, when Hardy uses this phrase in the third chapter of the novel (p. 24 in the Wessex Edition), he is specifically responding to Wordsworth who, in line 22 of 'Lines Written in Early Spring', speaks of 'Nature's holy plan'.
5. M. H. Abrams, 'English Romanticism: the Spirit of the Age', in *Romanticism and Consciousness*, ed. Harold Bloom (New York: Norton, 1970) p. 103.
6. Ian Gregor, *The Great Web: the Form of Hardy's Major Fiction* (London: Faber & Faber; Totowa, NJ: Rowman & Littlefield, 1974) p. 232. I should stress that this remark is in no way central to Gregor's splendid study.
7. William Blake, 'Introduction' to *Songs of Experience*, I, 2.
8. See Gregor, p. 164.
9. Although Friedman argues for a distinction between the two marriages ('The stream of Sue's conscience thus flows at the end into marriage; the stream of Jude's conscience flows beyond marriage into death' [Friedman, p. 70]), I would stress that remarriage and death are synonymous for both Jude and Sue.
10. *Joseph Conrad's Letters to R. B. Cunninghame-Graham*, ed. C. T. Watts (Cambridge University Press, 1969) pp. 56–7.

4

Speaking of Paul Morel: Voice, Unity, and Meaning in *Sons and Lovers*

I

Beginning with the earliest reviews of *Sons and Lovers*, Lawrence has been indicted for his 'inability to efface himself' and for giving us a 'narrative [that] reads like an autobiography'.[1] Later, Mark Schorer's provocative remarks about the confusion between Lawrence's 'intention and performance' sharply focused critical attention upon the crucial relationship between voice and form in *Sons and Lovers*. Schorer argued that *Sons and Lovers* should be considered a 'technical failure' whose 'artistic coherence' has been destroyed by its inconsistencies. Specifically, he observed 'the contradiction between Lawrence's explicit characterizations of the mother and father and his tonal evaluations of them'; he also remarked upon the novel's efforts both to 'condemn' and 'justify' the mother and both to expose and rationalize Paul's failures.[2]

Schorer's complaint about the novel's aesthetic unity reflects both his discomfort with a novel that implies conflicting and contradictory values, and his belief that if a reader has to engage in judging the reliability and perspicacity of a technically omniscient third-person speaker, the integrity of the novel is necessarily disturbed. In this chapter I shall argue that: (1) the discrepancies between the narrator's interpretations and ours create a tension that becomes an intrinsic part of the novel's form; (2) the fluctuating and complex relationship between the narrator and his major characters enables the reader to participate in the agonizing but wonderfully exciting *aesthetic* process by which an author tries to give shape and unity to his recent past; and (3) the failure of Lawrence to sort out the blame, to neatly 'master' his materials, is a major reason for the novel's subtlety and complexity.

Louis L. Martz has convincingly refuted Schorer. Arguing for the efficacy of Lawrence's technique in chapters 7 ('Lad-and-Girl Love') through 11 ('The Test on Miriam'), he writes:

> The point of view adopted is that of Paul; but since confusion, self-deception, and desperate self-justification are essential to that point of view, we can never tell, from the stream of consciousness alone, where the real truth lies. But we can tell it from the action; we can tell it by seeking out the portrait of Miriam that lies beneath the overpainted commentary of the Paul-narrator. This technique of painting and overpainting produces a strange and unique tension in this part of the novel.[3]

Though Martz's fine essay considerably furthers the discussion of the aesthetic unity of *Sons and Lovers*, I should like to take issue with him on several counts: (1) I do not believe Lawrence 'resumes' 'the method of the objective narrator' in chapters XII ('Passion') through XV ('Derelict'), and I do not perceive a tonal change in the narrator's voice in these later chapters of Part Two.[4] (2) I do not agree that the narrator in Part One is 'working with firm control, [setting] forth the facts objectively'.[5] (3) I think Martz's insistence on seeing a 'growth in [Paul's] self-knowledge' deflects him into a reading of the ending that blurs the negative implications of the final paragraphs.[6] (4) I feel that his term 'overpainting' ignores the temporal nature of the reader's perception of a work of fiction. Although a reader's impressions are continually qualified or even displaced by subsequent narrative commentary or dramatized scenes, two contrasting impressions do not really exist in the reader's mind simultaneously like a negative that has been double-exposed.

Lawrence's struggle to come to terms with his own experience is revealed in the novel's conflict between narrative incident and narrator commentary. This conflict reflects Lawrence's continuing re-evaluation of his experience as he rewrote *Sons and Lovers* at a time when he was torn between the desire to be true to the sacred memory of his mother and to respond to the views of first Jessie Chambers and later Frieda. To come to terms with his autobiographical material, Lawrence tries to divide himself into two separate characters: Paul and the narrator. Paul, a former self and the embodiment of his past, is a subjective creation; Lawrence immerses Paul in a narrative that mimes crucial events of his own life, but does not ask Paul to judge himself scrupulously. That task is left to the narrator, the embodiment of the present self who is supposed to be an objective figure charged with evaluating and measuring Lawrence's former self and tracing his linear development. But this dichotomy breaks down as Lawrence's objective self becomes empathetic to his former self, Paul Morel. Because Lawrence is not emotionally removed from the narrated experience, his superego has not grown sufficiently beyond the experience to evaluate and control his own mother-love. (In a December 1910 letter written while his mother was dying, Lawrence had said of the relationship with his mother: 'We have loved each other, almost with a husband and wife love, as well as filial and maternal.')[7] That his narrator's consciousness is incompletely developed and very much in the process of becoming is appropriate for a novel in which the protagonist's aesthetic rejects 'the stiffness of shape' for the 'shimmeriness' inside (p. 152).

The narrator is an apologist for Mrs. Morel and an adversary of Miriam. He takes distinctly different stances towards similar behaviour in the two women. If it is proper for Paul to resist having his 'soul' possessed by Miriam, why is the narrator rather tolerant of Mrs. Morel's 'root[ing]' her life in Paul and becoming 'the pivot and pole of his life, from which he could not escape' (pp. 141, 222)? Anxious to justify Mrs. Morel's behaviour, the narrator provides half-convincing excuses in which he desperately wishes to believe.[8]

The narrator perceives Mrs. Morel's insistent claims upon Paul within individual scenes, but he is unwilling to recognize the significance of the evolving pattern. He is aware how Mrs. Morel has substituted her sons for her husband, but refuses to acknowledge how individually organic moments with his mother, in which they share attitudes, ideas, and epiphanies of nature's beauty, add up to a perverse pattern. Nor does he acknowledge that Mrs. Morel's smothering and stifling maternity is often conscious, volitional, and willful. In the final scene in Part One, the narrator refuses to recognize the implications of what is occurring when Mrs. Morel transfers her affections from the recently deceased William to Paul while the latter is suffering from pneumonia. The narrator empathizes with both Paul and his mother and renders the scene without irony or detachment:

"I s'll die, mother!" he cried, heaving for breath on the pillow.
She lifted him up, crying in a small voice:
"Oh, my son – my son!"

That brought him to. He realised her. His whole will rose up
and arrested him. He put his head on her breast, and took ease
of her for love . . . .
   The two knitted together in perfect intimacy. Mrs. Morel's life
now rooted itself in Paul.

                                                    (pp. 141)

Their mutual passion is restorative for both of them. But this
apparently perfect moment of intimacy forges a fateful link that
severely impedes Paul's sexual and emotional growth. Subsequent
events make clear to the reader that it is Mrs. Morel's complicity in
the oedipal love – her willingness to fuse herself to him – that
blights Paul's maturation. But does the narrator acknowledge that
this fusion (a concept which Lawrence favourably contrasts in 'The
Study of Thomas Hardy' with the 'Two-in-one') of two lives is
potentially destructive? If there seems to be a hint of ambivalence
in the words 'rooted' and 'knitted', this is extinguished by the
insistence that the new relationship is restorative for both of them.
As he recalls this scene, Lawrence's speaker cherishes rather than
criticizes the intimacy between his younger self and his mother.
   Yet Lawrence undoubtedly meant to create a speaker who, while
sympathetic towards Paul, could detach himself enough from
Paul's oedipal love so as to be able to show the reader more about
the protagonist than Paul knew about himself. In the novel's first
part, Lawrence tries with some success to establish a discrepancy
between the narrator's perspective and Paul's and demonstrates
that Lawrence wishes to separate himself from Paul. But the
autobiographical material of *Sons and Lovers* resisted the convention
of omniscient narration in which Lawrence conceived it. When he
evolves Paul's responses to nature and sex, when he seeks to
translate the silence of Paul's unconscious into non-discursive
rhythms and images, Lawrence is completely empathetic towards
Paul and the narrative distance breaks down completely. The
objective voice, the evaluative superego with his gently ironic view
of Lawrence's younger self, is displaced by the urgent voice of the
vates seeking to transport the reader into a sensual, vitalistic
rapport with the young man who is finally discovering his long
repressed passional self.[9] For example, notice the texture of the
passage in which Lawrence renders Paul's and Clara's most
successful sexual consummation, the one that takes place in the
fields along the canal:

All the while the peewits were screaming in the field. When he came to, he wondered what was near his eyes, curving and strong with life in the dark, and what voice it was speaking. Then he realised it was the grass, and the peewit was calling. The warmth was Clara's breathing heaving. He lifted his head and looked into her eyes. They were dark and shining and strange, life wild at the source staring into his life, stranger to him, yet meeting him; and he put his face down on her throat afraid. What was she? A strong, strange, wild life, that breathed with his in the darkness through this hour. It was all so much bigger than themselves that he was hushed. They had met, and included in their meeting the thrust of the manifold grass stems, the cry of the peewit, the wheel of the stars.

(p. 353)

In such sexual and passionate moments, Lawrence is intruding into the ˙silence of unconscious physiological experience and inviting the reader to participate directly in the sensual life of his characters. His metaphors seek to transform the space in which the sexual act or passionate moment occurs into a place where the texture of life is sensuous, physical, instinctive and biological and where cognitive life is absent. Such metaphors, rather than creating objective correlatives, are lyrical explosions whose rhythms and images are supposed to engage immediately the reader's libidinous self without the intervening cognitive process by which a reader usually transforms a narrative episode into signification. A sentence such as 'They had met, and included in their meeting the thrust of the manifold grass stems, the cry of the peewit, the wheel of the stars' implies that during the sexual act the power of the participants' libidinous energy displaces the diurnal world in which they dwell and makes their world coterminous and spatially equivalent with the cosmos; in a word, microcosm becomes macrocosm. When it works, as I believe it does here, Lawrence's style *becomes* his argument. Sexual intercourse enables the participants to become part of the natural world and the energy that breathes through it; in Blakean terms, it restores if only temporarily the lapsed soul to Beulah.

II

While acknowledging the complexity of Part Two, Martz calls Part One 'A triumph of narration in the Old Victorian style' of objective omniscient narration.[10] But the fluctuating perspective of the first chapters is rather more complex than he allows. Desiring to render Mr. Morel with objectivity and to acknowledge his vitality, the narrator depicts him making his fuses, fixing his breakfast, and, especially, relishing his masculine holidays. The narrator does show how Mrs. Morel isolates Morel from his own children, and even briefly adopts a perspective sympathetic to Morel when analyzing the deterioration of the marriage. On rare occasions, the narrator depicts the frustrations of *both* ill-matched partners. When Morel cuts William's hair, the narrator catches the pathology of his wife's rage: 'I could kill you, I could!' (p. 15). Yet his sympathy is with Mrs. Morel. Basically, the narrator empathizes with her desire for a sanctuary from 'poverty', 'ugliness' and 'meanness', and he fails to stress – as the reader soon learns from dramatized scenes – that her dissatisfaction with her lot makes impossible a viable relationship with her husband (p. 5). Mrs. Morel's 'air of authority' and 'rare warmth' give her primacy within her home and within the lives of her children. While acknowledging her inability to accept her husband, the narrator minimizes how her willful desire to establish to her children that she is better than her husband pre-empts his position in the family. As she gradually establishes her dominant position, *she* assumes the role of father.

The first chapter establishes the pattern of the novel. Mrs. Morel evaluates her husband and his companions according to arbitrary social and economic standards. Mrs. Morel has a compulsion to improve herself and her family. In a perverse way that neither she nor the narrator understands, she equates material and social progress with blessedness. Trying in turn to shape Mr. Morel, William, and Paul, she creates for each of them expectations that they cannot meet. Mr. Morel's *manners* distress her, but her continual search for a surrogate husband begins when she learns that he does not take pride in his economic independence. That he actually pays his mother's rent disturbs her as much or more than that he has lied. Just like her father she is proud of her 'integrity', but integrity in a husband means something rather narrow to her: the ability to pay one's bills and to provide for one's wife. (She would not deign to take in mending like the other Bottoms' wives.) Morel's drinking is to her, above all, indicative of his economic and social irresponsibility which undermines her efforts to consider herself better than her neighbours. If ever Mrs. Morel indicts herself as niggling and petty, it is when she recalls: '[Mr. Morel] had bought no engagement ring at all, and she preferred William, who was not mean, if he were foolish' (p. 115). As she begins to allow William to play the role of surrogate husband, she unconsciously seeks to reduce her husband to a child; we recall how she mocks his efforts to run away after he had stealthily taken sixpence from her pocketbook. Meanwhile, as if she were a feudal 'queen' she accepts 'tribute' from William who 'gave all his money to his mother' (p. 52). William is subconsciously compelled to choose for a sexual partner someone who is the complete opposite to his mother–lover whom he has unconsciously dedicated himself to serving chivalrously. Mrs. Morel needs to control, dominate and subdue; yet one part of her despises her husband because he allows himself to be emasculated: 'She sat trembling slightly, but her heart brimming with contempt. What would she do if he went to some other pit, obtained work, and got in with another woman? But she knew him too well – he couldn't. She was dead sure of him' (p. 43).

Unconsciously at first, but later quite intentionally, she transfers her libidinous self – the nighttime self that in spite of her rationality and pragmatism responds to the sensuality of flowers and moonlight – to her children because she finds her husband's social, public self wanting. The first chapter shows how Mrs. Morel struggles between, on the one hand, the external norms that she has inherited from the Coppard tradition, and, on the other, her sensual and passionate potential. No matter how she would deny her biological self and renounce Morel, her libido expresses itself in her physical response to her husband and her narcissistic experience with flowers. As her orgasmic moment with the symbolically virginal lilies indicates (she 'melts out' of herself into 'a kind of swoon'), Mrs. Morel is no longer by the time chapter one ends completely dependent upon her husband to fulfill her sexual needs (p. 24). (Whatever Lawrence's intention, I think that the scenes in which Mrs. Morel, Paul, Miriam, and even Clara have passionate intercourse with flowers must be regarded in part as a function of their sexual frustrations.)

If Part One did have an objective narrator, would he not stress how Paul's class snobbery, self-righteousness, and ambition are shaped by the force of his mother's will? Mrs. Morel is obsessed with her sons' social and economic success because of her husband's failure to give her the vicarious recognition and economic status that she craves:

She felt . . . that where [Paul] determined to go he would get. . . .
Now she had two sons in the world. She could think of two
places, great centres of industry, and feel that she had put a man
into each of them, that these men would work out what *she*
wanted; they were derived from her, they were of her, and their
works also would be hers.

(p. 101; emphasis Lawrence's)

The narrator accepts Paul's view that his mother's 'hardness' and
defensive behaviour are rather understandable in light of the
disappointments she has endured. Explaining how she copes with
her anxiety about sending a 14-year-old boy to work at a factory,
where his health suffers from 'darkness' and 'lack of air', the
narrator explains: 'But she herself had had to put up with so much
that she expected her children to take the same odds. They must go
through with what came' (pp. 108–9). Mrs. Morel is aggressive and
even hostile to those with whom she enters an economic
relationship; one need only recall the waitress at Nottingham, the
man who drives the carriage to the cottage that the family has
rented, or even the man from whom she buys a decorated dish.
While Paul's response to the mine is aesthetic, imaginative, and
organic, hers is primarily economic. When Paul notices the beauty
of the pits, she can only think of the economic significance,
notwithstanding her prior observation that 'the world is a
wonderful place' (p. 123).

Once William indicates the extent of his attachment to Gypsy,
Paul begins to replace him as Mrs. Morel's surrogate husband.
When Morel breaks his leg, 'in her heart of hearts, where the love
should have burned, there was a blank' (p. 86). Even though she
continues to have intermittent if infrequent feelings of affection for
her husband, her attitude at this time gives special urgency to the
imploring question that she asks Paul: 'What do you want to be?'
(p. 88). At the age of fourteen, he accepts without protest her
charge that he make his way in the world, although the thought of
taking a job seems like 'bondage' to him and '[kills] all joy and even
life' (p. 89). But in her determination that he succeed, Mrs. Morel is
oblivious to his needs. Significantly, her concern for Paul's success
in the outer world corresponds to her gradual realization that
William is betraying her trust and her love. The emphasis on Paul
in chapter V ('Paul Launches into Life') alternates with brief, but
significant vignettes about William. Before Mrs. Morel sets off to

Nottingham with Paul, 'gay, like a sweetheart', she has begun to suspect that William, who sent her money only twice from London, is not fulfilling the acknowledged role of provider and the suppressed role of gallant knight that would make him a substitute for Morel (p. 92).

Although at first Mrs. Morel seems physically and psychically weakened after William's death, she recuperates when Paul's illness gives her an opportunity to transfer her affections to the next son. As William's relationship with Gyp had developed in intensity and as William had ceased to pay her economic homage, she already had begun turning towards Paul: 'Mrs. Morel clung now to Paul.... [S]till he stuck to his painting and still he stuck to his mother. Everything he did was for her. She waited for his coming home in the evening, and then she unburdened herself of all she had pondered, or of all that had occurred to her during the day.... The two shared lives' (p. 114). Perhaps in the choice of verbs ('clung', 'stuck', 'unburdened'), we can feel something of Lawrence's resentment as his narrator recalls how Paul was asked to play a role of surrogate husband that deprived him of much of his adolescence. Since Mrs. Morel teaches her children by example to be dissatisfied with spouse and home, William's disastrous choice of someone completely unsuited to him and the very antithesis of the people he has known, as well as Paul's dissatisfaction with the women in his life, can be in part attributed to Mrs. Morel's influence. How devastating is the effect on the young adolescent of his mother's speaking of the family parlour as 'a beastly cold, sunless hole' (p. 98).[11]

Just like the mother in 'The Rocking-Horse Winner' (1926), Mrs. Morel's economic discontent wrenches family relationships. Yet we see little to indicate that the Morels are ever so destitute that it interferes with their basic comfort. Mrs. Morel attributes almost magical significance to money. As in the later story, money becomes a virtual substitute for sperm. Money is the means by which Mrs. Morel accepts sexual fealty. Both her resentment of Gyp, and of Morel's male camaraderie and the concomitant drinking involves not only anger that money is being wasted, but sexual jealousy. Until his affair with Gyp, she takes special pride in William's salary. Money is a sanctioned sexual tribute that her sons may deliver without guilt on the part of giver or recipient. The narrator's voice has a touch of wonder and awe as he recounts how William becomes ill because he has delivered both his money and his actual sperm to Gypsy. Of course, to a considerable extent William is based on the actual history of Lawrence's brother Ernest. But within the fictive world William's sudden pneumonia and subsequent death have the parabolic, non-mimetic quality of Paul's death in 'The Rocking-Horse Winner', as if he were being punished for some mysterious transgression involving the mother.

Beginning with chapter IV ('The Young Life of Paul'), the structure of each chapter affirms the extent of Paul's bondage to his mother and the claustrophobic effect of these ties upon his emotional development. Characteristically, a chapter raises the hope of experience which will move Paul outward. But, gradually, Mrs. Morel's influence restricts and confines the possibility of new relationships and important self-discovery. Each movement outward is arrested by his obsession with his mother. For example, chapter VII, 'Lad-and-Girl Love', begins with the promise of exorcizing the intense but destructive passion between mother and son with which Part One ended. Paul and Miriam are both excessively self-conscious but they gradually establish a rapport. Throughout the chapter, Mrs. Morel's disapproval intervenes to block the natural development of his relationship with Miriam. This chapter's conclusion shows why 'their intimacy was so abstract' and why he 'suppressed into a shame' his sexual desire; his mother's rebuke for returning late punctuates a chapter in which his loyalty to his mother comes between Miriam and himself (p. 178). At crucial moments, when he is tormented by his passion for his mother and tortured by his inability to respond sexually to Miriam or his mother, his repressed libidinous urges find an outlet in antagonism to Miriam: 'He hated her, for she seemed in some way to make him despise himself.... He loved to think of his mother, and the other jolly people' (p. 179). (Of course, his mother is, with rare exception, a humourless figure.)

In the next chapter, 'Strife in Love', the narrator shifts his focus on Miriam and Paul to show briefly how the mother's influence continues. When Paul wins the painting contest, her joy has a self-indulgent aspect as she takes these victories as self-vindication: 'Paul was going to distinguish himself.... She was to see herself fulfilled. Not for nothing had been her struggle' (p. 183). The extent to which Mrs. Morel's perspective, which to the reader seems limited and self-serving, is given legitimacy and implicit endorsement by the narrator can be seen when the narrator anticipates Mrs. Morel's thought that Miriam 'wants to absorb him' with the comment that '[Miriam] loved him absorbedly' (pp. 189, 193). Paul's reasons for hating Miriam are illogical, implausible and revealing: 'If Miriam caused his mother suffering then he hated her – and he easily hated her. Why did she make him feel as if he were uncertain of himself, insecure, and an indefinite thing . . .?' (p. 193). Later in the chapter, after he seems to have found an outlet for his libido in adolescent sex play with Beatrice, Mrs. Morel rebukes him for failing to care for the bread while Miriam was there. His response is to remind her of his age: 'You're old, mother, and we're young' (p. 212). This is the catalyst for a quarrel which ends in Mrs. Morel's conclusive triumph over Miriam: their passionate incestuous embrace.

The narrator continually insists upon distinctions between Miriam and Paul, and between Miriam and Mrs. Morel, while the narrative shows that in many ways the Leivers family mirrors the Morels. If Miriam is a 'maiden in bondage, her spirit dreaming in a land far away and magical', Paul is a lad in bondage to his mother (p. 145). Considering the altercations and antipathy that divide the Morel family, it is astonishing that Paul criticizes the 'jangle and discord in the Leivers family' (p. 147). That Paul is immediately attracted to the rather supercilious and patronizing Leivers family at all shows how he has been educated by Mrs. Morel's social pretensions.[12] His attraction to someone whom he later suspects of wishing to dominate him and who imagines herself a 'princess turned into a swine-girl' shows that he responds to those qualities that suggest his mother (p. 142). That Miriam feels a need to 'swathe' and 'stifle' her 4 year-old brother recalls vividly how Mrs. Morel passionately encloses her sons. The narrator gives a motive for Mrs. Morel's jealousy by implying, without ever providing dramatic corroboration, that Miriam wishes to mother Paul: 'If she could be mistress of him in his weakness, take care of him, if he could depend on her, if she could, as it were, have him in her arms, how she would love him!' (p. 143). As Paul becomes dependent on Miriam for aesthetic stimulation and for bringing out his spiritual aspect, he almost gives her the status of his mother and creates competition between the two women within his psyche. On the other hand, there are substantial differences between the Leivers and Paul's own family. He is first attracted to Mrs. Leivers because she responds to the significance of an experience in other than economic terms. In contrast to his mother's expedience and pragmatism, the Leivers perceive spiritually and abstractly. Their effect on him is different: 'They kindled him and made him glow to his work, whereas his mother's influence was to make him quietly determined, patient, dogged, unwearied' (p. 149).

Within the narrative, it often seems that Miriam represents the 'shimmeriness' which is 'the real living', while it is the mother who is the 'shape' which 'is a dead crust' (p. 152). If Paul talks about 'shimmeriness', he does so in 'abstract' speeches, while it is Miriam's 'dark eyes alight like water that shakes with a stream of gold in the dark' (p. 152). When she yearns for him, he desires to kiss her in 'abstract purity' and then he criticizes her for not '[realizing] the male he was' (pp. 188–9). In 'Strife in Love', while he is watching his mother's bread and teaching Miriam French, Miriam is described in terms that suggest the bride in *Song of Songs* ('She was coloured like a pomegranate for richness') and only awaits Paul's sexual response to arouse her: 'Her dark eyes were naked with their love, afraid, and yearning' (p. 208). But it is Paul who cannot respond: 'He knew, before he could kiss her, he must drive something out of himself' (p. 208). As Paul stomps to the oven, Lawrence's narrator cannot but reveal how Paul has affected his vulnerable but complaisant friend: 'Even the way he crouched before the oven hurt her. There seemed to be something cruel in it, something cruel in the swift way he pitched the bread out of the tins...' (p. 208). Rather than allowing Miriam to complement his experience and enjoy her difference, he uses his mother's qualities as norms to judge the difference he discovers in Miriam: 'Her intensity which would leave no emotion on a normal plane, irritated the youth into a frenzy.... He was used to his mother's reserve. And on such occasions, he was thankful in heart and soul that he had his mother, so *sane* and *wholesome*' (p. 153; emphasis mine).

The narrator's distinction between Miriam's desire to shape Paul and his mother's need to will his future often seems a distinction without a difference. Like Mrs, Morel, Miriam 'gave him all her love and her faith' and wishes to 'guard' the best of him from the pollution of the outside world (p. 249). Deliberately mocking both Miriam's view of her sexual role and the hyperbolic conventions of platonic love to which (according to him) she subscribes, the narrator remarks: 'Nay, the sky did not cherish the stars more surely and eternally than she would guard the good in the soul of Paul Morel' (p. 249). Using ironic religious language, the narrator presents Miriam's self-sacrifice as perverse: 'Miriam [is] tortured ... [because] he [is] utterly unfaithful to her' (pp. 250–1). But Mrs. Morel is also a worshipper who denies herself so that her godhead might flourish. She is tortured by his need for a sexual partner. And she, too, transfers her sublimated passion into religious paroxysms; she 'prayed and prayed for him, that he might not be wasted' (p. 258). Even more than Miriam's prayers, hers derive from her compulsion to shape his life to her model, and to live through his achievements. Mrs. Morel's prayer is the expression of her will and, hence according to the values that pervade Lawrence's work, mechanistic and contrary to organic being. The reader understands that prayer is a socially sanctioned means by which she can direct her son's life. Intellectually, Paul knows 'that one should feel inside oneself for right and wrong, and should have the patience to gradually realise one's God' (p. 256). But because he has 'realized' his mother, his god – the individuating principle that makes each man himself and enables him to tap his latent potential – eludes him. The narrative dramatizes the tension between extrinsic standards inculcated by his mother and his inherent need to fulfil himself.

III

Our basic premise has been that Paul's inadequacies are unconsciously ignored and underplayed by the narrator, but that the dramatic events render a more complex vision of the human relationships that form the subject of *Sons and Lovers*. The preterite does not guarantee objectivity. That Lawrence was still coming to terms with the experience that forms the novel's raw material undoubtedly deflected him from objective analysis. The tension between the narrator's myth-making and the greater objectivity of much of the dramatic action may be part of the hold that the novel exercises upon its readers. We, as readers, participate in Lawrence's continuous and often ineffectual struggles with his mother's influence and his oedipal love. The concatenation of individual moments gives a different perspective to the scenes in which Paul and Miriam struggle with their inhibitions and psychic problems. The narrator's persistent efforts to attribute to Miriam insidious emotions that are not demonstrated within the dramatic action finally raise doubts about the quality of the narrator's analyses.

An example of how the narrative renders the complexities of the issues despite the narrator's insistent defence of Paul occurs in the early pages of 'Defeat of Miriam', a chapter that might just as appropriately be entitled 'Defeat of Paul'. After he makes his commitment to his mother not to marry while she lives, the degeneration of his relationship with Miriam accelerates. Although the narrator begins by rendering Paul's narcissistic reactions, he finally turns to Miriam's confused response to Paul's announcement that he cannot love her physically:

> [Paul] hated her bitterly at that moment because he made her suffer. Love her! She knew he loved her. He really belonged to her. This about not loving her, physically, bodily was a mere perversity on his part, because she knew she loved him. He was stupid like a child. He belonged to her. His soul wanted her.... She guessed somebody had been influencing him. She felt upon him the hardness, the foreigness of another influence.
>
> (p. 222)

Although the narrator starts by attributing to Miriam both an attitude of condescension and a sense of ownership, this distorted view gives way to a more sympathetic understanding of Miriam's plight. The preceding and subsequent events make clear that: (1) Paul's 'hatred' derives not from making her suffer, but from his obligations to 'another influence', Mrs. Morel; (2) his arrested sexual development does make him behave 'like a child'.

Lawrence's use of omniscience to render a spurious version of Miriam's thinking is an example of what we might call the aesthetics of distortion. A significant breakdown in narrative distance occurs when the narrator accepts Paul's interpretation of Miriam's response to his terminating of their relationship ('The Test on Miriam'). She protests that Paul has always been fighting to free himself. Neither Paul nor the narrator realize that her response is defensive, deriving from her 'self-mistrust'. Seeking a reason to make her the scapegoat, Paul becomes enraged that 'She had hidden all her condemnation from him, had flattered him, and despised him' (p. 297). Intellectually, the narrator knows that Paul's indignation is inappropriate and hyperbolic, but he cannot bring himself to condemn Paul. In consecutive paragraphs, he renders Paul's consciousness with gentle irony and Miriam's with bitter, scathing irony. Paul's adolescent and exaggerated response is presented in a series of short, almost choppy, declarative sentences to parody logical thought; the quality of his clichéd thinking is self-indicting. Yet, despite his guise of critically observing Paul, the narrator's presentation of her thoughts seem to confirm Paul's belief that he is the wronged party in the relationship:

> He sat in silence. He was full of a feeling that she had deceived him. She had despised him when he thought she worshipped him. She had let him say wrong things, and had not contradicted him. She had let him fight alone. But it stuck in his throat that she had despised him whilst he thought she worshipped him. . . . All these years she had treated him as if he were a hero, and thought of him secretly as an infant, a foolish child. Then why had she left the foolish child to his folly? His heart was hard against her.
>
> (p. 298)

But both this passage and the one that immediately follows are inconsistent with the Miriam whom we know. Can we believe that her mind has worked in Machiavellian ways to entrap subtly a man whom she regards as a 'foolish child' and as a 'baby':

> Why this bondage for her? . . . Why was she fastened to him? . . . She would obey him in his trifling commands. But once he was obeyed, then she had him in her power, she knew, to lead him where she would. She was sure of herself. Only, this new influence! And, he was not a man! He was a baby that cries for the newest toy. And all the attachment of his soul would not keep him. Very well, he would have to go. But he would come back when he had tired of his new sensation.
>
> (pp. 298–9)

According to the narrator, Miriam deliberately manipulates her 'bondage' into 'conquest' by seeming to obey while actually taking the lead. After experimenting with other relationships, Paul will return to her because he is a captive of her will, an instrument to fulfill her narcissistic needs, and a child who needs a tolerant mother figure. (Such a view of Miriam gives validity to the indignation that the narrator shares with Paul.)

The reader knows that Miriam does not think in these terms and realizes that the narrator is attributing these motives to her as a means of extenuating Paul, who has been increasingly exploiting her. Her love for nature, her idealism, and her spiritual quest make it clear that even if she were to lack vitality and passion (as Paul and the narrator incorrectly assume), she surely is not lacking in integrity and dignity. The Miriam of the novel may temporarily oversimplify her relationship to Paul as a 'battle' from the beginning, but she is not a Machiavelli of sexual politics capable of loving the man she *despises*. If she is bitter, sufficient reasons are found in the narrative. Paul cannot commit himself to her, while she can to him. Despite her self-mistrust and masochism, her bondage is the pathetic one of the woman who loves not wisely but too well. The above passages also inadvertently reveal how the Jessie–Miriam relationship in its non-sexuality helped compensate for the childhood of which Lawrence had been partially deprived by his mother's demands. That Miriam, the narrator, and even Paul use the child metaphor for Paul indicates that Lawrence suspected that his oedipal relationship had arrested his sexual *and* emotional development.

The narrator's insistence that Paul's infatuation with his mother is a representative rather than an idiosyncratic one, and that it typifies the 'tragedy of thousands of young men in England', derives from Lawrence's need to believe this. But the novel presents little evidence that others share Paul's particular problems. Morel, Baxter, and Arthur may have various forms of emotional difficulties, but they seem to function sexually. William's problem is not that he is diffident and shy, but that he becomes entrapped by a naive pursuit of what he has been taught by his mother to consider the Better Life. No, the polemic derives from Lawrence's need to generalize his surrogate's sexual difficulties with Miriam.[13]

In the crucial opening paragraph of 'The Test on Miriam', Paul wills himself to try to 'get things right' sexually and marry Miriam. (At this point, the intellectual, logical, and almost mechanical process by which he arrives at a decision mimics his mother's process of thinking.) Again we see that the test on Miriam is really the test of Paul's ability to break loose from his mother. In *Fantasia of the Unconscious* (1922), Lawrence might be addressing Paul's problem when he writes:

Every frenzied individual is told to find fulfillment in love. So he tries. Whereas, there is no fulfillment in love. Half of our fulfillment comes *through* love, through strong, sensual love. But the central fulfillment, for a man, is that he possess his own soul in strength within him, deep and alone. The deep, rich aloneness, reached and perfected through love and the passing beyond any further *quest* of love.[14]

(emphases Lawrence's)

Paul cannot find joy and fulfilment in an adult relationship because he is possessed *by his mother*.[15] The obtrusive ironic images – the four dead birds, and the remains of the cherries on which they had fed (the ripened cherries had at first seemed proleptic of the young couple's sexual maturity) – show how the retrospective narrator takes a morbid view of the sexual consummation and regards it as merely another mutual act of desperation to blur Paul's and Miriam's fundamental incompatibility. Although he uses these fictive devices to suggest that Paul is the *victim* of Miriam's frigidity, the narrator acknowledges that Paul found the coition reasonably satisfying: '[H]e felt as if nothing mattered, as if his living were smeared away into the beyond, near and quite loveable. This strange, gentle reaching out to death was new to him' (p. 287). If he achieves inner peace in the sexual act, surely Miriam is partly responsible. Intercourse divests him of the values his mother has rooted in him, neutralizes temporarily the urgency and intensity that she has given his life and career, and enables him to experience nature's rhythms and energy. Saying that he feels 'so strange and still', he explains to Miriam: 'To be rid of our individuality, which is our will, which is our effort – to live effortless, a kind of curious sleep – that is very beautiful, I think; that is our after-life – our immortality' (pp. 287–8). Moreover, he discovers the stillness and inaction of death and the unknown, aspects of existence that Mrs. Morel has increasingly denied, but that his father instinctively knows. That his mother refuses to accept death reveals her fundamental incompatibility with nature. She had tried to reincarnate William by shifting her love to Paul. Later, she willfully refuses to accept the natural cycle of life after she almost perversely lingers on when illness has reduced her body to a virtual skeleton. Because of his joyous sexual release, Paul does escape from his mother for a moment. His desire to eschew effort and will derives from the pressure of Mrs. Morel's compelling demands upon him. Temporarily, the sex act nullifies his mother's hold on him and makes her values irrelevant. But precisely because of this, he cannot admit that the sexual relationship is satisfactory. Technical omniscience gives Lawrence the sanction to plead his case. Considering what Paul seems to have achieved, the narrator's criticism of Miriam's giving herself as a 'sacrifice in which she felt something of horrors' should be taken as an example of Lawrence's need to believe that Miriam is incapable of passion (p. 286). In view of her prolonged virginity, her prior repression and self-denigration, we should hardly be surprised if she experiences a moment of awkwardness and self-doubt.

Their sexual consummation is the prelude to the demise of their personal relationship, and Lawrence's speaker must shift the onus to Miriam. Can one really trust his version of their meeting at Miriam's grandmother's house? Paul's perspective is a subjective one that reflects his own problems, and his interpretation of her looks is moot:

> [H]er hands lifted in a little pleading movement, and he looked at her face, and stopped. Her big brown eyes were watching him, still and resigned and loving; she lay as if she had given herself up to *sacrifice*; there was her body for him; but the look at the back of her eyes, like a creature awaiting *immolation*, arrested him, and all his blood fell back.
>
> (p. 289–90; emphasis mine)

That years of sexual restraint have marked their relationship is reflected by her slight sign of physical reluctance, but this does not necessarily indicate Miriam's disinclination for sex. Although Miriam says that she wants him, the narrator insists that she regards her sexual participation as 'sacrificial'. Since the religious terminology is within Paul's mind (he has just said to her: 'Your face is bright... like a transfiguration'), perhaps the terms 'sacrifice' and 'immolation' should be ascribed to *his* imagination (p. 289). Paul's need to criticize her at this point is intensified by his having just compared her with his mother: 'He thought she gave a feeling of home almost like his mother' (p. 289). The domestic arrangements within the cottage create a situation in which Miriam displaces his mother as the one responsible for caring for him.

Sex as a ritual between master and victim answers both their impulses. If Miriam's understanding of her sexual role involves sacrifice and submission, Paul does not discourage her from this. Paul

associates sex with death, because he feels guilty for betraying his
mother: 'As he rode home he felt that he was finally initiated. He
was a youth no longer. But why had he the dull pain in his soul?
Why did the thought of death, the after-life, seem so sweet and
consoling?' (p. 290). That Paul thinks of the word 'initiation' in
association with 'pain' and 'death' is revealing because it shows
that Paul regards sex as a ritual to be passed through at a cost to
oneself – indeed, as a sacrifice. If Paul and Miriam do not achieve a
mutual orgasm, is it not in part because his subconscious will not
allow him to replace his mother as his primary passion? Since a
fulfilling sexual relationship would give a benediction to his
friendship with Miriam, Paul has to find fault with it. The narrator
tries to muster evidence to support the view that the alleged sexual
failure is Miriam's responsibility when he has her cite the lesson
she has learned from her mother: 'There is one thing in marriage
that is always dreadful, but you have to bear it' (p. 291). But
Miriam disavows this rubric and is ready to respond to Paul's
tenderness and understanding if Paul can manifest these qualities.
The reader knows that Paul must severely criticize Miriam now
that he has been sleeping with her, because he already belongs to
his mother.

IV

No sooner does Paul begin his sexual relationship with Miriam,
than his subconscious requires that he discard her and turn his
thoughts to Clara. The narrator is not ironic about Paul's rapid
reversal of field: 'But insidiously, without knowing it, the warmth
he felt for Clara drew him away from Miriam, for whom he felt
responsible, and to whom he felt he belonged' (p. 292). As he
turns from Miriam to Clara, his anxiety and tension ease.
Interestingly, when Paul announces that he is breaking off with
Miriam, the narrator stresses natural and vital aspects of her
appearance that Paul has been ignoring: 'She has made herself
look so beautiful and fresh for him. She seemed to blossom for
him alone' (p. 295). Just as the narrator is on occasion grudgingly
fair to Mr. Morel in Part One, so in Part Two he will reluctantly
give Miriam her due. But the parallel is instructive precisely
because he purports to value Miriam, while he is obviously hostile
to Paul's father.

Martz argues that narrative objectivity is resumed in Chapter XII and speaks of Paul's 'remarkable self-understanding' in Chapter XIII. But neither Paul nor the retrospective narrator understands (1) why Paul is attracted to Clara, and then needs to reject her and to reconcile her to Dawes; (2) why he is tempted to revive his relationship with Miriam; and (3) why he is unable to posit a direction for himself after his mother's death. Martz oversimplifies the effect on Paul of his affair with Clara. If it really has a 'clarifying, purgatorial' effect, why is Paul as self-conscious, self-doubting, and fretful as he has always been?[16] Although Clara has helped him to discover that sex can be vital and healthy, has it really enabled 'them to find a truth' beyond sex?[17] His behaviour with Clara is hardly more logical than it is with Miriam. Paul's interpretation of Clara's attitudes and motives is not substantiated by her behaviour and conversations, and his criticism of her after their sexual relationship develops derives from his psychic need to separate himself from her, a need that is intensified by his mother's failing health. In chapters twelve through fifteen, as in chapters seven through eleven, and to a lesser extent in the first six chapters, the narrator engages in mythmaking, extenuation of *his* protagonist, and hypothetical theories of conduct that seem inadequate to the phenomena that he presents.

Paul does find limited sexual fulfilment with Clara. In a setting that looks backward to prehistorical time before man inhabited the earth ('The cliff of red earth sloped swiftly down, through trees and bushes, to the river that glimmered and was dark between the foliage.'), he has sex without real involvement (p. 308). As the sexual relationship continues and as an emotional tie begins to evolve, he feels that Clara, too, wishes to possess him. Once Mrs. Morel understands that Clara is not a real threat ('It would be hard for any woman to keep him. Her heart glowed; then she was sorry for Clara'), she is soon 'at her ease' (pp. 321–2). Yet the Puritanical Coppard value system has been inculcated in Paul, and he recognizes Clara as a lesser woman than Miriam 'if it came to goodness' (p. 326). When the narrator renders Clara's alleged sense of guilt ('After all, she was a married woman, and she had no right even to what he gave her.'), we cannot but feel he is really revealing his and Paul's discomfort for sleeping with a somewhat older woman who is married to a man not dissimilar to Mr. Morel (p. 352). When Paul arouses Clara as his father had his mother and displaces Baxter, a man who resembles his father in age, manner, and behaviour, he slips into the dialect of his father. Paul ritualistically restores Clara to her proper mate as if to compensate for his disloyalty to his father. The very title of the chapter most concerned with Paul's and Clara's sexual relationship, 'Baxter Dawes', may be indicative of Lawrence's unconscious need to palliate his father's memory even as he tells the tale.[18]

How revealing is the narrator's conception of the ideal sexual relationship; for that ideal involves the very self-sacrifice on the part of the woman that he had condemned in Miriam: '[Clara] took him simply because his need was bigger either than her or him, and her soul was still within her. She did this for him in his need, even if he left her, for she loved him' (p. 353). Because of his non-involvement with Clara's soul, because he regards her as a sexual object, he can remain comfortably separate from her once the sex act is complete. The narrator accepts Paul's distinctions between sex with Clara and with Miriam, even though the differences are not nearly as clear as they both make them. The sexual act is an 'initiation' and 'satisfaction' for each, because it transports them from their conscious selves into a timeless world where the processes of the intellect are suspended: 'To know their own nothingness, to know the tremendous living flood which carried them always, gave them rest within themselves.... There was a verification which they had together. Nothing could nullify it, nothing could take it away: It was almost their belief in life' (p. 354). But is this so different from Paul's original response to sex with Miriam? (See pp. 287–8). He becomes dissatisfied with Clara because she, too, cannot fulfil his need for impersonal sex (does he not really mean anonymous sex?). And she is much less satisfactory than Miriam at directing his passive energies – something that his mother has taught him both to expect and require from his women. According to the narrator's argument, Clara needs to arrest the sexual moment because she herself is incomplete. While Paul needs to keep his sexual life 'impersonal', she wants to 'hold him' and possess him (p. 354). Yet, paradoxically, he also wants someone to 'keep his soul steady' (p. 355). Neither Paul nor the narrator realizes that it is Miriam who would have come closer to Paul's emotional and sexual needs if Paul had been tender and responsive to her.

Paul, however, is uncomfortable *because* of the success of the sex with Clara: 'She made him feel imprisoned when she was there, as if he could not get a free deep breath, as if there were something on top of him' (p. 359). Paul cannot accept sexual satisfaction, and needs to discover the ways in which Clara is not quite as sufficient as their joyous coition might indicate: '[T]he baptism of fire . . . was not Clara. It was something that happened because of her, but it was not her' (p. 354). If 'baptism of fire' means the capacity to bring about sexual ecstasy and passionate fulfilment, how could any person be any more than a coequal partner? Does not Paul's expectation that Clara should be the autonomous means by which he achieves fulfilment show simultaneously how he places impossible demands upon his partners and how he sees himself as a rather passive participant to whom things are supposed to happen? Clara offers him passion, but he now must define her according to the very standards by which he had once found Miriam appealing but which he had rejected when he discredited her. Rather suddenly, the quest for the Good and Beautiful, the quest that was the catalyst for the evolution of the non-sexual relationship with Miriam, again becomes important. 'Here's the seacoast morning, big and permanent and beautiful; there is she fretting, always unsatisfied, and temporary as a bubble of foam. What does [Clara] mean to me, after all? She represents something, like a bubble of foam, represents the sea. But what is *she*? It's not her I care for' (p. 358; emphasis Lawrence's). Apparently, Clara is as wanting in soul and substance as Miriam had been in passion. His fear that Clara will 'absorb' him hardly seems appropriate since his kisses seem 'detached, hard, and elemental' and since Clara's 'mission' is described by the narrator as 'separate' from his (pp. 358, 361).

According to the narrator's myth, the passionate relationship with Clara enables Paul to grow and mature because his soul has been fertilized. But what about Clara? The narrator, Paul's surrogate, convinces himself that Paul has been the agent of Clara's revitalization: 'It was almost as if she had gained *herself* and stood now distinct and complete. She had received her confirmation. . . . [S]he *knew* now, she was sure of herself. And the same could almost be said of him' (p. 361; emphases Lawrence's). Once Clara realizes that she cannot meet his impossible expectations and that Paul will not accept her as she is, she wants to sacrifice herself to her former husband: 'She wanted to humble herself to him, to kneel before him. She wanted now to be self-sacrificial' (p. 384). If Paul's psychic games and subsequent rejection cause the experienced and considerably more self-sufficient Clara to lose her sexual pride (for, no matter what the narrator says, 'sacrifice' implies not only self-abnegation but submission), it is not surprising that the inexperienced adolescent Miriam had temporarily lost her sexual identity and had begun to worship perversely the young man who could not make love to her.

V

Paul and the narrator envision a linear pattern that dramatizes the development of Paul's consciousness, but the novel itself weaves an enclosing pattern that qualifies, if it does not parody, the final affirmation. The triumph of the mother *within the novel* is such that even Paul's turning away from death and acceptance of himself as a spark in the void are really an acceptance of his mother's notion that one can shape one's life by the sheer force of one's will: 'But no, he would not give in. Turning sharply, he walked towards the city's gold phosphorescence. His fists were shut, his mouth set fast. He would not take that direction, to the darkness, to follow her. He walked towards the faintly humming, glowing town, quickly' (p. 420). As he walked toward the city where his mother had dreamed of Paul's economic and social triumph, his expression (shut fists, mouth set fast) mirrors hers as she had approached death: 'Her mouth gradually shut hard in a line. She was holding herself rigid.... He never forgot that hard, utterly lonely and stubborn clenching of her mouth, which persisted for weeks (pp. 385–6). Grotesquely, Mrs. Morel's will continues to dominate him after her death. In turning from darkness, he turns to another kind of darkness because he has not yet exorcized the ghost of his destructive oedipal relationship. Thus the 'drift towards death', the description Lawrence used to describe Paul's plight in the famous letter to Garnett, is an apt description of Paul's final state within the novel.[19] The reader perceives that the narrator who renders the final scene as an affirmation is not yet free of the autobiographical sources. While Paul can withdraw from the Clara–Baxter–Paul triangle, he can never withdraw from the enclosing circle of his mother's influence. 'Sometimes he hated [Mrs. Morel] and pulled at her bondage. His life wanted to free itself of her. It was like a circle where life turned back on itself, and got no farther. She bore him, loved him, and his love turned back into her, so that he could not be free to go forward with his own life, really love another woman' (p. 345). That Paul perceives Mrs. Morel in strikingly sexual terms, after her death removes the incest taboo, shows her continuing hold on him: 'She lay like a maiden asleep.... She lay like a girl asleep and dreaming of her love.... He bent and kissed her passionately. But there was coldness against his mouth' (p. 399). When Paul whimpers 'mother' at the end of the novel, he completes the formal circle; he has finally and conclusively responded to Mrs. Morel's desperate cry with which Part One ended: 'Oh, my son – my son!' (pp. 420, 141).[20]

Sons and Lovers mimes Lawrence's psyche rather than his intent.[21] The unsuccessful struggle of the omniscient narrator to achieve objectivity is as much an agon as the tale of Paul's abortive quest for psychosexual maturity. Reading *Sons and Lovers*, one also experiences the author's creative problems. That the retrospective narrator is hardly more perceptive than the protagonist, that the narrator is an insistent, urgent and empathetic apologist for Paul, reveals the hold Lawrence's mother had upon his psyche. *Sons and Lovers* stares down the convention that technical distance and authorial omniscience imply objectivity or truth. It invites us to consider how obsessions and psychic needs penetrate a work of art, and transform and distort the intended form into something more complex, more disturbing, and more compelling.

Notes

1. The first quotation is from a review that appeared in *The Saturday Review* (London), 21 June 1913 and the second from an anonymous review in *The Athenaeum*, 21 June 1913. Both are reprinted in *Sons and Lovers: Text, Background, and Criticism*, ed. Julian Moynahan (New York: Viking, 1968). Page numbers in parentheses refer to the Moynahan edition.

2. See Schorer's brilliant essay 'Technique as Discovery', *Hudson Review*, I, (spring 1948) pp. 67–87; partially reprinted in *D. H. Lawrence and Sons and Lovers*, ed. by E. W. Tedlock, Jr (New York University Press, 1965) pp. 164–9.

   According to Schorer, the problem derives from Paul and his creator simultaneously loving the mother and hating her for 'compelling' his love:

   > This is a psychological tension which disrupts the form of the novel and obscures its meaning, because neither the contradiction in style nor confusion in point of view is made to right itself. Lawrence is merely repeating his emotions, and he avoids an

austerer technical scrutiny of his material because it would compel him to master them. He would not let the artist be stronger than the man....

... Lawrence could not separate the investigating analyst, who must be objective, from Lawrence, the subject of the book; and the sickness was not healed, the emotion not mastered, the novel not perfected. All this, and the character of a whole career, would have been altered if Lawrence had allowed his technique to discover the fullest meaning of his subject.

(Tedlock, pp. 168–9)

3.   Louis L. Martz, 'Portrait of Miriam: a Study in the Design of *Sons and Lovers*' in *Imagined Worlds: Essays on some English Novels and Novelists in Honour of John Butt*, eds Maynard Mack and Ian Gregor (New York: Methuen, 1968) p. 351.

4.   Martz, p. 364.

5.   Martz, p. 344.

6.   Martz, p. 367.

7.   From *The Collected Letters of D. H. Lawrence*, ed. Harry T. Moore (New York: The Viking Press, 1962). Reprinted in Tedlock, p. 14.

8.   She had to suffer the disgrace of poverty, while her sisters helped support her first son; her own father had been a Puritan who had browbeat her mother (so presumably she is excused for being on the offensive in her marriage); she had already been disappointed by one weak-willed man, John Fields.

9.   In Part Two, Lawrence is experimenting with the heightened imagistic language that becomes so characteristic of his technique. When Lawrence's prose becomes incantional and lyrical, and ceases to concern itself with presentation of dramatic scenes or with descriptions, *Sons and Lovers* most approaches the great prophetic novels, *The Rainbow* and *Women in Love*. The cancelled foreword shows how even in regards to his autobiographical novel, he was attracted to mystical and visionary explanations disguised as polemic and dialectical argument.

10. Martz, p. 345.

11. Rather grossly and insensitively she specifically calls William's failure to Paul's attention: 'But they're all alike. They're large in promises, but it's precious fulfilment you get.... They don't care about helping you, once they've gone' (p. 99).

12. 'Ordinary folk seem shallow to [the Leivers], trivial and inconsiderable. And so they were unaccustomed, painfully uncouth in the simplest social intercourse, suffering, and yet insolent in their superiority' (p. 147).

13. Twice within a few pages, the narrator tries to place Paul's situation within a dialectical framework. First, he argues that Paul's sexual problem is a common one: 'He was like so many young men of his own age. Sex had become so complicated in him that he would have denied that he could ever want Clara or Miriam or any woman that he *knew*' (p. 276; emphasis Lawrence's). A few moments later he pursues this point:

He looked around. A good many of the nicest men he knew were like himself, bound in by their own virginity, which they could not break out of. They were so sensitive to their women that they would go without them forever rather than do them a hurt, an injustice. Being the sons of mothers whose husbands had blundered rather brutally through their feminine sanctities, they were themselves too diffident and shy. They could easier deny themselves than incur any reproach from a woman; for a woman was like their mother, and they were full of the sense of their mother.

(p. 279)

14.   *Psychoanalysis and the Unconscious* and *Fantasia of the Unconscious* (New York: Viking, 1960) pp. 155–6.

15.   While writing his next novel, *The Rainbow*, he was still very much concerned with convincing himself of the frequency of sexual and passional relationships between parent and child of the opposite sex; witness Tom Brangwen's love for his step-daughter Anna and Will's for Ursula.

16.   Martz, p. 365.

17.   Martz, p. 365.

18.   The extent to which atonement to his father is important to Lawrence is indicated by both the substance and tone of the following remarks in *Fantasia of the Unconscious*: 'It is despicable for any one parent to accept a child's sympathy against the other parent. And the one who *received* the sympathy is always more contemptible than the one who is hated' (p. 131; emphasis Lawrence's).

19.   From the *Collected Letters* I, pp. 160–1. Reprinted in Moynahan, p. 492.

20.   As Harry T. Moore points out, the word should probably be 'whimpered' instead of 'whispered' because it occurs in Lawrence's final manuscript and 'in the first and several other editions published in his lifetime' (Tedlock, p. 63).

21.   One cannot dismiss Jessie Chamber's perceptive complaint:

> Either he was aware of what he was doing and persisted, or he did not know, and in that case no amount of telling would enlighten him. It was one of the things he had to find out for himself. The baffling truth, of course, lay between the two. He was aware, but he was under the spell of the domination that had ruled his life hitherto, and he refused to know. So instead of a release and a deliverance from bondage, the bondage was glorified and made absolute. His mother conquered indeed, but the vanquished one was her son. In *Sons and Lovers* Lawrence handed his mother the laurels of victory.

(Jessie Chambers, *D. H. Lawrence: a Personal Record, by 'E. T.'*, 2nd rev. edn, New York: Barnes & Noble, 1965; repr. in Moynahan p. 482)

5

Lawrence's Quest in *The Rainbow*

Now you will find [Frieda] and me in the novel, I think, and the
work is of both of us.

(22 Apr. 1914; *Huxley*, p. 191)[1]

A major subject of much modern literature is the author's quest for
self-definition. In particular, the search for moral and aesthetic
values is central to the novels of Joyce, Proust, Woolf, Conrad, and
Lawrence. Yet we have neglected how novels reveal their authors
because much modern criticism has been uncomfortable with the
expressive qualities of texts. Certainly, the New Criticism insisted
that texts be examined as self-referential ontologies which are
distinct from their authors' lives. Unwilling to commit the
intentional fallacy, Anglo-American formalism ceded discussion of
the author to biographers, psychoanalytic critics, and, more
recently, to phenomonologists, structuralists, and their successors.
Yet because the quest for values, form, and language is a central
subject in much modern fiction, it must be discussed as a formal
component within the text, separate and distinct from the narrator
or implied author. To neglect the dialogue between the creative
process and the subject matter of the story is to ignore a
fundamental part of the novel's imagined world. Lawrence's
struggle with his subject (his relationship with Frieda) is a major
aspect of *The Rainbow*, just as *Sons and Lovers* dramatizes his
struggle to come to terms with his relationship with Jessie
Chambers and his mother. Moreover, the author's quest for self-
understanding is central to other late nineteenth and early
twentieth century British novelists: Conrad in the Marlow tales,
Joyce in *A Portrait of the Artist* and *Ulysses*, and Woolf in *Mrs.
Dalloway* and *To the Lighthouse*.

Lawrence's quest within *The Rainbow* for values and for the
appropriate form is as important to the experience of reading the

novel as his polemic. Lawrence wanted to write about the passions of men and women in a new way. He also wanted to re-create himself and to urge his readers to re-create themselves. Lawrence felt that the novel is particularly suited in its spaciousness for proposing, testing, and discarding formulations as its author seeks truth.[2] *The Rainbow's* unfolding process presents a history of his struggle for fulfilment. Each phase of the Brangwens' history dramatizes a crucial episode in Lawrence's development. We must read *The Rainbow* with a pluralistic perspective that takes account of its prophetic and polemical impulses, but does not grant them an authority over the text. The reader must be attentive to the novel's oscillation between, on the one hand, its prophetic and mythic impulses and, on the other, its dramatization of Lawrence's own process of discovery. I shall argue that 1. *The Rainbow* dramatizes Lawrence's quest for the kind of fiction that is appropriate both for passionate sexual relationships between men and women and for the struggle within each man between, to use his terms, mind-consciousness and blood-consciousness; 2. *The Rainbow* enacts Lawrence's quest for self-realization. In one sense, each generation represents aspects of his psyche and is a means by which he uses the novel to discover his own individuality.

As with *Sons and Lovers*, the telling of *The Rainbow* is as crucial an agon as the tale.[3] Although the Ursula section was written first and the opening last, the book still roughly mimes the history of Lawrence's self-development. In the traditional novel narrated by an omniscient voice, one expects the voice to embody the values to which the characters evolve. But in *The Rainbow*, the narrator's values evolve and grow just like his characters, and the standards by which he evaluates behaviour become more subtle and more intricate as the novel progresses. What is good for Tom and Lydia would not necessarily be sufficient for Ursula, or even Anna and Will. Each generation must go beyond its predecessor to sustain itself; Lawrence seeks to discover new standards as the family chronicle moves forward toward the time when Lawrence wrote the novel in the second decade of the twentieth century.

Lawrence sought to dramatize the importance of sexuality but he also sought to discover an aesthetic that would embody his ideas. Proposing a Newer Testament to replace the extant one is part of the dialectical struggle that is at the centre of life. In life and in art, the best we can do is open up infinite possibilities. The climactic rainbow is not only for Ursula and for England, but represents an *enactment* of the aesthetic success achieved by writing the novel; Lawrence walks through the final arch to create anew in *Women in Love*. Like Ursula, his surrogate, he had to overcome dubiety and anxiety before he could go forward; hadn't he written in January 1915: 'My soul lay in the tomb – not dead, but with a flat stone over it, a corpse, become corpse-cold.... I don't feel so hopeless now I am risen.... We should all rise again from this grave.... I know we shall all come through, rise again and walk healed and whole and new in a big inheritance, here on earth' (30 Jan. 1915; *Huxley*, p. 222)? This pattern – a downward movement followed by an upward one – anticipates the closing scene when Ursula overcomes despair by rediscovering not only her biological self, but her potential to be alive passionately and sensually.

Lawrence wrote his novel to announce a credo to replace the Christian mythology and value system that dominated English life for several centuries. He conceived himself as prophet, seer, visionary, shaman, and Divine Messenger. Reduced to its simplest terms, his message is that mankind must rediscover the lost instinctive, biological, passionate self that has become sacrificed to democracy, imperialism, industrialism, and urbanization. Lawrence adopts biblical tales, images, syntax, and diction for the purpose of expounding a doctrine that undermines the traditional reading of the Bible. Yet he uses the biblical material to confer the stature of a Holy Book upon his novel, which argues for the centrality not of God but of the relationship between man and woman.

Given Lawrence's evangelical background, it was essential to his psyche that he come to terms with rather than reject the Bible. For Lawrence, the Bible itself was the prototypical novel because of its prophetic message. It has as its acknowledged purpose to announce God's Law, and to show by its dramatic incidents how man correctly and incorrectly should behave.[4] Influenced undoubtedly by Frazer's *The Golden Bough* and the turn-of-the-century's interest in ethnology, Lawrence understood that the Bible embodied the ethical archetypes of European civilization. As with Hardy, the shape and intensity of Lawrence's unorthodox beliefs are only possible because he had once been a believer. *The Rainbow* reflects the needs of Lawrence's Puritan conscience (which he owed to his mother's fastidious piety) to atone for the sacrilege of allowing his imagination to supplant faith and reason. Lawrence sought to create myths that would be more true to his generation than the ones it inherited.[5]

The Rainbow is Lawrence's quest to rediscover mankind's instinctive, libidinous, biological potential which he believed lay underneath the trappings of the social self that civilization has produced and required to play acceptable roles. While each novel contains its own genesis with its own physical and moral geography, few novels take us into such an extraordinary world as *The Rainbow* does. What Lawrence must do in his early chapters is nothing less than re-educate the reader to a new grammar of motives where the value of a character's behaviour is understood according to the degree it is true to its inner essence. Readers of *The Rainbow* are often baffled by what happens because the terms with which Lawrence describes behaviour are so strange. Often they read the novel in an undergraduate course after a series of English novels in which manners and morals are stressed. Just as the episodes of Genesis provide us with the standards – the grammar of motives – to measure the rest of the Old Testament, the purpose of *The Rainbow's* early chapters is to provide a grammar of passions so that in later chapters we will understand and recognize the deeper self beneath the conscious self.

Lawrence argues that passionate sexual relationships are not only beyond man's understanding, but beyond man's conscious control. That in *The Rainbow* Lawrence meant to propose a strikingly different kind of novel is clear from his oft quoted letter about characterization: 'I don't so much care about what the woman *feels* – in the ordinary usage of the word. That presumes an *ego* to feel with. I only care about what the woman *is* – what she IS – inhumanely, physiologically, materially...' (5 June 1914; *Huxley*, p. 200). But as he writes the novel, the characterization becomes increasingly complex until he does show us something of Ursula's feelings and ego.

The Rainbow shows how a writer's exploration of the potential of a genre can itself become part of his subject. Writing of an early draft of the then nameless book, he remarked: 'It is all crude as yet... most cumbersome and foundering... so new, so really a stratum deeper than I think anybody has ever gone in a novel' (11 Mar. 1913; *Huxley*, p. 113). He wished to write about '*the* problem of today, the establishment of a new relation, or the readjustment of the old one, between men and women' (17 Apr. 1913; *Huxley*, p. 120). Lawrence deliberately tries to reinvent the genre to address the passions of men and women. He writes of the unconscious life that he believed had escaped articulation by his predecessors and eschews, for the most part, the world of manners and morals that had provided the principal subject of the English novel. His prophetic voice displaces the ironic gentility of the traditional omniscient narrator of Victorian fiction. Nor does Lawrence adhere to the linear chronology of the realistic novel; he ignores references to the characters' ages and dates, and moves backwards and forward when he chooses. Highlighting certain episodes and details while overlooking others not only aligns him with the biblical tradition but also with cubism and post-impressionism, both of which had immense influence in England from the time of the major exhibitions in the period 1910–12.[6]

The structure and aesthetic of *The Rainbow* reflect his evolving relationship with Frieda who, in fact, gave the novel its title.[7] *The Rainbow* is part of his effort to destroy the old within him and to build a new self based on but not limited by his passionate marriage. Writing the novel became inextricably related to loving Frieda: 'I am going through a transition stage myself.... But I must write to live.... It is not so easy for one to be married. In marriage one must become something else. And I am changing, one way or the other' (29 Jan. 1914; *Huxley*, p. 180). For all the certainty of the prophetic voice, his love for Frieda created new anxiety and uncertainty: 'I seem to spend half my days having revulsions and convulsions from myself' (3 Apr. 1914; *Huxley*, p. 188). The concept of the novel as process and movement derives from Lawrence's personal needs. In the famous letter to Garnett in which he rejected the old concept of character, he commented scathingly on novelists' using a 'moral scheme into which all the characters fit'; he wrote of *The Rainbow* (which, in this letter, he still called by the earlier title *The Wedding Ring*): 'Don't look for the development of the novel to follow the lines of certain characters: the characters fall into the form of some other rhythmic form' (5 June 1914; *Huxley*, pp. 200–1).

Thus *The Rainbow* is a personal novel, even at those moments when it is most prophetic. The novel dramatizes Lawrence's quest for the myth of the passionate Elect. It is also an outlet for his frustrated messianic impulses, impulses that neither his wife nor friends took very seriously. Emile Delavenay speaks of Lawrence's 'constant search for disciples, which goes with the sense of a divine mission, of being predestined to make some revelation to mankind'.[8] No less than his romantic predecessors – Blake, Shelley, and Wordsworth – Lawrence sought refuge from the stress of life in the comfort of his fictions. The opening pages of *The Rainbow* express his fantasy of men who live purposeful, proud, sexually fulfilled lives and who are not inhibited by artificial social restraints. Each Brangwen generation 1. corresponds to an historical period; 2. to stages of growth in the passionate Elect; 3. to an historical phase of England's development – from rural (Tom and Lydia) to village (Will and Anna) to urban, industrial society (Ursula); and 4. to important phases of Lawrence's relationship with Frieda. The process of myth-making, the reaching out for biblical archetypes, is part of Lawrence's effort to cleanse and to refresh himself. Each generation of Brangwens registers a partial recovery of freshness for Lawrence.

In the very first pages, the anonymous pre-verbal Brangwens represent the reaffirmation of the primitive instinctive origins of man. They dominate the space they inhabit as if they were twenty times or fifty times the size of normal men. They are giants of the earth bestriding their land like Colossi (p. 2). For Lawrence this generation represents mythic forbears whose example still has meaning for modern man. Even as the opening renders the energy within nature and the men who are inseparable from nature, it announces the hyperbole, myth, and process that are central to the novel's aesthetic. After the canal and the railroad are introduced, the familial, agrarian life is no longer possible. Thus within Lawrence's myth of the giants of the earth, the Nephelim version of the creation myth, he also proposes a fortunate fall. The women are not content to live in 'the drowse of blood intimacy' (p. 2).[9] They feel that their world is anachronistic once industrialism touches it. They begin a quest for a richer life, for a life that contains an awareness of oneself and the world beyond the farm.

Lawrence is ambivalent towards the women's quest for knowledge and their turning away from a way of life where language and the life of the mind are secondary. Part of him wishes to return to the innocence of pre-history. But, as the novel evolves, he acknowledges that this existence may obliterate distinctions among men, prevent the growth of the individual, and limit people's possibilities to contribute to the community. On the one hand, a nostalgic Lawrence eulogizes a world that had never really been and longs for what that past represents. On the other hand, Lawrence, the contentious polemicist, wishes to change the world through his fiction and assumes the prophetic mantle to speak for the religion of the body.

Although, interestingly, she bears the first name of Lawrence's mother, Lydia, the experienced foreign woman, is a version of Frieda; Tom, the man aroused to his sexual and instinctual potential, is Lawrence's fantasy version of himself as a deeply passionate, intellectually unsophisticated figure. Their instinctive relationship corresponds to Lawrence's sense of the early stage of his relationship with Frieda. Their climactic consummation is a paradigm for the surrender of ego and rebirth that Lawrence sought. Tom's hesitant steps outward to acknowledge and fulfil his deepest needs, followed by his subsequent immersion in a passionate, sensual embrace, represent the kind of unconscious life flow that man must rediscover. *Sons and Lovers* left Lawrence with some residual effects of his mother-love and the frigid relationship with Jessie Chambers. Tom, I believe, represents another attempt to get things right sexually. (Nor should we forget, if we understand the personal nature of this novel, that variations on Lawrence's own Oedipal problems are central to Anna's relationship with her stepfather and Ursula's with her father.)

Tom and Lydia provide the first principle of Lawrence's grammar of passion. Lawrence uses the relationship between Tom and Lydia to show that *passionate* attraction takes place beneath the conscious level and disarms the intellect and the will. Lydia is roused to life despite her intention to withdraw from passionate attachments after the death of her husband. In Lawrence's Bible, passionate sexual attraction is akin to discovering Christ. On the basis of the most superficial acquaintance, of a few scant words between them, Tom feels her influence upon him: 'There was an inner reality, a logic of the soul, which connected her with him' (p. 36). Tom is 'nothingness' until he is completed and fulfilled by Lydia's acknowledgement. Stressing the impersonal physiological nature of this attraction, Lawrence uses pronouns which are adrift from their antecedents to describe the scenes of passionate interaction. Thus when Tom comes to announce his intention, she responds to his eyes:

> The expression of his eyes changed, become less impersonal, as if he were looking almost at her, for the truth of her. Steady and intent and eternal they were, as if they would never change. They seemed to fix and to resolve her. She quivered, feeling herself created, will-less, lapsing into him, into a common will with him (p. 40).

The scene is a deliberate parody of the traditional Victorian courtship scene where a man asks for the hand of the woman. Not only is the father absent, and the woman a widow with child; not only has the man's announcement preceded any social relationship; but the amenities and conventions of English proper behaviour are flouted at every turn. Lawrence's audience would have hardly been accustomed to the following dialogue in a relationship that took place in the 1860s:

> "You want me?" she said . . .
> "Yes," he said . . .
> "No," she said, not of herself. "No, I don't know".
>
> (p. 40)

Nor did it conform to conventions of 1915. Such a scene could serve as Lawrence's epigraph, if not epitaph, to the novel of manners and morals that continued to be England's dominant genre, despite the recent work of Joyce, an exiled Irishman, and Conrad, a Polish *émigré*.

As we read *The Rainbow* we experience Lawrence's search for the appropriate language with which to convey unconscious, physiological states. When the voice speaks in biblical diction, he provides a benediction for his characters; echoing Genesis to describe Tom's and Lydia's first passionate kiss, he implies that a new beginning is something that is continually possible for every individual soul: '[Tom] returned gradually, but newly created, as after a gestation, a new birth, in the womb of darkness. . . . And the dawn blazed in them, their new life came to pass, it was beyond all conveiving good, it was so good that it was almost a passing-away, a trespass' (p. 41).

Lawrence goes beyond *Sons and Lovers* in the use of nature imagery to confer value on his characters' sexual responses and to make human sexuality a microcosm of the natural cycle of the cosmos. In a realistic novel, the following sentence, describing Lydia's response to Tom, would not mean much: 'But she would wake in the morning one day and feel her blood running, feel herself lying open like a flower unsheathed in the sun, insistent and potent with demand' (p. 50). The gathering sexual energy of such words as 'running', 'open', 'lying', 'unsheathed', 'insistent', 'potent', and 'demand' charges the sentence with implication and power independent of its syntactical meaning. Furthermore, 'blood', 'flower', and 'sun' place the urgent sexuality in the context of nature's rhythms. The sentence's one metaphor, 'open like a flower', suggests that the opening of the woman for sex is akin to the receptiveness of the flower to the fertilizing bee. Beginning with the first use of 'feel', moving to 'blood', and continuing through 'potent' and 'demand', the heavily stressed prose (suggestive of Hopkins' poetry) gathers to a crescendo the sentence's power and urgency. As if to mime the arousing of her unconscious self, 'running' carries Lydia's awakened instincts through to 'potent' and 'demand'. The onomatopoeia of 'running' stands in a phonic tension with the slow, stately power of 'potent with demand'. Within the sentence the sexual act is encapsulated. Not only does the male sperm 'run' to the awaiting female, but the male, who feels incomplete, turns to the eternal female. And this is exactly what happens in the action of the novel. While it might be objected that the sentence describes only Lydia's awakening, the sentence is proleptic of the sexual act which her arousal makes possible. Once Lydia becomes awakened in her instincts and passion, she stands in readiness for the male. Lydia's awakening becomes a standard, albeit not the only one, by which Lawrence measures the more complex psyches of Anna and Ursula. Lydia is representative of immersion in sexuality and family, immersion that becomes increasingly difficult as England moves from agrarian to industrial society. The purity and simplicity of analogies with nature in the above passage disappear from the novel when the sexuality of later generations is described. Yet even Lydia's life is a quantum jump in complexity from the anonymity of the opening pages. Each of the four phases of Brangwen life takes Lawrence more time to describe because changing external conditions introduce new complexities into man's quest to realize his being.

A major difficulty in Lawrence's quest for form is that he wished to dramatize the continuing flux of passions for what he called an 'external stillness that lies under all movement, under all life, like a source, incorruptible and inexhaustible'.[10] He found this stillness in myth. *The Rainbow* depends on a tension between the movement of the narrative and the stasis of myth, which by its nature implies iteration of human experience. In the climax of the story of each generation, myth displaces process. The result is more like an elaborate rococo painting than a linear episode.

In the climax of the Tom and Lydia section, Lawrence proposes a parallel to the apocalyptic wedding in *Revelation*; Lydia as the Holy City comes down from Heaven as a bride adorned for her husband, Tom, who has heretofore held something of himself back and not fully accepted her otherness. Tom and Lydia surrender their egos and give themselves over to their passionate embrace, but something seems to be missing. Their victory comes at the expense of separateness and individuality. Part of the problem is the religious context: '[H]e relinquished himself ... losing himself to find her, to find himself in her' (p. 90). The very terms of the victory make us aware of the limitations of the biblical parallel. While the Bible moves toward apocalypse and the suspension of time, the displacement of *chronos* by *kairos*, the regenerate soul never comes to rest. It is always seeking but never finding *kairos* except during the sex act.[11] By definition, apocalypse implies that all become one in the kingdom of heaven, and distinctions will no longer be possible. But Tom and Lydia must return to the everyday temporal world.

Thus while they are born into another life, there is something unsatisfactory about their kind of union. On one hand, it provides a shelter for the children, or at least for Anna, in whom the Brangwens' passionate heritage resides, although she was not born a Brangwen. But, on the other hand, the children of blood-intimacy do not develop their full potential, as if there was something stifling to the growth of the soul in the marriage of Tom and Lydia. Their sexual passion creates a 'richness' of physiological energy at the expense of mental activity and awareness of the world (p. 100). Anna finally lapses into such a condition and Ursula is tempted by it when she is pregnant. While one part of Lawrence longed for this, another knew that such a life placed a constraint upon further development.

Lawrence is ambivalent towards Tom's and Lydia's victory, because their embrace *excludes* that part of him that must take part in the world of community and utterance. He moves on to the next generation in part because once he establishes the quality of Tom's and Lydia's passionate embrace, he is no longer interested in Tom and can no longer identify with him. Tom, who once had the need to explore new and strange experiences, lapses into the blood-intimacy of his forebears. Gradually, almost reluctantly, the voice acknowledges that Tom's achievement comes at the expense of giving up his quest into the unknown. Lawrence needs to extricate himself from his immersion in Tom because he is no longer an appropriate model for his own quest to resolve blood-consciousness and mind-consciousness. Tom has been the means of dramatizing one aspect of Lawrence to the exclusion of others. But Lawrence resists easy answers in defining his grammar of passions, and that resistance, that refusal to allow his myth to triumph over his own insights, is part of the novel's aesthetic, its meaning, and ultimately, its greatness. Competing for Lawrence's attention with the prophetic impulse is the nominalistic impulse which insists on making distinctions and undermining the simplifications of polemics.

Lydia articulates Lawrence's basic premise in the novel: 'Between two people, the love itself is the important thing, and that is neither you nor him. It is a third thing you must create' (p. 172). But neither the novel's opening dumb-show nor the story of Tom and Lydia speaks to the problem between Anna and Will. In his impulse to lose himself either in sexuality or religious mystery, Will is trying to go back to a simpler world. His effort to reconcile his aesthetic impulse with "passionate embrace" mimes Lawrence's. Except when they come together in passion, Anna and Will must inevitably remain separate; nor do they have, like Tom and Lydia, the teeming richness of the farm to sustain them.

II

The Anna and Will section corresponds to the passionate struggle that raged between Lawrence and Frieda while he wrote the novel. In the Will-Anna relationship, Lawrence explores the second principle of the grammar of passions: each person must bring an independent existence to marriage. The sheaf-gathering scene defines the essential problem between Will and Anna. Like Hardy, who uses the May-dance in *Tess*, he knew that, within rural life, vestiges of primitive rites survived in England. Lawrence implies that the way forward may be to reach back to man's anthropological origins when man was one with nature. Anna is defined in terms of extended space and of nature ('she called ... from afar ... like a bird unseen in the night' [p. 119]), but Will is restricted by something within him that keeps him from fully participating in the pagan sexual dance. Will cannot lapse out of consciousness; his name defines the quality that holds him back: will. By will, Lawrence means an active need to assert one's consciousness upon the world, a need he recognized in himself.

The chapter entitled 'Anna Victrix' defines the problem of man and woman after they have awakened to self-consciousness and are no longer in rhythm with nature in a pastoral world. Now that he has introduced new social and economic conditions, Lawrence must redefine the terms with which to describe physiological, passionate needs. Lawrence opens 'Anna Victrix' with a passage suggesting that Anna's and Will's marriage resembles both the expulsion from Paradise and the family of Noah after the old world has been destroyed (p. 140). But since Anna and Will do not fulfil the Brangwen promise, Lawrence discards these parallels and does not perceive them in terms of a consistent biblical pattern. Because their separation from the rest of the world mimes the dislocation caused by his own relationship to Frieda, there are passages in which the language strains to the point of breaking down. We feel Lawrence's excruciating pain embodied in the voice's narration of the difficulties between Anna and Will.[12] Will has the potential either to become alive passionately or to lapse into a kind of passional anomie, when, despite his sexual satisfaction with Anna, he does not fulfil himself and his passionate energy becomes corrupted. Deprived of his male pride and lacking an independent identity, Will's destructive passion is not so dissimilar from Uncle Tom's or from Gerald's in *Women in Love*. For a time the couple succeed in creating a timeless world within the diurnal world. As if to stress the parallel between generations, Lawrence echoes the earlier biblical language ('They were unalterably glad'). But the struggle between them is different and more complex. Will must come to terms with an industrial world that Tom and Lydia can virtually shut out. Will's dark intensity is a function of his need to believe in something more than the relationship between man and woman. He believes in the miracle of Cana and 'loved the Church' (p. 168); in defence, Anna, 'almost against herself, clung to the worship of the human knowledge' (p. 169). They never discover an equilibrium in which their separate selves enrich one another to form a union, a third entity stronger than the other two. Rather, each often becomes the other's emotional antithesis. As the passionate needs of one define contrary impulses in the other, the tension creates a destructive emotional friction that is never quite resolved.

Thus 'Anna Victrix' is an ironic title. By winning Anna loses. Anna is indifferent to the outside world, but, like Lawrence, she needs to find a balance between mind-consciousness and blood-consciousness. Just like Lawrence, Will requires his life in the world beyond; like Frieda, Anna is oblivious to these needs, and thus must share with Will the blame for the couple's problems. She needs to defeat him in body and spirit. She defeats him by despising his job, depriving him of his spiritual life, and taking away his pride. Will may be more the average sensual man than any other male figure, but he also objectifies Lawrence's fear that sexual passion will deprive him of his creativity. By abandoning his wood-carving of Adam and Eve, Will submits to the routine of the everyday world. In an ironic echo of the sheaf-gathering scene, during her pregnancy Anna dances alone in her search for the something that her life lacks: at an unconscious level, she is trying to 'annul' him by means of the primitive and atavistic dance. Anna's victory is not only Will's defeat, but ultimately her own.

Corresponding to the medieval period, the period between an agrarian and industrial society, the period in which villages and crafts dominate life in England, the Anna-Will section is the one in which religion is explored in its most personal form. Lawrence's evangelical conscience required that he explore the church as a putative source of values. At the centre of the novel is the very short chapter entitled 'Cathedral'. The cathedral, like the novel itself, is a man-made artifice that reconciles opposing dualities. But, to use Lawrence's terms, the cathedral, like Raphael's painting, arrests motion, while Lawrence's form, like the painting of Botticelli, is in motion.[13] In 'Cathedral', Lawrence shows the constraints that Christianity has placed upon man's efforts to realize fully his potential. Lawrence stresses how the Church denies process and movement and reduces everything to oneness. The Romanesque arch is a false rainbow because it reduces the variety of life to itself, something that Lawrence believed Christianity does by imposing arbitrary shibboleths ('Only the poor will get to heaven'; 'The meek shall inherit the earth').

The Cathedral represents an historical phase that man must put behind him if he is to continue the journey to fulfilment. Moreover, its geometric *resolution* is reductive. In Laurentian terms, the arch denies the Two-in-One and represents nullifying fusion, rather than union between two strong, contending souls that are independent in themselves. Like the blood-intimacy of the early Brangwens, it is another form of the dominance of what Lawrence called the Will-to-Inertia.[14] For Anna, as for Lawrence, God is something within and beyond one's self, but not within the Church. We may regard Anna as a Moses figure who has viewed the Promised Land, but will not enter. Before Anna lapses into child-bearing she carries on the Brangwen promise by refusing to submit her individuality to the church. Anna resists submission to 'the neutrality, the perfect, swooning consummation, the timeless ecstasy' of the Romanesque arches (p. 199). When she responds to the separateness of the gargoyles, she is compared to Eve. She seduces Will to a knowledge that he would deny; for him the church can no longer be a 'world within a world' (p. 202). Her resistance is described in terms of a bird taking flight, a striking image because it suggests the natural world that, Lawrence felt, was absent from the Cathedral and that has been shut out by the man-made rainbow (p. 200). Her desire to rise anticipates that of Ursula in the section when she assumes the mantle of Christ; her refusal to be fixed anticipates Ursula's refusal to submit to Skrebensky. The bird has freedom of movement in contrast to the Church's insistence on one direction. Anna's victory over Will's desire to use the Church as a spiritual womb to which they both might return is a significant step towards defining the Brangwens' values and creating Lawrence's consciousness.

III

Lawrence proposes as the third principle of his grammar of passions that certain elect souls can struggle by themselves to fulfilment, and can reconcile blood-consciousness and mind-consciousness, if they are true to their own impulses and if they avoid submitting to lesser beings and social conventions. Choosing a female as his surrogate enabled Lawrence to achieve distance and objectivity. Like Lawrence, Ursula is torn, on the one hand, between the female 'secret riches' of the body and, on the other, the 'man's world' of work, duty, and community (p. 333). When Lawrence's chronicle reaches the turn of the century, the Brangwen quest for symbols becomes more urgent because it mimes his own central concerns. Lawrence's surrogate, Ursula, seeks the symbols that will make her life whole. Her discovery of the appropriate one in the figure of Christ reborn to the life of the body parallels Lawrence's discovery of biblical archetypes as mythic analogues for his fictive characters. As the vessel of substantive insight, she becomes the central prophetic figure, just as Birkin is in *Women in Love*. Her quest is Lawrence's and that quest is enacted in the rushing, urgent form of the novel as well as in specific episodes such as Ursula's confrontation with the horses. Ursula's crises, defeats, and final victory mime Lawrence's own. Capable of growth and passion, she is Lawrence's ideal. Her role is not unlike that of Christ in the New Testament. She is the paradigmatic figure of Lawrence's secular scripture.

Ursula embodies both Lawrence's quest for a mental knowledge besides the knowledge of passionate embrace and his need to reconcile that quest with his marriage. Lawrence was not satisfied to fulfil himself apart from other men. He oscillated between the hope that he could transform England and the desire to subtract himself and a small number of the Elect into an enclave. Ursula's certainty that the mythical sons of God would have taken her for a wife expresses Lawrence's wish for a passionate Elect. She dramatizes Lawrence's own desire to leave behind the pedestrian life of modern England; she needs to go beyond the village life of her ancestors and existence as a provincial schoolteacher. Like Lawrence, she becomes increasingly iconoclastic about manners, morals, and social pressures. Like Lawrence, Ursula lives in a world of hyperbole. In a sense, 'the wave which cannot halt' (p. 2) defines Lawrence's growth; the telling of the Brangwen saga gave him the necessary energy, vitality, and confidence to transcend the limited world in which he found himself.

As Ursula imagines Christ speaking for the Law of the Body in the diction of the Bible, Lawrence's voice subsumes Ursula's. In the climax of Lawrence's quest for a new credo, Lawrence insists that Christ's return must be in the body and that man must be reborn in the body:

> The Resurrection is to life, not to death. Shall I not see those who have risen again walk here among men perfect in body and spirit, whole and glad in the flesh, living in the flesh, loving in the flesh, begetting children in the flesh arrived at last to wholeness . . . ?
>
> (p. 280)

This is the moment when Lawrence, at the centre of the novel, ascends his rhetorical Pisgah and looks to the future. As he speaks with urgency and intensity, we realize that the prophetic voice is a major character in the novel, that he is not only the teller but an essential character in the tale. Thus 'The Widening Circle', the

chapter in which the above passage appears (and the first of two
with that title), describes not only Ursula's expanding range of
experience, but that of the voice. He has progressed from
rendering the impersonal and anonymous life in the opening to
creating an individualized life where personal values and attitudes
are important. Just as the Brangwens lose their anonymity and
their individual quests become important, so Lawrence affirms
through his intrusive, prophetic, idiosyncratic voice the value of a
self-aware, unique personality. This is a value that was unknown
to the early Brangwens, but is crucial to Ursula as she seeks her
own identity even while responding to the demands of her body.

That her first love affair with Skrebensky is prolonged, unsatisfactory, and inhibiting reflects Lawrence's own view of his
relationship with Jessie. At twenty-one, Ursula has experienced
the kind of philosophical and psychological development Lawrence had achieved in his late twenties when he was creating her.
He takes pleasure in Ursula's unconventional attitudes towards
Christianity and in her flouting of traditional standards as, for
example, when she argues for making love in a Cathedral. Her
feelings of superiority and iconoclasm are Lawrence's as he sought
to define a new aristocracy of passionate Elect. Election should be
understood not only in terms of Evangelical theory that there are
men and Men, damned souls and saved souls, but also in terms of
Lawrence's snobbery and iconoclasm. The Brangwens, like Lawrence, have a pathological fear of being undifferentiated from the
mass of people.

Yet if Lawrence is Ursula, he is also Skrebensky. Skrebensky
embodies Lawrence's fear that he will not be able to fulfil Frieda.
Skrebensky is unformed and lacks the potential for growth and
fulfilment. In their first love-making under the moon, he needs to
'enclose' and 'overcome her' (p. 320). He lacks the passionate
energy that she requires: 'What was this nothingness she felt? The
nothingness was Skrebensky' (p. 320). Whereas Will has a problem
of unconsciously restraining and thus corrupting his passionate
potential, Skrebensky is inherently defective. While Will struggles
towards a kind of limited fulfilment, Skrebensky becomes a
factotum for the social system, a soldier who mindlessly fights for
the nation's political goals.

Ursula's oscillation between the demands of the conscious self
and the passional self continues in an upward spiral to the novel's
final pages as she moves toward the unreachable goal of what

Lawrence calls 'full achievement' of herself (*Phoenix*, p. 403). (It is Lawrence's version of Zeno's paradox that this goal recedes as it is approached, for there are always further levels of self-realization beyond the one that has been reached.) We recall in the Cathedral her mother's desire to take flight in order to escape Will's confinement. But Skrebensky holds her back. Because Skrebensky exists 'in her own desire only', she did not 'live completely' (p. 331); her first love baptizes her into 'shame' (the title of the ensuing chapter), as Lawrence believed Jessie had done to him.

Like her Brangwen forebears, Ursula is at ease in nature and open to experience. But at this point she does not have the independence that she will later have and desperately searches for someone to complete her. Yet her failure with Skrebensky, like Lawrence's own with Jessie Chambers, intensifies her quest. She turns her passion to a beautiful and proud young teacher, Winifred Inger. At first, Winifred seems to Ursula an example of one who has combined the best of female and male: 'She was proud and free as man, yet exquisite as a woman' (p. 336). But after a brief affair, lesbian love proves a dead end. (Lawrence, who would endorse Birkin's bisexuality, has a different standard for women.) While Ursula is associated with lions and later horses, Winifred is associated with moist clay and prehistoric lizards: '[Ursula] saw gross, ugly movements in her mistress, she saw a clayey, inert, unquickened flesh, that reminded her of the great prehistoric lizards' (p. 350). Lawrence is not above name-calling to denigrate characters who are unsuitable for his major figures. Winifred and Uncle Tom are arbitrarily aligned with the corruption of Wiggiston, although Lawrence does not *dramatize* why. It is as if Lawrence needed to turn against part of his creation and to expel it from the heightened passionate world he has created for the Elect: '[Uncle Tom's and Winifred's] marshy, bitter-sweet corruption came sick and unwholesome in Ursula's nostrils. Anything to get out of the foetid air. She would leave them both forever, leave forever their strange, soft, half-corrupt element. Anything to get away' (p. 350). Within the Brangwen strain and Lawrence's psyche is a struggle between the living, represented by Ursula, and the dead, represented by Uncle Tom. That the Brangwens have a corrupt line creates within the novel a viable threat to Ursula's and Lawrence's own quest.

At the close, Lawrence and Ursula are inseparable. When she agrees to marry Skrebensky, her capitulation to conventions mimes Lawrence's own fear that he lacked the strength to break free. But the horses represent the atavistic energy that he felt he needed to write *The Rainbow*. The painful activity of writing is mirrored by Ursula's terrible confrontation with an unacknow-ledged energy that must be expressed in spite of her conscious self. Just as Ursula must return from experiencing the 'hard, urgent, massive fire' of the horses to 'the ordered world of man', so must Lawrence (pp. 487–8). After she decides not to marry Skrebensky, her declaration prior to the final vision is also Lawrence's:

> I have no father nor mother nor lover, I have no allocated place in the world of things, I do not belong to Beldover nor to Nottingham nor to England nor to this world, they none of them exist. I am trammelled and entangled in them, but they are all unreal. I must break out of it, like a nut from its shell which is an unreality.
>
> (p. 492)

Very much like the dark night of the soul in traditional Christian-ity, this denial is a necessary prologue to her final vision. One must experience the Everlasting No on the road to the Everlasting Yea. Ursula is *enacting* the crucial prophetic passage where Lawrence has assumed the voice of Christ and imagined his own resurrec-tion:

> [Ursula] slept in the confidence of her new reality. She slept breathing with her soul the new air of a new world . . .
> When she woke at last it seemed as if a new day had come on the earth. How long, how long had she fought through the dust and obscurity, for this new dawn? (p. 492)

The 'new dawn' and 'new day' confirm the novel's insistence that the possibility of transfiguration is always present.

The final vision is not only Ursula's but Lawrence's. It is the moment to which the narrative and the narrator have moved. The novel has redefined God to be something remote, whose presence pervades nature but is indifferent to man's individual quest. (Ursula thinks: 'What ever God was, He was, and there was no need for her to trouble about Him' [p. 324]). Yet God also becomes the name of each individual's fullest potential, the aspect of life that is immune to Dr. Frankstone's mechanism. ('I don't see why we should attribute some special mystery to life' [p. 440]). Thus Ursula is recognizing the God within her when she understands that 'Self was a oneness with the infinite. To be oneself was a supreme, gleaming triumph of infinity' (p. 441). Such an insight is an essential prelude to the ending. Although Genesis is her favourite book, and her grandfather's death in a Flood established him as a Noah figure, she mocks God's command to Noah: 'be ye fruitful and multiply' (p. 323). Ursula must discover what Lawrence sees as the meaning of that myth – as a figuration of death followed by rebirth, despair by hope – if she is to carry out the Brangwen promise. Her vision of the rainbow is the fulfilment of God's Covenant that he will never destroy the things of the earth:

> And the rainbow stood on the earth. She knew that the sordid people who crept hard-scaled and separate on the face of the world's corruption were living still, that the rainbow was arched in their blood and would quiver to life in their spirit, that they would cast off their horny covering of disintegration, that new, clean, naked bodies would issue to a new germination, to a new growth, rising to the light and the wind and the clean rain of heaven. She saw in the rainbow the earth's new architecture, the old, brittle corruption of houses and factories swept away, the world built up in a living fabric of Truth, fitting to the overarching heaven.
>
> (p. 495).

Here the narrator and Lawrence are like a suspended series of intersecting circles. Ursula's vision is the fulfilment for Lawrence of the urgent quest that produced both *Study of Thomas Hardy* and *The Rainbow*; it signifies the continuing possibility of transfiguration for all men. Lawrence takes the worst case – the men of Wiggiston – and imagines them bursting forth, like the red poppy in *Study of Thomas Hardy*, with new life.[15] Lawrence's novel is the equivalent to Ursula's final vision, the rainbow that follows the terrible task of creation. If we recall Lawrence's denial of life after death, we see that heaven means, paradoxically, a transformed life on earth where men will be alive passionately. Each man must discover the God within himself, or in different terms, rewrite the Bible for himself.

However, the ending presents some difficulties. *The Rainbow* announces itself as an alternative to the novel of manners and morals. At the end of *The Rainbow* Ursula has cleansed herself of inhibiting manners and morals, but she has not formed any attachments on which the kind of community Lawrence desired could be based.[16] What precedes belies the final vision. Furthermore, the vision is an epiphany for Lawrence and Ursula of the possibility of transfiguration, but it does not dramatize a future. His novel does not prepare his readers for a new community and offers no more than the vaguest hope that such a community can occur within England. And *Women in Love*, by showing the world in disintegration, takes back the hope of a transfigured community that is offered by the ending of *The Rainbow*.

Like Hardy, Lawrence proposes a cosmology other than the traditional Christian one that dominates the English novel.[17] Lawrence appropriates the Christian myth stretching from Eden to the Apocalypse to define his passionate Bible. But does that myth also appropriate Lawrence's plot? What distinguishes Hardy is the fulfilment of a malevolent pattern. As if Lawrence could not sustain the implication of his insights, he imposes an apocalyptic ending on his material. Lawrence's ending undercuts and discards the novel's dramatization of the pervasive growth of a destructive strand of human life, represented by Skrebensky, Winifred, Uncle Tom, and Dr. Frankstone. His prophecy and his testimony are at odds. One cannot quite believe in the utopian simplification of Ursula's transforming vision because it is contradicted by the cumulative power of Lawrence's dramatic evidence. Within the novel, her triumph is hers alone. Lawrence's myth contradicts the novel's unfolding process. Moreover, by relying on the Judaic-Christian mythology for his epiphanies, Lawrence inadvertently restores some credibility to the very system that he is criticizing as anachronistic.

The movement of *The Rainbow* reflects Lawrence's efforts to clarify his own ideas and feelings, and to search for the appropriate aesthetic. Reading Lawrence, we must be attentive to the authorial presence embodied within the text. Knowing something about Lawrence's life and beliefs is essential. While *The Rainbow* nominally has an omniscient voice, we gradually realize that Lawrence's self-dramatizing voice reveals his values, emotions, idiosyncracies, and conflicts. Straining the convention of omniscient narration to its breaking point, Lawrence desperately tries to create a prophetic form out of his personal needs.

When we read *The Rainbow*, we participate in Lawrence's struggle to define his values and his concept of the novel.

Lawrence writes of his own passions and experiences even when he assigns them to invented characters. We respond to the process by which his subject is converted into art. Like Rodin in his sculptures, Lawrence never detaches himself from the medium in which he is working. But the novel is the more exciting for his involvement. This involvement is characteristic of other great innovators in British fiction in the 1890–1930 period: Conrad, Joyce, and Woolf. In these authors, the reader experiences a dialogue between the author's avowed subject and his effort to discover an appropriate language and form. These writers, like Lawrence, wrote to define themselves. And, as we know from the work of Picasso, Matisse, Pollock, and Rothko, the process of creation, the struggle to evaluate personal experience, and the quest for values become the characteristic concerns not only of modern literature but of modern painting and sculpture.

Notes

1. *The Letters of D. H. Lawrence*, ed. Aldous Huxley (New York: Viking, 1932).
2. *Phoenix: The Posthumous Papers of D. H. Lawrence*, ed. Edward P. McDonald (New York: Viking, 1936) pp. 529, 532. Published in 'Morality and the Novel' in *Calendar of Modern Letters* (Dec., 1925). Unless otherwise indicated, selections from *Phoenix* were unpublished in Lawrence's lifetime. See also *Study of Thomas Hardy and other Essays*, ed. Bruce Steele (Cambridge University Press, 1985).
3. See my chapter 4.
4. See *Phoenix*, p. 535.
5. See *Phoenix*, p. 296.
6. See Samuel Hynes, *The Edwardian Turn of Mind* (Princeton University Press, 1968) pp. 326–36.
7. For a splendid discussion of the evolution of *The Rainbow* and *Women in Love*, see Mark Kinkead-Weekes, 'The Marble and the Statue: the Exploratory Imagination of D. H. Lawrence' in *Imagined Worlds*, eds Maynard Mack and Ian Gregor (London: Methuen, 1968) pp. 371–418.
8. See Emile Delavenay, *D. H. Lawrence: the Man and his Work: the Formative Years 1885–1919*, trans. Katherine M. Delavenay (Carbondale and Edwardsville, Ill.: Southern Illinois University Press, 1972) p. 255.
9. Page references in parentheses refer to D. H. Lawrence, *The Rainbow* (New York: Viking, 1962).
10. Quoted in Kinkead-Weekes, p. 372, from an Autumn 1913 letter in

The Collected Letters of D. H. Lawrence, 2 vols., ed. Harry Moore (New York: Viking, 1962) I., p. 241.

11.   For a fuller discussion of *Kairos* and *Chronos*, see Frank Kermode, *The Sense of an Ending: Studies in the Theory of Fiction* (New York: Oxford University Press, 1967).

12.   Reading this novel, like reading many of the great innovative twentieth-century works such as *Ulysses*, *The Waste Land*, and *Absalom, Absalom*, means discovering the secret of what at first seems a partially closed semantic system. At times the correspondence of words to things and feelings is elusive. The text resists becoming part of the world of shared discourse and remains a lyrical overflow outside of recognized semantic codes. Yet even these passages have their own semantic logic. Take the one in 'Anna Victrix' in which two consecutive paragraphs beginning 'And ever and again' render Anna's and Will's perception of each other in rapidly changing images (p. 167). The essence of the passage is its movement. Lawrence is straining to invent the appropriate language to convey the passionate yet unconscious struggle between himself and Frieda. As important as the individual images is the process of metamorphosis, the rapid change in the vehicles of the metaphors. These images convey the struggle between Lawrence and Frieda that was the catalyst for these scenes. That Lawrence does not quite succeed in detaching himself from the struggle, does not move from immersion to reflection, becomes part of the reading experience for the reader who knows something about Lawrence's life.

13.   See *Study of Thomas Hardy, Phoenix*, pp. 446–8.

14.   For discussion of how *Study of Thomas Hardy*, written to 1914 but unpublished until after Lawrence's death, is central to Lawrence, see H. M. Daleski's *The Forked Flame* (Evanston, Ill: Northwestern, 1965) pp. 18–41. For discussion of how *Study* specifically informs *The Rainbow*, see Daleski, pp. 74–125.

15.   In *Study*, Lawrence writes, '[the wild poppy] has ... achieved its complete poppy-self.... It has uncovered its red. Its light, itself, has risen and shone out, has run on the winds for a moment. It is splendid' (*Phoenix*, pp. 403–4).

16.   In a letter to Lady Ottoline Morrell, he wrote of his utopian ideal:

> I want you to form the nucleus of a new community which shall start a new life amongst us – a life in which the only riches is integrity of character. So that each one may fulfill his own nature and desires to the utmost, but wherein tho' the ultimate satisfaction and joy is the completeness of us all as one.
>
> (1 Feb. 1915; *Huxley*, p. 224)

17.   See my chapter 3, originally published as 'Beginnings and Endings in Hardy's Major Fiction' in *Critical Approaches to Thomas Hardy*, ed. Dale Kramer, (London: Macmillan, 1979).

6
The Originality of E. M. Forster

I

Although his novels superficially resemble Victorian novels, it is not too much to say that E. M. Forster permanently changed the English novel. Perhaps his not having written novels for the last four decades of his life has inhibited our recognition of the seminal role Forster played in the transformation of the Victorian novel into what we know as the Modern novel. For example, Lionel Stevenson[1] barely mentions E. M. Forster's contribution, and Walter Allen asserts that Forster cannot 'be regarded as a pioneer' and places him 'in the older English tradition which, beginning with Fielding, ends, we normally assume, with Meredith'.[2] In this chapter, I shall make rather more substantial claims for Forster's originality as an artist than are usually made.

Forster's originality is based on four major achievements:

1. In the guise of writing objective novels, he wrote personal, subjective ones. He used the conventional omniscient narrator in novels which have a large expressive component. For Forster's novels, like those of the other great Modern British novelists – Joyce, Lawrence, Woolf, and Conrad – are the history of his soul, are metaphors of the self. His novels not only dramatize his characters' search for values, but structurally are quests for values, quests that reflect his own doubt and uncertainty.

2. He conceived of the structure of a novel as a continuous process by which values are presented, tested, preserved or discarded rather than as the conclusion of a series that clarifies and reorders everything that precedes. Thus his final scene is merely one in a series of events; it just happens to be the last that the reader will experience. Consequently, the issues raised

in the novel remain unresolved and the future directions of the surviving characters are often open to speculation.

3. In his novels, Forster not only challenges the artistic and thematic conventions of the novel of manners, but the traditions of manners and morals on which British life and fiction depended. His novels test accepted Victorian shibboleths about proper and decorous behaviour, about the importance of reason as necessary to control unruly passions and instincts, and about the relationships among social classes. His characters do not discover a place within the community but remain outside the community. When his characters acknowledge their sexuality in the face of conventions, they are not, as in prior novels, punished for it. The plots establish the validity of instinct, passion, and inner life.

4. He expanded the novel's range beyond the drawing rooms that provide the setting for so much of the English novel. In his effort to reach for poetry and passion, he expanded the novel geographically (India, Italy), sociologically (Leonard Bast; the schisms that divide classes, races, and religions), and cosmologically (the mysterious Marabar caves and the Hindu perspective in *A Passage to India*).

II

The debt of the Victorian novel to the eighteenth century novel includes a debt to Neo-classic – what we think of as Aristotelian – assumptions about plot's central role in a novel's form. But Forster is not an Aristotelian. He thinks of plot as a series of circumstances – often arbitrarily selected and arranged – which enables the author to explore the characters' personal lives and values. In a Forster novel, plot is important, but no more than voice or setting, and less than the moral and emotional life of the characters. Forster's plots, in fact, mime the quest of his principal characters to escape social entrapment by expressing feelings and passions and by creating personal ties. It is characteristic of Forster that the ending is another in a series of episodes in which man's limitations are exposed rather than an apocalyptic episode which resolves prior sound and moral problems. In *Aspects of the Novel*, he wrote rather critically: 'Nearly all novels are feeble at the end. This is because the plot requires to be wound up' (p. 66).[3] But Forster ended his novels without resolving them in order to imply that life was a continuous process that could not be arbitrarily summarized by a climactic incident (other than death) at the end of a narrative.

Like the other major British modernists – Conrad, Lawrence, Joyce, and Woolf – Forster understood human character as a continually changing flux of experience rather than fixed and static, as in the traditional novel of manners, and sought to dramatize states of mind at crucial moments. The essence of a Forster novel is contained in crystallizing moments that give that flux meaning. He believed, however, that within the flux of each person's experience were crucial symbolic moments, watersheds of experience, when, as he put it in *Aspects of the Novel*, 'life in time' gives way to 'life by values' and the significance of a character's life revealed itself. But these moments, akin to Joyce's epiphanies, are often not complete in themselves or clearly understood by the character experiencing them, even though the narrator and reader understand them. In part, his novels are a concatenation of these significant moments in the lives of his major characters.

For Forster, fiction provided the only possible principle of order in the face of major historical forces that seemed to have deprived man of his significance – the Industrial Revolution, imperialism, urbanization, and the intensifying organization and systemization of English life. He is interested in these historical phenomena insofar as they affect the quality of man's feelings, imagination, and personal relationships. Flux is both an inevitable part of life with which we must come to terms and an enemy which we must combat. It makes anachronistic the social solutions of the past. And Forster thought that the kind of novel that a conservative, hierarchical society produced is also anachronistic. In the face of the instability of personal relations, of class structure, and of accepted standards of social behaviour, the novel of manners, which depends upon the author's reliance upon his audience to recognize violations of decorum and propriety, begins to break down. In Lawrence, Joyce, and Woolf, as well as in Forster, characters are judged more on whether they are true to their best impulses rather than on how they function in the community.

Forster's novels enact his quest for the inner life as well as his attempt to rescue himself from the curse of modernism.[4] In a sense, his novels are elegiac and nostalgic. Like Eliot, Joyce, Conrad, and Lawrence, he juxtaposes the present to the past, in part to define the present, in part out of nostalgia for the past.

Forster's novels, like Hardy's and Lawrence's, seek to create, nostalgically, an English pastoral, a mythology with tales of English heroes, which would invigorate the culture and the language. Like Lawrence, Conrad, and Hardy, Forster stands with the Coleridgeans against the Utilitarians. Thus, rural life – the myth of the English countryside – is a source of values. In *Howards End* he writes:

> In these English farms, if anywhere, one might see life steadily and see it whole, group in one vision its transitoriness and its eternal youth, connect – connect without bitterness until all men are brothers.
>
> (*HE*, p. 266)

Like Arnold, Forster's goal was 'to see life steadily and see it whole'. Forster is, above all, a humanist who does not believe that a God directs human destiny. As for Arnold, art was a surrogate for religion.[5] With its carefully constructed patterns and symbolic scenes, the artificial order of the novel was for Forster an alternative to disbelief.

Beginning with Hardy and Conrad, the major British writers frequently examine the events of the narrative in the context of vast historical perspectives. Lawrence, Conrad, Joyce (and, of course, Yeats and Eliot) also dramatize the present through the lens of the past. Frazer's *The Golden Bough* (1890) extended the range of the past beyond biblical time and even beyond historical time; later Jung's emphasis on archetypes stressed that all cultures share common anthropological experience and psychological traits. And Forster wished to show that, despite differences in breeding, customs, and values, a common heritage united mankind. Crucial aspects of Forster's values rest in what he calls 'the inner life' and the 'unseen', both of which resist language. By the 'inner life', he means passions and feelings, those aspects of life in which man may experience poetry and romance. For Forster, the 'unseen' means not the traditional Christian God but a world beyond things that can be reached by passions, imagination, intelligence, and affection. Like Conrad, Lawrence and Joyce, Forster sees the need to revivify family ties and personal relationships that form the basis of both ancient cultures and British civilization. Forster wants the novel to move beyond local, nominalistic insight and toward universal truths. As he puts it in *Aspects of the Novel*, he wants his fiction to '[reach] back ... to join up with all the other people far back' (*Aspects*, pp. 92–3).

Whereas Victorian novelists usually wrote of how man lived in the community and examined the values for which man lived, their successors, including Forster, wrote about themselves. Influenced by Impressionism and post-Impressionism, which stressed the uniqueness of each man's perception, as well as by the dissolution of moral and political certainties in the 1890–1910 period, Forster wrote fiction that expressed his private feelings, the idiosyncracies of his personality, and the anxieties and frustrations of his psyche.[6] Like Conrad, Lawrence, Joyce and Woolf, he wished to create the order in art that the world lacked; like them, he wished to create himself in his art and to export that created self back into his life; like them, writing fiction became his means of defining himself. Forster reveals his psyche and values on every page, and yet he is a far less prominent presence than Conrad, Lawrence, Joyce, and Woolf. Forster's own spiritual quest determines the form of his novels. Rather than establishing a fixed standard of values by which he measures his characters, his technically omniscient voice undergoes a quest for values.

Forster's aesthetic values cannot be separated from his moral ones. With their elegant phrasing, tact, balance and sensibility, Forster's novels enact his values. They are the objective correlative for the keen sensibility, the personal relationships, the delicate discriminations of feeling that he sought. Within sustained creative activity, the artist discovers unity and coherence in his own life and the completed work of art provides unity and coherence for others. Forster sought to move beyond the subjective and to create an impersonal art out of his own experiences and feelings. But he never quite succeeded in getting outside of himself, and it may be that his novels are more exciting because of this. Although Forster grew as a novelist and gradually enlarged his scope, he never suppressed his own doubts and anxieties simply to create an objective vision for himself and his reader.

In *Aspects*, he expressed his admiration for Hardy: 'The work of Hardy is my home' (*Aspects*, p. 66). This has been taken to mean Forster is an heir to the Victorian novel, but Forster, like Lawrence, realized that Hardy was one of the great innovators in the English novel. Hardy taught Forster, particularly in *Jude*, that the author did not have to separate the omniscient narrator from the protagonist's perspective. Like Hardy, he uses an omniscient voice that often becomes an empathetic spokesman for major characters. Like Hardy, he creates an alternative to the benevolent Cosmos that dominated English fiction prior to Hardy. Like Hardy, Forster gave up writing novels in the middle of his career. Forster not only was influenced by Hardy's skeptical world view and his sense of story, but by his stress on various kinds of sexual exploitation. Forster transfers Hardy's sexual themes primarily to the upper middle class. *Howards End* is a kind of retelling of *Tess*, with both Jackie and Helen playing variations of Tess's role with Wilcox; Wilcox's son, Paul, is a version of Alec, and Leonard Bast is a parody of Angel. Forster is criticizing the hypocrisy and insanity of sexual morality which allows Henry Wilcox, twice a seducer, to condemn Helen Schlegel's sexual peccadillo.

Forster's view of man is somewhere between Hardy's pessimism and Lawrence's optimism; he doubts man's capacities, but believes that man will muddle through, and that the artist provides a model for the potential of the individual imagination to create meaning and of the individual heart to respond, on occasion, in a humane way. Forster shares with the other great modernists the belief that language could create meaning, could exorcise chaos when all else fails. Forster is often a polite version of Lawrence, of whom he wrote admiringly in *Aspects*.[7] Like Lawrence, he saw himself in the tradition of English Romantics who sought to combine the visionary and realistic mode, the prophetic and the personal.[8] Both frequently sound an elegaic and nostalgic note. Both regretted that man was no longer in harmony with nature and that the industrial revolution had deprived man of his individuality. Forster anticipates Lawrence in dramatizing what industrialism and commercialism had taken from the modern world. Doesn't Wilcox suggest Gerald Crick? The former thinks that the force of his will can reshape the world to his own image; he is 'broken' when circumstances, in the form of a manslaughter charge against his son, get beyond his control.

III

Discussing how Forster's novels differ from their predecessors not only enables us to appreciate Forster's uniqueness as an artist, but places the relationship between Forster's values and techniques in a new perspective. Because Forster's two masterpieces, *Howards End* and *A Passage to India*, are also his most innovative novels, I shall stress those works. But, because my implicit and explicit argument is that Forster's novels are strikingly original in concept, theme, and execution, I shall discuss the entire canon.

In *Where Angels Fear to Tread* (1905) Forster begins the process of turning the English novel of manners upside down. He recognizes the role of sexual passion in human behaviour and eschews moral judgement about such passions. Lilia Herriton and Caroline Abbott are attracted and aroused by the primitive energy of Gino, the young Italian son of a dentist, who by English standards lacks culture and civilization.

Where Angels Fear to Tread also introduces Forster's characteristic theme of a conflict between two cultures. Forster believes that place shapes character. Here it is Italy versus England. England, as epitomized by Mrs. Herriton and even more by the next generation in the person of her daughter Harriet, is depicted as sexually repressed, emotionally sterile, and impotent in personal relations. Philip, the self-conscious, disengaged man who has difficulty feeling and suffers from a kind of anomie, introduces a new character into English fiction. By contrast, Italy retains passion, poetry, sexuality, and thus offers the possibility of 'intimacy' and 'perfect friendship' (p. 140). Gino represents an older tradition of instinctive life that survives in spite of civilization's conventions and restraints. Certainly Caroline and Philip are changed by their days at Monteriano. The passions of Lilia, Gino, and finally Caroline overwhelm the traditions that would restrain them. The novel shows that feelings and passions are the essence of being alive.

Until *A Passage to India* and *Howards End*, Forster's voice rarely has the certainty of the authoritative omniscient voice of Victorian fiction. Thus the reader of a Forster novel must be especially attentive to irony and to the psychological nuances of character. Part of Forster's modernity is his expectation that the reader will discover relationships and significance. Forster's reticence, the sparsity of his analysis in comparison to such contemporaries as Bennett or Galsworthy, is part of his technique; as illustration, let us look at the climax of *Where Angels Fear to Tread*:

She said plainly "That I love him". Then she broke down. Her body was shaken with sobs, and lest there should be any doubt

she cried between the sobs for Gino! Gino! Gino!
He heard himself remark "Rather! I love him too!".

(p. 145)

Caroline's hysterical surrender to sexual passion and Philip's latent homosexuality introduce something new in English fiction. Forster's range of sexual emotions goes a step further than Hardy's, even in *Jude the Obscure*. Forster's poised balance and irony reveal the limitations of characters who do not quite know themselves. No sooner does Philip move away from the aesthetic view of life than he lapses back when his love is unrequited. After his declaration he becomes inhibited by his learning, his snobbery, his self-irony, and his lifelong subservience to his mother.

Forster's novels open up possibilities but do not resolve them. In his first novel, he emphasizes that the structure is a process by which characters search for values. Caroline's return to England alone is a kind of defeat. Unlike Lilia, Caroline does seem to compromise with her passion. Given her strength of character and her ability to influence Gino, would she have failed with him had she declared her passion? Although Forster has shown us that Gino quickly has fallen into the stereotypical Italian marriage, Caroline has a depth that Lilia lacked and that Gino acknowledges. Yet Caroline has too readily submitted to convention and perhaps let the presence of Philip and Harriet check her passion. At the close Forster leaves the reader to ponder whether not only Philip, but even the more open Caroline will revert to their Sawston personalities. As Caroline and Philip go to nurse Harriet, we wonder whether either of them is open to experience.

Philip looks upon life as spectacle. He is a voyeur of the passions. His aesthetic view of life objectifies an impulse Forster both despised and feared he possessed. Forster felt that moral engagement was the essence of art and life. When Philip finally declares his passion, Caroline Abbott's response exposes his limitations (although, to be fair to Philip, she does not realize that he is changing): 'You're without passion; you look on life as a spectacle: you don't enter it; you only find it funny or beautiful' (p. 145). Philip's aestheticism may be part of Forster's efforts to imply obliquely his character's latent homosexuality and to define a male figure who is ambivalent about heterosexual passion (we might recall *Maurice* where Clive's aesthetic sense and reading of *The*

Symposium place Maurice's and Clive's love beyond carnal intercourse).

Thus can we not tentatively conclude that Forster's presence becomes part of the novel's imagined world? The incompleteness of heterosexual relationships, in part, represents the emotional reticence of the homosexual Forster to dramatize sexual fulfilment. The potentially fulfilling heterosexual relationship is necessarily discarded in *Where Angels Fear to Tread*, when Philip cannot reach the obvious decision to rescue himself and Caroline. And this is part of a pattern in Forster's work. In *The Longest Journey*, Gerald, an appropriate mate for Agnes, dies, and Maud and Rickie never connect. *Howards End* shows marriage and heterosexual relationships as a series of missed opportunities. As we shall see, only the ending of *A Room with a View* shows that conventions might be rejected. And, because Lucy and Young Emerson seem to have turned their backs on England, their triumph is purely personal and offers little hope for England.

In *The Longest Journey* (1907), Forster is unable to separate himself from Rickie. If the reader knows Forster's biography and other works, the reader understands the tension within the text, a tension which is heightened at crucial times within Rickie's narrative.[9] Rickie's problem as a character is that he cannot maintain his iconoclasm and independence. An author himself, Rickie is unable to separate himself from the roles that society demands. Here, as in all Forster's novels, social conventions stifle the imagination, blunt the feelings, inhibit the passions, and ignore the demands of the inner life. Rickie diminishes as a character until he is subsumed into the very role he despised. He becomes another Pembroke, his wife's philistine brother. Symbolically Ansell and Stephen Wonham may be, as Stone contends, the 'intellectual and physical halves of Rickie's estranged soul, the Apollonian and the Dionysian', and of Forster's also.[10] But they become more substantive characters in the novel's imagined world. For, unlike Rickie, who cannot sustain his identity, they maintain their authentic selves.

One of Forster's principal themes is how conventional sexual morals restrict the development of the inner life and stifle the very possibilities of growth and fulfilment. In a way, *The Longest Journey* is a whimsical retelling of *Jude the Obscure*. Forster places Rickie in the role of Jude, the man whose aspirations are continually adjusted downward in a world beyond his control, and places

Agnes in the peculiar role of an Arabella who poses as a Sue. Of course, the real salvation for Rickie rests in implicit sexual connection with Stewart Ansell (a male Sue) and Rickie's bastard brother Stephen (a male Arabella). When Stewart holds on to Rickie's ankle in the meadow on the day that he is captured by Agnes (I think 'captured' is exactly how we are supposed to regard her conquest in the dell), the homosexual relationship with Stewart represents the road not taken, the better path. The form of the novel rejects not only conventional marriage but the formal resolution of life in marriage that characterizes the novel of manners; perhaps, among other things, the epithet 'the longest journey' ironically applies to conventional marriage and the genre that testifies to its efficacy.

In the final section after saving Stephen's life, Rickie ironically recreates Stephen in his image as Herbert has done for him. The ending reaches for prophecy, but unfortunately achieves bathos and fustian when Forster writes, 'Though he could not phrase it, [Stephen] believed that he guided the future of our race, and that, century after century, his thoughts and his passions would triumph in England' (p. 310). Nothing that precedes justifies Stephen's naive faith in himself, and his erratic character hardly bodes well for the future of England or for himself.[11]

Passion, instinct, and spontaneity surge through *A Room With A View* (1908) and challenge the formalism of Victorian manners dramatized within the novel. This formalism represses and controls the passion and energy that threaten it. It does so by imposition of stereotyped roles and conventional relationships – Charlotte not only as guide for Lucy in Florence, but protector of her purity; Cecil, as the potential husband for Lucy, the supposedly submissive young virgin. Although we can trace Lucy Honeychurch back to George Eliot, she represents a continuation of another stage in the evolution of a new character in English fiction, the independent, self-possessed, sexually mature, and responsive woman. Her soul becomes a room with a view because she discovers passions. Sexuality becomes respectable in an upper-middle-class woman.

English upper-middle-class conventions obtrude to shape Lucy's experience while she is taking the obligatory grand tour. But Florence arouses her need for something more. Lucy gradually develops in her personal life the passion and imagination that she had projected into her music. She discovers her authentic self and becomes not a product of social artifice shaped by conventions, but a creative intelligence. By contrast, Cecil, like Philip, understands beauty but does not respond to people. He has allowed society to create his character; he lives in a world of forms and phrases. Lucy welcomes George's passionate kisses; but she disdains Cecil's formal kisses after their engagement, an engagement which represents a vestige of the claustrophobic tradition that Forster is indicting.

In Forster's novels accident and coincidence are the ways that the not-I world intrudes into the hubristic illusions of proud, narrow-minded, selfish people that they can control the cosmos in which they live. The Emersons represent to Mrs. Honeychurch and the Vyses forces they would like to purge from their complacent Sawston world, but the Emersons' reappearance and persistence flout that wish. Yet Forster's poised and assured ironic detachment creates a continuing substantive alternative to Sawston's values. For example, Forster uses the traditional picnic of the novel of manners, a picnic which would be an expected part of an Austen novel, to show the emptiness of Victorian social conventions and their irrelevance to personal relationships. Mr. Eager's aesthetic arrangement of the expedition is undermined by human passions, culminating in George's kiss. The polite traveller's phrase, 'a room with a view', expands into the concepts of living more passionately, seeing more clearly, and breaking out of social restraints.

Typically in Forster, the novel proposes a number of apparent endings, which later events reveal as merely a resting place in the narrative's evolving process. Thus, after Lucy breaks her engagement with Cecil, which is her necessary Everlasting Nay on the path to the Everlasting Yea, Forster writes of her temporarily abandoning her quest for self-fulfilment in terms which suggest the nemesis that everyone must avoid:

She gave up trying to understand herself, and joined the vast armies of the benighted, who follow neither the heart nor the brain, and march to their destiny by catch words. The armies are full of pleasant and pious folk. But they have yielded to the only enemy that matters – the enemy within. They have sinned against passion and truth . . .

(p. 174)

Gradually, the violence in the Piazza Signoria, the two impulsive and impassionate kisses of George Emerson, the spontaneity of the elder Emerson, and the ladies encountering George, Freddie, and Mr. Beebe in the nude, anticipate the dénouement. The reappearance of the Emersons represents the passionate self that Lucy repressed when she agreed to marry Cecil, and the libidinous energy that Windy Corner and Mrs. Honeychurch have tried to ignore.

Howards End (1910) turns the novel of manners upside down, and dramatizes that in the modern world there is a separation between, on the one hand, culture, tradition, and courtesy, and on the other hand, wealth. Indeed *Howards End*, like *The Rainbow*, is conceived in terms of dualism between the forces of light and those of darkness: the Schlegels and the Wilcoxes, manners and money, love and truth, things as they are and things as they ought to be, personal life and the world of commerce and industry, imagination and reason, the surface life and the inner life. In this book, Forster goes beyond the novel of manners to examine the relation of public life to private values. England becomes a character and its health is a central subject. Forster shows that the impossibility of the Schlegels' desire 'that public life should mirror whatever is good in the life within' (p. 25). The Schlegel sisters are unable to stop the advance of materialism, mediocrity, and the empirical intellect that responds only to facts. In the character of Leonard Bast, Forster uncharacteristically reaches down into the lower middle class to show how the energy and pretension of the new urban class are synonymous with that of London; we cannot but think of Eliot's line, 'I had not thought death had undone so many.' The Schlegels want to create Leonard into one of their sort, but they pathetically fail.

Like *Nostromo, Women in Love* and *The Magic Mountain*, the plot of *Howards End* is a vision of a world in disintegration. As it moves from house to house, *Howards End*, like *Women in Love*, gradually discards or discredits major aspects of English civilization. The manorial and feudal life style at Oniton, indicted in part because of its absentee landlord who is disinterested in the property or life among the people in the environs; the recently built Ducie street house, with its utilitarian plan and overfurnished look and its location too close to stables; Swanage, representing suburbia, soon to become the 'most important town of all, and ugliest of the three' with which it forms a cluster; and Wickham Place, about to be swept under by the 'gray tides of London' (pp. 106, 166). As in *The Waste Land* and *The Secret Agent*, London is as much a condition of mind as a place. And that condition of mind expresses Forster's anxiety. London has become an impersonal juggernaut, stalking the beleaguered outposts of civilization, like Wickham Place. In *Howards End*, Forster elegized a world that he had lost.

Margaret is Forster's surrogate. Her credo of balance and proportion as a last resort is not only central to the moral values of the novel, but defines Forster's concept of the form of the novel. Margaret keeps alive the potential for inner life and personal response. At the outset, she has a 'profound vivacity, a continual and sincere response to all that she encountered in her path through life' (p. 7). Like Margaret, Forster felt 'that those who prepare for all the emergencies of life beforehand may equip themselves at the expense of joy' (p. 57). For a time she seems to be shrinking under the pressure of Wilcox's moral obtuseness, but she survives because of her openness to experience and her ability to respond in personal terms.

Yet Margaret, finally, has her limitations. Her inner life is in danger of becoming, like Mrs. Wilcox's, virtually her whole life. Margaret moves to Mrs. Wilcox's position within the novel. Both have renounced not only their social roles, but their social selves. Forster understands that this reliance upon spirituality can result in indifference not only to the concept of community as a social and political entity, but even to friends. (He pursues this in *A Passage to India* in the characters of Godbole and Mrs. Moore.) Forster's voice oscillates between striving for an inclusive humanistic perspective and settling for a more iconoclastic voice that empathizes with Margaret's complacency, nostalgia, and snobbery. Forster does not always view with irony Margaret's categorizing and supercilious sensibility or realize that her aesthetic, voyeuristic view of life (not unlike Philip Herriton's) results in her frequent indifference to other people.

The ending implies the possibility of establishing an enclave of affection and sensitivity, but the enclave exists with even less hope of renewing itself than had the earlier enclave at Wickham Place. Not only does the fecundity of the crude Charles Wilcox threaten that precarious enclave, but Helen's child, in whom the novel's promise rests, is, after all, partly a Bast. Mr. Wilcox is an invalid, Margaret cannot love children, and the novel ends with the senior Wilcox's revelation of his keeping Margaret in the dark about his first wife's wish that Margaret be heir to Howards End. What adult relationships other than the ties between Margaret and Helen survive? Industrialization and progress continue to extend their range, while the Schlegels' 'triumph' is something of a defeat for the values in which they believe. But the collapse of the Wilcox family will not deter the forces that are changing England. Henry epitomizes commercial, social, and sexual values that are pervasive in England. Helen's response to Beethoven defines not only her 'panic and emptiness', but that of England's. Finally, the title of *Howards End* becomes a pun on death and destruction, a pun that reverberates throughout the novel.

Writing in 1960 in the 'Terminal Note' to *Maurice*, Forster remarked:

> A happy ending was imperative. I shouldn't have bothered to write otherwise. I was determined that in fiction anyway two men should fall in love and remain in it for the ever and ever that fiction allows, and in this sense Maurice and Alex still roam the greenwood.
>
> (p. 250)

In this homosexual novel which Forster did not publish for nearly six decades (1913; pub. 1970), Forster's ending is not idyllic but inconclusive. How much of a victory is it if these single men are forced by conventions to become 'outlaws' (p. 254)? Are we not left with the impression that future Maurices will experience his confusion and loneliness and will seek advice from intolerant and incredulous doctors and well-meaning but often ineffectual hypnotists? Isn't the 'disgusting and dishonourable old age' of the person who propositions Maurice on the train a real possibility for a man who himself was, in a parallel scene, once tempted to make similar advances to a man? Forster shows that because the homosexual is denied love and must repress his needs, he desperately seeks love in any way that he can. (Of course the fundamental irony is that, had these been heterosexual scenes, there would have been barely cause for remark. In one scene, a man would have stifled an unfortunate impulse for an adolescent girl; and in the other he would have resisted the advances of a lewd woman.) If Maurice did not have financial means, his course of action would have been far more difficult.

Indeed, Forster presents his penultimate ending as another in a series of catastrophies for the increasingly isolated and alienated title character. After Clive turns from Maurice, the latter's life is a sequence of disasters. The plot has dramatized the hopelessness and loneliness of a homosexual in England. Maurice alternates between, on the one hand, guilt and disgust (when he accepts and internalizes society's image of the homosexual) and, on the other, acknowledgement of the legitimacy of his own needs. After Alex, the Laurentian gamekeeper with whom he experiences full physical love, at first rejects his idea that they go off together, Maurice despairs that 'Love had failed' (p. 233). Given what has preceded and the dramatic intensity of the crucial episodes in the novel, it is the penultimate ending, rather than the fairy tale of the last paragraphs, that reflects Forster's emotional engagement and artistic energy.

IV

We best understand the originality of *A Passage to India* (1924), a seemingly traditional novel, if we compare it briefly with an Austen novel. *A Passage to India* is a modern version of the novels of manners. It is based on Forster's desire to show that it is no longer possible to write an Austen novel without sacrificing artistic integrity.[12]

Forster not only shows how the tradition of manners fails when it leaves the insularity of an English village, but hints at its obsolescence. The English and Indians are in an imperialistic relationship where members of both the conquering and conquered nations are corrupted and diminished because a relatively small number of representatives of one nation keeps the entire population of another in a subservient position. (But we should note that this relationship echoes a less rigorous, but nonetheless stifling class system that he has presented in his prior novels.) Heaslop's comment, 'We're not out here for the purpose of behaving pleasantly!' shows how the credo of Austen's England has been abandoned (p. 43). Forster implies that the politics of imperialism and the sociology of a backward country – where the European finds 'humanity grading and drifting beyond the educated vision' – undermine English personal relations and the standards on which they depend. What, for example, do these standards have to do with the non-verbal, handsome untouchable who turns the fan at the trial?

Austen, like many of her contemporaries, believed that characters in novels, like people in real life, could approach ideals of self-understanding and self-control. But Forster's fiction testifies that contemporary man lives in a world which has lost its grace, dignity, and humanity, and that loss is accentuated in India, which restlessly strives to find its identity while under the control of the British. Adela's poignant and ironic complaint underlines Forster's nostalgia for a time when personal relationships flourished among an aristocracy that had leisure for them: 'What is the use of personal relationships when everyone brings less and less to them?' (p. 188).

Because the omniscient narrator expresses Forster's quest for values, he is a different kind of figure from the omniscient narrator of Victorian or eighteenth-century fiction. While Austen's values within the novel's imagined world are static, Forster's evolve. Unlike Austen, he tests and sympathizes with a variety of value systems. While Austen *knows* from the outset the standards by which Emma falls short and tells us on the first pages, Forster tentatively adopts, *seriatim*, the perspective of Fielding, Mrs. Moore, and Godbole as he searches not only for the way to solve the Anglo-Indian problem, but for his own values. Whereas Austen's focus is on the moral development of her characters, Forster's is on making sense of the imagined world he has created. His omniscient narrator seeks to understand what he presents. Forster dramatizes the transformation of the narrator as new circumstances come into the narrative. It is as if his learning that evil is as much in the human psyche as in the Caves shows him that Austen's England is irrelevant to India. The tale becomes a *passage* to enlightenment for Forster's surrogate, and ultimately, for us. That he has changed his values becomes part of the rhetoric and urges the reader to change his attitudes to India and to reconsider his values.

At first Forster embraces the code of Fielding, a code that would not at first glance be out of place in an Austen novel: 'The world, he believed, is a globe of men who are trying to reach one another and can best do so by the help of goodwill plus culture and intelligence – a creed ill suited to Chandrapore, but he had come out too late to lose it' (p. 56). Forster admires his self-control, decency, and fundamental courage (what he called 'pluck' in the essay 'What I Believe'). After Forster's voice adopts the values of Fielding, he steps back and re-examines them when he realizes that Fielding lacks the emotional range of Aziz. The self-styled 'holy man minus the holiness' is the spirit of Bloomsbury, the epitome of liberal England, and the heir to the tradition of manners and morals, represented in Austen by Knightley: 'I believe in teaching people to be individuals, and to understand other individuals. It's the only thing I do believe in' (p. 112).

Even while his book is a room with a view of India and provides what he believes is a necessary education for the English, Forster is redefining the equation of travel with learning and moral growth that is an essential premise of much eighteenth and nineteenth-century fiction and travel literature from *Moll Flanders* and *Tom Jones* to *Jane Eyre* and *Great Expectations*. The equation is a version of the Protestant myth of self-improvement through experience and hard work. We think of Fielding's self-image as a traveller, and we realize the concept of travelling as an experience of learning but not necessarily growth or self-development is central to *A Passage to India*. Fielding's education is not of the kind that makes prior fictional characters more integrated and responsive people. He bathetically returns to England, marries, and becomes part of officialdom, ironically proving his own contention that 'Any man can travel light until he has a wife or children' (p. 112).

Unlike Highbury, India is more than a background for events in an imagined world. The difference between Austen's Highbury and Forster's India is the difference between Constable's eighteenth-century landscapes, depicting a scene such as Salisbury Cathedral as it might have looked at an ideal moment, and the landscapes of such post-Impressionists as Cézanne and Van Gogh, who express the emotions of the painter more than they depict the actual physical scene. Thus the Caves are a metaphor for the non-verbal world that precedes and will survive mankind. Like Hardy's Egdon Heath, they are immune to and indifferent to man's life. As Forster describes them, we feel both an imaginative effort and a personal agony unlike anything in Austen. It is as if they resist human description, even though Forster tells us they are 'readily described': 'Nothing, nothing attaches to them and their reputation – for they have one – does not depend upon human speech' (p. 117). But of course they depend on oral and written language to extend their reputation; even the very inadequacy of the language illustrates the mind's limitations as it confronts the unknown.

Forsyth sees the irony of showing that the human mind, when seeking the ultimate comparison, uses personification to contain and to try to comprehend the Caves:

> Fist and fingers thrust above the advancing soil – here at last is their skin, finer than any covering acquired by the animals, smoother than windless water, more voluptuous than love. The radiance increases, the flames touch one another, kiss, expire. The cave is dark again, like all the caves.
>
> (p. 118)

Yet, paradoxically, Forster's perspective places human events in a geological context and reduces their proportion. For him India is not a fiction, a metaphor for British imperialism, but an essential and troubling reality that gives significance to the world he occupies.

Even before the trial Forster begins to separate himself from Fielding, to reveal that Fielding's truth is only a partial truth, and that he lacks imagination, spirituality, and passion. The crucial moment occurs when Fielding sees the Caves from a distance; he fails to apprehend the beauty or significance of the Caves and questions his life and values: 'He felt he ought to have been working at something else the whole time – he didn't know at what, never would know, never could know, and that was why he felt sad' (p. 181).

If I were to choose a paradigmatic episode to show how Forster turns the novel of manners upside down, it would be this moment when he exposes the limitations of his erstwhile surrogate Fielding. Could we imagine Knightley in a moment of self-doubt, alone in a moral desert bereft of values? Finally Fielding has no tradition of manners on which to rely; nor does he believe in a benevolent cosmos. Fielding is exposed and contained in a fiction in which, by tradition, he should be the hero. He has spoken for the novel's values as Forster's surrogate. He has risked career and physical well-being in the interest of truth and fairness. Yet this is not enough.

In prior novels Forster wrote for the most part of the plagues of moral relativism and materialism, plagues which could be defined and perhaps partially controlled, if not rectified. After the trial, the voice indicates that Fielding's Western values are only one of several sets of values with which man may equip himself. In the last part of 'Caves' and in 'Temple', Forster questions not only Fielding's values, but the values to which he had dedicated his prior novels – the primacy of personal relationships and the necessity of understanding one another; these values are epitomised by the famous epigraph to *Howards End*, 'Only Connect'.

Yet finally in *A Passage to India* humanism triumphs, if in a reduced and more modest version. As Godbole and Mrs. Moore are tested and ultimately discarded as prophets, the voice again becomes the spokesman for the values of humanism – moderation, tolerance, tact, integrity, respect for others. His own language presents the unity and balance that life lacks. Despite Mrs. Moore's insight, a schism between her vision and her behaviour undermines for the reader the possibility that she is a prophetic character. Mrs. Moore's selfish desertion of Aziz shows how she has put aside relations with people in her quest for spiritual self-realization. Whatever the excuse, she commits what for Forster is the heresy of deserting her friend. Seen from the standards of traditional values, her self-immersion represents a serious failure of the moral fabric that binds one man to another.

A fundamental paradox of the novel is that Forster's own prose has difficulty aligning itself with mystery and spiritual values, and Forster knows this. Yet the celebratory and static religious ritual of 'Temple' is an effort to move beyond the concatenation of events on which traditional western narrative is based. Within that section, the narrator (Forster's surrogate) adopts a double perspective: the external perspective of a secular skeptic, whose view, like Fielding, is predicated on interest in other cultures and a desire to understand something different; and the inner vision of someone experiencing a spiritual revelation – Godbole. For Forster, Godbole, with his cosmic perspective, is a prophetic figure, but his failings also undermine the thrust of his ideas. He is no help to Aziz when he is falsely accused; later he allows Aziz to believe Fielding had married Adela, a belief which leads Aziz to foolish and humiliating behaviour, because he, as a Brahman, 'had never been known to tell anyone anything' (p. 295). Godbole's olympian perspective resembles one aspect of the narrator, the one which takes an historical and geographical view of the action. But the long view seems irrelevant to the manners and passions of individual human beings:

"When evil occurs," says Godbole, "it expresses the whole of the universe. Similarly when good occurs.... Good and evil are different, as their names imply. But, in my humble opinion, they are both of them aspects of my Lord."

(p. 169).

And just as the English mind's rationalism and control has limits, so does Godbole's ascetic spirituality and ability to thrust himself out of himself; for he cannot meditate upon the stone.

If Forster adopts Lawrence's bardic voice and prophetic vision, he faces with Conrad the problem of how to cope with a purposeless, amoral, indifferent universe. He views Godbole's spiritualism as another of mankind's working arrangements. The Hindu celebration is an outlet for very human and even animal passions and instincts; to perform his holy journey after the Rajah dies, the Hindus simply (and to Western eyes bathetically) make an effigy of the Rajah. If at first the novel seems to reject Fielding's liberal humanism, it gradually shows that the alternatives are no better. That religion as a living force has its limits is illustrated by Godbole's human failures. Like Mrs. Moore, he has subtracted himself from a human community in his search for something more. Thus Fielding's humanism may have a qualified triumph, after all, when we realize the effects of being 'one with the universe' as exemplified by Mrs. Moore's and Godbole's indifference to other people (p. 198).

Mrs. Moore's son Ralph is the western correlative to the 'untouchable' Indian who turns the fan in the courtroom. Yet his simple vocabulary, his depth of feeling, and his intuitive understanding of the elaborate Hindu rituals comment upon the verbosity of the Moslems and the complicated motives of the English. Although he 'appeared to be almost an imbecile' (p. 297), he instinctively understands Aziz's hostility; by telling Aziz that his mother, Mrs. Moore, loved him, he is the catalyst for Aziz's temporary reconciliation with Fielding. And he anticipates Forster's final verdict – 'not yet' – on the possibility of lasting reconciliation. That wisdom becomes the province of the unwitting in Ralph – as it has in the Emersons, Stephen, and Gino – is an aspect of Forster's rebellion against utilitarianism, progress, and moral education.

V

Forster's originality has to be seen in the context of the other major writers of the period – Conrad, Joyce, and Woolf. In Victorian fiction, characters are defined by their relationship within a community. In modern British fiction the characters are defined by alienation from that community.[13] They are, like their creators, iconoclasts detesting the community that has created them. The major character's quest for self-understanding is the essence of the English novel from 1890 to 1930, but the focus is on the desperation of that quest, not the attainment of that goal. That quest reflects the author's own uncertainty, frustration, and anxiety. The stress on private values, on restoring family relationships, and on developing personal relationships that matter is another characteristic of the novel in the 1890–1930 period; it is an alternative to the Victorian novel's faith that community life can provide a social and moral fabric for each individual. The traditional novel's omniscient narrator depends for its effects upon the incongruity between what the narrator says and what the character thinks. But when the narrator's values are not stable and consistent, that irony breaks down and we feel the author as a formal presence within the text. Like his contemporaries Conrad, Lawrence, and Joyce, Forster believed that human truth must inevitably be partial, a matter of perspective.

Writing in 1925, Virginia Woolf insisted in 'Mr. Bennett and Mrs. Brown' that the Georgian writers needed to abandon the 'tools' and 'conventions' of their Edwardian predecessors because the latter 'have laid an enormous stress on the fabric of things':

> At the present moment we are suffering, not from decay, but from having no code of manners which writers and readers accept as a prelude to the more exciting intercourse of friendship.... Grammar is violated, syntax disintegrated.[14]

Forster does not violate grammar and syntax. Forster's style has more in common with Austen, Fielding, and James than with the comparatively pedestrian journalistic prose of Bennett, Wells, and Galsworthy or the experiments with diction and syntax of Joyce and Lawrence. He shows how polished, precise use of literate discourse can both render the inner life – feelings, passions, subconscious needs – and, particularly in his last two novels, create the prophetic note that he sought. Forster's conversational prose, his leisurely pace, his self-confidence, his lucid, unpretentious diction and poised syntax, imply the very humanistic values he espoused. While Conrad, Lawrence, Joyce, and Woolf sought new forms and syntax, Forster shows that the English language and its novel genre already had the resources to examine the life of instincts and passions.

Notes

1. Lionel Stevenson, *The English Novel: a Panorama* (Boston: Houghton Mifflin, 1960).
2. Walter Allen, *The English Novel* (New York: E. P. Dutton, 1954) p. 400.
3. Except for those volumes that have yet to appear, *The Longest Journey* and *Maurice*, page numbers in parentheses refer to *The Abinger Edition of E. M. Forster*, ed. Oliver Stallybrass (London: Edward Arnold, 1972–   ). For those volumes not yet in the Abinger edition, the page numbers in parentheses refer to *The Longest Journey* (New York: Alfred A. Knopf, 1962), and *Maurice* (New York: Norton, 1971).
4. Forster wrote in 'The Challenge of Our Time':
   I belong to the fag-end of Victorian liberalism, and can look back to an age whose challenges were moderate in their tone, and the cloud on whose horizons was no bigger than a man's hand. In many ways, it was an admirable age. It practised benevolence and philanthropy, was humane and intellectually curious, upheld free speech, had little colour-prejudice, believed that individuals are and should be different, and entertained a sincere faith in the progress of society.
   (*Two Cheers for Democracy*, p. 54)
5. In *The Cave and the Mountain: a Study of E. M. Forster* (Stanford University Press, 1960), Wilfred Stone writes:
   [Forster's] art, and his belief in art, are his religion.... The religion *is* a coming together, of the seen and the unseen, public affairs and private decencies. Another name for this religion is humanism.
   (pp. 18–19)
6. As Stone writes:
   His novels are not only chapters in a new gospel, they are dramatic installments in the story of his own struggle for selfhood – and for a myth to support it. They tell of a man coming out in the world, painfully emerging from an encysted state of loneliness, fear, and insecurity.
   (p. 19)

7. According to Forster, Lawrence is 'the only living novelist in whom the song predominates, who has the rapt bardic quality' (*Aspects*, p. 99).

8. See Stone, p. 381.

9. Stone writes:

    [Rickie] exists to be sacrificed; he is a totem for all those childish disabilities that his creator hates in himself – the weakness, self-contempt, and repressed hostility that must be got rid of if he is ever to achieve a man's estate.

    (p. 213)

    The dissolution of distance between author and protagonist in autobiographical novels recurs in other fiction of this period ('The Secret Sharer', *Jude the Obscure*, *Sons and Lovers*, and *A Portrait of the Artist*). For, in the face of rapid social changes and the resultant confusion of values, authors are trying to create themselves and rescue versions of their youthful selves.

10. Stone, p. 209.

11. Thus I cannot agree with Stone that 'Stephen the hero is apparently never to backslide again' or that 'at the heart of [the book's] revelation is the vaguely adumbrated faith that the real hero is yet to come – a synthesis of Stephen's body, Ansell's mind, and Rickie's soul into a new being and perhaps into a new sex' (pp. 212, 214).

12. We recall that in *Aspects of the Novel*, Forster respects Austen as a writer who 'pass[es] the creative finger down every sentence and into every word' (p. 50).

13. In *The Turn of the Novel* (New York: Oxford University Press, 1966), Alan Friedman has written:

    It may not be too soon to suggest that whatever the causes, older assumptions about character, society, and career have already given place to newer ones; that self and world, sequence and consequence, if not in life at least in fiction, have been restructured; that, in short, we have been witnessing a mutation in the form of the novel which corresponds to a mutation in the ends of culture.

    (p. xiii)

14. Virginia Woolf, 'Mr. Bennett and Mrs. Brown', *The Captain's Death Bed and Other Essays* (New York: Harcourt, Brace, 1950); pp. 112, 115.

Part Two

7
The Case for Humanistic Formalism

I believe that we are on the threshold of a return to the concerns of traditional humanism – what a work means, who created it and why, and how it reflects the world beyond it. Moreover, it is the purpose of my *The Humanistic Heritage: Critical Theories of the English Novel from James to Hillis Miller* and *Reading Joyce's 'Ulysses'* to contribute to that return.[1]

At many major universities, deconstruction basks in the consensual glow conferred by a dominant trend. With the influence of deconstruction spreading like fire in dry grass on a windy day, we are in a feisty time when we have the opportunity to debate the values, purposes, methods, and future of literary studies. We should be grateful to deconstruction for opening up the canon and for questioning the notion of one authoritative reading; we should also be grateful for its raising fundamental questions about the direction of literary studies in America and England. Yet we must thoughtfully consider in what directions deconstruction is taking literary studies. We must do more than querulously assert, as many traditionally oriented critics do even at our major universities, that deconstruction has reached high tide and, if I may change metaphors, that a benign critical teleology will express itself by – in a critical version of the Big Bang theory – expunging the evil influence of deconstruction.

By promising nothing less than a new ideology of reading, deconstruction has brought excitement to literary studies. In its efforts to apply philosophic texts and linguistics to the study of literature, it offers the seductive appeal of the complex and learned. Its major American practitioners – de Man, Miller, Hartman, Bloom – are often brilliant in their insights, if elusive in their argument. Deconstruction has transformed the way we talk about our literary experiences and given us new and fresh stories of reading. But I believe that we need to take stock of the current critical mindscape and retrieve some important principles that have become submerged.

In this chapter, my goals are to define what I believe to be valuable in deconstruction and to help clarify and define the principles of what I call humanistic formalism. In discussing deconstruction, I shall focus on Jonathan Culler's *On Deconstruction* because it has become the explanatory midrash for deconstruction, especially for the puzzling works of Derrida and de Man. I would like to play the role of the English Brother William of Baskerville in Eco's *The Name of the Rose* and make a rather pragmatic and Aristotelian inquiry into the mysteries and thickets of continental theories; like the tolerant Brother William, I am less concerned with heresies than fallacies. After reviewing the claims of deconstruction – and taking a brief glance at the claims of Marxist criticism – I shall articulate my own humanistic credo.

It behooves traditional Anglo-American humanistic criticism to resist the onslaught of deconstruction and to defend the ground of its own formalism. It is essential to define the theory and method of a criticism that owes its roots to Plato and Aristotle and that has in its various guises stimulated the serious study of literature in the twentieth century. We should begin by acknowledging what we have learned from deconstruction. Deconstruction has introduced the valuable idea that interpretations are stories of our reading experience – that is, interpretations are shaped by our particular personality and historical situation. Furthermore, it has warned us that these stories of reading, although they may pose as objective commentaries, are really, like all writing, to some degree at least a disguise for idiosyncratic troping. But its practitioners have not sufficiently stressed the infinite gradations of metaphoricity within a complex work, nor how our reading involves a continual process of determining the precise gradations of the literal and the figurative. As readers, we organise even the most literal and the realistic language into narrative units of reading experience; these units always have something of a metaphorical component because they represent our understanding of the absent world and of the absent author who breathed life into that world and represents himself in it. As we read and organize the literal and determine the degree of metaphoricity, our reading process resembles the author's original organization of his experience.

One of deconstruction's virtues is that it reminds us to question the concepts of monolithic explanations for complex literary texts and issues; in a passage Culler twice quotes approvingly, de Man tells us: 'The possibility of reading ... can never be taken for granted'.[2] Deconstruction has been helpful in its stress on the process of reading, on the dialogue between text and reader, on the need to stand outside a work. It has helped us understand that moral hierarchies within imagined worlds are in flux, particularly within the spacious worlds of novels where subsequent episodes modify prior ones and vice versa.

Deconstruction reminds us that we cannot use language to summon reality absolutely. Using the English positivist William as his mouthpiece, Eco puts it nicely in *The Name of the Rose*: 'I had thought each book spoke of the things, human and divine, that lie outside books. Now I realized that not infrequently books speak of books; it is as if they spoke among themselves.'[3] To be sure, we read better when we know what is in other books, particularly the books that the author has read. Textuality, the idea that books take their meaning from other books, challenges the assumption that language summons reality and contends that such an assumption is an example of the logocentric fallacy.

Deconstruction has become a cult with its own prophets – Barthes, Foucault, and Derrida – who speak a strange language. It has its own history and its own critical rites. One seminal rite is to quote obscure passages of Derrida, often translated into ungrammatical English, and to pretend that these statements are readable – as in the following passage: 'for we have read *in the text* that the absolute present, Nature, what is named by words like "real mother" etc., have always already escaped, have never existed; that what inaugurates meaning and language is writing as the disappearance of natural presence'.[4] Like other élite cults, deconstruction has fathered and mothered its own exotic vocabulary; it has also generated an extremely fullsome syntax which yields its meaning only to its acolytes and devotees. Perhaps most dangerously, it has created modes of inquiry which consign the literary work to the back burner.

Let us turn briefly to the Derridean idea that western culture has privileged the 'metaphysics of presence' by allowing itself to believe that language can summon or evoke a prior reality. If I, for example, write 'Derrida', he does not appear in the room as a presence; nor does his name mean exactly the same thing to every reader. But it does not follow that his name is merely a series of sounds, a moment of pure textuality, whose significance can derive from its play on 'derision' or 'dadaism' or an inversion of 'arid' or 'Ariadne' (as in, to use a favourite deconstructive trope, 'Ariadne's thread'). Even though words cannot absolutely summon reality, they can approach reality.

In its search for absolute distinctions and definitions, Deconstruction at times totalizes and becomes conservative if not totalitarian. While acknowledging that meaning cannot be stable and determinate, we do not need to go the much further distance and concede that meaning is impossible. Just because a text fails to yield one unambiguous reading does not mean that most skilled readers do not agree on the major formal and thematic principles of most works. Merely because one can argue that language does not invoke presence, it does not follow that – to recite a shibboleth of recent theory – 'There is nothing outside the text.'[5] Or as Michael Riffaterre puts it, 'Representation of reality is a [merely] verbal construct in which meaning is achieved by reference from words to words, not things.'[6]

I am calling for a new humanism that – without abandoning its stress on such formal matters as rhetoric and close scrutiny of narrative codes – turns its attention to the content, meaning, and significance of imaginative literature. Rather than using literature as an occasion for speculation about the *text's* implications for semiotics, Marxism, or deconstruction, this new humanism would seek to understand the essential experience of the *work's* imaginative world. I imagine that this humanism would unembarrassedly ask, 'What happens to characters within an imagined world?'; 'What is the nature of the voice that speaks to us; specifically, what are her or his attitudes, values, and feelings, and how does the artist convey them?'; 'What do we learn from the representation of human behaviour within that world?'; 'What happens to the reader experiencing the imagined world?'; 'What is the relation of form – including structure (especially beginning and ending), mode of narration, patterns of language – to meaning?'; 'What does the imagined world reveal about the author and the actual, historical world in which she or he lived?'

I am a formalist in the sense that I believe content and meaning are an inextricable function of form. My credo is based on the belief that an interest in the contents of literary works is *a priori* to the reason we read, and that sophisticated readers respond to an inextricable relationship between form and content. When reading or when listening, we respond to the thoughts, feelings, and values of an ego or a consciousness or a presence. We hear a human voice that has tone, timbre, attitudes, gender, and values.

Literary theory, I believe, is important only insofar as it addresses methods of reading literary works, and only insofar as it enables us to think conceptually about how literary works cohere. Insofar as theory produces readings of literary works and helps us to understand how the works we read behave and how we behave when we read, it has a valuable function. In my judgement, a criticism that fails to produce powerful interpretations of complex works and fails to give us a fresh reading of major authors, is not very important. Among other things, one feels in reading Culler that deconstruction is not sufficiently interested in works of literature. Or, as Eco's nominalist Brother William puts it, '[T]rue learning must not be content with ideas, which are, in fact, signs, but must discover things in their individual truth.'[7]

It may be time to propose the term 'Theoretical Fallacy' for the phenomenon of speculating about works from such a remote distance and at such an abstract level of discussion that the theories do not help the reader understand what is within such works. Culler writes, 'Critical categories are not just tools to be employed in producing sound interpretations but problems to be explored through the interaction of text and concept.'[8] But all too often the concepts and categories are privileged over the critical activity of recreating what it feels like to read a work. But, then, Culler has told us in 'Against Interpretation' (the opening essay of *The Pursuit of Signs*): 'One thing we do not need is more interpretation of literary works.'[9] Surely the title, 'Against Interpretation', throws down the gauntlet to Anglo-American formalism to define its purposes and goals. For I believe that interpretation is central to the study of literature. In *On Deconstruction*, Culler writes, 'The notion that the goal of analysis is to produce enriching elucidations of individual works is a deep presupposition of American criticism.'[10] I proudly share that benighted notion.

I DECONSTRUCTION AND ITS IMPLICATIONS

Deconstruction depends upon rejection of the possibility of moving towards an authoritative reading; it rejects the idea that reading can recover the author's intent, values, themes, or understanding of the world which his work imitates. By contrast, what I call humanistic formalism believes that we can approach the author's values and vision by attending to the rhetorical effects within the imagined world created by the author. In its disbelief in the hermeneutical circle – the circle by which the reader recreates the text that the author wrote through the mediation of the literary work – deconstruction is cynical. Even while disagreeing among its practitioners about the importance of intentionality, humanistic formalism recognizes the folly of the effort to deconstruct the author; thus Culler writes 'If, as Barthes claims, "the birth of the reader must be at the cost of the death of the author," many have been willing to pay that price.'[11] I wonder if anyone who has tried to teach *Ulysses* without having read Joyce's prior work or Ellmann's biography could write that. Put baldly, a work more readily yields a determinate meaning to those who know about the author's other works, life, and historical context.

A revitalized humanistic formalism would eschew such New Critical orthodoxies as the biographical fallacy and the shibboleth 'exit author' and discover how to speak of the author as a formal presence in the text in ways that go beyond equating the omniscient narrator or implied author with the biographical author. For we need an aesthetic that takes account of how, particularly in such modern works as *The Rainbow* and *Ulysses*, the author's struggle with his subject becomes a major determinant of fictional form. In the process of reading we respond to an *imitation*, a *representation* of the real creator of the work. He or she is in the imagined world as a distortion – at times, an idealization, a clarification, a simplification, an obfuscation – of the creating psyche. I admire Patricia Meyer Spacks formulation: [If authors] create themselves as figures in their poems, readers choose, consciously or unconsciously, to accept such figures as more or less appropriate to reality.'[12]

Thus the new humanistic formalism must part company with a parochial formalism – either New Critical or deconstructive – that excludes authors from the critical dialogue. The process of locating a human being within a work recognizes that reading is not merely a verbal game but a shared experience between reader and writer. Do we not seek and respond to a human voice within a work because it expresses the energy and values of the author? Voice validates language, gives it shape, connects it with our experiential world. Even when reading letters and newspapers, we ask 'Who is speaking to whom?' and 'On what occasion?' and 'For what purpose?' For this reason, esoteric discussions that ignore authorial voice or reduce speech to a kind of writing should be met with great skepticism. Because a complete explanation of the relationship between authors and both their alter egos and their characters is not possible, because we cannot provide a mathematical equation for each work, does it follow that we should abandon our inquiry into such matters?

In its quest to undermine, to question and to displace, deconstruction is a kind of radical skepticism. Both deconstruction and skepticism depend on the quite accurate perception that nothing is perfect and that certainty is impossible. Put another way, deconstruction is a modern urban phenomenon in an age of anxiety and disbelief. Just as the urban Wise Guy (the modern picaro) lives on the margin and knows how to exploit every event for a profit, the deconstructive picaro is an academic wise guy who sees the fly in the ointment, the problem with any idea, and the faults in every person or situation; he verbally transforms the spectre of a remote possibility into what might actually happen and makes us aware that the inconceivable might happen just this once. He inverts the meaning of meaning, the significance of significance, by (to use one of deconstruction's terms) 'valorizing' the marginal, the inessential, the digressive, the false. For example, Culler writes in praise of misunderstanding and misreading:

> Reading and understanding preserve or reproduce a content or meaning, maintain its identity, while misunderstanding and misreading distort it.... We can thus say, in a formulation more valid than its converse, that understanding is a special case of misunderstanding, a particular deviation or determination of misunderstanding.[13]

What Culler is doing is inverting the meaning of the words understanding and misunderstanding. If we are going to reassign meanings to words and reinvent the language, then of course there will be a free play of signifiers and of course we will be hard put to make connections with the world outside the text.

In *Saving the Text*, Hartman coined the word 'derridadism'; if not 'dada', surely deconstruction is a *fin de siècle* movement which responds to boredom and ennui.[14] Yet deconstruction adds excitement to reading because it makes the inconceivable possible. It not only discovers patterns of sexuality and violence which import into reading repressed emotions that may be lacking in real life, but in its conceit of the critic's controlling the text, deconstruction offers fantasies of power: 'The effect of deconstructive analyses, as numerous readers can attest, is knowledge and *feelings of mastery.*'[15]

For Culler, the major task of criticism has always been

> that of making the text interesting, of combating the boredom which lurks behind every work, waiting to move in if reading goes astray or founders.... A semiological criticism should succeed in reducing the possibilities of boredom by teaching one to find challenges and peculiarities in works which the perspective of pleasure alone would make boring.[16]

But for humanistic formalism, the critic's task is to discover meaning and significance within the imagined world, often by focusing on how the author has created a structure of effects for the reader. The critic's task is to recover meaning and report it intelligibly to other readers who have shared with her or him the experience of reading a work. The critic seeks to explain literature in terms of experiences that authors, fictional characters, and readers might possibly share. Such a criticism believes that words signify and that they can create an imagined world which temporarily displaces the reader's consciousness of the real one. For this criticism, reading – entering into the imagined world of another – is itself pleasurable.

Humanistic formalism does not believe that the critic creates the pleasures of a work; no, the pleasure of reading comes from the work itself. Ultimately, while not indifferent to the calls of textuality, humanistic formalism stresses the signified over the signifier; the text's silences, gaps, and opacities are important for the most part because they, too, signify something about the imagined world outside the text. For this criticism, the representational is important, but it seeks to include in its concept of the representational what Culler calls 'the strange, the formal, the fictional'.[17] Indeed, humanistic formalism stresses the necessity for including the strange (experiences, particularly psychological ones, that defy ordinary experience or reflect the dimly acknowledged needs of characters and authors); the formal (the aesthetic organization of experience), and the fictive (imaginary experience which, in the form of dreams, fantasies, and plans for the future, is part of human life).

Deconstruction stresses that each reading contains the seeds of its own undoing. It privileges the reader rather than the author without quite acknowledging that it does so. Put another way, the text is consubstantial with the reader rather than the author and/or the anterior world on which the text is based. Deconstruction emphasizes that every reader discovers heterogeneous readings in the same text which lead the reader to an irreconcilable paradox or *aporia*. Deconstruction believes that all reading is misreading because no reading can take account of all the possibilities of a text. Humanistic formalism believes that reading is a quest towards the goal of an accurate reading, even though, like Zeno's paradox, it is a goal which we can only approach but never reach. But we can make very substantial progress toward that goal. Deconstruction views accurate reading as a mirage which continually recedes in proportion to which it is seemingly approached.

In *On Deconstruction*, Culler writes: '[T]o deconstruct a discourse is to show how it undermines the philosophy it asserts, or the hierarchical oppositions on which it relies, by identifying in the text the rhetorical operations that produce the supposed ground of argument, the key concept or premise.'[18] But why does *identifying* its rhetorical operations undermine a discourse? If one identifies the rhetorical operations in *Emma* or *The Rape of the Lock*, isn't one finding what reinforces or supports the philosophy it asserts? For most works, identifying the rhetorical operations will show how a coherent, organic work is produced. But even if one identifies tensions within the rhetorical operations – tropes that pull in diverse directions – are we moving in a direction necessarily different from the old formalism? Finally, the act of identification is only a prelude to the imposition of some pattern of reading or interpretation, even if it is a pattern of reading that challenges prior readings. As the excesses of the New Criticism taught us, cataloguing tropes for its own sake has little real value; I can recall reading in critical articles and books in the early 60s such banal sentences as the following: 'In this poem, there are four kinds of color imagery (blue, green, red, and white) and three kinds of animal imagery.'

We may even want to reconsider whether it is best that we use the term 'text' for novels. Isn't text a term which blurs the difference between signifier and signified and between foreground and background and deflects us from thinking of a novel as an 'imagined world'? It may also be time to ask whether in novels order and unity are not preferable to disorder and incoherence. We should also be concerned with the standard that privileges works that tear themselves apart and regards as hierarchically superior those works that say something other than what they mean to say.

One problem with the concept of textuality is that it releases the critic from the responsibility of describing what a work says; when language is merely the interplay of signifiers, canniness and wit become the goals rather than truth or mimesis. Those who lost families in the Holocaust or their friends in the Viet Nam war will find it puzzling to have experience reduced by Deconstruction to a rhetorical figure: ' "experience" is divided and deferred – already behind us as something to be recovered, yet still before us as something to be produced.'[19] What I find most striking about *On Deconstruction* is its failure to deal with both political and social causes and effects and with human behaviour – its causes, personal motives, and its consequences.

Much of what deconstruction claims as 'advances' is not so different from the progressive strains of humanistic criticism. Empsonian ambiguity as well as the New Critical emphasis on tension and paradox are more like than unlike *aporia*. Nor is it news that the history of the criticism of a literary work will repeat the tensions within the work; it would be surprising if many, if not most, important critical readings did not in some way enact if not 'repeat the structures it is analyzing', since much good criticism seeks to enact the process of reading.[20] Nor did we have to wait for deconstruction to tell us that the best literary criticism often 'enacts what it asserts'.[21]

What is new is the change in the critic's stature from humble middleman who is midwife to meaning created by the author in his work to a kind of imaginative *Übermensch* who uses the work as a stimulus for whatever re-creation – I use the pun on 'recreation' deliberately – occurs to her or him. Just as Romantic poets perceived the world according to the lamp of their imagination, these critics perceive literary works in light of their imaginative needs. They use the work or text as a pretext for their own text; the test is not whether a reading is true but whether it is 'interesting'. But we should be wary of the implications of Culler's next move:

> Where one text claims to analyze and elucidate another, it may be possible to show that in fact the relationship should be inverted; that the analyzing text is elucidated by the analyzed

text, which already contains an implicit account of and reflection upon the analyst's moves.[22]

For what Culler is doing is giving the critic's commentary equal status with – if not privileged status over – the original work. And we should also acknowledge an important difference between the older and newer formalism: unlike deconstruction, which values *aporia* and heterogeneous readings, the New Criticism valued the resolution of the contending readings into a unified one.

Do we feel while reading that 'experience... has always already occurred and yet is still to be produced – an indispensable point of reference, yet never simply there?'[23] If, as I believe, the human mind seeks coherent, logical explanations for its experiences, including its reading experiences, then it is a rather damaging admission for Culler to tell us that 'deconstructive readings show scant respect for the wholeness or integrity of individual works'.[24] Again, in the following assertion, where is the joy in reading about the representation of human experience, or, indeed, where is the joy in either language or aesthetic form? 'The deconstructive questioning of categories and assumptions leads back repeatedly to a small group of problems and gives conclusions that function as knowledge.'[25] But knowledge *of what* and *for what*? Can we really hold out the possibility of a morphology of the marginal, the illogical, and the fissures within either a text or an intellectual tradition? As soon as such phenomena are 'regularized' in a deconstructive grammar, is not deconstruction in danger of adopting the codification and unilateral explanations that deconstruction objected to in structuralism? Does not deconstruction create its own Platonic models by the very nature of its abstract speculations about how texts behave?

II THE EFFECTS OF DECONSTRUCTION ON LITERARY STUDIES IN ENGLAND AND AMERICA

The appeal of the New Criticism was that it made works accessible and exciting to high school students and young undergraduates; in a way, it was an enticement to two generations of students who were taught that if they used their analytic powers, sensibility, and judgement, they would be able to understand a work of literature as a coherent, self-contained ontology that related to their own experiential world. I have always told my students that my courses were subtitled 'In Defense of Reading' and urged that learning how to read well was as important as learning the details of an interpretation. What, we should ask, does deconstruction *say* to freshmen who are studying literature at a college or university for the first time? Among other things, it says that a negative process – 'deconstruction' – is more important than a positive one – 'reading' or 'construing'. It encourages the student to describe her or his reading in abstract terms that belie his or her experiential base. Does it not often teach, by practice, that abstract and vague diction should take precedence over specific, detailed discussion? In its efforts to privilege the reader, it deflects the students' attention from the literary work to their own responses and implies that any story of reading is as good as any other.

Why are we embarrassed to say that we read both to understand and to increase our experience? Is deconstruction not part of the tendency in the late 1970s and 1980s to define ourselves in private terms, to become more passive about asserting our own individuality, to take our lives as given and follow through the culturally accepted patterns? In its stress on *response* to prior readings and undoing what has been done, I wonder if deconstruction is not a reactive, conservative, limiting epistemology. Is it not the humanistic critic who has been seduced to read powerfully and joyfully, while the deconstructionist critic by choice remains at the margins of a work as something of a voyeuristic outsider?

I have heard reports of less-than-successful sections of freshman humanities where young teachers deconstructed poems that have not been first construed and used arcane language to discuss such moving love poems as 'To His Coy Mistress' in terms of exotic rhetorical phenomena, codes, 'moves', and intertextual resonances. Yet does not the appeal of such poems to undergraduates derive from their resemblance to questions of love and sexuality that students recognize as having something to do with their own lives? Deconstruction fathers/mothers abstractions in the classroom which make young undergraduates feel that the instructor has reached his or her thirties without ever having been eighteen, nineteen, twenty, or twenty-one; this apparent experiential gap creates the feeling in freshmen that their teacher has no empathy for their responses to the literature being read. While I would hasten to add that deconstruction has no monopoly on puzzling freshmen, it is rather a striking irony that deconstructionist colleagues often acknowledge that they have had their greatest success in teaching undergraduates when they use traditional methods of reading, including the very 'thematizing' that they disdain in graduate seminars.

We can roughly divide the brief history of deconstruction into two phases. In the first, the concept of the critic as intellectual midwife fostering the dialogue between work and audience was replaced by the concept of the critic as Genius discovering patterns, epistemologies, and semiologies of which the artist is unaware; in other words, beneath the novel or poem that the author thought he had written was another one far more complex, less unified, and much less mimetic. In the second phase, the critic seriously engages the prior criticism of the work in the hope of discovering why vital issues in the critical dialogue have been discussed in a particular way. If the first phase gave the critic equal stature to that of the author, the second stage has the parodoxical effect of *privileging* the critic's intellectual activity, even while effectively *reducing* the critic to a marginal position from where he does little more than carp at the readings of prior critics.

In what is now regarded as 'advanced' literary studies, graduate students are encouraged to indulge in the kind of textuality which fuses one's own reading onto a prior reading without any regard to the original text; the effect of this process is to give the critical article or book more prestige than the work it analyzes and to claim in the name of semiotics that the critical activity of analyzing the secondary material is equal to if not greater than the activity of powerfully reading complex works. Thus in supposedly 'state-of-the-art' graduate courses, whole seminar sessions are spent applying Foucault's or Barthes's theories to a work or in discussing the critical 'strategies' and rhetorical 'moves' of a single critical essay. In a kind of parody of traditional criticism, the language of the critical article or book is analyzed in depth to discover meanings of which the critic was unaware. For the first time in my teaching career, two of the graduate papers in a seminar devoted to Joyce's *Ulysses* – papers which were described to me beforehand in vastly different terms – focused almost exclusively on analyzing one or two 'texts' of prior critics rather than the actual text of *Ulysses*.

A healthy interest in recent theory should be accompanied by a healthy scepticism that literary criticism has had in recent years a Great Leap Forward. We should be wary of a criticism that speaks in arcane diction and neologisms – indeed, at times, in tongues. In addition to replacing 'work' with text, and relying heavily on Derridianisms such as 'supplement' and 'difference', deconstruction adds 'ize' to nouns to create 'thematize', 'dichotomize', 'naturalize', 'problematize', and, of course, 'marginalize'.

Of course, deconstruction offers an enticement to graduate students who no longer have to worry about the massive amount of secondary material that has been produced by the cottage industry of academic publishing. In its freeing readers to do what they wish with works and to redefine the canon as they please, it offers a handy tool for graduate students – who are overwhelmed by the plethora of scholarship and criticism – to say something *different* and seemingly original. For we should not underestimate how awed graduate students are by the sheer volume of critical materials that have accumulated in the past two decades. Deconstruction also offers an enticement to American and English professors of foreign literatures and European and Third World students of English and American literature for whom questions of tone and irony are very difficult. Is it possible that we are developing a generation of graduate students who are tone-deaf – who, rather than respond to the voice and irony of *Emma* will be interested primarily in indicting the novel for what is omitted in the way of sociological analysis of the class structure? The canon of the traditional English and American novel, with its emphasis on the incongruity between the values of a narrator who has a coherent self and the major characters – an incongruity dependent on subtle irony and nuances of voice – is particularly resistant to deconstructive readings.

The question of why we should spend endless hours and course time reading Derrida is a real one. Once we have learned the basic lessons of deconstruction, are we not better off reading literary texts? After spending several hours reading 'Cogito and the History of Madness' (in *Writing and Difference*) for an informal colloquium, I asked myself whether this does not deflect us from attention that should be spent elsewhere. Once one knows the basic distinctions of deconstruction, is it worth the time to read volumes of Derrida with the same attention as Yeshiva students read Torah? I think I speak for many university literature professors when I say that, had I been confronted in my undergraduate or graduate years with Derrida, Nietzsche, and Marx as primary texts – instead of *Paradise Lost, Hamlet, Crime and*

Punishment, Lord Jim, and *Ulysses* – I would not be teaching literature today.

In literature as in life we find what we look for. This is another way of saying that theory is disguised autobiography. Just as Aristotelian critics such as R. S. Crane and Wayne Booth found in eighteenth-century texts the order and meaning that they sought in their criticism and discovered that authors built into texts both the rhetorical effects and moral values that they admired, deconstructive critics find *aporia* – moments of irreconcilable impasse – in modern texts. On the one hand, reading is defined by critics such as Barthes in terms akin to sexual orgasm; on the other, reading enacts the angst, marginality, frustration, and self-division that at times we are all prone to feel not only in our own critical and teaching activities, but in our lives. Perhaps, for deconstruction, interpretation has become in some instances no more than, to paraphrase T. S. Eliot, fragments that we each create to shore against our fears that our reading, like our lives, may end in ruins.

Questioning and redefining the canon to include works by women and minorities and works that have been undeservedly neglected is one of the exciting developments of the last decade; without canon re-evaluation, the study of 'modern literature' would have remained confined to the period from the sixteenth century through the Victorian era, with the heavy stress on the 1500–1880 years. But, believing as I do that some works have more artistic value and interest than others, I worry about using minor works as the centre-pieces of syllabi for students who take a very finite amount of literature courses. I also worry about the current practice of using eccentric and idiosyncratic works to make vast statements about cultural history.

III THE NOVEL AS MIMESIS: THE QUESTION OF REALISM

To return to *The Name of Rose*: Eco knows that there is a reality beyond words, even if one cannot quite define or reach it. Brother William's quest for the murderer of real dead bodies is a quest to go beyond signs to discover the anterior reality – what Marianne Moore would call 'imaginary gardens with real toads in them'. Within the abbey in Eco's novel there are texts, but there are dead bodies – mysterious bodies – which make a mockery of immersion in the world of books. As Brother William puts it, 'If the [foot]print exists, there must have existed something whose print it is.'[26] Or perhaps more to my point, 'The good of a book lies in its being read. A book is made up of signs that speak of other signs, which in their turn speak of things.'[27]

As we read, we enter into an imagined world whose significance depends on some relation to the world we recognize. The very conventions of grammar and syntax are mimetic of writing and speech patterns with which we are familiar; these conventions help embed us comfortably in the text. The things of the world – chairs, apples, sunny and rainy days – conform to what we know prior to the text. To reduce reading to linguistic games falsifies and trivializes what happens when we read and when we write. In concluding his section on the novel in *Structuralist Poetics*, Culler writes of Structuralism's contribution:

> By focusing on the ways in which it complies with and resists our expectations, its moments of order and disorder, its interplay of recognition and dislocation, it opens the way for a theory of the novel which would be an account of the pleasures and difficulties of reading. In place of the novel as mimesis we have the novel as a structure which plays with different modes of ordering and enables the reader to understand how he makes sense of the world.[28]

I know of no novelist who, in the above passage, finds anything recognizable in his stories of writing novels, and few readers who find much that is recognizable in their own stories of reading novels. What happens to the passion of Ursula Brangwen, the pride of Leopold Bloom, the perspicacity and sensitivity of Mrs. Ramsay, the disillusionment of Mrs. Dalloway, and the subtle cowardice of Conrad's Jim? What does criticism that refuses to discuss the human characters and moral issues in literature say about itself?

E. D. Hirsch, one of the most eloquent defenders of the mimetic function of literature and one of the most thoughtful about how literature means, writes in *Validity in Interpretation* that 'Validity implies the correspondence to a meaning which is represented by the text' and '[T]he only compelling normative principle that has ever been brought forwards is the old-fashioned ideal of rightly understanding what the author meant.'[29] Where he oversimplifies is in his failure to distinguish between the historical and ahistorical aspects of reading. For good readers stand outside the work and think about what the author means to contemporary readers as well as what the work means to the original audience. We try to recuperate the original work – the world it represents as well as the world which shaped its creation (which may as in Eco's tale about the fourteenth century be quite different) – as much as we can, but as time passes the attempt to do so becomes more difficult. But we also read in terms of our own historical and personal position and, from that perspective, are aware of changes and similarities between the author's *Zeitgeist* and ours. To the extent that books liberate us from a sense of the tick-tock of time in our worlds and put us inside an imagined world where we are immersed in the narrative time of that world and of the people who inhabit it, reading is ahistorical.

In his later study *The Aims of Interpretation*, Hirsch writes, 'Meaning ... refers to the whole verbal meaning of a text, and "significance" to textual meaning in relation to a larger context, i.e. another mind, another era, a wider subject matter.'[30] But can 'meaning' be separated from 'significance'? As soon as one describes what is inherent in the text it becomes significance; the 'isness' or meaning of a work cannot be separated from its 'doesness' or significance. To use Hirsch's distinctions, literary criticism should not be content with meaning, but needs to concern itself with significance. Literary theory purports to codify the search for meaning as a kind of knowledge. But is this kind of knowledge possible except insofar as a trained reader will respond with greater sensitivity and perspicacity? If knowledge means knowing which are the right critical questions, then theory can teach it. But if it means constructing elaborate hypotheses by which literary works are tested and subsequently organized, then I am skeptical.

In his important recent study, *A New Mimesis: Shakespeare and the Representation of Reality*, A. D. Nuttall has defined the principles for his version of a new mimesis. He believes that major topoi – such as recurring moments in the literary tradition when the poet speaks of the generations of dead – need be read not simply as recurrences of the same formal conventions but as genuinely felt emotions. He calls for both a 'renewed sense of the variety of reality' and 'a renewed sense of evidence', as well as what he calls 'the license to ask "Is this true?" or "Is this likely?" when reading fiction'.[31] For Nuttall realism includes 'precise visual description and psychological insight', but it also responds 'to the more fugitive aspects of the real; in particular to shifting *appearances* as distinct from more stable entities'.[32] He is not arguing for the superiority of realistic fiction, but for the premise that 'no form of literature be regarded as wholly insulated from this varying world'.[33] What we need is a criticism that understands that 'text' includes *the texture* of the moral and emotional experience it describes.

Some authors wish to approximate reality more than others; traditionally, we have called them realists. By the very nature of its selection and arrangement of its data from all the possible data, realism presents a perspective which is inevitably something of an illuminating distortion. But all authors depend on some recognition on the part of the reader that an act of mimesis is occurring. To again invoke my model of Zeno's paradox, even the most realistic texts can approach but never quite reach reality. (The contrasting metaphor for deconstruction is a mirage where reality continually recedes by approximately the distance that language seems to approach it.)

While I believe all literature has *some* realistic component, I want to stress that realism is not an evaluative term and that we should not assume that the more realism the better. On the contrary, I understand realism as a descriptive term. Moreover, realism is more a process than an end. It involves the attempt to approach an historical or individual world. While ultimately language will not create a world prior to the text, the world evoked by language will have its own verisimilitude. As we read, the reality of the imagined world continually modifies and transforms itself. But always the imagined world will have a continually changing relation both to the anterior world which provided the tentative ground for the imagined world and a continually changing relation to the anterior world in which the reader lives – the world that provides the ground for his or her responses.

Obviously within any work some aspects are more grounded in reality than others. For example, the depiction of a character depends upon the selection of one individual from among many possible residents of a city or geographical area, among many possible professions, among many members of the social class. By convention we understand that a major character – say, in Hardy's *Jude the Obscure* – a young, aspiring, uneducated male from the lower social classes who would rather be a scholar or clergyman than a stone carver – represents or typifies various groups and categories to which he belongs. In other words, under certain circumstances created by the author, readers perceive characters as signs with referents. By contrast, the simple descriptions of objects within a room generally have much less of a signifying function. Representation of humans is of such a different kind of mimesis that it almost becomes different in kind not degree. Representing human beings is both more metaphorical than other kinds of representation because of how we understand characters in their typifying function, and less metaphorical because the creation of people often short-circuit their putative metaphorical function and creates odd kinds of empathy with readers. Moreover, within novels characters are often so individualized and so idiosyncratic that they in fact represent only themselves and undermine the author's patterns of signification; put another way, the infinite variety of complex characters may deflect them from their signifying function. (As I argue in my *Reading Joyce's 'Ulysses'*, Leopold Bloom is an example.)

Realism has been recently called into question on the grounds that there is no possible agreement about what constitutes reality since we as modernists believe that each person perceives in terms of his own experience and psychic needs. This is another version of Conrad's insistence that 'Another man's truth is a dismal lie to me.'[34] We not only all read a different text, but we are aware that even authors who thought they were creating omniscient narrators are really only creating anonymous first-person perspectives since what the omniscient narrator tells us is really only one possible explanation. (As my use of the word 'tells' indicates, I believe that the mimetic model of a storyteller, of a person speaking to another through the written word, more adequately explains what happens than elaborate theories that insist on writing as a sharply *different* recondite activity.)

Readers and authors do their work in isolation from their fellows and are always lone perceivers; yet rhetorical convention depends upon an author creating a social reality based upon the possibility of implied mutual understanding of author and reader. Rhetorical convention implies that the author is a representative of a larger community – the omniscient narrator, in particular, calls attention to the author as a representative figure. The reader is a representative of a larger community of readers who are being addressed. Realism depends upon the possibility of creating a hermeneutical circle in which author and reader participate. It depends on the possibility of a shared ontology, an agreed upon system of language – usually with a varying but relatively low metaphorical quotient. It depends on the belief in an *a priori* world even if the relation between the anterior world and the imagined ontology continually varies.

In addition to the empirical world, realism also needs to address dreams, hopes, and plans whose linear narratives may have more in common with the simplified plots of fictions than with the disruptions, abundance, and plotlessness of everyday life. Among other things, what makes *Ulysses* so compelling is its substituting for a traditional monolithic plot the presentation of Bloom's, Molly's, and Stephen's fantasies, hopes, and dreams – often in the form of half-told, dimly acknowledged, and contradictory plot fragments. One reason that twentieth-century writers such as Lawrence and Joyce return to myths for their plots is that our lives seem more and more to lack the kind of coherent forward movement that plots require. As Eliot understood, the mythic dimension orders the futility and anarchy of contemporary history. But myth also introduces a level of metaphoricity that breathes new life and gives greater complexity to what may at first seem lifeless or sterile reality.

In the face of the threat of nuclear war, the breakdown of moral and religious certainties, the proliferation of divorces, the proclivity for multiple and simultaneous relationships, and even for overnight encounters, our lives no longer follow traditional linear plots. While our parents followed – indeed, were shaped by – the plots of marriages that were expected to last to the death of one partner, with the mother in the role of caretaker and the father in the role of provider, the uncertainties of our culture have made it much more difficult to embrace a monolithic plot. If the English novel is a genre of manners written by and for a culture whose paradigmatic plot is the quest for the appropriate marriage partner, then the so-called sexual revolution has changed not only the novel's authors but its readers. The fictions produced by our unstable culture reflect the intrusion of uncertainty, qualification, and disruption, but I think humanistic formalism has demonstrated that it has the critical tools to cope with the challenges of modernism and post-modernism.

Marxist critics want to expand reality to include the historical and social patterns implied by the imagined world and to stress how that imagined world's circumstances relate to the anterior one. They want to find a pattern behind the 'real' world, a kind of historical grammar that would give an explanation for what is presented as 'reality' or, put another way, would provide a kind of knowledge for explaining the individual instances of realism within a novel. Fredric Jameson has been calling this reality beyond or behind the empirical reality the 'political unconscious'.[35] This conceptual pattern is a hypothetical schematic version not merely of what happens within the novel's imagined world, but of both what has happened prior to the events of the novel, and what might happen after the events of the novel are over. It has the same relation to the actual presence of history – say, the Napoleonic Wars in *War and Peace* or the first World War in *To the Lighthouse* – as form does to content. But like form, history cannot be described except in the most metaphorical terms; thus historicity always has about it something of the ineffable.

On the whole, the current critical emphasis on historicity in novels is an attempt to bridge gaps that have not been articulated and fill in spaces that the novelist with his compulsive concern for human life has ignored. At times is not the hypothesis of an historical pattern beyond the experiential level of the literary work a kind of New Platonism? Novels may be able to make some progress in creating an historical or economic cause and effect; surely, some novels do this much better than others. But we must differentiate between, on the one hand, discussions of the historical dimensions of such novels as *War and Peace* or *Ragtime* in which historical events are dramatized or described with the same degree of verisimilitude as characters and episodes and, on the other, discussions of the historical implications drawn from a scintilla of material within the novel and then elaborated, developed, and indeed, *created* by what the reader knows about the period in which the novel is written. In these latter discussions, it seems as if critics were drawing lines to invisible dots.

IV THE MARXIST TELEOLOGY OF EAGLETON'S *LITERARY THEORY: AN INTRODUCTION*

Given its influence, we should briefly examine Terry Eagleton's *Literary Theory: an Introduction*. Eagleton's study is shaped by a teleology which concludes with a spirited and polemical defence of Marxist criticism in the final chapter. His goal is to deconstruct the possibility of discussing theory and method:

[L]iterary theory ... is really no more than a branch of social ideologies, utterly without any unity or identity which would adequately distinguish it from philosophy, linguistics, psychology, cultural and sociological thought; and secondly in the sense that the one hope it has of distinguishing itself – clinging to an object named literature – is misplaced. We must conclude, then, that this book is less an introduction than an obituary, and that we have ended by burying the object we sought to unearth.[36]

It is surely ironic that a book that ignores Chicago criticism – which more than any other Anglo-American criticism focuses on what literary works do – concludes by calling for the study of 'the kinds of *effects* which discourses produce'.[37] It would be hard to exaggerate Eagleton's oversimplification or neglect of American criticism; failing to mention the American literary tradition – as defined by such diverse figures as Richard Chase and D.H. Lawrence – deflects him from the realization that the criticism of the English novel and English poetry has been created in part by the canon it addresses. He does not even mention the names of M.H. Abrams, Wayne Booth, R.S. Crane, Mark Schorer, Dorothy Van Ghent, Ian Watt, Frank Kermode, Percy Lubbock, E.M. Forster, Arnold Kettle (the most important British literary Marxist before Williams). The one sentence devoted to Kenneth Burke is facile to the point of feeble, and R.P. Blackmur, mentioned once, is indexed as R.P. Blackbur. Nor does he discuss the strong political strand of American criticism dating back to Edmund Wilson and *The Partisan Review*.

Eagleton claims that literary theory does not have a subject, only an arcane vocabulary which it uses to define its domain:

Literary theorists, critics and teachers, then, are not so much purveyors of doctrine as custodians of a discourse.... The discourse itself has no definite signifiers, which is not to say that it embodies no assumptions: it is rather a network of signifiers able to envelop a whole field of meanings, objects and practices.[38]

But he is assuming that because the process of reading a work or describing the ingredients of an imagined world cannot be perfectly or fully described, it follows that there is no point making the effort. By contrast, I believe that the interpretive history of complex modern texts such as *Ulysses, The Rainbow, Lord Jim,* or *Mrs. Dalloway* shows that the goal of full description can be approached – although, of course, never reached – by careful subtle reading, and that we can describe how and why we are most successful in our interpretive quests. If we discuss the behaviour of a group of works or the process of reading in terms of specific texts that would enact the method or concepts, our discourse will have signifiers and signified objects. Literary theory becomes pure textuality only when it fails to ground its argument in specific works.

Eagleton has a sense of humour and writes lucid, readable, albeit polemical prose. His language, notwithstanding occasional anecdotes, does not have anything to do with individual experience, either of reading or life. By using abstract language remote from reading experience, we must indict him for the 'Theoretical Fallacy'. Rather than presenting a reasoned defence of Marxist criticism, Eagleton's final chapter, 'Conclusion: Political Criticism', is an ideological polemic that complains that departments of literature are part of the 'apparatus' of capitalist states.

Eagleton wants to see literature as not only the product of historical and social effects but also as one of the causes of historical and social events. As a Marxist, he sees literature as determined by conditions in which the artist lives. In its decentring of the author, in its questioning of the assignment of a privileged place among kinds of writing to literary texts and its insistence on a dialogue between literature and other writing produced in the same period, in its focus on writing as cause and effect, Marxism has a good deal in common with deconstruction. In his desire to see works historically produced, Eagleton deconstructs the author: 'Its "anonymity" is part of its very structure, not just an unfortunate accident which befalls it; and in this sense to be an "author" – the "origin" of one's own meanings, with "authority" over them – is a myth.'[39] I believe that we should acknowledge that we respond to a speaking presence while we read; for me, the lived life of a work depends upon the process of experiencing a human voice within the imagined world. Our challenge is to find ways of discussing the author as a formal presence within a work without committing reductive versions of the biographical fallacy.

Eagleton objects to the isolation of art from other kinds of productivity. He wants to study literature and, indeed, all writing, as a function of the historical process operating upon it; for him the historical process is economically determined. Romanticism and symbolism are seen as ways for élitist artists to escape social realities in their lives and in the subject matter of their art:

> For Romanticism, indeed, the symbol becomes the panacea for all problems. Within it, a whole set of conflicts which were felt to be insoluble in ordinary life – between subject and object, the universal and the particular, the sensuous and the conceptual, material and spiritual, order and spontaneity – could be magically resolved.... The concrete and the universal seemed to have drifted apart: an aridly rationalist philosophy ignored the sensuous qualities of particular things, while a short-sighted empiricism (the 'official' philosophy of the English middle class, then as now) was unable to peer beyond particular bits and pieces of the world to any total picture which they might compose.... The symbol fused together motion and stillness, turbulent content and organic form, mind and world.[40]

Eagleton's strengths are his discussions of major twentieth century critical movements in the five chapters between his 'Introduction: What is Literature' (appropriating the title of Sartre's inquiry by that name) and his 'Conclusion: Political Criticism'. But, given the influence of traditional humanistic approaches on English departments in England and America, how can one justify devoting a single chapter – a chapter entitled 'The Rise of English' – to them? Since 'liberal humanism' is a kind of bogeyman for Eagleton, it is perhaps hardly surprising that he gives short shrift to the various approaches of traditional humanistic criticism. Chapters two to five are entitled respectively 'Phenomenology, Hermeneutics, Reception Theory', 'Structuralism and Semiotics', 'Post-Structuralism', and 'Psychoanalysis'.

Indeed, in his discussion of liberal humanism, Eagleton strongly misreads his oedipal predecessors – almost 'fetishizes' them (to turn one of his favourite words against him). Far more than he would acknowledge, he is a successor to Leavis, a successor who wants to take English studies from the moral ground which is Leavis's focal point to the political realm: ' "Mass" culture is not the inevitable product of "industrial" society, but the offspring of a particular form of industrialism which organizes production for profit rather than for use, which concerns itself with what will sell rather with what is valuable.'[41] For Eagleton such shibboleths as

'social and historical realities' or 'the sociality of human life'
replace the Leavisite phrases 'lived experience' and 'morally
serious'.[42] Eagleton has his own anxiety of influence about Leavis;
and he adopts the Leavisite tone of English evangelicalism when
dealing with him or with liberal humanism. We recall the
Arnoldian strain in Leavis and Eagleton's immediate academic
father, Raymond Williams, another anxiety-ridden son of Leavis.
Does not Eagleton raise the standard of high seriousness in the
guise of 'social and political realities' and vent his annoyance with
what he regards as contemporary Philistines?

A non-Marxist deconstructionist might notice that what Eagleton forgets is that the arbitrariness of signs undermines his Marxist
rhetoric. But for Eagleton words do signify, and, for him, the work
of Derrida is a search for 'a wider and deeper history – of
language, of the unconscious, of social institutions and
practices'.[43] Like Fredric Jameson, Eagleton implies that there is a
deeper, more profound realism than humanistic critics perceive.
But the approach to this ineffable reality, like the approach to the
Congo – and the inner reality – in *Heart of Darkness*, is fraught with
difficulty. Indeed, the effort to discover reality in Marxist criticism
recalls the Myth of Sisyphus; just as one seems to be in reach of
one's goal of rolling a large boulder uphill, one finds oneself and
the boulder at the bottom of the hill. Jameson forewarns us that
our only approach to reality will be through what he thinks of as
the insufficient medium of language:

> We would therefore propose the following revised formulation:
> that history is *not* a text, not a narrative, master or otherwise, but
> that, as an absent cause, it is inaccessible to us except in textual
> form, and that our approach to it and to the Real itself
> necessarily passes through its prior textualization, its narrativi-
> zation in the political unconscious.[44]

But can one really propose a concept of history that is without
ground in reality? Is history really a concept removed from the day
to day events of individual lives? Do Eagleton and Jameson write in
the optative about what criticism might be *because* they lack a
vocabulary and epistemology for dealing with the historical
dimensions of texts except in utopian terms? Is ideology always
utopian in a Marxist framework? Does the abstract vocabulary of
Eagleton and Jameson interfere with *their* reading works as unique
individuals with passions and motives – individuals who belong to

a fabric of lived relationships that is produced by social and historical reality?

While Eagleton's concern with world events is a nice release from the claustrophobic world of post-structuralism, he is hardly the first to worry over the lack of relevance. Moreover, readers of Van Ghent, Burke, and *The Partisan Review* know that American formalism insisted on giving its formalism a political dimension. Do American literary theorists assume, as Eagleton contends, 'that at the centre of the world is the contemplative individual self, bowed over its book, striving to gain touch with experience, truth, reality, history or tradition'?[45] Liberal humanism believes in self-knowledge and self-growth; it believes that pursuing the life of the mind may lead one to moral maturity, and it believes that entering into the imagined world of books may improve one's perspicacity. It believes in a continuity between reading texts and reading lives.

Eagleton does not discuss individual works in terms which enact his conception of historical process. I want to know what kinds of readings his political criticism produces when it turns to specific works. (To be fair, Eagleton has done his share of such 'practical criticism', but doesn't the absence of substantive examples here make his last chapter polemical?) How anyone can propose a kind of historical criticism without mentioning Auerbach's *Mimesis* is also puzzling, for Auerbach, although he does not restrict himself to economic causes, addresses the very dialogue between real and imaginative worlds that is Eagleton's concern. A lynchpin of Eagleton's argument is that all readings are shaped by ideology – which he defines as 'those modes of feeling, valuing, perceiving and believing which have some kind of relation to the maintenance and reproduction of social power'.[46] But in this book he does not show what kinds of reading specific ideologies produce or how his Marxist perspective will produce fresh readings. I would like to see examples of his historically variable readings. He should not merely dismiss theories that discuss 'the poem itself, organic society, etc', but demonstrate what should be discussed by reference to specific texts. In Jamesian terms, Eagleton, like Culler, prefers to tell rather than show.

V   FEMINISM AND HUMANISM

Deconstruction has sought to appropriate the position of beleaguered minorities and to claim that it speaks on behalf of Third

World nations and economically exploited masses. The implication that aligning oneself with socially progressive opinions somehow validates one's way of reading or one's way of discussing theory might be called the Fallacy of the Good and Beautiful.

While welcoming their support of enlightened positions, traditional humanistic critics should resist the polemical contention that in opposition to a 'conservative' benighted humanism, deconstruction not only aligns itself with, but also is the intellectual counterpart and offensive arsenal for, the women's movement, minorities, and the socially oppressed. Recently deconstruction has sought to adopt anti-apartheid and divestment as its own, although these positions were strongly advocated well before the arrival of deconstruction by humanists in literature departments who were often in the vanguard of the civil rights movement, minorities, and the socially oppressed. Recently, lated among True Deconstruction Believers is Derrida's statement on apartheid, as if his Word legitimized a political position and as if he spoke *ex cathedra* from the Holy See of Deconstruction. Indeed, his opinions have the very authority and presence that are anathema to deconstruction in other moments. Isn't Derrida cited by his followers as an apostolic text in day-to-day teaching and critical discourse?

In *On Deconstruction* Culler claims that feminist studies are a branch of deconstruction. But surely in England and America most work in feminist studies is concerned not with textuality and rhetorical moves but with the representation of experience: with the social implications of how women characters and authors have been and are being treated; with criticism that reduces women to passive objects and consigns women characters to the cupboards of male imagination; and with the need to adjust the canon to take account of women writing and women reading.

Indeed, feminist criticism often assumes the presence of an author and an historical cause and effect both between texts and the anterior world, and within imagined worlds. Certainly, Anglo-American feminist criticism is rooted in what Joanne Fry has called 'its experiential basis' and 'a concern for women's lives';[47] it examines representation of women in literature and takes account of cultural change. In their seminal *The Madwoman in the Attic*, Gilbert and Gubar proceed on the assumption that a self-conscious 'I' can be defined: 'For all literary artists, of course, self-definition necessarily precedes self-assertion: the creative "I am" cannot be uttered if the "I" knows not what it is.'[48] Their concerns are the difficulty and necessity of recovering that female "I" from an antagonistic or indifferent literary culture and society.

Moreover, it is worth noting that the humanistic study of the English novel has recognized the strong contribution of women writers and critics. It was almost a shibboleth of the late 1950s and early 1960s that the three greatest – or, in a less provocative version, three of the greatest – English novels of the nineteenth century were written by women: *Emma, Wuthering Heights,* and *Middlemarch.* In her essay, 'Emphasis Added: Plots and Plausibilities in Women's Fiction', Nancy Miller writes that '"sensibility", "sensitivity", "extravagance" – so many code words for feminine in our culture that the attack is in fact tautological – are taken to be not merely inferior modalities of production but deviations from some obvious truth.'[49] But in fact the humanistic tradition has valued in the English novel the very qualities of sensibility, sensitivity, and even, 'extravagance' – if I understand the term correctly as implying idiosyncratic and excessive behaviour that exceeds the norms. More than any single book in America, Dorothy Van Ghent's *The English Novel: Form and Function* defined the canon of the English novel. In a prior generation, Virginia Woolf's *The Common Reader* had much to do with shaping the traditional canon of English fiction; and, as soon as the modern novel became a subject, Woolf's fiction was widely taught in England and America. Q. D. Leavis and Muriel Bradbrook were vital parts of *Scrutiny* which up until recently set the canon in England.

Culler's equation of logocentricism and phallocentricism is simply the creation of a word world based on little or no evidence. At times, 'phallocentric' is less a concept than a kind of name-calling in an academic version of the rhetoric of insult. One problem of textuality, of writing for its own sake rather than with reference to an origin or a presence, is that it relieves writing of the responsibility of accuracy. Culler's assertions proceed on the simplistic equation of male with Bad and Female with Good:

> [Feminist Readings] demonstrate the limitations of male critical interpretations in terms that male critics would purport to accept, and they seek, like all ambitious acts of criticism, to attain a generally convincing understanding – an understanding that is feminist because it is a critique of male chauvinism. . . . Men have

aligned the opposition male/female with rational/emotional, serious/frivolous, or reflective/spontaneous: and feminist criticism of the second moment works to prove itself more rational, serious, and reflective than male readings that omit and distort.[50]

While objecting to simple oppositions, Culler in the above and following passages speaks as if deconstruction requires a binary perspective and needs to propose ideas in terms of dichotomies:

> The more convincing its critique of phallic criticism, the more feminist criticism comes to provide the broad and comprehensive vision, analyzing and situating the limited and interested interpretations of male critics. Indeed, at this level one can say that feminist criticism is the name that should be applied to all criticism alert to the critical ramifications of sexual oppression, just as in politics 'women's issues' is the name now applied to many fundamental questions of personal freedom and social justice.[51]

But arms control, support for humane regimes in South America, opposition to Apartheid, the plight of the homeless, the reverse Robinhoodism of the Reagan government are not 'Women's Issues', but human issues requiring the energy and engagement of both genders. What Judith Fetterley, focusing on the woman reader, writes of feminist criticism is true of homosexual, Black, Third World, Jewish, Marxist, deconstructive, psychoanalytic criticism – or, indeed, of my apologia for humanistic formalism: 'Feminist criticism is a political act whose aim is not simply to interpret the world but to change it by changing the consciousness of those who read and their relation to what they read.'[52]

Feminist criticism performs a valuable function in reminding us of the biological, cultural, and historical reasons that women read differently. But to propose a dichotomy in which half the world reads as women and the other half as men is reductive. We all belong to several groups that shape our responses. For the most part women, like men, write and read as part of multiple intersecting and constantly evolving identities. Men and women from similar cultural background reading an Ann Beattie or a John Updike story in *The New Yorker* have far more in common than with readers of the same sex who have different cultural backgrounds.

Jews who have suffered through the Holocaust, blacks who have lived through the era of Jim Crow laws and customs, those who were raised in the Mississippi delta, Japanese-Americans who were (dis)placed in camps in World War II have common bonds that transcend sexual differences. For how many people outside the academy is the sexual difference the dominant factor – as opposed to one of several important factors – in the way they read and experience?

Thus my responses are an intersection of my experience and personality. Major factors in my reading responses include my teaching and writing about the novel for the past twenty years. But this professional self at times gives way to a self defined by my Jewish heritage; by my growing up in a middle-class community on Long Island and my access to theatre and museums; by parental influences; by my relatively cosmopolitan background, including travel experiences; by my relatively provincial life in Eastern university English departments for more than two decades as a graduate student and teacher; by my life in rural Ithaca these past twenty years; by my marriage to a school administrator of a quite different background with whom I shared twenty-two often satisfying and at times tumultuous years trying to define a relationship in which each of us (at best) helped the other grow, but (at worst) bogged the other down in carping and failure to provide an adequate support system; by my complex relation with my adolescent children, particularly my independent and iconoclastic elder son who says 'no' before doing 'yes'. (The above sentence, it will be noted, not only gives some clues as to what it is like to read as Dan Schwarz, but enacts my credo by giving the author a human voice to which the reader must respond; it is meant to be in striking contrast to critics whose polemical abstractions are themselves an attack on reading and writing as a living experience.)

VI THE HUMANISTIC CRITICAL LEGACY

While Anglo-American critics have not articulated a philosophic basis for their criticism, they have developed a methodology and principles – even, indeed, an implicit theory – that interprets, analyzes, and judges novels effectively. I have written at length about this tradition in my *The Humanistic Heritage: Critical Theories of the English Novel from James to Hillis Miller*. I have called this tradition humanistic formalism, and have cast a wide net to include critics as diverse as Forster, Booth, Van Ghent, Watt, Kermode, and even appropriated Auerbach, Raymond Williams, and some aspects of the work of Hillis Miller. Despite some failures, this tradition has explicated the texts of major novelists of the past three centuries and made these texts more accessible to readers. That complicated and problematic novels, like *Lord Jim, The Golden Bowl, The Sound and The Fury,* and *Ulysses,* have become part of the consciousness of educated people and that major English and American eighteenth and nineteenth-century novels have been better understood – more subtly and fully read – is a tribute to the efficacy of this criticism.

The concerns of this tradition have been accuracy, inclusiveness, and the quality – the maturity and sincerity – of its mimesis, and its mimesis represents how people live in a social community. Perhaps from an historical perspective this criticism should be seen as a response to the British novel's interest in content and its moral effects on readers. For this body of criticism would usually subscribe to what Gene Thornton wrote in another context: '[A]rt is about something other than art, and subject matter is important precisely because it distracts the viewer's attention from art and focuses it on something outside the picture – life, the world, God – that is more important than art.'[53] Humanistic novel criticism also takes seriously the importance of subject matter, and believes that the doing – technique, structure, and style – is important *because* it reveals or discusses the meaning inherent in the subject.

The differences that separate various strands of Anglo-American criticism seem less significant than they once did. Now we are able to see that the New Critics, Aristotelians, the *Partisan Review* group, contextualists, and literary historians share a number of important assumptions: authors write to express their ideas and emotions; the way man lives and the values for which he lives are of fundamental interest to authors and readers; literature expresses insights about human life and responses to human situations, and that is the main reason why we read, teach, and think about literature. While the emphasis varies from critic to critic, we can identify several concepts that define this criticism:

1. The form of the novel – style, structure, narrative technique – expresses its value system. Put another way: form discovers the meaning of content.

2. A work of literature is also a creative gesture of the author and the result of historical context. Understanding the process of imitating the external world gives us an insight into the artistry and meaning of the work.

3. The work of fiction imitates a world that precedes the text, and the critic should recapture that world primarily by formal analysis of the text, although knowledge of the historical context and author are often important. This criticism believes that there is an original meaning, a centre, which can be approached, and at times reached, by perceptive reading. The goal is to discover what the author said to *his* intended audience *then* as well as what he says to us now. Acts of interpretation at their best – subtle, lucid, inclusive, perceptive – can bring that goal into sight.

4. Man's behaviour is central to most works, and should be the major concern of analysis. In particular, these critics are, with the exception of Northrop Frye, interested in how people behave – what they fear, desire, doubt, need. Although modes of characterization differ, the psychology and morality of characters must be understood as if they were real people; for understanding others like ourselves helps us to understand ourselves.

5. The inclusiveness of the novel's vision in terms of depth and range is a measure of the work's quality.

In the last several years, humanistic criticism has made several advances; specifically, it became more attentive to the role of the reader and to the temporality of the structure of literary works. By seeing the structure as an evolving process, rather than as a static and spatial architectonic shape, and by conceiving of the reader as an active figure who is constantly testing, discarding, and modifying his impressions, the dialogue between reader and work has taken on another dimension. It should be noted that well before deconstruction, humanistic formalism was moving in similar directions in its stress on the process of reading (in the work of Burke, Booth, and Kermode) and in its close analysis of the tensions and ambiguities within modern novels (in the work of Van Ghent, Schorer, Watt, and Guerard as well as in a host of their successors). The idea that works are not seamless organic wholes and that works have fissures and tensions which undermine unity is not new. Critics working in the tradition of humanistic formalism have taught us that Esther Summerson is a different kind of narrator than the omniscient narrator; that Father Time as an allegorical figure depends on a different kind of mimesis than either the socially representative Jude or psychologically idiosyncratic Sue, and that the catalogues in 'Cyclops' do not occupy the same status in the imagined world as Bloom's reveries.

Humanistic formalism calls into question deconstruction's insistence on the arbitrariness of signs in the only sense that such a concept matters to literary criticism. It assumes that in specific circumstances readers share similar recognition of signs and thus respond in approximately similar ways. Of course, the more readers share the same cultural background as the author, the more they will share her/his experience and the less arbitrary will appear the author's signs. Readers who have been reading similar works and studying in the same field will share a greater recognition of the signs I am now writing on this page. Thus the arbitrariness of signs is not absolute but rather a function of the reader's experience, the author's intent, and, of course, historical circumstances, which render some signs far more arbitrary to a contemporary audience than they were for the original reader. For example, Conrad would have expected contemporary readers of 'The Secret Sharer' to understand the British maritime code; he would not have expected them – as many of his readers today do – to extenuate Leggatt or to be reluctant to pass judgement about the captain's providing refuge for an escaped murderer. Nor would he have expected us to be taken in by Marlow's empathetic reading of Jim's abandoning the native passengers and crew in *Lord Jim*.

In terms of my own personal aesthetic, let me propose directions that a revised humanistic novel criticism – a criticism that builds upon the above concepts – might take. I assume that the author has created an imagined world, an ontology separate and distinct from the real one, and that the created world of a good novel is organized according to orderly principles and is apprehensible by orderly principles, although the reader's concepts of order may be different from those of the author. The structure of a novel is an evolving process in which the reader participates with the author. After all, the author embodies in his work a structure of affects that arouses expectations and subsequently fulfils, modifies, transforms, postpones, or deflates them. Since each novel generates its own aesthetic, we need to inquire into how a particular novel signifies. We must define the voice of the novel by continually asking, 'Who is speaking to what implied audience and with what intended effects?'

Finally, the language of a novel presents a concatenation of events or episodes that comprises a narrative. And this narrative enacts a meaning. Notwithstanding the deliberate efforts to subvert the expectations of traditional narrative by disrupting chronology and doubling every action (a technique that paradoxically calls attention to both the fictionality of the text and the inevitability of the events within the imagined world), the narrative that we find in a novel like *Lord Jim* makes a coherent statement about the way life is lived in the imagined world within the text. Just as we value the integrity of literary works that account for the complexity of life and language, we should value the integrity of readings that provide coherent explanations of the infinite variety of the multiple dimensions of a complex work. Moreover, our interest in imagined worlds depends upon their relation to real ones; although that relation may be oblique, we do look for kinds of representation in our fictions, and we do understand events in fiction in terms of signification beyond as well as within the imagined world of the novel. Thus it is not only appropriate but necessary to inquire into the relationship between the presence embodied in the form of the novel and the real author. Reading is a mode of perception, a mode of construing, and reading about characters within an imagined world appeals to us because such reading is an extension of how we perceive and understand the events in our own lives. Of course, we must understand that characters in fiction are functions of the formal properties of a novel's imagined world. But, despite some recent attacks on the 'metaphysics of presence', we should not be apologetic for, or embarrassed by, thinking of characters in literature as if they were human within the 'hypothesis' of their imagined worlds, or as reflections, distortions, or parodies of their creators.

Without abandoning interpretation of literary works, a revised humanistic criticism should develop concepts about how novels behave and how readers respond. It should perceive reading as an active quest to discover what words mean and signify within the imagined world. It should seek to understand how these words function within their own ontology and how the rhetorical effects – usually, but by no means always, consciously built into the world by the author – affect the reader in her or his world.

Notes

1. *The Humanistic Heritage: Critical Theories of the English Novel From James to Hillis Miller* (London: Macmillan; Philadelphia: University of Pennsylvania Press, 1986); *Reading Joyce's 'Ulysses'* (London: Macmillan; New York: St. Martin's Press, 1987).
2. Jonathan Culler, *On Deconstruction* (Ithaca, NY; Cornell University Press, 1982) p. 224.
3. Umberto Eco, *The Name of the Rose*, trans. William Weaver (New York: Warner Books, 1983) p. 342.
4. From *De la Grammatologie*, quoted in *On Deconstruction*, p. 106.
5. Thus the work is 'an intertextual event', and the reader becomes a 'space', a 'place' or a 'function'. See Culler, pp. 32–3.
6. Quoted by Wayne Booth, *Critical Inquiry*, 3:3 [spring 1977] p. 408; from Michael Riffaterre, 'Interpretive and Descriptive Poetry: a Reading of Wordsworth's "Yew-Trees"', *New Literary History* 4 [winter 1973] p. 230.
7. Eco, p. 382.
8. Culler, p. 180.
9. Culler, *The Pursuit of Signs: Semiotics, Linguistics, and the Study of Literature* Ithaca: Cornell University Press, 1981) p. 6.
10. *On Deconstruction*, p. 221.
11. Ibid., p. 31.
12. Introduction to *The Author in his Work*, eds Louis L. Martz and Aubrey Williams (New Haven and London: Yale University Press, 1978) p. xii.
13. *On Deconstruction*, p. 176.
14. Geoffrey Hartman, *Saving the Text: Literature/Derrida/Philosophy* (Baltimore: Johns Hopkins University Press, 1981) p. 33.
15. *On Deconstruction*, p. 225; my emphasis.
16. Culler, *Structuralist Poetics* (Ithaca, NY: Cornell University Press, 1978) p. 262.
17. Ibid., p. 134.
18. *On Deconstruction*, p. 86.
19. Ibid., p. 82.
20. Ibid., p. 133.
21. Ibid., pp. 138–9.
22. Ibid., p. 139.
23. Ibid., p. 63.
24. Ibid., p. 220.
25. Ibid., p. 223.
26. Eco, p. 381.
27. Ibid., p. 478.
28. Culler, *Structuralist Poetics*, p. 238.
29. E. D. Hirsch, *Validity in Interpretation* (New Haven and London: Yale University Press, 1967) pp. 10, 26.
30. E. D. Hirsch, *The Aims of Interpretation* (University of Chicago Press, 1976) pp. 2–3.
31. A. D. Nuttall, *A New Mimesis: Shakespeare and the Representation of*

Reality (New York: Methuen, 1983) p. 182.
32.   Ibid., p. 186.
33.   Ibid., p. 193.
34.   2 Nov. 1895 letter to Edward Noble in G. Jean-Aubry's *Joseph Conrad: Life and Letters*, 2 vols (Garden City: Doubleday, 1927).
35.   See Fredric Jameson, *The Political Unconscious* (Ithaca, NY: Cornell University Press, 1981).
36.   Terry Eagleton, *Literary Theory: an Introduction* (Minneapolis: University of Minnesota Press, 1983) p. 204.
37.   Eagleton, p. 205.
38.   Eagleton, p. 201.
39.   Eagleton, p. 119.
40.   Eagleton, p. 21.
41.   Eagleton, p. 34.
42.   Eagleton, pp. 196–7; see chapter 4 of my *The Humanistic Heritage*.
43.   Eagleton, p. 148.
44.   Jameson, p. 35.
45.   Eagleton, p. 196.
46.   Eagleton, p. 15.
47.   Joanne Frye, *Living Stories, Telling Lives* (Ann Arbor, MI: University of Michigan Press, 1986) pp. 21, 24.
48.   Sandra M. Gilbert and Susan Gubar, *The Mad Woman in the Attic: The Woman Writer and the Nineteenth Century Literary Imagination* (New Haven: Yale University Press, 1979) p. 17.
49.   *PMLA* 96:1 (Jan. 1981) p. 46.
50.   *On Deconstruction*, p. 58.
51.   Ibid., p. 56.
52.   Judith Fetterley, *The Resisting Reader: a Feminist Approach to American Fiction* (Bloomington: Indiana University Press, 1978) p. vii.
53.   Gene Thornton, 'P. H. Polk's Genius Versus Modernism', *New York Times' Leisure*, 12 Feb. 1982, pp. 25–6.

8

Modes of Literary Inquiry: a Primer for Humanistic Formalism

I think we are entering a period in which a fruitful dialogue between traditional humanistic study and recent theory will address the challenges posed by deconstruction and Marxism, even while returning to a focus on literary works not as texts but as imagined worlds. Using Lawrence as my prime example and Conrad as my secondary example, I want to examine how humanistic formalism addresses a number of issues pertaining to literary study. By examining some recent scholarship and critic- ism, I shall locate some topics and issues that need to be reconsidered in the light of recent theory. In particular, we shall consider how we can discuss the author in the text.

It has been one of the triumphs of literary study in England and America that the wildly experimental and boldly innovative authors of the early twentieth century have been made accessible. No longer the avant-garde, Joyce, Lawrence, Conrad, Eliot, and Woolf now occupy a comfortable place in the canon of English literature. It was in part by showing us how to read complex modern works that the New Criticism established the power and value of its method. Subsequently, literary scholarship, with its publication of impressive biographies, authoritative editions, collections of letters, and studies that examined virtually every aspect of these writers' thoughts, vastly increased our knowledge of twentieth-century literature.

I THE USE OF LITERARY AND HISTORICAL CONTEXTS

As New Criticism has waned, humanistic formalism has become increasingly attentive to how historical and intellectual contexts shape the author's imaginative work. It rightly assumes that neither authors nor works exist in an historical, literary, or

177

intellectual vacuum. It assumes that we understand an author better if we know about the world in which he lived and the ideas to which he responded. The paradigms for this kind of work are the great contextual studies of modernism by Ellmann (*James Joyce; Yeats: the Man and the Masks;* and *The Identity of Yeats*) and Kenner (*The Pound Era*).

More recently, Ian Watt's *Conrad in the Nineteenth Century*[1] is a triumphant combination of scholarship and criticism that has permanently affected the way we read Conrad. Although he only goes up to 1900, Watt has written the most significant book on Conrad since Albert J. Guerard's *Conrad the Novelist* (1958). Watt neither imposes a thesis nor isolates an aspect of Conrad's art, but instead comes to terms with the totality of Conrad's early achievement in the way Ellmann does with the careers of Yeats and Joyce. The book's importance derives from his combining sensitive and insightful responses to Conrad's works with profound knowledge of intellectual, literary, and social history and the modernist movement in literature. Watt not only provides splendid readings of major works, especially *Heart of Darkness* and *Lord Jim*, but also places Conrad's work in the context of his Polish background, European literary and intellectual history, and the English world in which he settled in 1894.

By defining Conrad's work in the context of his life as well as intellectual and literary history, Watt makes an important methodological statement to those critics who would restrict their attention to the text and emphasize the reader's response to the text. Thus, in a sense, the book's method is its most important argument. Watt shows that a work takes its meaning from the world that produced it. He demonstrates how to read literature in terms of contexts without sacrificing formal analysis of the work's imagined world. Implicitly and explicitly he is responding to critics who believe that every work is about the writing and reading of itself, and who believe that the possibility of meaning is a fiction in which authors and readers participate. Literary works are, for Watt, expressions of the author's psyche and of his culture. Watt believes that historical and biographical knowledge not only enables us to retrieve the text the author wrote but also enables us to understand patterns of cultural history of which the author and his original readers might have been unaware. Watt believes that, while interpretations may vary, literary criticism can be as true as other kinds of knowledge insofar as it provides the *correct* material for understanding the text and insofar as it *accurately* reads the text.

While no critic in fact can exclude his own biases from his method, the intrusion of comments on how human beings behave, unless wrapped in Freudian or Lacanian terms, is thought by many to be sentimentalism, or as one of my colleagues might dismissively put it, 'old-fashioned humanism'. But Watt enacts in his criticism the argument that a literary critic must also be an experienced, mature, judicious observer of human behaviour. Watt is a traditional humanist who believes literature tells us something about ourselves and the world in which we live. Believing that literature is, among other things, a criticism of life, Watt draws upon his life experience to make comments on the behaviour of Conrad and his characters. Thus he generalizes about Conrad's friendship with Ford: 'The challenge, under conditions of easy and intimate dialogue, to be articulate about matters which have hitherto been more or less private or unconscious, is perhaps the commonest way in which to clarify our own perceptions and convictions' (p. 257).

In *Conrad in the Nineteenth Century*, Watt accomplishes the purpose announced in the first sentence of his preface: 'To provide a comprehensive account of Conrad's literary career [in its] three main aspects: biographical, historical, and interpretative' (p. ix). As in *The Rise of the Novel*, he deftly combines historical criticism with formal criticism. For Watt, biographical, sociological, and historical facts are explanations for the forms of works of art and necessary for understanding the meaning of them. Moreover, literature is important because it not only expresses the *Zeitgeist*, but also in turn becomes a significant part of cultural and intellectual history. Influenced at Cambridge by the Leavises and the *Scrutiny* group, Watt believes that the literary critic has simultaneously the modest task of serving the author he interprets and the magisterial task of speaking in defence of culture and civilization. With his standards of 'moral intensity' and 'total sense of human life', F. R. Leavis preserved the Arnoldian strain of high seriousness which, along with his stress on close reading, influenced Watt. Like Mark Schorer, Albert Guerard, and Dorothy Van Ghent, Watt sought in his fiction criticism to use the techniques of the New Criticism to ask larger questions about the author's values, psychology, and intellectual milieu.

Watt's study is a significant response to the tendency to regard Conrad as a nihilist or a metaphysician of darkness. Speaking of

Heart of Darkness, Watt writes: 'Neither Conrad nor Marlow stands for the position that darkness is irresistible: their attitude, rather, is to enjoin us to defend ourselves in full knowledge of the difficulties to which we have been blinded by the illusions of civilization' (p. 253). Watt's discussion of *Heart of Darkness* should put to rest the view that Conrad's texts more generously yield their mysteries to formalism, whether of the New Critical or more recent European varieties. Watt shows how Conrad's scientific knowledge affected his presentation of Marlow, presents the parallel between Marlow's work ethic and Carlyle's, and demonstrates how Conrad is responding to both imperialism and Social Darwinism.

Imaginative and powerful scholarship such as Watt's has been complemented by more modest work in which scholars examine an author or authors in the context of a strand or two of the warp and woof of the authors' lives or of intellectual and literary history; what results is a slightly revised – rather than a bold, new – perspective. An example of such a study is Kim Herzinger's *D. H. Lawrence in His Time: 1908–1915.*[2] His premise is 'that an understanding of Lawrence's cultural context, and his responses and reactions to it, is essential to a fuller comprehension of his work' (p. 18). Carefully researched and well-written by a scholar who has full control of the details of his argument, Herzinger's book establishes Lawrence's affinities with the Georgians, and, less emphatically, with the Edwardians and Imagists. He also discusses Lawrence's tenuous connections with several other groups, including Futurism and Bloomsbury. Lawrence enthusiastically reviewed *Georgian Poetry 1911–1912*; according to Herzinger, he found the work of Abercrombie, Brooke, Drinkwater, and company to be, in contrast to the weariness of Edwardians, 'passionate, personal, constructive, and joyful' (p. 52). I wish Herzinger had gone beyond the rather early cut-off date of 1915, at least for a chapter or two. Given that the modest tone and naive and joyful hopefulness of the Georgians are so very different from Lawrence's hyperbolic, iconoclastic voice and rapid oscillations of mood, it is not surprising that Herzinger's most compelling pages are about Lawrence's effort to kick over the vessels of the literary culture in which he lived. Thus he demonstrates compellingly that in the story 'England, My England' Lawrence rejects aspects of the Georgian sensibility.

Herzinger's understanding of the period on which he writes is impressive, although he often seems to have a parochial interest in literary life in England at the expense of both the social and political ingredients of English culture and the larger European cultural milieu of which England was becoming a part. For example, although he mentions the 1910 post-Impressionist exhibit, he fails to relate Lawrence's experimental representation of action and character in *Sons and Lovers, The Rainbow,* and *Women in Love* to the fundamental change in perception illustrated by the various forms of post-Impressionism, including Cubism and Fauvism. Since Lawrence as a painter had a keen awareness of the visual possibilities of scene, and the need for highlighting or distorting some details while neglecting or minimizing others, it would be surprising if the post-Impressionist exhibits in 1910 and 1912 were not major events in shaping Lawrence's sensibility. In *Sons and Lovers,* is not Paul's preference in his paintings for 'shimmeriness' over traditional shapes and forms partly based on Lawrence's understanding of Impressionism and other alternatives to realism?

II   LAWRENCE AND TRADITION

Influence study has had a respectable heritage in literary studies. The Church fathers were interested in the presence of the Old Testament in the New; the Renaissance acknowledged the importance of the Western classical tradition. As English emerged from the classics as an independent area of study in the early twentieth century, it sought to define the historical and linguistic antecedents of the canon of English literature that it was fashioning. Adopting the philological methods employed by students of Greek and Roman literature, researchers in English departments pursued sources with the same urgency that classical scholars looked for Greek antecedents in Roman literature. In the twentieth century, English departments have devoted much energy to developing authoritative editions which include elaborate discussions of possible sources.

T. S. Eliot's 'Tradition and the Individual Talent' gave impetus to a more complex view of influence than that derived from simple interest in sources:

No poet, no artist of any art, has his complete meaning alone. His significance, his appreciation is the appreciation of his relation to the dead poets and artists. You cannot value him alone; you must set him, for contrast and comparison, among the dead. I mean this as a principle of aesthetic, not merely historical, criticism.

Eliot not only proposes a diachronic and vertical concept of tradition by which earlier works father later ones, but suggests an ahistorical or synchronic approach. The impetus of Eliot's views removed the study of influence from narrow historicism which often stressed the recurrence in later works of themes or verbal patterns that appeared in earlier ones. Instead of merely searching for historical iteration, Eliot pointed the way to the comparison of two writers for the purpose of learning not so much how one influenced the other, but rather of seeing what new insights could be gained about both writers by reading them next to one another. Eliot's concept of tradition redirected attention to the way that major works participate in both a synchronic and diachronic dialogue among masterpieces. In other words, he supplemented the vertical paternal concept of literary influence with a lateral juxtaposition which was not based on diachronic principles. In the late sixties in some influential English departments, such lateral juxtapositions were known as 'literary encounters'. At the time, these encounters were among the projects on the critical frontier; they spawned in the graduate students of the time such humourous titles as 'The Influence of Eliot on Arnold' or 'Pope as Reader of Wordsworth'.

The concept of intertextuality, which now basks in the consensual glow of many major English departments, has gone a giant step further in its ahistorical assumptions; it has extended the lateral version of tradition by seeing each work – or at least the reading of each work – as a linguistic configuration in which any and all other written work potentially intersects. Put another way, the text is the nodal point to which readers bring their prior reading; we all create our own text based on the intersection of the text we are reading with all the other texts which we have read.

Recent theory has called into question the very function of literary history and its intellectual cousin, literary influence. Furthermore, it has questioned the very possibility of the concept of authorial originality by suggesting that the author's language is a function of his temporal and spatial definition. According to this line of argument, the author – to the extent that we can speak of such a construct – creates his own text from the texts available to his imagination. But he is less a strong creative presence than the function of what he has been reading, of the way language is behaving at particular historical moments, and of the historical and social circumstances in which he lived. Thus one reads in so-called 'advanced' criticism that the concept of the author is obsolete because an author is less the life he leads than the language he reads and hears.

With some justice, Harold Bloom is often thought of as a member of the Yale deconstruction group, and humorously classified with Hartman, Hillis Miller, and the late de Man as 'The Gang of Four'. But Bloom does not surrender the concept of the author; rather, he argues that the author – deeply engaged in an Oedipal struggle with his literary father – may be creating a different work than he imagines, one that bears the traces of the masterwork to which he as a strong reader is responding in his creative act. Bloom argues that major writers by their very act of strongly responding to those they regard as their most significant predecessors subsume the imitated literary ancestors in a new creation; the strong response – by its very Oedipal nature – *must* be a violent misreading. The resulting new creation, however, is also a recreation which leaves the creator with a strong sense of indebtedness and often an equally strong need to deny influence. Every major work, Bloom contends, is a misrepresentation of a literary ancestor.

Let us examine a recent collection of essays on literary influence. Although Jeffrey Meyers' introduction to *D. H. Lawrence and Tradition*[3] gives a perfunctory nod to some of the issues I sketched above, including a mention of Bloom's theory, the contributors proceed on relatively traditional conceptions of what influence means. They assume the possibility of a positivistic narrative – a linear story of influence – in which we see not merely the presence of an earlier writer in a later one, but actually conceive the later writer's work as an *effect* for which the cause is the *earlier* writer. For some reason there has been a particular urgency to find influences in Lawrence – usually among traditional figures in English studies but sometimes in rather obscure places such as the occult or the Futurists – as part of the academic effort to domesticate him from his rightful position as a bull in the china shop of English literary studies.

Published in the Lawrence centennial year, Meyers' useful collection contains some fine essays by major critical figures, but it does not do much to help us re-evaluate Lawrence's achievement in his major work. The essays are more solid and erudite than brilliant or seminal. Those pieces written by such eminent critics as Robert Langbaum, George P. Landow, and H. M. Daleski do not represent their best work. The most important contributions are Langbaum's 'Lawrence and Hardy', Roberts W. French's 'Whitman and the Poetics of Lawrence', and Kingsley Widmer's provocative and contentious essay, 'Lawrence and the Nietzschean Matrix'. But, in saying this, I do not mean to discredit the other four contributions, the most interesting of which are Landow's 'Lawrence and Ruskin: the Sage as Word-Painter', and Daleski's 'Lawrence and George Eliot: the Genesis of *The White Peacock*'.

It is worth noting that this volume lends some credence to Bloom's theory. For many of the contributors, Bloom becomes a critical father figure in matters of influence, and they contest him on grounds not dissimilar from the process – the anxiety of influence – that Bloom describes. But in these essays the contest with Bloom is a mild one, and Bloom's strong Freudian model is not really confronted. Except for Widmer, Lawrence's use of his predecessors is described not in terms of Bloom's *agons*, but in the distinctly muted tones of academic debates that would have made Lawrence smile with rancour.

Langbaum's excellent and often elegant piece draws lines between the expected dots. The dots were placed on the critical mindscape by Daleski who showed in *The Forked Flame* (1965) – the critical book which still towers over the landscape of Lawrence scholarship – how important 'Study of Thomas Hardy' was to *The Rainbow*. (A quibble: my reading of *The Rainbow*, especially the scene with Dr. Frankstone, makes me sceptical of Langbaum's claim that Lawrence is a 'Darwinian'.) Given Lawrence's Whitman essay in *Studies in Classic American Literature*, it is not surprising that French makes a compelling case for the Whitman influence on Lawrence's poetry. Yet, despite some admirable specificity, he often relies on scattered quotations to support generally accepted thematic generalizations ('As Whitman's statements make clear, his conception of sex went beyond male/female relationships to include all human relationships, homosexual [or homoerotic] as well as heterosexual' [p. 108]). Landow, whose book on Ruskin is of major importance, reminds us of Lawrence's position in the line of Victorian sages, while pointing out valuable similarities between Lawrence and Ruskin. Whether we read the major novels in the canon any differently now that we know about the Ruskin influence or parallel is moot, but the essay does help us to understand Lawrence's tone in such travel books as *Sea and Sardinia* and *Twilight in Italy*.

But although Daleski convincingly shows us that 'The White Peacock* may be read rewardingly as Lawrence's rewriting of *The Mill on the Floss*', is it possible for an essay that spends its energy on *The White Peacock* to be of much interest to any but the most devoted Laurentians (p. 53)? The virtue of the Daleski essay is that it alone of these essays presents a sustained examination of a Lawrence work and gives us a feeling of what it is like to live as a reader in a fictional world created by Lawrence. In contrast to Daleski's detailed argument, John Colmer's 'Lawrence and Blake' focuses on general similarities; but he does not really analyze the prophetic and vatic strain in Lawrence's voice in specific contexts. To be sure, he points out some important resemblances:

> A belief in the liberation of man and society through love and the wisdom of the body is common to both writers but it takes rather different forms in each. In Blake we do not find that emphasis on the preservation of separateness in love that is a major theme in Lawrence's novels, especially *Women in Love*.
>
> (p. 16–17)

What would give life and meaning to his generalizations would be a discussion of the Blakean strain in crucial passages of *The Rainbow*, say, the opening pages or the ending of the tenth chapter – the first of the two chapters entitled 'The Widening Circle'.

What I find encouraging in this volume is that it shows an interest in literary history and the history of ideas – an interest on which humanistic study must rest some of its claims. What is discouraging, however, is the failure to support arguments about influence with powerful and attentive readings of Lawrence's most significant fictional work. Such readings would give us more of a sense of Lawrence's originality as a creative artist whose medium is words.

Because in these essays close reading is often ostentatiously subordinated to sweeping generalizations, claims of parallels belong at times to a word-world, a word-world lacking specificity and the closely woven fabric of a lived process of reading and of coming to terms with complex literary works. While the use of what might be called a middle level of critical discourse shows how far we have come from the nominalism and occasional pedantry of old-fashioned source studies, I am concerned lest we stray from the necessary task of using our reading skills to discover evidence for our generalizations. For me this lack of rigour at times takes us close to what I call 'reminds me of' criticism – as in the locution 'x reminds me of Lawrence' or 'Lawrence reminds me of x'.

It is notable that in this volume the most striking Laurentian qualities are attributed to several different sources; these claims made by each contributor for the writer he pairs with Lawrence *remind* me a little of a poker game where each player raises the ante in the hopes that the other players will drop out before the cards are shown. Indeed, in some of these essays, the cards are never really shown. For example, depending on whom one is listening to, Lawrence's apocalyptic and prophetic vision as well as his delight in life and the natural world, comes from Whitman or Blake or Ruskin. Thus French writes:

> At the close of *Apocalypse*, at the close of his life, Lawrence gathers strength in the reassurance of Whitman's great prophetic message. In one last magnificent outpouring he sounds the essential themes: the mysterious beauty of life in a physical world; the joy of living, the mere being; the inescapable bonds of the human community; the merging of the one in the many; the organic relationships connecting all that exists, the smallest part with the greatest, each part with every other part.
>
> (p. 114)

But now let us turn to the concluding paragraph of the Colmer essay on 'Lawrence and Blake':

> [In Blake and Lawrence] there is the same combination of innocent eye and apocalyptic fervour, the same sense of being involved in a life and death struggle with mysterious forces within oneself and in the external world, the same vision of the polarities of existence that transcends the distinctions between good and evil, natural and supernatural, male and female; finally, the same firm grounding of the mystical and mythopoeic in the concrete world of physical sensation.
>
> (p. 20)

And Landow puts in his bid for Ruskin's importance to similar aspects of Lawrence, while Paul Delaney and Widmer respectively find 'apocalyptic fervour' in Carlyle and Nietzsche.

The reason the Hardy and Whitman essays are most compelling is that they are the writers who really engaged Lawrence's critical and intellectual attention and on whom he has written. The letters and non-fiction prose only sustain the impression that for figures like Ruskin and Carlyle there is not enough supporting evidence for the claims of significant influence. Except for Hardy and Whitman, the contributors need more factual evidence to establish that Lawrence engaged the writers who allegedly influenced him. Recently I reviewed *The Letters of D. H. Lawrence, Vol. III 1916–21.*[4] As the dates 1916–21 indicate, these letters were written at the height of Lawrence's intellectual and literary career. Yet I found little evidence in that volume that Lawrence lived within an intellectual and literary fabric of the kind that is explicitly claimed in these essays.

Meyers' introduction might have been more to the point had he differentiated between kinds of influence – between the major and primary influence of a Hardy, Lawrence's major mentor in English fiction, the strong 'misreading' of whose work hovers over his major achievements, and of the more intangible secondary or tertiary influence of a Carlyle. Notwithstanding Delaney's able essay, surely the difference in the importance of Hardy and Carlyle is so great that we are talking not merely of a difference of degree but of a difference of *kinds* of influence. (In a telling remark very early in Lawrence's career, he writes, 'I am suffering acutely from Carlyliophobia' [I. 47].) Reading these essays makes clear that the challenge of recent theory is not the only reason that we might need to reconsider the terms 'source', 'influence', 'tradition', and 'resemblance'; the various contributors and the editor disagree among themselves about the meaning of these terms.

The attribution of the same qualities to different sources begins to become iterative if not silly to the reader, and to give an unintended irony to Meyers' claim that his volume could have had chapters on Wordsworth, Byron, Keats, the Brontës, Dickens, 'Bennett and urban realism', Melville, 'Cooper and the American Indian', Stevenson, 'Edward Carpenter and homosexuality', 'Freud and German literature', 'Tolstoy and the idea of love', 'Verga and primitivism', and 'Renaissance and modern painting'. Such claims make us begin to wonder facetiously, 'What about

Machiavelli, Maimonides, and Marco Polo?' and to be reminded of Joyce's hilarious catalogues in 'Cyclops'.

Cumulatively, this book convinces me that we have done what we could to place Lawrence in the English tradition; my own view is that he resists this domestication, that he is something of an English primitive, and that he is more morbid, more eccentric, and less of an original *thinker* than we like to admit. But he is a more original *creative artist* than we dare acknowledge. For his daring imagination and brilliant and at times excessively figurative language speak to us in compelling ways, precisely because he was not only a powerful misreader but at times a virtual *non-reader* of his predecessors; by a non-reader, I mean a man whose egotism and obsessions enabled him to go beyond his contemporaries or predecessors into the vast uncharted lands – the unwritten white spaces of his imagination – that only true geniuses explore with success.

My guess is that in the next decade the kind of traditional influence study represented in Meyers' collection – based on the assumption that because A precedes B, and because A and B have similar ideas or have at times similar tones, A must in some way be the cause of B – will be complemented by studies of the interrelationships among the major writers of the period and how these writers simultaneously create and reflect their historical and cultural contexts. Rather than trying to cultivate the worked-over terrain of vertical influence studies, critical attention will turn to lateral and contiguous relations among writers and among their contemporaries in other arts and in far different fields. Thus we shall see Lawrence not only among the writers he most resembles, Yeats and Hardy (who actually died only two years before he did), but among those significant voices of his period with whom he seems most to differ, such as Joyce, Conrad, and T. S. Eliot. And we shall begin to think more seriously about the English modernist movement as part of the larger pattern of European modernism.

III THE USE OF LITERARY LETTERS

Dissatisfied with the shibboleth 'exit author' provided by the New Criticism, but unwilling to settle for naive correspondences between life and text, the more progressive strains of what I call humanistic formalism are seeking to develop an aesthetic that accommodates the authorial presence within a text. It is no longer self-evident that we commit an egregious critical *faux pas* – the dreaded biographical fallacy – when we use letters to establish a reading or to propose an argument about the writer's themes and values. As the concept of the author is challenged in different ways by deconstruction and Marxism, we must seriously consider the question of how we should use literary letters. What exactly do literary letters tell us? Should letters be regarded, like the author's literary works, as psychic and moral gestures of the author? Do they have the same 'textual' status as literary works? From a Marxist perspective, are letters, like literary works, the function of historical forces, or can they be regarded as more idiosyncratic and personal, and therefore less important for understanding the *Zeitgeist* than for understanding their author's uniqueness?

Letters, I think, should be regarded as another of the author's linguistic creations, albeit an individual letter is clearly a very minor performance in comparison to a literary work. Yet often letters not only reveal something about authors' psyches, views of anterior reality, and aesthetic theories, but may dramatically enact their quest to define the themes, values, and formal principles of their art. Letters may enable us to understand the very essence of the creative process. They may give us a perspective on a personal relationship that affected the creative process, although unless the letters of both participants in a correspondence are published, the letters are more like a series of monologues – and occasionally discontinuous ones at that – than a dialogue. Within the informal confines of letters, authors may work out their philosophic and aesthetic positions. If the recipient is a trusted friend, the letter gives the writer an opportunity to present an informal working paper. At times, letters also serve a therapeutic function. A letter can provide an opportunity to share – and even to transfer to a sympathetic other – frustrations and anxieties that interfere with creativity.

Put in contemporary terms, a *signified* presence is evoked by the letters; even if such a presence is never *fully* realized, it can be approached by sustained reading and study of the works, letters, and non-fiction. While deconstruction thinks of this presence as a mirage that continually recedes as we approach it, we should think of the authorial presence as something that we continually approach but never reach; this process resembles Zeno's paradox that we can never bisect our way across a room.

In the case of Lawrence, the letters have contributed to the contextual approach that has helped bring him into focus the past two decades. Beginning with H. M. Daleski's *The Forked Flame* (1965), Lawrence criticism has stressed that understanding the major novels requires knowledge of Lawrence's aesthetic ideas and grammar of passions (or love ethic). Undiluted if not always transparently logical or precise statements of his positions can be found in his letters and, in particular, his non-fiction prose, most notably 'Study of Thomas Hardy' and the diverse essays that make up both volumes of the *Phoenix* papers. In a major essay entitled 'The Marble and the Statue: the Exploratory Imagination of D. H. Lawrence' in the invaluable 1968 collection *Imagined Worlds*, edited by Maynard Mack and Ian Gregor, Mark Kinkead-Weekes demonstrates how *The Rainbow* and *Women in Love* reflect Lawrence's own passionate quest in his relationship with Frieda and how his personal values and his aesthetic values affected one another.

There can be no doubt that the ongoing publication of the seven-volume Cambridge edition of the letters is providing an invaluable resource not only to Lawrence scholars but to students of modern English literature and culture. It is another step towards bringing Lawrence scholarship to maturity; or, put somewhat more ironically, into domesticating the revolutionary, cantankerous voice of Lawrence into the polite world of academic manners. Taken together with the three-volume Lawrence biography that is being written for Cambridge University Press under the general editorship of Kinkead-Weekes – who, as I understand it, will write the middle volume and pull together the work of the three diverse hands, including his own, into a one-volume version – this elegant edition of Lawrence's letters continues the process of transforming Lawrence from an eccentric genius into a central canonical figure. And that process – along with a similar process that has taken place in the study of Joyce, Yeats, Conrad, Eliot, Woolf, and Forster – has given respectability and definition to a remarkable period in British literature. But of course respectability and definition are just what Lawrence wished to avoid and might have regretted as limiting and confining. (One recalls Lawrence's sympathy with Anna Brangwen's desperate need to escape the confining and claustrophobic Cathedral in the crucial chapter of that name in *The Rainbow*.)

Prior to the Cambridge edition, we had the very useful one-volume edition, *The Letters of D. H. Lawrence* (1932), edited by

Aldous Huxley and *The Collected Letters of D. H. Lawrence* (1962) edited by Harry Moore. While lacking in completeness, both collections enabled us to hear – often in a more provocative and often outrageous tone than the fiction, but also at times in more moving and poignant strains – the distinctive, sometimes prophetic voice of Lawrence. But with superb notes, careful editing, and an informative introduction, the three volumes of letters that have already been published are of a scholarly magnitude that makes Huxley's and Moore's volumes superannuated after long and useful lives. While admiring the scholarship of the editors and welcoming the necessary documentation for further study of Lawrence, we should not ignore the implications of what Lawrence is saying.

My focus will be on the most recently published volume of *The Letters of D. H. Lawrence – Vol. III 1916–21*.[5] At best, these letters demonstrate how Lawrence's personality is inseparable from his values and philosophy; thus in a rather provocative November 1916 letter to Forster where Lawrence seems to have created a hyperbolic, intemperate persona to annoy his understated, civilized, liberal, humanist correspondent, he bitterly asserts:

> People today want their senses gratified in art, but their *will* remains static all the time with the old, and they would rather die than face a conclusion out from the senses to the mind. There ought to be a flood to drown mankind, for there is no health in it, and certainly no *proud* courage. Plenty of the slave courage of death, but no proud courage of life, no independent soul anywhere. Lord, let there be a flood to drown them all. (#1303; beginning with the first volume, the letters in the Cambridge edition are numbered consecutively)

Interestingly, in this letter written following the suppression of *The Rainbow* – which ends with the strong use of the optative and optimistic rainbow image, representing God's Covenant to Noah that he will never again destroy the earth – Lawrence returns to an earlier phase of the Noah myth: 'The process of violent death will possess humanity for many a generation yet, till there are only a few remaining of all these hordes: a slow, slow flood of death will drown them all. I am glad, for they are too corrupt and cowardly' (ibid.). It would be just as much a mistake to overlook in this letter Lawrence's moral irresponsibility when he embraces violence as it would be to ignore his fascism in *Apocalypse*.

It is not unusual for the persona in the letters to be something of a querulous eccentric. He can be a misanthrope: 'To learn plainly to hate mankind, to detest the spawning human-being, that is the only cleanliness now' (#1455). He can be an anti-Semite: 'Best cease to be a Jew, and let Jewery disappear – much best' (#1442); 'I have a horror of the dreadful hosts of people, "with noses"' (#1729). Alas, on more than several occasions we hear the voice of a self-pitying, self-indulgent, and self-important crank: 'In fact I here and now, finally and forever leave off loving anything or everything or anybody' (#2228).

The letters in this volume include the vatic (and, one might say, hubristic) strain in Lawrence's fiction. Lawrence really believed that he could change the world. Writing of the essays that would become *Studies in Classic American Literature*, he remarks: 'Of course I think the world ought to hold up its hands in marvelling thankfulness for such profound and relieving exposition. And of course I see the world doing it' (#1542). But as the letters progress from 1916 to 1921, they become at times tediously concerned with publication details and money matters. On the one hand, Lawrence speaks of his weariness with materialism; but, on the other hand, the letters become increasingly concerned with economic matters.

As we read this volume as an evolving collection, Lawrence lurches from the most pedestrian details of his life and petty observations of others to grand conceptual theories, but rarely stops at the middle level of discourse which would integrate the fabric of details into his theoretical framework. Often we see minor details and sweeping generalizations within the same letter. In the early letters of this volume, occurring after the suppression of *The Rainbow* and the outbreak of the war, he oscillates between rage and between seeing himself as a prophetic *Übermensch* and seeing himself as an alienated, marginalized figure who has no place in English culture. Reading these letters confirms my view that it is very difficult to take Lawrence very seriously either as a political or moral philosopher or as a psychologist. He is to be valued because he invented a language and a fictional form to render our unconscious, biological, physiological, sexual, and passionate feelings – or, at least he made vast strides towards rendering those inarticulate aspects of ourselves. Do we not value Lawrence because within his best fiction and poetry his *performances* of the aforementioned aspects of human life touch our suppressed, inarticulate, and dimly acknowledged passions and feelings? But the reader of Boulton's and Robertson's introduction would hardly guess at the peculiar opinions, responses, and judgements that are within the letters that follow the introduction.

As we can see from a March 1921 letter, Lawrence's political views are at times not much more elegant than Pound's:

> As for binding men together in a new spirit of Internationalism, of which you speak in your letter, alas, I doubt it is no good trying that any more. The only active internationalism is the Soviet sort, the Moscow manifestoes. And these are dead against the internationalism of the cultured spirit.... League of Nations is as ridiculous as a poor vaudeville.... And when there is a mob unison – as between France and England, or between all socialists – it is now a unison founded on the low interests and the lowest passions of greed and spite.
>
> (#2181)

With characteristic bravura and belief in his own ability to envision the *real, real truth* behind the facade of surface reality, Lawrence asserts his views without providing evidence or even the appearance of logical argument. Lawrence is a Platonist who reads the text of the world according to a group of controlling principles: 'If you kill all tigers still the tiger-soul continues' (#2228). Yet before we become too smug and begin to consider Lawrence as a kind of political Grandma Moses, we should recall the grim fulfilment of at least one of his 1921 political prophecies: 'Italy is really pro-German: but is frightened. But she hates France and England deeply. The hate accumulates everywhere. It means war ahead: not love and peace' (#2181).

In several of the volume's most eloquent letters, the First World War plays the role of antagonist. But sometimes, as in the following November 1916 letter, it is also seen as a necessary purgative process within a cyclic theory of history in which the end will herald a new beginning. Lawrence has an ambivalent attitude to war, at once welcoming it as a precursor to, if not the fulfilment of, a necessary destruction and disliking it because of what it does to the passionate possibilities between man and woman:

> The whole crux of life now lies in the relation between man and woman, between Adam and Eve. In this relation we live or die. –

The soldier-spirit is fatal, fatal: it means an endless process of death. A man who has a living connection with a woman is, ipso facto, not a soldier, not an essential destroyer, but an essential creator.

(#1307)

This passage gives us another example of the prophetic strain in Lawrence's voice as well as of his hyperbolic and conceptual imagination. In many of the 1916 letters, we hear a voice that in its rhetorical bullying closely resembles the narrator of *Women in Love* and its protagonist, Birkin. Do we not hear that insistent, wilful, polemical, relentless voice which increasingly uses fiction as a pulpit? Thus, of Americans he writes, '[P]erhaps they are nearer to the end, and the new beginning.... America, being so much *worse*, falser, further gone than England, is nearer to freedom' (#1306). Indeed, he sees *Women in Love* as enacting this cyclical view of history: 'The book frightens me: it is so end-of-the-world. But it is, it must be, the beginning of a new world too' (ibid).

Even those of us who are familiar with Lawrence's basic 'philosophic' premises will have to concede that he often seems to occupy his own word-world. His style and voice depend upon excess – upon something other than mimesis – upon intratextual moments that define them. The logic of his letters does not stand much looking into. His language is usually metaphorical, and, indeed, long before Derrida and de Man, Lawrence taught us about how supposedly literal and objective language is really disguised figurative language.

It is characteristic of Lawrence's imagination to propose what I call a sacred reading of the world – that is, a reading which fits every perception into *a priori* categories. I use the term 'sacred' to imply a reading that mimes the unity and totality that earlier periods used to attribute to God's creation. By contrast, in its stress on momentary immersion in life and language and the nominalistic, disparate details of experience, realistic art (and we know from *Sons and Lovers* and the sexual scenes in *Lady Chatterley's Lover* that Lawrence can be a realist) offers what I call a profane reading of the world; such a reading stresses the gratuitous, serendipitious, incongruous nature of life. (A very different kind of profane reading – which occurs rarely in Lawrence – is interested in the free play of language as signifier rather than in its mimetic or signified potential.)

What is left out of this third volume of letters is often as revealing as what is included. For in the 1916–21 period, Lawrence is virtually oblivious to most of the literary and intellectual movements of the period, never even mentioning James, Joyce, T. S. Eliot, or Yeats and barely mentioning Conrad. Less surprisingly, he does not mention the major painters such as Picasso or Cézanne. While we find no mention of Nietzsche or Marx in the index, I did come across a passing reference in #2241 to Nietzsche. But this volume of letters certainly challenges the recent view, epitomized by Herzinger's *D. H. Lawrence in His Time: 1908–1915*, that Lawrence was less of a primitive and more of an intellectual than had been thought.

However, at their most interesting and eloquent, the collected letters are a threshing ground for Lawrence to test his ideas and fictional voice. They remind us that the author's quest for self-definition is a major theme in modern literature, particularly in Lawrence. They call attention to the need in Lawrence studies for an expressionist approach that shows how Lawrence's themes and techniques are related to his personal struggles. Lawrence used his letters, like his fiction, to recreate himself. For despite his seeming certainty, Lawrence's personal life was a quest for values and his artistic life was a quest for the appropriate aesthetic form to render those values. We might, in closing, recall that in a 1914 letter he wrote of *The Rainbow*: 'Now you will find [Frieda] and me in the novel, I think, and the work is of both of us' (#718).

IV READING LAWRENCE'S NON-FICTION: *STUDY OF THOMAS HARDY AND OTHER ESSAYS* AND *APOCALYPSE AND THE WRITINGS ON REVELATION*

In mid-1914, Lawrence agreed to write a short critical study of Hardy for the publisher James Nisbet and Co.; as the writing progressed and the focus changed, Lawrence soon began to think that the appropriate title for his unfinished work would be *Le Gai Savaire*. For 'Study of Thomas Hardy' developed into a quest to define – or perhaps we should say a performance of – Lawrence's philosophy. As Bruce Steele tells us in his introduction to the Cambridge edition of *Study of Thomas Hardy and Other Essays*:[6] 'Despite Lawrence's spelling "Savaire," which is neither modern French "savoir" nor a medieval dialect of French "savair," the meaning – The Gay Science (or Skill) – is clear' (p. xxxvi). Since it originally was published posthumously in *Phoenix* (1936) under the title 'Study of Thomas Hardy', Steele has rightly decided to use both titles.

In his major study *The Forked Flame* (1965), H. M. Daleski first realized the vast importance of Lawrence's idiosyncratic, digressive, but intermittently brilliant and compelling book-length essay 'Study Of Thomas Hardy' for understanding Lawrence's major novels, particularly *The Rainbow*:

> The most striking feature of Lawrence's *Weltanshaung* is its dualism; and in the essay on Hardy Lawrence sets out his concept of duality in terms of the 'male' and 'female' principles, insisting that all creativity is dependent on the fruitful interaction of the two principles.... Lawrence, though believing intensely in himself as a male, was fundamentally identified with the female principle as he himself defines it in the essay on Hardy.
>
> (Daleski, p. 13)

Daleski extrapolated from the 'Study' crucial concepts of Lawrence's dualism:

> The male principle is almost exactly coextensive with all that Lawrence spent most of his life fighting against: abstraction, idealism, what he called, generically, the 'mental consciousness'; and conversely (and of course paradoxically), the female principle comes close to subsuming what he termed the 'phallic consciousness,' which he fiercely espoused.
>
> (Daleski, p. 35)

Steele's scholarly apparatus and editing skills are typical of the high order of erudition that to date have marked the ongoing publication of the authoritative Cambridge edition of the Letters and Works of D. H. Lawrence. In his introduction, he provides a history of the text as well as some important contextual information, including a brief discussion of how in 'Study of Thomas Hardy' Lawrence is responding to both Lascelles Abercrombie's *Thomas Hardy: a Critical Study* (1912) and to Futurism. In keeping with the scrupulous resistance to making any critical or speculative comment that typifies the Cambridge edition, Steele does not discuss the relation of the works in this volume to the rest of the

Lawrence canon or show any familiarity with the critical issues that are central to reading Lawrence – his highly metaphorical and extravagant language, his prophetic tone, and his conception of character as a function of unconscious passionate and physiological needs rather than as a function of conscious motives and processes of reason. To be sure, because the Cambridge edition is written to survive critical fashions, this diffidence about speculation is not unbecoming; yet a demure approach to such a bold, high-spirited, digressive work as 'Study of Thomas Hardy' seems to miss the very point of Lawrence as a rebellious, contentious, experimental figure.

According to Steele, Lawrence later completed a now lost philosophic text from the work which began its life as the little book on Hardy. But we must regard what we have as a work in progress, as part of the quest for values and ideas of what Mark Kinkead-Weekes has called Lawrence's 'exploratory imagination'. 'Study of Thomas Hardy' is a threshing ground for Lawrence's ideas about relationships and passions. We should think of the 'Study' as an exploratory canvas rather than as a finished project; it bears the relation to *The Rainbow* that sketches bear to finished oil paintings. Lawrence is a strong misreader of Hardy, but his responses to Hardy's work enabled him to discover and refine the love ethic – or what I call the grammar of passions – in *The Rainbow*. Rereading 'Study', do we not feel that its prophetic voice, its hyperbolic language, its use of writing as performance and quest are aspects of the artistry of *The Rainbow* – aspects that are usually but not always controlled by the formal demands of that masterwork?

If one reads the first chapter of 'Study' expecting to learn anything about Thomas Hardy, one will be disappointed. But as a conceptual probing of ideas that are important for understanding *The Rainbow*, the 'Study' is significant. In the first chapter we read: chapter we read:

> The final aim of every living thing, creature, or being is the full achievement of itself.... Not the fruit, however, but the flower is the culmination and climax, the degree to be striven for. Not the work I shall produce, but the real Me I shall achieve, that is the consideration; of the complete Me will come the complete fruit of me, the work, the children.

(pp. 12–13)

Such a passage makes more sense if we remember the urgency to Lawrence of the mechanism-vitalism debate and his desire to part company with the Social Darwinists; recall the caricature of Dr. Frankstone, the female biologist, in *The Rainbow* who thinks that she can reduce everything to stimulus–response. (Does not her name deliberately echo Frankenstein's?) By contrast, Lawrence is arguing that every living thing, including 'the common wild poppy', has a life force, an energy, which will resist analyses. When at the end of *The Rainbow*, Lawrence takes the worst case – the men of Wiggiston – and has Ursula join with his prophetic voice in imagining them bursting forth with new life, we might recall what he says of the poppy in 'Study': 'The common wild poppy', has a life force, an energy, which will resist analysis. uncovered its red. Its light, its self, has risen and shone out, has run on the winds for a moment. It is splendid' (p. 13). And 'Study of Thomas Hardy' helps us to understand what he means by the union of two strong figures, each of whom is independent in himself or herself:

> When there is any union of male and female, there is no goal of abstraction: the abstract is used in place, as a means of a real union. The goal of the male impulse is the announcement of motion, endless motion, endless diversity, endless change. The goal of the female impulse is the announcement of infinite oneness, of infinite stability. When the two are working in combination, as they must in life, there is, as it were, a dual motion, centrifugal for the male, fleeing abroad, away from the centre, outward to infinite vibration, and centripetal for the female, fleeing in to the eternal centre of rest.
>
> (p. 69)

Yet it is well to remember that in *The Rainbow* the perfect union is an unreachable goal, a deferred presence that is at odds with the often pedestrian demands of actual living.

Lawrence's reading of Hardy and, in particular, of *Jude the Obscure* in terms of his values is very much in the current vogue of textuality where the 'text' is conceived as a nodal point for the intersection for all the reader's prior reading experience. For Lawrence responds to Hardy's characters not in terms of Hardy's realized intention as it appears in his works and as it is conveyed to his readers, but as an enabling condition – a kind of literary catalyst – for his own creative efforts. Does he not see Sue Bridehead as a female precursor of Skrebensky?:

> Jude's marriage with Sue was over before he knew her physically. She had, physically, nothing to give him. Which in her deepest instinct, she knew.... She was unhappy every moment of her life, poor Sue, with the knowledge of her own non-existence within life. She felt all the time the ghastly sickness of dissolution upon her, she was a void unto herself.
>
> (p. 113–14)

And he probably has Lydia in mind when he writes of Arabella: 'She takes him, and is gratified by him. Which makes a man of him' (p. 105). (Hardy specialists may be in the forefront of those who will regret the lack of an index which efficiently directs them to the provocative comments about aspects of their subject; but they will not be alone in wishing that Steele had provided an index for the entire volume.)

It may be that deconstruction is proposing an ideology of reading that will give a work such as 'Study of Thomas Hardy' new life. Traditional humanistic criticism – with its emphasis on accepted genres, organic unity, a controlled and often ironic voice, and its assumption that language is grounded in an anterior world – has little place for a work like 'Study'. Thus, from the perspective of humanistic criticism, 'Study' has been thought of as an awkward, if not bizarre work that one tastes and samples but reads through only if one is pursuing a Lawrence project. Perhaps with its blurring of traditional genres, its disregard for formal argument, its vatic tone, its privileging of the critic's voice over the author's, its implicit acknowledgement that a text need not necessarily be read or organized linearly, and its tendency to fuse one 'text' onto another (as Lawrence does not only with Hardy's novels but with his impressions of Renaissance painters and sculptors), 'Study of Thomas Hardy' may arouse new interest. It is the kind of marginal text that deconstruction likes to address; in its rapid movement, its disdain of traditional argument, its sweeping generalizations without supporting evidence, does not 'Study of Thomas Hardy' – as in the following vatic pronouncement – resemble some of deconstruction's own texts? 'In the degree of pure maleness below Shelley are Plato and Raphael and Wordsworth, then Goethe and Milton and Dante, then Michael Angelo, then Shakespeare, then Tolstoi, then St. Paul' (p. 71).

This volume includes a number of other essays, the most interesting and eloquent of which is 'Why the Novel Matters' (1925; first published in *Phoenix*) and 'Morality and the Novel' (1925; first published in the December, 1925 issue of the *Calendar of Modern Letters*). While not as strikingly original or conceptually challenging, these shorter essays do have the virtue of being of an appropriate length for a non-specialist reader to respond to Lawrence's odd combination of heavily metaphorical language, repetitiousness, and polemical and prophetic tone. In 'Morality and the Novel' Lawrence places himself in the Romantic tradition and turns traditional notions of morality on their heads when he writes: 'Morality is that delicate, forever trembling and changing *balance* between me and my circumambient universe, which precedes and accompanies a true relatedness' (p. 172). As Margot Norris has written in her important recent study *Beasts of the Modern Imagination* (1985), Lawrence is part of a 'biocentric tradition' (along with such diverse figures as Nietzsche, Kafka, and Max Ernst) that subverts 'the anthropocentric premises of Western philosophy and art' and invents 'artistic and philosophic strategies that would allow the animal, the unconscious, the instincts, the body to speak again in their work' (Norris, p. 5).

In 'Why the Novel Matters' Lawrence writes, 'The novel is the one bright book of life. Books are not life. They are only tremulations on the ether. But the novel as a tremulation *can* make the whole man-alive tremble. Which is more than poetry, philosophy, science or any other book-tremulation can do' (p. 195). He also explains (performs?) why he needed to rewrite the Bible in such diverse works as *The Rainbow* and *The Man Who Died* (1929; it was originally published under the title *The Escaped Cock*): 'The novel is the book of life. In this sense, the Bible is a great confused novel. You may say, it is about God. But it is really about man-alive.... Even the Lord is another man-alive, in a burning bush, throwing the tablets of stone at Moses' head' (p. 195). In a sense, Lawrence spent his life trying to write a body of fiction – a New New Testament – which would undermine the Christian hierarchy of values, a hierarchy that privileges mind over body, chastity over sexual gratification, reason over passion, and community over individual self-fulfilment.

Let us briefly turn to another volume of the Cambridge edition, *Apocalypse and the Writings on Revelation* (1980) edited by Mara Kalnins. Published posthumously and inaccurately, *Apocalypse* grew out of what was originally intended as an introduction to *The Dragon of Apocalypse* by Frederick Carter. Lawrence's non-conformist upbringing made the Bible a living and intimate part of his imagination. Only a man steeped in Christianity could compose such apostate visions as *The Rainbow* and *The Man Who Died*; only former believers could disbelieve with the imaginative intensity that Hardy, Lawrence, and Joyce did. Kalnins' judicious introduction presents the history of the book's development and a brief discussion of the ideas and values which occupied Lawrence's attention. Yet I would have found the introduction and, indeed, the explanatory notes more compelling had they related *Apocalypse* to the later fiction and to Lawrence's prior prophetic books with which it has striking parallels. For example, when Kalnins speaks of *Revelation* as 'the revelation of the undying will-to-power in man, and its sanctification, its final triumph' (p. 67), don't we need a reference to specific passages in 'Study of Thomas Hardy' as well as a brief discussion of this theme in the novels? After all, a minor work like *Apocalypse* does not exist in a vacuum, and its interest depends on the light it throws on the canon.

Since, like 'Study of Thomas Hardy', *Apocalypse* has limited value as imaginative literature, it has been read mostly by Lawrence specialists. But it is revealing about Lawrence's authoritarian temper and his hostile attitude to democracy. Nor is it to the credit of humanistic scholarship to ignore the implications of his disreputable ideas, as Kalnins seems to do:

> Lawrence's distinction between 'aristocrat' and 'democrat' does not involve any of the undertones of authoritarianism or of what, since Mussolini coined the word for us, we have loosely termed 'fascism.' Lawrence's view of man is deeper; it is not political but spiritual, not a denial of men's individuality but a confirmation of it based on an acceptance of the innate and inexplicable differences between men.
>
> (p. 23)

Lawrence does not require hagiographers, and we should admit that, beginning with *Women in Love*, if not *The Rainbow*, there is often something unpleasant in the implication that some people are inherently superior to others and should be acknowledged as such. In *Apocalypse* itself Lawrence writes, '[I]f the weak are not ruled, they will rule, and there's end of it. And the rule of the weak is *Down with the strong'* (p. 65). Is this the 'acceptance' of the 'differences between men'? Or this: '[t]he democracy of thou-shalt-not is bound to be a collection of weak men. And then the sacred "will of the people" becomes blinder, baser, colder, and more dangerous than the will of any tyrant' (p. 72)? Unless we have historical amnesia, we know that in the context of the late 1920s and the early 1930s Lawrence's writing lent support to those advocating totalitarian regimes. One need not be a devout liberal to object to the following bogus Russian history that provides a rationale for dictatorship: '[E]very peasant was consummated in the old dash and gorgeousness of the nobles, and in the supreme splendour of the Tsar. The supreme master, and lord and splendid one: their own...' (p. 71).

It is appropriate to consider the question of the potential importance and usefulness of eccentric works of non-fiction that few readers besides Lawrence specialists will read from start to finish and only then for the clues they yield about his philosophy. While one can argue that letters reveal an anterior reality in which the author lived and thus can be somewhat privileged as more real than fiction if only because they usually were meant to define something that seemed true to the writer, can we make the same claims for a writer's non-fiction – particularly works which eschew conventional expository and discursive methods? Wilde (*De Profundis*), Yeats (*A Vision*), and Lawrence wrote what might be called fictional non-fiction that expressed their visions and philosophies. These works not only have to do with presenting what most of us would regard as an anterior world, but use techniques which are more performative than mimetic. But these literary oddities provide imaginative evidence to complement and qualify what we know from the fiction, even if they can make no pretenses to contribute to a factual understanding of the historical contexts in which the writer wrote. Yet, because these eccentric works are moral and psychological gestures of the author whose presence defines the imagined space of the fictional world, we must take them seriously. Certainly, in Lawrence's case they are very much part of his effort to define himself through his writing. In their very metaphoricity and hyperbole, in their emphasis on process not stasis, in their vatic tone and extravagant self-dramatization, do not the essays in the volume under review point both toward the fictional works and to the creative presence that informs them?

IV THE USE AND ABUSE OF LITERARY BIOGRAPHY

The study of the major British modernists is becoming one of the most fruitful fields for the kind of literary criticism that imaginatively and creatively takes advantage of the work of literary scholarship. This trend is all the more striking when one recalls that in the forties, fifties, and even sixties among the texts that the New Criticism privileged in its efforts to establish the credentials of their supposed objective methodology were the poems of Eliot and Yeats as well as the fiction of Conrad and Joyce. In this section I should like to compare Zdzislaw Najder's successful literary biography of Conrad with Ross Parmenter's rather unsuccessful one on a brief period of Lawrence's life. I might have discussed Robert Gittings' two-volume re-evaluation of Thomas Hardy, which is more of a traditional biography and less of a literary biography – a genre that assumes literary works mime the author's life. What we miss in Gittings is a complex understanding of how Hardy's imagination works as it transforms fact into fiction, and why he draws repeatedly on the same incidents and discards so much other seemingly crucial life experience.

Najder's authoritative study *Joseph Conrad: a Chronicle*[7] is a significant contribution to the study not only of Conrad but of literary modernism. It is part of an important scholarly development that in the past two decades or so has been providing historical and biographical grounding for modern studies. Stimulated by Ellmann's work on Joyce and Yeats, the publication of biographies, scrupulous editions, letters, diaries, journals, and non-fiction gradually have discredited the critical shibboleth 'Exit Author' that dominated modernist studies well into the 1960s.

Modern biographers often have such a wealth of factual material, sometimes including enormous quantities of letters, that they must decide whether to stress – as a novelist would – the pattern of significant turning points and crystallizing events, or whether to try to recreate the life in all its diurnal detail, variety, and richness. In the first method, practised by Samuel Johnson and Lytton Strachey, the author selects every episode and fact to reveal a significant form to the subject's life as if the subject were a major character in a novel; the biography becomes a metaphor or an allegory of the life. In the second method, anticipated by James Boswell in his *Life of Johnson*, the author seeks to be as inclusive as possible. He is a nominalist, believing that the details, friendships, and backgrounds of life accumulate to represent a full, multidimensional portrait.

Like Ellmann's *Joyce* and Painter's *Proust*, Najder combines the best of both methods. It does not discredit the important contributions of the other two major biographies of Conrad, Jocelyn Baines's *Joseph Conrad: a Critical Biography* (1960) and Frederick Karl's *Joseph Conrad: the Three Lives* (1979), to say that Najder's book far surpasses those works. A Pole who himself recently followed Conrad into exile, Najder's work, especially his invaluable *Conrad's Polish Background: Letters to and from Polish Friends* (1964), has long been respected by Conradians. An earlier and mostly similar version of the book under review was published in Polish in 1977 – two years before, Najder reminds us, the publication of Karl's book. Najder and Karl continue the process begun by Baines of correcting the simplified romantic view of Conrad that he himself created in his non-fiction, especially *The Mirror of The Sea* and *A Personal Record*, and which Richard Curle and G. Jean-Aubry perpetuated in early biographies.

Avoiding the kind of psychological speculation that informs Karl's study and the far more egregious Bernard Meyer's *Joseph Conrad: a Psychoanalytic Biography* (1967), Najder separates biography from criticism and focuses on factual material. With a minimum of jargon, he brilliantly discusses Conrad's private personality and psyche, including his recurring depression. As he puts it, a literary biographer:

> establishes the meaning of signs used by the given author by pointing not only at his intentions but, much more important, at his cultural background and resources. The biographer's textual function does not essentially consist in explaining private allusions or subconsciously used codes but in identifying the scope within which we can define the meanings of words, images, and conventions employed.
>
> (p. vii)

Rather than, as Karl sometimes does, presenting a smorgasbord of everything he knows, Najder selects and arranges his material into tautly argued chapters about the causes and effects of Conrad's behaviour.

Najder's first chapter on Conrad's Polish background and influences convincingly and efficiently defines the revolutionary,

romantic, and literary influence of his father, Apollo Korzeniowski, and contrasts that influence with the role of his rationalistic,
practical, and reserved uncle, Tadeusz Bobrowski, who became
Conrad's surrogate father after Apollo's death in 1869 when
Conrad was twelve. Since all biographies contain some element of
disguised autobiography, should we not see in Najder's extremely
sympathetic treatment of the idealistic but apparently impractical
if not otherworldly Apollo an understandable attempt on Najder's
part to place himself and the recent history of Solidarity in the
tradition of Apollo Korzeniowski? Thus he writes: 'What literature
and politics were to Apollo, laws, regulations, and accounts were
to Tadeusz' (p. 29). His discussion of the *szlachta*, the Polish ruling
class to which Conrad's family on both sides belonged, helps
explain Conrad's cultural heritage and fastidious pride: 'Polish
szlachta and Polish intelligentsia were social strata in which
reputation, one's evaluation by one's own milieu, was felt to be
very important, even essential for one's feeling of self-worth' (p.
38). In the splendid second chapter, Najder's discussion of
Conrad's 1874–78 Marseilles years, including his attempted
suicide, judiciously separates fact from fiction; in particular, he
shows the folly of reading *The Arrow of Gold* as disguised
autobiography. His mastery of Conrad's maritime career enables
us to understand how Conrad's imagination and psyche work to
reshape the factual origins of his sea tales.

Meticulously researched, elegantly argued, and masterfully
organized, Najder's biography of Conrad should remain, notwithstanding the long-awaited publication by Cambridge University
Press of the collected letters of Conrad, the definitive biography
for decades to come.

In recent years, Lawrence scholarship has probed into every
nook and cranny of Lawrence's life. Two biographies – Leo
Hamalian's *D. H. Lawrence in Italy* and Jeffrey Meyers' *D. H.
Lawrence and the Experience of Italy*[8] – addressed his periods of
residence in Italy: September 1912–June 1914; November 1919–
February 1922; September 1922–June 1929. The assumptions of
these studies seem to be that *all* the personal experiences of writers
are important for understanding their works, as if in some
mysterious way the authors' creative imaginations draw on every
aspect of *their* life. (To be fair, Meyers is more critically sophisticated than Hamalian.)

In his *Lawrence in Oaxaca: A Quest for the Novelist in Mexico*,[9] Ross

Parmenter has taken as his subject Lawrence's 1924–25 sojourn in Oaxaca, Mexico, and has written an incredibly detailed, chatty, and digressive study of over 400 pages about a period that lasted a little more than three months. To be sure, during those months Lawrence not only wrote four of the pieces in *Mornings in Mexico* and rewrote *The Plumed Serpent*, but suffered in January 1925 a serious illness.

A retired former music editor of *The New York Times*, Parmenter has been living in Oaxaca since 1965. Reading between the lines of his justification for writing this study, I suspect that not too many figures whose lives would be of interest to an English reading audience have lived in Oaxaca: 'It was fortunate that the Lawrence chapter I wanted to write for love of Oaxaca had validity as a biographical unit' (p. 346). While Parmenter's interviews of people who were living in Oaxaca during that period some sixty years ago may at times, I am afraid, recall the Woody Allen movie *Zelig*, his major resource is Lawrence's own words from his fiction, letters, and non-fiction as well as the written testimony of the two women who accompanied him to Oaxaca, Frieda and Dorothy Brett.

To his credit, Parmenter has a real interest in his subject and avoids jargon. He can tell a story, has read Lawrence carefully, and has done some serious research. But that is not enough to rescue this prolonged and repetitious book from being consigned to the margins of Lawrence study. Perhaps the best way to give the flavour of Parmenter's idiosyncratic volume is to quote the entire dedication: 'To the memory of Luisa Linder de Martinez (1894–1984) creator and animator of the Pension Suiza in Oaxaca within whose sheltering tranquility this book was written.'

Parmenter's premise is that he has discovered an exciting and neglected chapter in the life of one of the more flamboyant writers of the twentieth century. He oscillates between addressing a general audience and a scholarly audience who would be interested in the minor tributaries of Lawrence's literary career. Parmenter's focus shifts uneasily from writing about Lawrence to writing about the history and current life of Oaxaca, including his own responses to the practices and customs of that city. After quoting a letter of Brett's, Parmenter writes: 'Meanwhile, any one who has enjoyed the friendliness and quick understanding of the vendors and appeal of their big-eyed children will recognize how precisely Brett caught elements that make marketing such a pleasure in Oaxaca' (p. 47). Or, he writes: 'I have often wished

Lawrence had seen and described the ancient ritual dance' (p. 223). Often Parmenter writes in a journalistic style as if he were addressing an audience of non-professional readers who would care how accurate Lawrence's descriptions of local customs were. But will he find such an audience when much of his book depends in part at least on knowledge of Lawrence works which are not widely read? Certainly, the chapter on *The Plumed Serpent* would make far more sense to someone who has read the novel.

Parmenter's other putative audience – the one composed of Lawrence specialists – may find superfluous Parmenter's interest in Oaxaca for its own sake; his ingenuous first person intrusions, including tedious narrative accounts of how he came upon evidence in the University of Texas library ('I asked to see the tray of index cards for the library's manuscripts. When I got to the M's my eyes popped' [p. 228]); and the interviews with those who knew Lawrence almost sixty years ago.

Since I have always been troubled by Lawrence's misanthropy, anti-Semitism, and penchant for violent political solutions, I am somewhat sceptical of Parmenter's hagiography of Lawrence as a human being: 'Surely few men have walked the earth with such intense aspiration towards goodness. . . . He was a great and good man' (p. 346). Indeed, as Parmenter himself notes of *The Plumed Serpent*, 'Lawrence's own moral scheme put him on the side of his repellent protagonists' (p. 302). While he finds 'Huitzilopochtli's Night' – the chapter in *The Plumed Serpent* in which Ramon and Cipriano preside over ritual murder – a 'stumbling-block', before concluding that '*The Plumed Serpent* emerges high among the novels of its period, high even among the novels of Lawrence', I believe that Lawrence veers into a sociopathic fascist vision where self-proclaimed *Übermenschem* are allowed to let their atavistic psyches roam free (p. 304).

Parmenter obviously enjoyed writing the book, and his enjoyment sometimes is enough to rescue it from a tedious read – provided that one is such a committed Laurentian that every crumb of new evidence is scholarly manna, and that one enjoys rereading quotations from Lawrence's letters, non-fiction, and fiction and from Frieda's and Brett's reminiscences. While not being a charter member of this group, my strong interest in Lawrence's artistic achievement makes me something of a fellow traveller. From a critical perspective, this book is an unsophisticated performance. Parmenter naively quotes from fiction as if novels and stories were autobiographical documents; for example, he can write: 'Lawrence's own beliefs about marital fidelity are embodied in one of the new sections he wrote in *The Plumed Serpent* in Oaxaca' (p. 266); he then proceeds to quote what he takes as the crucial paragraph. Nor does he consider the theoretical questions involved in a project that assumes a one-to-one correlation between life and art. To test Lawrence – who writes in a metaphorical mode even when he pretends to be writing literally – by the standards of factual accuracy is itself a task of dubious interest. I am not sure that Laurentians require a paragraph on the local custom of eating boiled grasshoppers to correct Lawrence's remark in a letter about the natives eating 'squashed fried locust-beetles' (p. 46).

It ought to be high on the agenda of humanistic formalism to define how we can speak about the presence of the author within the form of a literary work. The interest of literary biography depends in part upon the assumption that literature is in some way mimetic of the author's life. The great literary biographies such as the monumental work of Leon Edel on James or Richard Ellmann on Joyce have a significant form; they rhetorically urge us to see the relationship between life and art and implicitly convince us that what is included in their studies is based on a process of selection and arrangement of those life events that were crucial in shaping their subject's art. By contrast, one major problem of Parmenter's book is its excess of information and explanation; put another way, its combination of travelogue, reminiscence, and biography does not cohere into a taut, efficient significant form. To fulfil the needs of all but the most compulsive Laurentian, *Lawrence in Oaxaca* could be condensed into a chapter or at most a monograph of less than half its length. It will certainly not change the way we read Lawrence's fiction.

Although virtually every aspect of Lawrence's life and art seems to have been given microscopic examination, the fact remains that it has been a good while since we have had a major critical study which forces us to reconsider our basic assumptions about Lawrence's fiction. On the whole, Lawrence criticism has not been seriously touched by the deconstructive ethos or the more progressive strains of what I call humanistic formalism.

V PHENOMENOLOGICAL CRITICISM; THE ROAD NOT TAKEN

We might recall that in the feisty days of the late 1960s and early 1970s, when it seemed in some major literature departments as if intellectual and political revolution was never more than a few insights away, phenomenology became an appealing course on the critical menu. It was perceived as an antidote to the logical positivism and pretenses to objectivity of the New Criticism and Chicago Neo-Aristotelianism. It urged that we understand both the author's encounter with his experience and the reader's encounter with the text in terms of an epiphanic revelation which dissolves the distinction between 'I know' and 'I have seen'.

According to phenomenological criticism, just as the author must efface his ego to confront the world, so must the reader surrender his ego; he must achieve something akin to negative capability in order to enter into the privileged world of the author's consciousness or *cogito* and thus be able to read with understanding and sensitivity. The literary text becomes the mediating agency between the subjective interior world of the reader and the privileged vision of the author. In the reader's search for the *real, true* artist beyond the surface reality in the work, do we not see an unintentional parody of the True Believer's search for the Holy Spirit? Indeed, is not the reader perceived as a kind of acolyte to the author?

It was J. Hillis Miller who, after coming into contact with Georges Poulet at Johns Hopkins, was most responsible for importing phenomenology into the Anglo-American critical tradition. He adopted phenomenology as his dominant critical approach in such influential studies as *The Disappearance of God* (1963), *Poets of Reality* (1965), and *Thomas Hardy: Distance and Desire* (1970). Poulet describes how in a room full of Tinterettos, he discovers 'the common essence present in all the works of a great master, an essence which I was not able to perceive, except when emptying my mind of all the particular images created by the artist. I became aware of a subjective power at work in all these pictures and yet never so clearly as when I had forgotten all their particular configurations'.[10] Similarly, Hillis Miller focused not on discovering the form and meaning of individual works, but on defining the common consciousness or *cogito* that informed the writer's canon.

Hillis Miller, Edward Said, and their followers moved on to less subjective and more methodologically rigorous kinds of criticism such as structuralism, post-structuralism, deconstruction, and semiotics. But for a small number of talented scholars, including Bruce Johnson and Philip Weinstein, phenomenology still occupies the central position in the critical firmament. Thus we shall briefly examine Johnson's *True Correspondence: a Phenomenology of Thomas Hardy's Novels* and Philip M. Weinstein's *The Semantics of Desire: Changing Models of Identity from Dickens to Joyce.*[11]

A major impetus for Poulet and his followers was Edmund Husserl. According to Johnson's introduction, we should understand Husserl and Hardy as early moderns who shared a common epistemology:

> My sense ... is that both Husserl and Hardy emerge from late-Victorian contexts that, for whatever reason, encourage a 'primordial form of apprehension,' a new humility allowing glimpses under the 'nets' of theory and preconception, and that the best phenomenological approach to Hardy is precisely a reconstruction of those original contexts and of that original spirit shared by both men.... For Hardy, as for Husserl, the modern world seemed to demand new ways of perceiving that were most new because most primordial.
>
> (pp. 2–3)

I suspect that a good many people who pick up a book on Thomas Hardy will have no earthly idea what Johnson is talking about when he plunges into Husserl's *Ideen zu einer reinen Phänomenologie und phänomenologischen Philosophie* and quotes a few translated phrases without providing either an explanatory context or a passage sufficiently long to clarify Husserl's argument.

A querulous reader might complain that for the most part Johnson's introduction belongs to a book that he has not yet written. For he really does not fulfil his promise to examine the common 'late-Victorian, early modern phenomenological bias' shared by Husserl and Hardy, or show how Husserl's *Ideas* 'cries out for interpretation as a period piece, as an eloquent cultural artifact more expressive of 1913 ... than many an Edwardian novel or Futurist painting' (pp. 3, 1). Indeed, Husserl, who seems so central to the argument in the introduction, only appears twice more in passing.

But such criticism of Johnson's provocative and insightful book would not do justice to his considerable success in placing Hardy in the context of his intellectual milieu. At his best, Johnson presents important historical material about the world in which Hardy wrote and to which his fiction responded. He recreates the ontology of each of the major Hardy novels and some of the crucial ingredients of Hardy's consciousness that shaped that ontology. Thus, building on David DeLaura's argument that Angel in *Tess* is associated with Matthew Arnold, he writes: 'Angel, in short, is deliberately set up as a possible answer to the ache of modernism, and he fails utterly, whatever combination of intellectual positions of the seventies and eighties he may be seen to represent' (p. 112). Johnson demonstrates that Hardy's work depends upon a dialogue between the pastoral world of his imagination and the post-Darwinian modern world which he inhabited. Johnson is particularly astute on the biological and evolutionary contexts, especially Hardy's response to Darwin. Building on the argument of Elliot B. Gose, Jr.,[12] he convincingly argues for the importance of 'the impact of Darwin and the comparative and evolutionary anthropologists' not only on *Tess* but on the entire Hardy canon (p. 115). By making good use of Hardy's *Literary Notes*, he establishes how Hardy 'comes to the *The Return of the Native* full of recent anthropological orientations and queries and that foremost in his mind is the issue of survivals so important to Tylor's *Primitive Culture*' (p. 64).

That Johnson, author of the important study *Conrad's Models of Mind*, is working towards a phenomenology of the early modern period in England is demonstrated by the frequent comparisons of Hardy and his world to that of the contemporaries of his later years, especially Conrad and Lawrence. Indeed, one regrets that he did not write at least one chapter, perhaps a concluding one, on that subject because the discrete comparisons scattered throughout the text do not add up to a substantive evolving argument. Typical is the following one sentence aside when discussing the visual effect of 'the snow-filled dusk of Fanny's visit' in *Far from the Madding Crowd*: 'Although this may be only a good description of a particularly turgid night, I suspect Hardy is frightening himself in the manner of Joseph Conrad, whose characters often find themselves in fogs where all distinctions drop away to produce a primitive apprehension of the world laid naked' (p. 24). Do we not need further discussion about how these two figures 'frighten' themselves? Sometimes the brief discussions of other writers are splendid, but on occasion they are digressive and forced; for example, amidst a convincing discussion of Hardy's use of the past and his 'diachronic sense of man's identity', Johnson introduces a laboured contrast of Hardy's sense of the past to that of T. S. Eliot (p. 66).

Johnson's critical agenda includes presenting an alternative to what he believes is the pretense of objectivity claimed by the New Criticism. Thus he announces in the second paragraph: '[T]he phenomenological method can be seen as the last passionate defense of pure subjectivity against the deluge of logical positivism' (p. 1). What appeals to Johnson is the subjectivity of phenomenology – its insistence on understanding the author's encounter with his experience and the reader's encounter with the text in terms of an epiphanic revelation which dissolves the distinction between 'I know' and 'I have seen'.

Johnson's interest in Hardy derives in part from his conviction that Hardy, too, would have disliked logical positivism and the New Criticism. Thus he writes of *The Return of the Native*, '[Meaning], however, is a quasi-rational term that we need not impose on the obvious [involvement] of these people in the great symbolic cycles and rhythms of existence that make Clym's high thinking seem the most arrogant presumption' (p. 67). At times Johnson presents his own subjective responses and speaks of his own feelings and impressions as if to call attention to his lack of pretensions toward objectivity: 'The descriptions of early mornings at the dairy reinforce my feeling that Angel makes of Tess something that she simply is not' (p. 107). He contends that his reading of Hardy recreates the essence of Hardy's response to his experience and the world. But, despite his claims to the contrary, he is often applying his 'own version of phenomenology to Hardy' rather than recreating the phenomenology that he claims Hardy and Husserl share (p. 3).

If Johnson's method is to be taken as an enactment of his ideology of reading, he is arguing that the reader's 'primordial' response must be educated by a strong sense of the historical milieu and the literary culture in which the author wrote. Johnson's approach is vulnerable to objections from both sides of the critical mindscape. On one hand, more recent theory can take issue with him on the grounds that he is relying on a metaphysics of presence and pursuing an identity that is always deferred. I suspect that, much to his chagrin, post-structuralists will consign him to the group of old-fashioned humanists who are less interested in language than the values implied by a novel and the psychology of its personae. On the other hand, more traditional formal critics can rightfully object that Johnson does not pay enough attention to such aesthetic issues as the voice and evolving form of the novels that he discusses.

Combining a sophisticated mind, knowledge of the intellectual backgrounds and literary culture, and sensitive readings of important passages, Johnson has produced an interesting, perceptive, and valuable critical work. But finally, despite some splendid moments, his readings are not sufficiently original or striking for his book to change the way that we read Hardy's major fiction.

The unifying premise of Weinstein's ambitious and thoughtful exploration of six major British novelists – Dickens, Eliot, Hardy, Conrad, Lawrence, and Joyce – is that as we move from Victorianism to Modernism, the body and its desires increasingly become a larger factor in human identity at the expense of the mind: 'To move from Dickens to Joyce is to encounter a virtual revolution in which the body's propensity and the mind's restraint exchange roles as primary indices of identity' (p. vii). Weinstein's strengths are his insightful discussions of individual novels, his frequently subtle understanding of the imagination of the writers he discusses, and, notwithstanding a somewhat confused introduction, a readable and often elegant prose style. But, because he does not sustain his method, concepts, and arguments from chapter to chapter, his book tends to become a series of discrete essays. Furthermore, in his reliance on Nietzsche and Freud, he does not adequately define the specific cultural contexts that pertain to the development of the Modernist movement in England. Finally, often he both disregards the evolving form of a novel as a temporal reading event and fails to discuss what a novel's rhetoric does to its readers and why.

Weinstein is trying to create a dialogue between traditional formal criticism and recent movements in criticism. He is properly skeptical of what he calls the 'hermeneutics of suspicion' (read: Deconstruction) which urges that 'The critic's job is not to cooperate with the text but to expose it' (p. 12). But he chooses to place his methodological emphasis on phenomenology which had its heyday in the early 1970s when he began this study. In terms that readers of Georges Poulet, the European patriarch of Anglo-

American phenomenology, and the Hillis Miller that permeates *The Disappearance of God* and *Poets of Reality* will recognize, Weinstein speaks of 'approach[ing] the self-understanding of the novelistic universe in question, to identify its nodal and enabling assumptions, those creative premises that have generated its characteristic shape and concerns and that intimate what can and cannot be achieved within its contours' (p. 13).

In between the Introduction and a brief Afterword, Weinstein's book has a tripartite structure; all three parts contain two chapters, each of which is devoted to a major author. Under the subtitle 'Mid-Victorian: Constraints and Masquerades', the first and most successful part discusses Dickens (*David Copperfield* and *Little Dorritt*) and Eliot (*The Mill on the Floss* and *Daniel Deronda*). In a splendid chapter, Weinstein captures the essential spirit of Dickens's imagination. The second part, entitled 'Late Victorian: Tragic Encounters', discusses Hardy's *Tess of the d'Urbervilles* and *Jude the Obscure* and Conrad's *Lord Jim* and *Nostromo*. Notwithstanding an interesting discussion of the ineffectuality of the spoken word in *Jude*, neither the perceptive Hardy chapter nor the capable, if not strikingly original, Conrad chapter will change the way that we read these writers.

The final part is entitled, 'Modernist: Beginning the Revaluation', and includes a fine chapter on Lawrence (*Women in Love* and *Lady Chatterley's Lover*) and one on Joyce which Weinstein calls 'a meditation ... on *Ulysses* as a Modernist novel' (p. 188). Claiming that in *Ulysses* 'the plot does not matter' and failing to engage *Ulysses* as an evolving novel, the Joyce chapter illustrates some of Weinstein's problems with rhetoric and with literary theory (p. 280). When he writes that in *Ulysses*, 'the realm of Meaning and the realm of phenomena continuously, provocatively engage each other', he seems to sense how Joyce's interest in the momentary quirks of life and his fascination with language for its own sake threaten to deflect the reader from imposing an order upon the events of the narrative (p. 271). But he does not understand that the rhetoric of *Ulysses* urges two conflicting ways or ideologies of reading it: the ideology of reading that focuses on plot and characterization and insists that the reader move from immersion in the phenomena of a text to stories or allegories about reading, and the opposing ideology of reading that stresses the free play of the reader's imagination without thinking of the interpretive consequences. And, of course, these conflicting ways of reading anticipate the dialectic struggle on today's critical mindscape between the two major ideologies of reading – humanistic formalism and deconstruction.

VI DECONSTRUCTION: THE USE AND MISUSE OF THEORY

More than any movement since the New Criticism, deconstruction has had an enriching effect on literary studies. It reminds us that complex texts resist monolithic interpretations and that we need to take account of seeming marginalia. It stresses that each reading contains the seeds of its own undoing. It privileges the reader rather than the author without quite acknowledging that it does so. Put another way, the text is consubstantial with the reader rather than the author and/or the anterior world on which the text is based. Deconstruction emphasizes that every reader discovers heterogeneous readings in the same text which leads to an irreconcilable paradox or *aporia*. Deconstruction believes that all reading is misreading because no reading can take account of all the possibilities of a text. Deconstruction depends upon rejection of the possibility of moving towards an authoritative reading; it rejects the idea that reading can recover the author's intent, values, themes, or understanding of the world which his work imitates. By contrast, what I call humanistic formalism believes that we can approach the author's values and vision by attending to the rhetorical effects within the imagined world created by the author. Humanistic formalism believes that reading is a quest towards the goal of an accurate reading, even though, like Zeno's paradox, it is a goal which we can only approach but never reach. But we can make very substantial progress toward that goal. Deconstruction views accurate reading as a mirage which continually recedes in proportion to which it is seemingly approached.

According to deconstruction, our critical 'stories' of reading necessarily become oversimplified and inaccurate allegories of reading, because they can never do justice to the full possibilities of meaning disseminated by a work. Deconstruction believes that the Age of Interpretation is over and that the critic is a kind of poet who can pursue any connections to which his reading leads him. Since his mind is the nodal point for the meeting of 'texts', the critic can – in the name of intertextuality – weave his own web. The enemy of deconstruction is alternately or collectively perceived as reason, humanism (with its emphasis on discovering the values the author embodied in his work), organic unity, the belief that language signifies, the quest for knowledge, liberalism, and the traditions and institutions that support these values and activities.

Evidence is accruing that many of us who are fascinated by the theoretical questions raised by deconstruction and have become familiar with its basic concepts are demanding that it provide subtle readings of complex texts or important discussions of recurring patterns over a range of texts. Thus, recently, the influential and theoretically sophisticated journal *Novel* published an editorial entitled 'Why the Novel Matters', called for papers under the rubric 'Still towards a Humanistic Poetics?', and organized a 1987 conference to address these subjects. It may be time to propose the concept of the 'Theoretical Fallacy' to describe works that propound abstract formulations and speculations which never adumbrate the works they purport to consider. Perhaps those of us who believe that the function of criticism is to move towards the goal of discovering both what a work said to a contemporary reader and what it says to today's reader should begin to question the value of 'theoretical texts' that fail to create a dialogue between concepts and works.

I would like to discuss three books that reflect the consensual glow cast by the noonday sun of Deconstruction: Margot Norris's *Beasts of the Modern Imagination: Darwin, Nietzsche, Kafka, Ernst, and Lawrence*; Debra A. Castillo's *The Translated World*; and Steven G. Kellman's *Loving Reading: Erotics of the Text*.[13] For reasons that I shall make clear, only the one by Margot Norris will continue intellectually to shine if, as I believe, deconstruction is beginning to move past its high point in the intellectual firmament. Using the lessons of recent theory without abandoning the traditional concerns of humanistic criticism, Norris proposes that the artists she discusses – Nietzsche, Kafka, Ernst, and D. H. Lawrence – represent a 'biocentric tradition' that originated in Darwin: 'For Darwin himself revolutionized the concept of form, demonstrating that Nature produces form, not vice versa, and that form is engendered by force and desire rather than by mind' (p. 15). To be a member of this tradition, one must combine, on the one hand, the subject matter of 'an antiidealistic, antirational, antimetaphysical conception of Nature; a self-referential critique of anthropocentricism, a vitalistic equation of life with power and energy rather than with matter' with, on the other hand, such 'stylistic strategies' as 'performative prose: devious logic or aggressive polemic; the use of animal or organic metaphors amid perspectival shifts; and the text's refusal to seduce, concede, or ingratiate' (p. 236).

Norris effectively argues that these artists reverse the traditional hierarchy that sets man above animal. To be sure, she sometimes engages in deconstructive cant as when she claims that the artists in this tradition eschew the mimetic: 'Mimesis is the negative mark, the mark of absence, castration and death, an insight that required artists to reevaluate the ontological status of their media as negative being, as mere simulacra of life' (p. 5). More to the point, she ·claims, 'The biocentric thinkers recognized that, although Nature remains largely inaccessible to language (that is, it is impossible for language to speak Nature), figurative language can nonetheless function as an arena for biocentric performance' (p. 224). But one of the most valuable lessons of recent theory is to remind us that all language, even that of the most nominalistic realists, is more or less metaphorical. Moreover, is it not a paradox that as we approach what we think is the essence of realism, we find traces of metaphoricity, while when we approach what we think of as allegory, romance, or purity of form, we often discover underpinnings of the empirical impulse? In their quest to express the body, the animal, the libido, do not – must not – these artists substitute one kind of mimesis for another?

Norris has written an important and elegantly argued major work, one that adds to our understanding of intellectual history as well as of the writers she discusses. Among other things she transforms the shibboleths that graduate students learn about the nineteenth century mechanism–vitalism debate into a rich, intricate context of intellectual and literary history. Her discussion of Darwin is particularly perspicacious, especially her distinction between Darwin and Herbert Spencer. In a brilliant chapter she excludes Hemingway from her tradition because he is guilty of 'the aesthetic and idealistic rationalization of violence' (p. 196). I am least comfortable with the Lawrence discussion, which is overly grounded on the reading of one work in a canon that is not as homogeneous as she supposes. Although it is an oversimplification to say that Lawrence 'seems to measure human strength by the ability to dispense with meaning', her discussion of *St. Mawr* is compelling (p. 17).

Debra Castillo conceives of the library as a metaphor for the categorizing sensibility inherent in the concept of culture: 'The proliferating catalogue takes off toward infinity, overwhelming the library it was intended to organize, developing a will and a purpose of its own that only make reading more obscure than it was before the advent of such an organizing mania' (p. 80). Classification is itself an instance of man's corruption and sterile positivism as well as a power move that inevitably leads to ossification.

The quest for order is seen not merely as a fiction but as somehow pernicious. Thus she writes of Joyce's search for what he called 'the perfect order of the words in the sentence': 'There is, nevertheless, an unnerving political implication in this clear assumption of an absolute value standard based on Joyce's background and culture, an implicit claim of aesthetic superiority over other cultures. It represents, in a sense, the tacit colonialization of the world of print, subjecting the word to a history of increasing rigor and control' (p. 21). One would have thought that the use of allusions in *Ulysses* and of the encyclopedic cataloguing in 'Cyclops' and 'Ithaca' would be fruitful soil on which to work an analysis of her library trope, but she eschews close reading for vague, often pretentious speculations whose accuracy is difficult to determine. In the above passage, are not words like 'political', 'colonialization', 'subjecting ... to', and even 'control', part of the tendency – under the aegis of Foucault – to transform the neutral concept of 'rhetoric' into the highly charged concept of 'power'? While some readers may respond to raising the stakes of academic life by importing the language of economics, sexuality, and international politics, is not the price of this inflation often a loss of clarity in the way we speak about the effects of our reading experience?

Similarly, following the example of Foucault (and other Marxists), Castillo applies the language of economics and production to works which often have little apparent focus on these matters. Let us, for example, look at her comments on Conrad's famous 1897 image of the universe as an indifferent, amoral knitting machine which refuses to embroider the patterns of man's aspirations: 'It knits us in and it knits us out. It has knitted time, space, pain, death, corruption, despair and all the illusions – and nothing matters. I'll admit that to look at the remorseless process is sometimes amusing.' The first sentence of Castillo's discussion shows how she transforms a passage to her own purposes and ignores the context in which Conrad was speaking or the person whom Conrad was addressing (in this case, Cunninghame-Graham who believed with the Fabian socialists and Social Darwinists in an upwardly evolving teleology):

> The economic processes not only resist the insertion of bodies into the machine: in the development of critical capitalism the machinery of production becomes ever more alienated.... There is no end to its productivity, no end and no exit, only the inexorable knitting, the piling up of one book on top of another in the library.... To comment upon these commentaries is to give the knitting machine new fuel.
>
> (p. 323)

Castillo writes for the true believers in deconstruction. She has read widely and deep; but, notwithstanding some penetrating and even brilliant insights, if the goal of criticism is to produce subtle readings of complex texts, she has not succeeded. To give the full flavour of her flamboyant, excessive, and often arcane rhetoric, let me quote from her discussion of Nietzsche: 'Nietzsche calls for a new science unlike the old, odd scratchings of scholiasts and critics, seeing in the library that strange hell where man reads on palimpsests the phantom of the original, hidden discourse.... Logophilia begets logorrhea, begetting in turn taxonomies' (p. 41). Or perhaps I should cite the following passage which imports the language of sexuality – or sexology – into her discussion:

> Since the librarian's own immortality is ensured only if the books he writes are preserved for his heirs, he must repress that part of him that is drawn to fire, emphasizing only the living, spermatic stream that cancels and controls the flames.... Books are bodies, are flames, are lovers; they are also desexualized dead objects.... The librarian is not a libertine but a necrophiliac.
>
> (p. 198)

Can we rely on someone as a guide through books and culture who has so little respect for language that she produces the above passages and a plethora of neologisms such as 'decorporalization' (p. x) and 'monumentalization' (p. 324)?

Perhaps taking his cue from Barthes' *Le Plaisir du texte*, Steven Kellman has written a readable, fascinating study on the relationship between erotic and creative impulses: 'The poet and the lover are of imagination compact, and where they come together is in what they would do with us. The creation of a text is a labor of love, not only for want of other wages. And reading, like love, aims at dissolving personal boundaries. Both reading and loving are processes that are betrayed when reified' (p. 4). Reading and erotic experiences vary not only with invidiuals but with 'period' and 'culture'; thus he differentiates between modernism and Post-modernism in terms of his sexual trope: 'Modernism rejects an aesthetic experience that is in effect a frontal, immodest, and promiscuous embrace. Post-modernism with its nostalgia for the tribal community and with its blatant sexuality, will substitute a very different model for reading' (p. 85).

If Castillo's digressive, undisciplined study is too long, Kellman's modest book needs to be expanded. Some of his chapters – and especially the discrete sections into which his chapters are divided – are more like telegrams than sustained arguments. Excluding notes, his *essay* is ninety-three pages of text (and that is stretching things because he not only has eleven pages that are either blank or contain only a chapter title but also many half-pages). Despite some perceptive comments on a number of writers such as Mailer and Thoreau, Kellman does not really explore major works or give us a critical concept for doing so. He clearly has a relish for sexual subjects and metaphors; his delight in discussing Sade's violent and scatological *Les 120 Journees de Sodome* may put off some readers. If Kellman has a goal to which he is taking his readers, he needs to bring it into focus; for the book is foreplay without consummation.

Notes

1. Ian Watt, *Conrad in the Nineteenth Century* (Berkeley and Los Angeles: University of California Press, 1979).
2. Kim Herzinger, *D. H. Lawrence in His Time: 1908–1915* (Lewisburg, Pennsylvania: Bucknell University Press, 1982).
3. Jeffrey Meyers (ed.), *D. H. Lawrence and Tradition* (Amherst: University of Massachusetts Press, 1985).
4. James T. Boulton and Andrew Robertson (eds), *The Letters of D. H. Lawrence, Vol. III, 1916–21* (Cambridge University Press, 1984).
5. Ibid.
6. Bruce Steele (ed.), *Study of Thomas Hardy and Other Essays* (Cambridge University Press, 1985).

7.   Zdzislaw Najder, *Joseph Conrad: a Chronicle*, trans. Halina Carrolle-Najder (New Brunswick, N.J.: Rutgers University Press, 1983).

8.   Leo Hamalian, *D. H. Lawrence and the Experience of Italy* (New York: Taplinger, 1982), and Jeffrey Meyers, *D. H. Lawrence and the Experience of Italy* (Philadelphia: University of Pennsylvania Press, 1982).

9.   Ross Parmenter, *Lawrence in Oaxaca: a Quest for the Novelist in Mexico* (Layton, Utah: Gibbs M. Smith, 1984).

10.   Georges Poulet, 'Criticism and the Experience of Interiority' in *The Structuralist Controversy: the Languages of Criticism and the Sciences of Man*, eds Richard Macksey and Eugene Donato (Baltimore: Johns Hopkins University Press, 1970) p. 72.

11.   Bruce Johnson, *True Correspondence: a Phenomenology of Thomas Hardy's Novels* (Jacksonville: Florida State University Press, 1983); Philip M. Weinstein, *The Semantics of Desire: Changing Models of Identity from Dickens to Joyce* (Princeton University Press, 1984).

12.   David J. De Laura, ' "The Ache of Modernism" in Hardy's Later Novels', *ELH*, XXII (1967) pp. 380–99; Elliot B. Gose, Jr. 'Psychic Evolution: Darwinism and Initiation in *Tess of the d'Urbervilles'*, *NCF*, 18 (1963) pp. 261–72.

13.   Margot Norris, *Beasts of the Modern Imagination: Darwin, Nietzsche, Kafka, Ernst, and Lawrence* (Baltimore: The Johns Hopkins University Press, 1985); Debra A. Castillo, *The Translated World* (Talahasee: Florida State University/University Press of Florida, 1985); Steven G. Kellman, *Loving Reading: Erotics of the Text* (Hamden, Conn. Archon: The Shoe String Press, 1985).

9

Reading Conrad's *Lord Jim*: Reading Texts, Reading Lives

I shall argue that the experience of reading *Lord Jim* enacts a dialogue between the major ideologies of reading on the current critical mindscape – deconstruction and what I call humanistic formalism – and that *Lord Jim* privileges the reading of humanistic formalism, which urges an absolute judgement on Jim's behaviour and an organic and coherent text, over the deconstructive reading which raises questions about the possibility of formal unity, explanations of behaviour, and standards of judgement. Ultimately, *Lord Jim* affirms the possibility of significance and values, and refuses to endorse the relativity of Marlow or the solipsism of Stein.

Since J. Hillis Miller is perhaps the most influential of the deconstructionists working in prose fiction, I would like to take a moment to look at his argument about *Lord Jim*. In his chapter on *Lord Jim* in Fiction and Repetition, Hillis Miller has proposed that the repetition – the structural and thematic doubling that dominates the language and form of *Lord Jim* – implies that Jim's behaviour cannot be explained. By contrast, I shall contend that Jim's behaviour can be *judged*. *Lord Jim* proposes – and Conrad expects the reader to perceive – a hierarchy of explanations. But to see the hierarchy, one has to understand that the omniscient narrator proposes an absolute judgement, just as surely as Marlow proposes a relative one based on his complex and often sympathetic understanding of Jim. When Miller contends that *Lord Jim* lacks the reliable narrator of Victorian fiction, he is misreading the first four chapters. Miller argues that *Lord Jim* 'reveals itself to be a work which raises questions rather than answering them.... The indeterminacy lies in the multiplicity of possible incompatible explanations given by the novel and the lack of evidence justifying a choice of one over the others'.[1] By contrast, I shall be arguing that

Lord Jim in its complex and eccentric way answers the questions it raises.

Our first critical task is to recall that *Lord Jim* has three separate tellings: First, the omniscient narrator's presentation of Jim in the first four chapters; on occasion this voice returns to remind us of his presence; Secondly, Marlow's long monologue from chapters five through thirty-five; and Thirdly, Marlow's response to Jim's demise on Patusan which takes the form of an epistle received by one of the listeners to his monologue.

Conrad believes that 'another man's truth is a dismal lie to me'.[2] To understand why Conrad thinks each of us is locked into her or his own perceptions and that all values are ultimately illusions, perhaps we should examine Conrad's ironic image of the cosmos as created by an indifferent knitting machine – an image which he proposed in an 1897 letter to his optimistic socialist friend Cunninghame-Graham:

> There is a – let us say – a machine. It evolved itself (I am severely scientific) out of a chaos of scraps of iron and behold! – it knits. I am horrified at the horrible work and stand appalled. I feel it ought to embroider, – but it goes on knitting. You come and say: 'this is all right; it's only a question of the right kind of oil. Let us use this, – for instance – celestial oil and the machine shall embroider a most beautiful design in purple and gold.' Will it? Alas no. You cannot by any special lubrication make embroidery with a knitting machine. And the most withering thought is that the infamous thing has made itself; made itself without thought, without conscience, without foresight, without eyes, without heart ...
>
> It knits us in and it knits us out. It has knitted time, space, pain, death, corruption, despair and all the illusions – and nothing matters. I'll admit however that to look at the remorseless process is sometimes amusing.[3]

Conrad uses this elaborate ironic trope to speak to the late Victorian belief that the industrial revolution is part of an upwardly evolving teleology; this belief is really a kind of Social Darwinism. According to Conrad, humankind would like to believe in a providentially ordered world vertically descending from a benevolent God – that is, to believe in an embroidered world. But we actually inhabit a temporally defined horizontal dimension within an amoral, indifferent universe – or what in the above passage Conrad calls 'the remorseless process'.

Conrad dramatizes that humans always judge one another in terms of their own psychic and moral needs at the time that they are making judgements. But notwithstanding the fallibility of all judgements, we must strive to make objective judgements and to sustain values and ideals, even if we know that we will always fall short of them. Thus when Conrad writes that all is illusion, he means that all we can do is make working arrangements with the cosmos, and that there are no absolute values derived from an external source. But he does not mean that all values are equal. Similarly, merely because we cannot discover an absolute, final, original reading, it does not follow that all readings are equal. Rather, as readers, even while acknowledging that our readings are a function of our limitations, we must strive to establish judgements and values within complex texts. By affirming the value of the search for meaning in the lives of his characters within his imagined world, Conrad is rhetorically enacting the value of this search in reading texts.

The process of reading *Lord Jim* involves the reader in the remorseless process of responding to different judgements of Jim's behaviour. First, there is the judgement of the omniscient narrator that precedes not only our meeting Marlow, but our learning what happens on the *Patna*. Does the reader ever forget the original rigorous judgement established by the omniscient narrator in the first three chapters, a judgement that is based on adherence to absolute standards? Does not that judgement accompany the reader as he wends his way through Marlow's narrative of his own efforts to find some terms with which to understand Jim's terrible failure on the *Patna* when Jim, along with the rest of the white officers, abandons the native crew and passengers? And, of course, the reader must sort out the significance of Stein's oracular but hazy pronouncements. No sooner do we hear Marlow's judgement delivered in his long monologue after knowing that Jim has succeeded on Patusan and, at least in Marlow's eyes, justified Marlow's confidence in him, than we are confronted with Marlow's final, inconclusive judgement after Jim has failed; this judgement is halfway between the rigorous one of the absolute narrator and the empathetic one that had informed Marlow's telling.

Let me conclude my introduction by outlining the programme for the rest of my chapter. In my next four sections I shall focus respectively on the function of the omniscient narrator in the novel's opening chapters; Marlow's complex response to Jim; the role of Stein, that odd figure who inhabits the middle of the novel; and the implications of the ending for shaping our final response to the novel. Finally, in the last section I shall offer suggestions for reading *Lord Jim* which has implications for reading other novels.

I THE FUNCTION OF THE OMNISCIENT NARRATOR

Prior to Marlow's first words in chapter five, the omniscient narrator in the opening chapters judges Jim by fixed standards and shows him wanting. Without any ambiguity, Conrad uses this narrator to show us that Jim's jump from the *Patna* is a characteristic one rather than – as Jim would like to believe and as Marlow is at times tempted to accept – a gratuitous action that just happened to an unfortunate young man.

Lost in his fantasies of heroism, Jim fails to respond to an emergency on the training ship. Because Jim has not internalized the proper responses, when he is faced with an actual chance to take part in a rescue he becomes physically and morally paralyzed: 'He stood still. It seemed to him he was whirled around' (p. 5).[4] But he rationalizes that he had not really failed: 'The gale had ministered to a heroism as spurious as its own pretence of terror. ... [A] lower achievement had served the turn. He had enlarged his knowledge more than those who had done the work. When all men flinched, then – he felt sure – he alone would know how to deal with the spurious menace of wind and seas' (p. 7). The strength and resilience of Jim's imagination enable him to forget his failure, and to transfer – in the phrases 'the pretence of terror' and 'the spurious menace' – the *pretence* of his courage and the *spurious* quality of his fantasies to the physical events which revealed his pretence. We should note that, at this point before he succumbs to the temptation of the exhortation to 'Jump', Jim is a kind of magician with language – a poet – who can arbitrarily rearrange words as he sees fit.

Jim's second failure is when, while serving as first mate, he loses his nerve. The omniscient narrator tells us that until then Jim had never been tested by 'those events of the sea that show in the light of day the inner worth of a man, the edge of his temper, and the fibre of his stuff; that reveal the quality of his resistance and the

secret truth of his pretences, not only to others, but also to himself'
(p. 7). Notice how the narrator ironically applies to Jim the term
'pretence' – the very word Jim had used to describe the gale on the
training ship. When the storm strikes, Jim is disabled: '[He] spent
many days stretched on his back, dazed, battered, hopeless, and
tormented as if at the bottom of an abyss of unrest.... He lay there
battened down in the midst of a small devastation, and felt
secretly glad he had not to go on deck... [He felt] a despairing
desire to escape at any cost' (p. 8). The 'abyss of unrest' looks
forward to the abyss or 'everlasting deep hole' into which Jim
jumps, while the word 'secretly' not only scathingly echoes and
exposes the 'secret truth of *Jim's* pretences', but reinforces our
sense of the immense schism between the man Jim would be and
the man he is (p. 68). With bitter irony and without any
interrupting transition, the omniscient narrator concludes the
above paragraph: 'Then fine weather returned, and [Jim] thought
no more about it' (p. 8). In the 'despairing desire to escape at any
cost', do we not sense a foreshadowing of Jim's suicide at the
novel's end? Like Jukes in Conrad's 1902 novella 'Typhoon', Jim's
imaginative ability to think of *what might possibly happen* leads him
through corridors of terrible fantasies and finally to a nervous
exhaustion indistinguishable from catatonia. Didn't Conrad himself, the seaman who would be an author, fear that what the
omniscient narrator calls 'Imagination, the enemy of men, the
father of all terror' would prey upon his own capacity for action (p.
8)?

Conrad's narrative coding continues to create a concatenation of
episodes that judges Jim's moral dereliction and psychological
incapacity. Each episode iterates the prior one's indictment, even
while it adds another piece of evidence to the charge that Jim has
not internalized the fixed moral standards of the merchant marine
– the code, stipulating honour, fidelity, courage, and a highly
developed sense of responsibility – on which civilized life in the
colonies depends. Thus Jim, after he recovers from his leg injury,
throws in his lot with those who eschew the 'home service' of the
merchant marine for easier employment:

> They loved short passages, good deck-chairs, large native
> crews, and the distinction of being white.... They talked
> everlastingly of turns of luck ... and in all they said – in their
> actions, in their looks, in their persons – could be detected the

soft spot, the place of decay, the determination to lounge safely
through existence.

(p. 9)

As in the above passage, it is characteristic of Conrad to introduce
parallel phrases with recurring words; within a sentence these
phrases often increase in intensity as they move to an explosive
conclusion; thus in the first of the above sentences, Conrad's
appositional phrases move from the rather neutral descriptive
phrases to the morally intense and scathing indictment (in the
climactic phrase 'the distinction of being white') of those who
believe they are privileged on racial grounds. While Jim assumes
that he will not be tarnished by the company of the kind of men
who choose to work on boats like the *Patna*, the ironic narrator
places Jim among these men with soft spots and places of decay.
Conrad's adjectives here do not so much describe an internal
condition as they participate in a structure of effects to give the
reader a sense of Jim's moral flaw. We cannot visualize a soft spot
or a place of decay any more than we can see an *'invisible* halt' in
Jim's gait.

The fourth episode or vignette that inexorably illustrates that,
contrary to Jim's contention, his jump was a characteristic rather
than a gratuitous action is his behaviour on board the *Patna*; as on
the training ship his mind is wooed from his duty to the 'human
cargo' of pilgrims by fantasies of accomplishment: '[H]is thoughts
would be full of valorous deeds: he loved these dreams and the
success of his imaginary achievements. They were the best part of
his life, its secret truth, its hidden reality' (p. 13). That the words
'achievement' and 'secret' echo prior passages documenting his
flawed nature shows how Jim is iterating his past as he will
throughout his life. Repeating the term 'secret', – which has, as
Stephen Marcus has shown in *The Other Victorians*, a sexual
connotation (as in *My Secret Life*) – underlines how Jim has
separated himself from reality and has paradoxically created *in his
actions* – as opposed to his dreams – a self that has no social role to
play; Conrad thus gives the nuance of narcissism to Jim's self-
indulgent fantasies. Living in the world of his fictions rather than
in the world of actual duties and responsibilities, Jim is a
hopelessly divided self unfit for his tasks.

Cumulatively, these four vignettes stand as an absolute judgement of Jim, a judgement based on applying the rigorous

standards of the merchant marine which, Conrad believed, were the essential underpinnings to life at sea and to colonial life in primitive areas. Even as Marlow becomes an apologist for Jim, even as he uses Jim's case to look into his own case and the moral nature of all men, these vignettes retain their validity and accompany our reading, just as surely as Jim's past experience accompanies him after he abandons ship and wanders from place to place trying to catch up with his irrevocably lost self.

Conrad uses the omniscient narrator to establish that, contrary to Jim's argument to Marlow, Jim's jump was not something that could have happened to anyone but was, rather, the inevitable results of a character flaw. The omniscient narrator conducts his trial – performs Jim's trial for the reader – before the actual trial at which Marlow meets Jim. By beginning the novel with an omniscient voice which clinically and ironically shows that Jim's jump is characteristic of a morally flawed person, Conrad gives the reader a standard – a moral barometer – from which he cannot escape. Just as Jim feels imprisoned by a 'serried circle of facts' after he has jumped and must explain what happened, to the human community and, in partcular, to a tribunal of his peers, Conrad has created in the remarkable opening chapters a narrative code which uses 'a serried circle of facts' to indict Jim and imprison him. Conrad thus prevents the reader from fully joining Marlow's subsequent apologia for Jim. Moreover, by scrupulously alerting the reader to Jim's process of rationalization and self-delusion, Conrad rhetorically prepares the reader to judge Marlow's myopia when he, Marlow, begins to rationalize both his own responses to Jim and, increasingly, his own behaviour.

II MARLOW'S ALL-TOO-HUMAN JUDGEMENT

Originally, Marlow wanted to judge Jim by absolute standards. Marlow would have liked to read Jim as if he, Marlow, were the omniscient narrator, and, indeed, for a brief moment, Conrad teases us into thinking that we have been listening to Marlow – or at least an omniscient double of Marlow – all along. In the first moments of his monologue about Jim, Marlow aligns Jim with beetles, criminals, alloyed metal, and 'to men with soft spots, with hard spots, with hidden plague spots' as if he were going to continue the narrator's indictment (p. 21).

But the self-dramatizing Marlow soon reveals that he is vulnerable to those who, like Jim, claim extenuating circumstances because Marlow does not sufficiently believe in himself to uphold absolute values. Marlow cannot, as Stein will advise, shut his eyes and see himself as a fine fellow, a saint. He must face the ambiguity of living in a relative world which lacks anterior concepts of order. Because of his own needs, he begins to read Jim as Jim would like him to. In Marlow's evolving sympathy with Jim as 'one of us', in Marlow's taking up a position as Jim's apologist, in his gnawing and disturbing suspicion that he may not be able to claim a superior moral position because anyone might do what Jim did, Marlow begins to abandon the credo of the merchant marine and British imperialism and increasingly allows Jim to become a standard by which he, Marlow, measures himself. But the omniscient narrator has taught us not to be a Jim-reader of Jim, and when Marlow becomes a Jim-reader of Jim, we back off from accepting Marlow's authority as a reader of himself. In Marlow's world, once he loses his beliefs in fixed standards, there are no sources or origins and everything exists – as the replicating text indicates – as a variation of the other; such infinite variation makes judgements difficult.

As Marlow becomes an apologist for Jim, the reader is expected to adopt a stance of judgement towards Marlow – is expected to see that Marlow, too, is a fallible human being who is different in degree but not in kind from Jim. On three occasions Conrad undercuts Marlow's pretensions to moral authority:

1. first, when during Jim's trial, Marlow offers Jim Brierly's plan to evade the trial and escape the rituals of civilized judgement (p. 93);
2. secondly, when Marlow goes to Stein because he wishes to 'dispose' of Jim, in part to avoid his bizarre fear of having Jim – in the role of a common vagrant – confront him in London;
3. and, finally, when during his visit to Patusan, Marlow loses control in his interview with Jewel for no reason other than his own need to assure himself that he is better than Jim at a time when Marlow's ability to make moral distinctions is threatened: 'I felt the sort of rage one feels during a hard tussle ... 'You want to know [why the world does not want him]?' I asked in a fury. 'Yes!' she cried. 'Because he is not good enough', I said brutally' (p. 194). Marlow's self-indulgent indiscretion – what

purpose is served by telling Jewel that Jim is not good enough? – strikingly contrasts with the climax of *Heart of Darkness*. There, we recall, when an embittered and disillusioned Marlow returns to Europe, he is, although he hates a lie, willing to lie to the Intended and to let her think that Kurtz's last words were her name in order that she have the sustaining illusion of Kurtz's undying devotion.[5]

The novel questions the possibility of absolute standards in other ways. That Brierly, the precociously successful young captain who seems to have achieved everything that Jim dreams of, and who seems to be the very man most suitable to judge Jim, kills himself after serving on the tribunal at Jim's trial, structurally illustrates the impossibility of one man judging another. Who could have had better personal and professional credentials to judge Jim than Brierly, whose career trajectory was the exact opposite of Jim's? Yet looking into Jim's case, Brierly begins to look into his own and begins to believe that what one person does any person can do. Does not Brierly's radical empathy become a warning to the reader of what could happen to Marlow if he allows the distance between himself and Jim to close? (We recall 'The Secret Sharer' where the captain irrationally identifies with the escaped murderer Leggatt with whom he has very little in common and whose values are diametrically opposed to his own.) Isn't Conrad using Brierly's strong misreading of Jim's life to issue a rhetorical warning to the reader to strive for distance and judgement and to avoid the radical empathy that leads to flagrant misreading? Within the text, we are being told to attend to the rhetoric of the text and not to create our own text. To recall my subtitle: 'Reading Lives, Reading Texts'.

Throughout the novel, the omniscient narrator's judgement co-exists with Marlow's inevitably human, somewhat sentimental, and finally flawed perspective. Even when we as readers participate in Marlow's search for explanations, even when we are moved by his efforts to make sense of Jim's behaviour and his, Marlow's own life, the original, objective judgement of Jim remains engraved on our minds. While Marlow's judgement is wavering, relative, and unsure of its ground, the omniscient narrator's judgement is absolute, and refers to anterior standards. To read *Lord Jim* properly, one must hold in mind these contradictory perspectives.

Do not the absolute judgement of the omniscient narrator and the relative, human judgement of Marlow revolve around one another as we read Lord Jim? As humans with our doubts and anxieties, with the memories of our failures, and fears about our shortcomings, we are prone to the kind of humane, and, yes, on occasion, sentimental sympathy and radical empathy with which Marlow responds to Jim. In current terms, it is tempting to say that these judgements deconstruct one another so that neither becomes privileged. Indeed, Marlow's reading of Jim can be taken as a model for intratextual reading based on contiguous relations within a text, while the omniscient narrator's reading depends on a belief in anterior standards. The paradox is that here it is the humanistic reading that *is* deconstructing the novel's – and the reader's – quest for unity.

But while Marlow enacts the moment of irreconcilable impasse or *aporia* of modernism, Conrad, I am arguing, does not. For, as we have seen, Conrad's omniscient voice stands in judgement of Jim's behaviour and of Marlow's understandable efforts as one of us – lonely, doubting humans in a confusing world that Conrad thought of as a 'remorseless process' – to explain Jim's behaviour. Conrad expects the reader to understand that Marlow's confidence in absolute values has been undermined by his own experience, and that we readers must, like judges, sift through the data as objectively as possible, even while recognizing that, like Brierly and Marlow, we are all prone to skewed judgements based on our own needs. But while the novel tempts us to be a Jim-reader of Jim, or a Brierly-reader or a Stein-reader, and even more urgently to being a Marlow-reader – who at times is a Jim-reader, a Brierly-reader, and a Stein-reader – it finally insists on our being an omniscient reader and as unforgiving and unyielding in our judgements as the omniscient narrator.

The taut organic unity of the novel in which every part echoes every other part and in which every word rings with resonance is the significant form for establishing a world dense with meaning and judgement. It is the form – including the relationship between the romantic second part in unexplored Malaysian islands and the realistic first part within the colonized East where western maritime values have gained a foothold, between the part dominated by the *Patna* and the part dominated by Patusan – that enables Conrad to reclaim the subject, centre the meaning, and reject *aporia*. Does not even such a small matter as the name 'Patusan' being an anagram of the letters of *Patna* plus 'us' remind the reader of the community commitment which Jim lacked on board the ship? Does not the novel's doubling call attention to the almost reflexive nature and organic form of Conrad's fictive world?

III   THE FUNCTION OF STEIN

The oracular Stein makes a claim for omniscience or, rather, Marlow, in search of a telos or ultimate meaning, seeks to apotheosize Stein. By placing Stein in the centre of the novel, by endowing his life with heroic proportions which make him an image of what Jim would like to be, by giving him a history which in many ways echoes that of Jim (excluding, of course, jumping ship), and, finally, by giving him the ambiguous speech of an oracle figure, Conrad arouses the reader's expectations that Stein may solve the novel's moral issues.

Let us look briefly at Stein's argument. Stein proposes that man must existentially commit himself to one's ideals as a means of dealing with the 'destructive element'. Shouldn't we think of that element as the necessary result of an indifferent, amoral cosmos that Conrad conceived in terms of a machine that insisted on knitting rather than embroidering? Because Jim has not internalized his dreams, because they do not support his ego-ideals, he cannot sustain his dreams. Man has a need to fulfil anterior ideals and at the same time has baser impulses which may result in cowardice and mediocrity. But if one shuts one's eyes to reality and embraces one's dreams, then one has a chance of sustaining oneself in the destructive element or remorseless process:

> [Man] wants to be a saint, and he wants to be a devil – and every time he shuts his eyes – he sees himself as a very fine fellow – so fine as he can never be.... In a dream ... and because you not always can keep your eyes shut there comes the real trouble – the heart pain – the world pain. I tell you, my friend, it is not good for you to find you cannot make your dream come true, for the reason that you not strong enough are, or not clever enough. *Ja!* ... And all the time you are such a fine fellow, too!
>
> (p. 130)

In an ironic reversal of Jim's jump which occurs when Jim abandons his dreams and sees that he will certainly drown, dreaming – closing one's eyes and living one's dreams and illusions – is equated by Stein with falling into the sea: 'A man that is born falls into a dream like a man who falls into the sea. If he tries to climb out into the air as inexperienced people endeavor to do, he drowns – *nicht war*? ... No! I tell you! The way is to the destructive element submit yourself, and with the exertions of your hands and feet in the water make the deep, deep sea keep you up' (p. 130). Climbing into the air is a metaphor for failing to keep oneself afloat in one's dreams; if one does climb into the air, then one opens one's eyes to one's own limitations and sees the world as it is – as a destructive element. The way to survive, according to Stein, is 'To follow the dream, and again to follow the dream – and so – *ewig* – *usque ad finem*' – which translates 'until the end' (p. 131). When Jim opens his eyes on the *Patna* to the real danger, he abandons his dream of heroism and the merchant marine credo that insists that he stick to the ship under all circumstances. When he lets the scoundrel Gentleman Brown insinuate a kinship with him, he abandons his position as the political and ethical leader of the Patusan community. In both cases, his self-image is not strong enough to stand up to his collision with circumstances in the not-I world which represent the destructive element or remorseless process.

Something more of an 1890s figure than is usually noticed, Stein understands the nature of masques and fictions; he knows the value of adhering existentially to one's dream or values as a way of making sense of a meaningless world. But has it sufficiently been stressed how Stein is preaching a form of solipsism and that he says nothing at all about the failure of Jim to sustain traditional community values? Critics have mistakenly privileged Stein's remarks because they have failed to notice that Conrad no sooner raises expectations that Stein might be a Wisdom Figure than he deflates those expectations. For one thing, what he says in his broken English is rather ambiguous. For another, no sooner does he deliver his advice than his pretensions to sphinxian wisdom are undermined; Marlow notices that Stein loses his poise and confidence: 'The hand that had been pointing at my breast [like a pistol] fell.... The light had destroyed the assurance which had inspired him in the distant shadows' (p. 130). And, finally, that Stein is depicted by Marlow in the novel's last paragraph as aging and ineffectual shows us that he not only has not found any absolute knowledge, but that he may not even retain faith in the credo that he has articulated in the above passage. The Stein episode teaches that there can be no one centre of meaning in texts or in life. Just as neither Stein nor Jim can be the key to meaning for Marlow, so Marlow cannot be the source of meaning for his listeners; and, for us readers, no one character or scene can be privileged over the others.

Of course, discrediting Stein as a Prospero figure does not invalidate the human search for meaning; nor does the absence of ultimate meaning suggest that there cannot be hierarchies of relative meaning. The reader is expected to understand Stein's advice as another working arrangement that individual humans make with the cosmos. Even Marlow does not arrive at formulations that would replace Stein's, for ultimately Conrad does not believe in static philosphic formulations.

IV   THE ENDING OF *LORD JIM*

Jim's betrayal of his followers in Patusan derives from his inability to believe in his own triumph – or, put another way, to read the text he himself wrote about the hero that makes good on his second chance. He alone does not believe in his triumph and believes that his accomplishments are apocryphal. (Doesn't he say at the height of his triumph: 'If you ask them who is brave – who is true – who is just – who is it they would trust with their lives? – they would say, Tuan Jim. And yet they can never know the *real, real, truth* ...' [emphasis mine; p. 185]?) Because Jim does not believe in his own redemption, words cannot be part of what Marlow calls 'the sheltering conception of light and order which is our refuge' – a conception that, as Marlow puts it, protects us from 'a view of the world that seemed to wear a vast and dismal aspect of disorder' (p. 190); do we not hear in these words an echo of Stein's destructive element? Once Jim responded to the word 'Jump' on board the Patna, he had leapt into an abyss where belief in the innocence of language as an ordering principle in a fundamentally hostile world is no longer possible. Like a voice from within insidiously suggesting to Jim that he *belongs* to Jim as part of his imprisoning fate, Gentleman Brown convinces Jim that they are moral and emotional brothers and that Jim must provide him a safe departure. But Brown and his murderous band betray Jim's trust and slay Jim's followers. In Marlow's words, '[Jim] had retreated from one world, for a small matter of an impulsive jump, and now the other, the work of his own hands, had fallen in ruins upon his own head' (p. 248).

In the imagined world of *Lord Jim*, Conrad – that non-Derridean – gives voice and speaking precedence over writing. For Marlow, who has used spoken language to summon almost magically what is past and to put his back to the future, who has used telling to recreate himself, the written word is a kind of deferral of the immediacy of spoken language and an indication that he is giving up his inquiry into himself. Thus the written language of the epistolary section becomes itself a metaphor for the moral weariness and resignation he feels and a recognition of mortality and defeat. Now Marlow too seems to have lost faith in language. Marlow's valedictory passage defers meaning and leaves him without that presence or epistemological counter which Jim had provided for Marlow's quest for moral and spiritual meaning:

> And that's the end. He passes away under a cloud, inscrutable at heart, forgotten, unforgiven, and excessively romantic.... For it may very well be that in the short moment of his last proud and unflinching glance, he had beheld the face of that opportunity which, like an Eastern bride, had come veiled to his side.
>
> But we can see him, an obscure conqueror of fame, tearing himself out of the arms of a jealous love at the sign, at the call of his exalted egoism. He goes away from a living woman to celebrate his pitiless wedding with a shadowy ideal of conduct. Is he satisfied – quite, now, I wonder? We ought to know. He is one of us – and have I not stood up once, like an evoked ghost, to answer for his eternal constancy? Was I so very wrong after all? Now he is no more, there are days when the reality of his existence comes to me with an immense, with an overwhelming force; and yet upon my honour there are moments, too, when he passes from my eyes like a disembodied spirit astray amongst the passions of his earth, ready to surrender himself faithfully to the claim of his own world of shades.
>
> (p. 253)

Does Marlow forgive him? Note how Marlow sometimes forgets Jim, while in *Heart of Darkness* he never could forget Kurtz who haunts his memory. When he describes Jim in such terms as 'under a cloud, inscrutable at heart, forgotten, unforgiven and excessively romantic', Marlow is describing his response to Jim, rather than Jim. (As readers of Heart of Darkness recall, this is not unusual in Conrad, where such adjectives as 'abominable' or 'unbounded' are used more to create a structure of effects for the reader than to describe an objective situation within the imagined world.) But these non-referential adjectives enact how, since the omniscient narrator turned over the narration to Marlow, he has moved from reflection to self-immersion. Perhaps Marlow's final judgement (especially 'unforgiven') is a step towards reasserting the rigorous code from which he had departed. While Marlow withholds judgement – 'I affirm nothing' – does he not send his packet to a listener whose views are not only close to those of the omniscient voice, but also to those Marlow had held when he first met Jim (p. 206)? For the privileged recipient is chosen because he believed in the imperialistic dream that the white Europeans are emissaries of enlightenment 'in whose name are established the order, the morality of an ethical progress?' (p. 206).

Surely, we readers moving outside the linguistic circle of Marlow and Stein understand that the cloud, like the invisible halt of Jim's gait and his spot of decay, is a metaphor for Jim's moral blemish; we cannot see Jim clearly because, for Marlow, his morally ambiguous behaviour places him in the shadows of Marlow's imagination. And do not the above adjectives call attention finally to Jim's moral emptiness and raise questions about whether Jim is still worth the effort? Marlow understands that Jim is still wooed by his fantasies; Jim leaves behind the reality of the woman who loves him, and to whom he has human ties, for a romantic ideal of honour. Isn't Marlow's final stance, as much as Stein's ageing, a reassertion of the impossibility of permanently suspending time and of creating an imaginative world? But this impossibility paradoxically gives the omniscient narrator's positivistic judgements validity.

Poignantly, in his allowing Doramin to shoot him, Jim chooses the masculine world of physical action, represented by the pistol (recall how he had entered Patusan 'with an unloaded revolver in his lap'), over the alternative, more feminine world of values represented by the talismanic friendship ring given to him by Stein – the ring that he gave to his messenger, 'Tamb Itam, to give to Dain Waris as a sign that his messenger's words should be trusted' (p. 149). Just as his achievements in the native black world can never be as real to Jim as the failures in the white home world, feminine values – that of romantic loe and personal ties – cannot be as real to him as the world of male heroism. Jim can love Jewel in his romance world of 'knight and maiden', but not in the relative world of partial failures and relative successes (p. 189). By choosing to face the male pistol, Jim, in fact, ironically closes the eternal circle implied by the feminine ring. After Doramin shoots Jim:

> People remarked that the ring which he had dropped on his lap fell and rolled against the foot of the white man, and that poor Jim glanced down at the talisman that had opened for him the door of fame, love and success within the wall of forests fringed with white foam, within the coast that under the western sun looks very like the stronghold of the night.
>
> (pp. 252–3)

Is not Jim's suicide – along with Jim's jump from the *Patna* and his trusting Gentleman Brown – a third betrayal? Do not the moral absolutism and breakdown of distance that propel him to suicide repeat Brierly's suicide? In Conrad's moral universe a man's character is his fate and Jim has not fundamentally changed. But this does not invalidate meaning. Indeed, what happens is that Jim accepts the verdict of the omniscient narrator, the verdict that had judged Jim's jump from the *Patna* not as a gratuitous act but as part of a concatenation of events that revealed Jim's flawed character. More than Marlow, Jim had continued to judge himself according to absolute standards from which he had departed – the very standards articulated by the omniscient narrator at the beginning of the novel. Doesn't Jim's internalizing of these judgements make the circular ring an appropriate image for the form of the novel? In retrieving the original standards by which he had failed, Jim most certainly weds himself to what Marlow calls 'a shadowy ideal of conduct' (p. 253). But that shadowy ideal is in fact the credo of the novel that is articulated by the omniscient narrator in the opening chapters.

In the ending, then, we see not an abandonment of values but a reassertion of the original values articulated by the omniscient narrator. To be sure, individual voices – whether Stein's, Brierly's, or Marlow's – are unable to establish authority. In Marlow's and the novel's last paragraph, Stein is reduced to speaking vacuously of 'preparing to leave ...', and seems to lack both the imaginative and rhetorical energy of his prior appearance. Marlow no longer imposes his all-too-human order on his experiences (p. 258). Jim dies 'with his hand over his lips', an emblem – or a statue – of his estrangement from language. Conrad himself will no longer rely on Marlow as a surrogate for his epistemogical quests; he moves on to other voices and techniques, returning in *Chance* (1912) to a Marlow who resembles the earlier Marlow more in name than in intellect or the ability to make subtle moral discriminations. But the words of the novel and, in particular, of the omniscient narrator survive to communicate their judgements to the reader.

V   SUGGESTIONS FOR READING *LORD JIM*

Like any complex work, *Lord Jim* teaches us how to read itself. We should think of our experience – our process – of reading it as the reader's odyssey. We should be aware of what the novel does to us as we read it and how its disrupted chronology and multiple modes of narration establish an unusually complex relationship between text and reader. In my view the principal interest of Lord *Jim's* chronological disruptions, its multiple perspectives, its structural doubling, and its stylistic idiosyncracies should be how they shape a reading of the novel. Just as Marlow is engaged in a moral odyssey as he repeats the journeys of Jim's physical odyssey, so the reader takes part in an odyssey of judgement in which she or he is presented with an abundance of evidence and opinions. The reader must establish a perspective for both Marlow and Jim that survives and transcends the novel's plethora of judgements, its wealth of detail, and its protean transformations of characters. Conrad's use of adjectives – in, for example, the passage we examined from the ending – as a kind of subjective correlative for which the reader must fill in the space between signifier and signified is a kind of linguistic model for the necessary corrective judgement that the reader must provide. In Conrad, style is inseparable from what it *does* to the events and characters it describes and what it *does* to the reader as he negotiates his journey through the novel to his final destination, the novel's end. Since Conrad's focus always returns to the characters and their meaning, we should assume that the effects of his language upon the reader – what we might think of as the *doesness* of the text as opposed to the *isness* – were never far from his mind.

The odyssean reader must wend his way through a variety of experiences, but these experiences can best be understood in terms of *Lord Jim*'s major formal principle. This formal principle urges the reader to see *Lord Jim* as a completely organic and integrated novel in which one can conceive in every part some aspect of the meaning and harmony of the whole. In his book Gödel, Escher, Bach, Douglas Hofstadter describes the graph of a mathematical function INT[eger] (x), every section of which is a replica of the whole.[6] Since every individual part of each section is also a replica of the whole, the graph consists of an infinite number of copies of itself. Thus INT[eger] (x) becomes an apt metaphor for a humanistic reading of *Lord Jim*, because it expresses the humanistic idea that within the specific narrative about a few characters can be perceived universal truths or at least important evidence of what a culture values. Another model for organic unity is the genetic code which determines the macrostructure of an organism, but which is contained in every separate part of the organism.

Opposed to this totalizing perspective is the formal principle which insists that, as Geoffrey H. Hartman puts it, 'literary language displays a polysemy, or an excess of the signifier over the signified'.[7] While for the most part, *Lord Jim* insists that its readers interpret every detail in terms of larger patterns, one must acknowledge a secondary and subordinate story of reading *Lord Jim*. At times, the novel's focus on isolated moments of life and ingenious linguistic pyrotechnics may temporarily deflect the reader from stories of reading that propose organic unity. At some points in our reading experience, the text seems to be questioning the reader's quest for meaning with troubling data, as in the passage where Stein's oracular stature is undermined or when Marlow loses control. On occasion, focusing on the quirky and idiosyncratic aspects in human behaviour, *Lord Jim* does immerse the reader in the nominalistic world of the lives of a few characters; furthermore, by presenting Jim through Marlow's explanatory and apologetic lens, Conrad does raise the possibility that some of the novel's implications cannot be resolved.

Throughout *Lord Jim*, Conrad is aware that the possibility of meaninglessness is inseparable from the probability of significance. By constantly proposing, testing, and discarding multiple explanations for Jim's behaviour and by presenting Marlow as an evolving self-dramatizing character, Conrad urges us toward such a complex response. He wants us to read profanely and to experience the agony of Jim's demise through Marlow's puzzled eyes; he wants us to entertain the possibility that *Lord Jim* is not merely inconclusive, but that it is skeptical about discovering significance from the plethora of details within his novel – and, by implication, as skeptical of our own efforts to come to terms with crucial events in our own lives.

But ultimately the narrative form of *Lord Jim* privileges the original judgement – the prologue narrated by an omniscient voice preceding Conrad's elaborate orchestration of the multiple but limited and self-interested perspectives of the novel. And Conrad re-integrates those moments of seeming *aporia* into his pattern of moral significance. By doing so, he establishes a hierarchy of meanings in which the relative, marginal, or deconstructive reading is subordinated to the novel's moral judgement as revealed by the novel's organic form.

The dialectic between the two modes of reading – the formally coherent humanistic one and the skeptical deconstructive one – is crucial not only to the experience of reading *Lord Jim* but to reading many modern novels. While nineteenth century novels are more likely to use the omniscient speaker and to propose a unified artistic and moral vision, modern novels as diverse as *Ulysses* and Eco's *The Name of the Rose* characteristically carry seeds of their own self-doubt about the possibility of meaning and coherence. For the sake of intellectual housekeeping, it would be neater either to give the two modes of reading *Lord Jim* – the one that insists on moving from immersion to interpretive reflection and to acts of construing, the other that stresses immersion in the text for its own sake – equal importance, or to claim that the linguistic reading deconstructs the humanistic one. But it is more accurate to say that for the most part *Lord Jim* invites the first mode of reading, the traditional humanistic mode of reading that stresses unity of form and content, rather than the latter, deconstructionist mode of reading which questions meaning, coherence, and significance. Put another way, in *Lord Jim* the humanistic reading is dominant and the deconstructive reading is subordinate. Although Marlow's empathetic involvement, Brierly's fallibility, and Stein's obscurantism challenge and ironically undermine our desire for order, Conrad depends upon the reader's expectations of coherence and unity – what Wallace Stevens in 'The Idea of Order at Key West' calls our 'rage for order'. For, finally, Conrad wants us to read *Lord Jim* as a sacred text – as his own embroidery – in which every episode signifies and in which the words on the page represent the possibility for unity and wholeness in the modern world.

Notes

1. J. Hillis Miller, *Fiction and Repetition: Seven English Novels* (Cambridge: Harvard University Press, 1982) pp. 39–40.
2. G. Jean-Aubry, Joseph Conrad: Life and Letters 2 vols (Garden City, N.Y.: Doubleday, Page & Co., 1927) I. 184.
3. Ibid., I. 216.
4. Page numbers in parentheses refer to the Norton Critical edition of *Lord Jim*, ed. Thomas Moser (New York: Norton, 1968).
5. I discuss Marlow's shortcomings in greater detail in my book *Conrad: 'Almayer's Folly' Through 'Under Western Eyes'* (Ithaca, N.Y.: Cornell University Press, 1980). See my Lord Jim chapter, pp. 76–97.
6. Douglas Hofstadter, *Gödel, Escher, Bach: an Eternal Golden Braid* (New York: Basic Books, 1979).
7. Geoffrey Hartman, 'The Culture of Criticism', *PMLA*, 99:3 (May 1984) p. 386.

10

'Tell Us in Plain Words': an Introduction to Reading Joyce's *Ulysses*

As my title's playful use of Molly Bloom's response to Leopold Bloom's explanation of metempsychosis (the transmigration of souls) indicates, I shall stress – as I do in my recent study *Reading Joyce's 'Ulysses'*[1] – that *Ulysses* is a readable novel rather than an elaborate puzzle or a Rosetta Stone or a hieroglyph (U.64; IV.343).[2] Indeed, there is a danger that the study of *Ulysses* has become like ground that has been farmed for so long that it now only supports exotic crops like persimmons.

Just as the explanatory Talmud has become part of the Torah for observant Jews, and just as for believing Christians biblical interpretation is as much a part of God's message as the New Testament, the biographical and critical apparatus produced by the cottage industry known as Joyce scholarship has become part of the process of reading *Ulysses*. By distributing his schemata for the novel, and by helping both Frank Budgen write his early biography and Stuart Gilbert write his critical study, Joyce deliberately and wilfully shaped the interpretation of *Ulysses*. It is as if God had given both the Holy Word and the subsequent exegeses. Nevertheless, if we approach *Ulysses* as a novel which has important continuities with other novels and with Joyce's prior work, we discover that its meaning and significance depend – like all literary works – on the relationship among the three basic ingredients of literary criticism: author, work, and audience.

In the first two sections of this chapter, I shall discuss the continuity between *A Portrait of the Artist as a Young Man* and Ulysses in terms which try to posit a formal approach to Joyce while acknowledging the biographical grounding of Joyce's work. For in Ulysses, Joyce transforms the ordinary events of one day, 16 June 1904 in the lives of this three major characters – Stephen Dedalus, Leopold Bloom, Molly Bloom – into significant form;

these events are often based on details of Joyce's own life. In my third and concluding section, I shall then propose some suggestions for reading *Ulysses*.

I THE AUTHOR IN THE TEXT AND THE MOVEMENT FROM LYRICAL TO DRAMATIC AND EPICAL FORM

Reading Joyce raises messy questions about the relationship between an author's life and work. For Stephen Dedalus, the major character in *Portrait* and one of the three major figures in *Ulysses*, is based definitively, yet ambiguously, on Joyce's life. To read Joyce, we need to define the formal relationship between author and novel and to propose an aesthetic which includes the principle that a book's significance may depend in part on knowing something of what happened to the author between the time of the action and the time the book was written. However, we must ask whether we can read *Portrait* or *Ulysses* as if it were possible for Joyce to recreate his life in fiction and to stand objectively detached from the emotional bonds that tie him to the represented experience of his own life. Or, is the explicit and subjective relationship between *Ulysses* and Joyce's life – a life with which we are familiar in great detail because of Richard Ellmann's remarkable biography *James Joyce* – inevitably part of our reading experience? Do we not respond to the teller of *Portrait* and *Ulysses* as a character within the imagined world of the novels whose full significance depends on a dynamic and varying relationship with the creator?

If we turn to Joyce's own discussion of genre in *Portrait*, we shall see how the relationship between author and work is crucial to Joyce's aesthetic; Joyce writes:

> [A]rt necessarily divides itself into three forms progressing from one to the next. These forms are: the lyrical form, the form wherein the artist presents his image in immediate relation to himself; the epical form, the form wherein he presents his image in mediate relation to himself and to others; the dramatic form, the form wherein he presents his image in immediate relation to others ... The lyrical form is in fact the simplest verbal vesture of an instant of emotion. ... He who utters it is more conscious of the instant of emotion than of himself as feeling emotion. The simplest epical form is seen emerging out of lyrical literature when the artist prolongs and broods upon himself as the center

of an epical event and this form progresses till the center of emotional gravity is equidistant from the artist himself and from others. The narrative is no longer purely personal. The personality of the artist passes into the narrative itself, flowing round and round the persons and the action like a vital sea ... The dramatic form is reached when the vitality which has flowed and eddied around each person fills every person with such vital force that he or she assumes a proper and intangible esthetic life. The personality of the artist, at first a cry or a cadence or a mood and then a fluid and lambent narrative, finally refines itself out of existence, impersonalizes itself, so to speak. The esthetic image in the dramatic form is life purified in and reprojected from the human imagination.

(P. 214–15)[3]

In applying Joyce's aesthetic to his own works, we should think of literary works not as purely lyrical, epical, or dramatic, but as mixed modes that contain aspects of more than one genre. *A Portrait of the Artist as a Young Man* begins in the lyrical mode, but, to the degree to which it is ironic, approaches the epical mode. If we understand the relationship in *Ulysses* among the three genres as a dynamic process – as a trialogue among them – we can better understand the novel's form and meaning.

Thus in *Ulysses* Joyce progresses from the lyrical to the epical and finally to the dramatic. The first three chapters oscillate between the lyrical perspective of Stephen and the epical perspective of Joyce's omniscient but not entirely distanced narrator, a narrator who is never far from Stephen's consciousness and who does not enter into the consciousness of any other characters. By using the lyrical mode, Joyce establishes the continuity with *Portrait* of both Stephen and of the narrative presence, and calls attention to the process of fictionally re-examining and re-creating his own life. By allowing the lyrical mode to dominate over the epical mode with which *Portrait* had concluded, he shows that Stephen has taken a step backward in his artistic development, for the mature artist needs the objectivity Stephen lacks.

In *Ulysses* Joyce progressively distances himself from Stephen and establishes him as a potential character in an epic – the character of the young artist trying to find himself amidst personal and historical confusion so that he might develop into the writer of a novel like *Ulysses*. Presenting Bloom, his intelligent, sensitive, uneducated, empirical, sensual, middle-aged Irish Jew, is the means by which Joyce places his characters – not only Bloom, but Stephen, too – at a distance from himself. Joyce conceived Bloom as a character that would enable him to achieve the epical mode or, in the words from the passage in *Portrait* that we have been discussing, to 'prolong and brood upon himself as the center of an epical event'.

Perhaps the most notable aspect of the dramatic mode is the protean speaker whose virtuosity enables him to assume various and conflicting voices. For the unique styles that Joyce writes for each chapter can be equated with the voices of characters in drama. This ventriloquy calls attention to the presence of an objective artist impersonalizing himself and looking from a detached, ironical perspective at the personae of the plot and at the various tellers. Does not the recurrence of Stephen Dedalus, the major figure of *Portrait*, make particularly striking the contrast between the diverse voices of *Ulysses* and the third person omniscient narrator of *Portrait*, who renders Stephen's perspective almost exclusively?

Joyce's desire to objectify part of himself in Bloom, a character who seems to be the diametric opposite of Stephen, the artist based on Joyce's younger self, was probably influenced by Oscar Wilde's theory of masques; Wilde believed that we must assume a masque in order to liberate ourselves from our customary conventional daytime selves. Yet for the very reason that Bloom is still enough of the mature Joyce who is living in Europe and writing *Ulysses*, Joyce had to struggle to achieve the objectivity and distance that are the prerequisites for his dramatic mode, the mode in which, as Joyce puts it, the 'personality' of the artist 'impersonalizes itself'.

Beginning with the fifteenth chapter, 'Circe', and climaxing with the eighteenth and last one, 'Penelope', the artistic personality becomes – to use Joyce's terms from the passage from *Portrait* I quoted above – 'impersonalized' and 'reprojected from [Joyce's] human imagination'. Indeed, it is Molly, based on the physicality and ingenuousness of Joyce's beloved Nora Barnacle that allows him to achieve the necessary objectivity and impersonality to use comfortably the dramatic mode. Molly Bloom displaces the narrative presence or, to say the same thing, the ventriloquy of the voice in 'Penelope' is so complete that we almost – but not quite – forget that the narrative presence contains all the varied voices, including some, such as the snarling ally of the Citizen in the

'Cyclops' episode and the speaker of sentimental pulp in 'Nausi-caa', that he assumes only to discredit.

The reader understands that the possibility of discovering an appropriate fictional form for the modern epic novel is itself one subject of *Ulysses*, a subject that self-consciously hovers over the entire novel. Since, for Joyce, inclusiveness is itself an essential prerequisite and a value for the modern epic, he wished to include within *Ulysses* not only his epic mode, but also the lyrical and dramatic. (Given the current critical climate, it is worth noting that Joyce's own definitions of form focus on narrative distance; that they insist on the relation of work to author; and that they assume the imitation of an *a priori* world.) Central to Joyce's inquiry into the putative form for the modern epic was what voice to assume, what style to employ, and what kind of characters could possibly imply the universality he required.

Since, at the end of *Portrait*, Stephen, as Ellmann nicely puts it in his biography, 'could no longer communicate with anyone in Ireland but himself', Joyce could not rely on Stephen's consciousness.[4] In *Ulysses*, Joyce decided to make the creation of the *mature* artist the subject. But how? Why not dramatize how the warmth and generosity of an obscure Middle-class Jew – a man as marginal as Stephen, the egotistical but self-doubting young artist who has not fulfiled his potential – open doors and windows of experience to the latter? Why not demonstrate that on one crucial day (16 June 1904), Stephen began the journey from an immature artist to the mature epic artist who was now writing *Ulysses*? Why not show that Shakespeare, the artist that Joyce regarded as his major precursor in the English language, also used his own life as his subject? And Joyce does all of these things in *Ulysses*.

Indeed, Joyce's creative imagination works, very much in the way that in 'Scylla and Charybdis', the ninth episode of *Ulysses*, Stephen defines Shakespeare's. Stephen praises Shakespeare for qualities that are essential to the artistic conception of *Ulysses* and the narrative presence Joyce creates to tell it. Notwithstanding Stephen's hyperbole and self-doubt about his own argument, Joyce uses this chapter to educate his reader to read his novel in terms of the aesthetic principles with which Stephen interprets Shakespeare; these principles argue that, for the creative genius, the personal past is as important as the historical past because the genius can universalize his own idiosyncratic and nominalistic experience.

From his 1922 vantage point, Joyce has Stephen predict the relationship between his 1904 self and his retrospective fictionalized self: 'In the intense instant of imagination, when the mind, Shelley says, is a fading coal, that which I was is that which I am and that which in possibility I may come to be. So in the future, the sister of the past, I may see myself as I sit here now but by reflection from that which then I shall be' (*U.* 194; IX. 381–5). By defining the relationship between the creative imagination of Shakespeare and the biographical Shakespeare whose actual experience is the crucial source for the activity of his creative imagination, the above passage educates the reader to understand that Joyce viewed Stephen as an immature version of the author who wrote *Ulysses*. But with the necessary experience – and for Joyce that included the kind of heterosexual experience that Bloom and Molly, as well as Shakespeare and Ann Hathaway have shared – Stephen has the potential to become a mature artist.

We should not think that the fictionalized presence is simply a more mature version of Stephen. Rather, the retrospective 'future' self is Joyce fictionalized, within the imagined world of the novel, as a mature omniscient presence whose experience is more inclusive and whose knowledge of life is more profound than we have any reason to believe that Stephen's could ever become. For the creative imagination of this presence not only embodies Stephen's creativity and artistic values, Bloom's experience and humanity, and Molly's female perspective and acceptance of the body, but also is an artistic crucible for discovering universal and epic implications within the ordinary lives of these three characters.

Writing to his brother Stanislaus, Joyce remarked:

Don't you think there is a certain resemblance between the mystery of the Mass and what I am trying to do? I mean that I am trying ... to give people some kind of intellectual pleasure or spiritual enjoyment by converting the bread of everyday life into something that has a permanent artistic life of its own ... for their mental, moral, and spiritual uplift.[5]

Joyce believed in the significance of seemingly trivial details, and wanted to show that significance to the reader. Thus he establishes parallels between different historical eras, such as turn-of-the-century Dublin and Homeric Greece, and between such radically different characters as Bloom and Stephen.

As we read *Ulysses* and feel the presence of Joyce trying to transform his fictionalized reminiscence into a significant form and to define a voice and values that transcend the perspectives of Bloom, Stephen, and Molly, we understand that, like the reader, Joyce had to struggle between, on the one hand, the pleasures of immersion in the local details of his tale and of his language and, on the other, the demands of interpreting those details. In other words, the reader's odyssey recapitulates in important ways the author's odyssey. Do we not experience an active fictionalized presence not merely trying to transform fact into fiction, but trying to transform the bread and wine of ordinary daily experience into an imagined world with its own teleological significance?

To the extent that we see Stephen as a representation of the younger Joyce, we as readers proceed from the fictional *towards the real*. Thus Stephen becomes an immature, self-immersed Joyce who must mature before *Ulysses* can be written, and Bloom represents that part of Joyce which in 1904 still had to be discovered and developed. That the book progresses from Stephen to Bloom and Molly – from Stephen's inexperience to Bloom's worldly and practical experience and Molly's sexual experience – illustrates the maturity that must occur before Stephen can become someone who might hope to write *Ulysses*. Even without the knowledge that reading Ellmann's *James Joyce* gives us of the historical Joyce, we understand that the three major figures signify the fictionalized Joyce who is now speaking to us and that, in this crucial sense, to recall a phrase that the narrator uses to point up the amazing parallelism between the minds of Stephen and Bloom, 'One life is all' (*U.* 202, 280; IX. 653, 907–8).

But even if our sense of the biographical Joyce and the Joyce we import from his other works and letters signifies and is signified by the fictionalized presence, we can only say that we as readers define the character and values of the speaking voice we hear from within the novel as the 'real' Joyce. For as novel readers we can never journey from the fictional to the real, only from the seemingly more fictional to the seemingly less fictional. In a literary version of Zeno's paradox, the real is always outside the imagined world and thus, finally, unreachable to readers. One can approach but never reach the 'real' Joyce, and Joyce knew this without needing Derrida to teach him about the metaphysics of presence.

Our sense of the 'real' voice in novels is based on our own selecting and ordering principles for the words we read. Paradoxically, the more real the voice within the imagined world, the more fictive – in the sense of distorting the biographical or historical reality that precedes the novel – the voice may actually be. Thus while we might speculate about the 'real' Joyce in 1922, *Ulysses* is calling attention to the values of the fictional teller and his relationship to the characters and actions he describes. Does not the novel teach us that, just as Shakespeare can be recreated as a metaphor for Stephen's aesthetic ideology, and just as the artistic presence recreates Odysseus and Elijah to make sense of his world, we readers can and should recreate whatever image of the Joyce artist figure that helps us to make sense of our lives? For more than any other major novel except Finnegans Wake, reading Ulysses depends upon our actively creating our own narrative form – our own coherent interpretive 'story' of reading – to give shape and form to the data that we are collecting piecemeal.

II   RE-ENTER STEPHEN: THE OPENING OF *ULYSSES*

As soon as we enter into the imagined world of *Ulysses*, we realize that Stephen is a man in trouble. He is living with Malachi Mulligan, a man he dislikes and who patronizes him, in a Martello tower which was intended to be a British fortress against a French invasion during the Napoleonic era. Although it is early morning in late spring, a time of hope and promise, the artistic expectations aroused by the ending of *Portrait* are unfulfilled. By providing a traditional omniscient narrator whose voice is separate and distinct from Stephen's, Joyce uses the opening of *Ulysses* to propose a critique of the lyricism and subjectivity of *Portrait*: 'Stately, plump Buck Mulligan came from the stairhead, bearing a bowl of lather on which a mirror and a razor lay crossed' (*U.* 2–3; I. 1–2).

In *Portrait* Joyce oscillates between objectifying Stephen and using him as a thinly disguised autobiographical figure in a fictionalized reminiscence – a reminiscence that contains a quirky combination of Joyce's moral and spiritual autobiography, confession, and artistic credo, even as it provides an occasion for his stylistic experimentation. From the outset of *Ulysses*, Stephen is clearly the result of Joyce's conscious effort to dramatize with some detachment and objectivity a character within the imagined world of the novel.

Put another way, in the opening chapers of *Ulysses*, Stephen has become, in terms of Joyce's genres, less of a lyrical figure and more of an epical figure. As Telemachus setting out on his journey in search of his father and ultimately his mature identity, Stephen must be a distinct objectified character rather than a lyrical figure whose thoughts and emotions reflect Joyce's. Thus, although Stephen's stature within the imagined world is sharply reduced, Joyce's narrator – as opposed to Stephen – has made vast progress towards achieving the artistic goals, defined in *Portrait*, of impersonality, detachment, and stasis.

Reading the first three chapters of *Ulysses*, we inevitably refer back to *Portrait*. In other words, *Portrait* is a special case of Joyce's use of the literary and historical past. That is, we not only measure Stephen against Homer's Telemachus and Shakespeare's Hamlet, the creation of whom was – according to Joyce – pivotal to Shakespeare's development from a lyrical to an epical and dramatic artist, but we hold him up against the younger version of himself who had first left Ireland in spring, 1902 only to return in August 1903 to see his dying mother.

The richness of these first three chapters depends in part on our responding to echoes of prior language and incidents from *Portrait*. It is as if for the reader the past were accompanying Stephen as, to recall what George Eliot wrote about Bulstrode in Middlemarch, 'a still quivering part of himself'. Or, as Stephen puts it in the closing pages of *Portrait*, '[T]he past is consumed in the present and the present is living only because it brings forth the future' (*P*. 251). In a process not unlike pentimento, where images of an earlier and supposedly painted-over version peek through the painting that we are examining, Stephen's past, as we know it from *Portrait*, insists on intruding its shadows upon our perception of Stephen in *Ulysses*. At times Stephen is aware of how he is partially reiterating and reliving the past. But he is not aware, as we are, that Joyce is rewriting it.

What I want to stress is that the meaning Joyce imposed upon Stephen's experience in *Portrait* is undone by subsequent events which cause Stephen to lose hold of some of his imaginative gains and to slip back into artistic and moral confusion. This meaning was earned not only at a very great cost to Stephen's psyche, but its order and form were imposed at a great expense of Joyce's imagination and energy. Let us leave aside the personal cost to Joyce the creator as he unweaves the pattern of meaning he had imposed on his surrogate self, and consider the formal implications of rewriting Stephen's story. The echoes in *Ulysses* of prior passages and incidents in *Portrait* are very much part of our reading experience. Do not our minds read with the prior novel always at the forefront of our memories? Because *Portrait* had moved teleologically towards Stephen's escape from Ireland and his self-definition as an artist, the opening chapters of *Ulysses* are all the more poignant and bathetic. We refer back continuously to what in the context of these first chapters is a searingly ironic conclusion to *Portrait*. Do we not at times feel that Joyce is rewriting what we have already read, opening up experience that we thought was behind us? Does not this process raise questions about whether we can consign any experience to the past or even whether we can impose order on past experience? When, as *Ulysses* progresses, it dramatizes Stephen's and the speaker's movement to maturity as a man and an artist, does not the reader remember the process by which such gains were radically modified and indeed, in large part, erased? In other words, the modification of the teleology of *Portrait* calls into question the reliability of the teleology of *Ulysses*.

If, in *Portrait*, the narrator had viewed with gentle irony both Stephen's concluding dialogue with Cranly and his subsequent diary entries, now Stephen regards himself with bitter self-conscious irony. In place of the ebullient brilliance and confidence in his role as an artist, which we saw in his dialogue with Cranly that precedes the diary entries in *Portrait*, Stephen reveals, in his opening dialogue with Mulligan, self-hatred, loneliness, and cynicism: 'You behold in me, Stephen said with grim displeasure, a horrible example of free thought' (*U.* 20; I. 625–6). Not completely undeserving of Mulligan's diagnosis, 'General paralysis of the insane', Stephen is paralytically self-conscious; looking in the mirror he thinks, 'As he and others see me. Who chose this face for me? This dogsbody to rid of vermin' (*U.* 6; I. 128–9, 136–7). In a sense, Stephen is back where he was at the beginning of the last section of *Portrait* when, partly in response to the devolution in the family fortunes, 'his heart was already bitten by an ache of loathing and bitterness' (*P.* 175). Now, living on his own with Mulligan, a deeply resented pretender to the role of father, Stephen is in the same mood; it is as if the liberation of the concluding pages of Portrait, in which he defined himself as a priest of the imagination who would discover the conscience of his race, had not occurred.

When we recall the euphoric expectations of the penultimate diary entry in *Portrait*, we realize that Stephen's artistic career has become stalled: 'Welcome, O life! I go to encounter for the millionth time the reality of experience and to forge in the smithy of my soul the uncreated conscience of my race' (*P*. 253). Because the reality of experience in the form of passionate feelings and empirical knowledge of life is what he lacks, Stephen is not yet ready to be the writer of the epic that Ireland requires. For Joyce, Stephen's apostasy is his inability to transform his personal and cultural experience into epical and dramatic art. Before Stephen can write an epic of modern Ireland, he must turn his back on various forms of aestheticism that preached 'art for art's sake' and glorified a separation between life and art. In his 1922 *Ulysses* Joyce is rejecting the aestheticism and solipsism of Stephen's credo in the 1916 *Portrait* where he wrote: 'I will try to express myself in some mode of life or art as freely as I can and as wholly as I can, using for my defence the only arms I allow myself to use – silence, exile, and cunning' (*P*. 247).

Unlike his mythical namesake Daedalus, who has adopted the arts to the reality of experience, Stephen is lost in the world of his own dreams. Unlike Daedalus and his son, Icarus, who were imprisoned by Mino in a labyrinth, Stephen is imprisoned in a labyrinth of his own making. He is an Icarus figure who has flown too near the sun rather than, like his namesake, Daedalus, a man who has flown successfully. At the end of *Portrait*, Stephen had wanted to adopt Daedalus as his mythic father without taking on the inevitable identity of the drowning Icarus: 'Old father, old artificer, stand me now and ever in good stead' (*P*. 253). The emphasis on drowning images in the first chapter, 'Telemachus', underlines Stephen's ironic position here as an Icarus figure rather than the Daedalus figure that he had defined as his model in *Portrait*: 'He would create proudly out of the freedom and power of his soul, as the great artificer whose name he bore, a living thing, new and soaring and beautiful, impalpable, imperishable' (*P*. 170). In the ninth episode, 'Scylla and Charybdis', Stephen, the man who desperately wants to be his own father, acknowledges his identity as the poignant son who did not heed his father's advice: 'Fabulous artificer. The hawklike man. You flew. Whereto? Newhaven- Dieppe, steerage passenger. Paris and back. Lapwing. Icarus. *Pater, ait*. Seabedabbled, fallen, weltering. Lapwing you are. Lapwing be' (U.210; IX.952–4; see I. 453). Although Daedalus successfully escaped into exile in Sicily and lived a creative life, Joyce would have also expected the reader to remember that the jealous Daedalus had murdered his nephew Talus whose inventiveness threatened to rival his own. Perhaps the ironic parallel to the murder is Stephen's need to demean his artistic rivals; just as in the 'Cyclops' chapter, Bloom does not murder the modern Polyphemus, the Citizen, but rather uses words, so Stephen slays his rivals with the lancet of his art.

For some time Stephen seems to have acceded to Mulligan's patronizing dominance. He had returned from his exile in Paris for his mother's death, but it is not clear why he remains in Dublin. Morbidly savouring his own misery, he has been wearing black since his mother's death ten months ago and is still locked in bitterness, self-pity, and melancholy. Like Hamlet with whom he identifies, Stephen realizes that he is paralyzed but he does not know what to do about it. Like Claudius, Mulligan is a false father who would usurp his affections, were Stephen, like Hamlet, not intent on rejecting him. Stephen's awkward relationship with Mulligan, in which Stephen is displeased with himself and always on guard, explains his need for an alter ego to help him overcome loneliness and a sense of isolation, a need which explains his later responsiveness to the kindly, sympathetic Bloom.

Stephen desperately needs an empathetic other, someone who will provide the responsive consciousness that prior generations found in a prayerful relation with God. Should we not see the parallel between Stephen's need for a double, a secret sharer, with whom he might communicate in an amoral indifferent cosmos, and the needs of Conrad's Captain in 'The Secret Sharer' and of both Jim and Marlow in Lord Jim, as well as the needs of Hardy's Sue and Jude in *Jude the Obscure* and Lawrence's Paul and Miriam in *Sons and Lovers*?

Our response to the morbid, humourless Stephen would be different and less sympathetic had we not read *Portrait*. But because we have responded to the development of his creative imagination, we do not so readily abandon him and, at least in part, see him as a victim of an indifferent father, insensitive and at times predatory friends, and a narrow-minded and repressive culture. And by the second half of the second episode, 'Nestor', he does become more sympathetic in the conversation with the bigoted and myopic Deasy, an Orangeman who represents the mediocre and materialistic English culture that is infesting Ireland.

III   READING JOYCE'S *ULYSSES*

Ulysses should be read as a social, political, and historical novel. *Ulysses* is Joyce's inquiry into the question of what values are viable in the twentieth-century urban world where, according to Joyce's view, God does not exist and traditional notions of heroism are obsolete. Among other things, *Ulysses* is an effort to redefine the concept of the hero. Joyce uses the marginal Jew Bloom to redefine heroism in secular humanistic terms. As he examines recent Irish history and culture, Joyce proposes Bloom as an alternative to the contemporary xenophobia and fantasies of the Celtic Renaissance as well as a successor to Parnell.

Ulysses teaches us how to read itself. We should think of our experience of reading it as the reader's odyssey. We should be aware of what the novel does to us as we read it and how the ventriloquy of its various styles establishes an unusually complex relationship between text and reader. Unlike some recent critics who believe that Joyce's interest in style deflects the reader from his characters, I believe that the focus in every chapter returns to the subjects of Stephen, Bloom, Molly, and the Dublin world they inhabit. To be sure, in the chapters from 'Sirens' through 'Oxen of the Sun', we are aware of a tension in Joyce's imagination between interest in style and interest in character, but in the climax of every chapter his focus returns to his major figures and their significance. As odyssean readers turning the pages of the novel and progressing through one crystallizing day in the lives of the major figures, we must overcome the difficulties of style and the opacity of content – just as the modern Ulysses, Bloom, must resist temptations to deflect him from his journey home.

In my view the principal interest of Joyce's stylistic experiments should be how they shape a reading of the novel. For the odyssean reader is invited to see that Bloom and Stephen survive and transcend the wealth of detail and the protean transformations of style. Style in *Ulysses* is not, as some recent critics have assumed, something that is embodied in the text separate and distinct from the effects it creates. For Joyce, as for Conrad, style is inseparable from what it does to the events and characters is describes and what it does to us readers as we negotiate our journey through the novel to our final destination, the novel's end. Since Joyce's focus – notwithstanding frequent rhetorical flourishes and word-play for their own sake – always returns to the characters and their meaning, we should assume that the effects of his language upon the reader were never far from his mind.

In 'Ithaca', Joyce's objective scientific voice takes an ironical tone to Bloom's acts of interpretation and, by implication, to the kinds of reading that Ulysses requires; the voice speaks of 'the difficulties of interpretation since the significance of any event followed its occurrence as variably as the acoustic report followed the electrical discharge and of counterestimating against an actual loss by failure to interpret the total sum of possible losses proceeding originally from a successful interpretation' (U. 676; XVII. 343–7). Here Joyce understands that interpretations are often subjective moves posing as objective facts. Yet the passage has other implications. For, if every event has resonance, does not the passage argue for the significance of the relatively trivial events of 16 June 1904? Do we not achieve a kind of immortality in the endless sequence of events that derives, in a kind of ripple effect, from our actions and words?

Ulysses urges the reader to see that if only Bloom's deeds and Stephen's words touch one person, they have an effect because that one person's behaviour and words in turn affect another and so on in an endless sequence. Indeed, that is one reason why the Greek and Hebraic cultures have survived. It is because these cultures – their myths and values – survive as a living tradition that Joyce's metaphors can call them forth from across Lethe and become, as Stephen says, 'lord and giver of their life' (*U.* 415; XIV. 1116). When prior myths are abused or misused – as, for example, in 'Aeolus', when Taylor uses ritualistic hyperbole to compare the bondage of the contemporary Irish with that of the Jews in Egypt – they refuse to answer the call and thus remain among the dead.

Throughout Ulysses, Joyce is aware that the possibility of meaninglessness is inseparable from the probability of significance. Put another way: Joyce depends upon the reader's expectations of coherence and unity, even as he challenges and ironically undermines our desire for order with discrete details, catalogues, neologisms, and nonsense. Joyce wants us to read *Ulysses* as a sacred text in which everything signifies and in which the words of the page represent the possibility for unity and wholeness in the modern world. Yet at the same time he wants us to read profanely and not merely see the book as inconclusive, but as skeptical about the possibility of discovering significance from the plethora of details within his novel – and, by implication, as sceptical of our own efforts to come to terms with even one day in our own lives. By constantly proposing, testing, and discarding multiple identities for Bloom and Stephen, Joyce urges us toward such a complex response. Thus in the hallucinatory episode, 'Circe', no sooner does Bloom imagine himself as the Messiah of the New Jerusalem than he has to be crucified. Moreover, the crucifixion, like its parallel in 'Cyclops', is really a verbal one – a stylistic event – created by Joyce at the expense of Bloom and performed for the reader.

As odyssean readers, we must wend our way through a variety of experiences, but these experiences can best be understood in terms of the novel's two major and contradictory formal principles: on the one hand, its insistence on integration and, on the other, its refusal to allow every word to signify in terms of coherent thematic or structural patterns. Resisting the odyssean reader's efforts to understand *Ulysses* in terms of organic unity are a plethora of catalogues, barely relevant details, marginalia, false clues, linguistic games, and playful attempts to undermine the reader's quest for unity. On the one hand, *Ulysses* insists that its readers interpret every detail in terms of larger patterns, and thus urges the book's own argument that even the most particular details of the individual lives of Bloom and Stephen are important because Bloom and Stephen iterate major historical and mythical figures in western civilization. But, on the other hand, does not Joyce's insistence on exploring the eccentricities of style for its own sake – its local wit, word games, catalogues, neologisms, and odd typography – urge the reader to pause and enjoy, without imposing interpretive patterns or judgements upon, the peculiarities and oddities of either language or human behaviour? Does not the temporary focus on quirky and idiosyncratic aspects in human behaviour and ingenious linguistic pyrotechnics temporarily immerse the reader in the local pleasures of the text that resist interpretation and deflect the reader from stories of reading that propose organic unity?

As with reading *Lord Jim*, we see that reading a complex modern work is enhanced by understanding it in terms of a dialogue between the two modes of reading – the humanistic one that insists on moving from immersion to interpretive reflection and the deconstructive one that stresses immersion in the text for its own sake. For the dialectic between the two modes of reading – a dialectic which enacts more vividly than any other literary work I know the contending claims of the two dominant ideologies of reading on today's critical mindscape – is crucial to the experience of reading *Ulysses*. But it is more accurate to say that at most points *Ulysses* invites the first mode of reading, the traditional humanistic mode of reading that stresses unity of form and content, rather than the latter, deconstructionist mode of reading which questions meaning, coherence, and significance.

Notes

Daniel R. Schwarz, Reading Joyce's 'Ulysses' (London: Macmillan; N.Y. St. Martin's Press, 1987).

2. Quotations refer to *Ulysses: a Critical and Synoptic Edition*, eds Hans Walter Gabler with Wolfhard Steppe and Claus Melchior (London and New York: Garland, 1984). I have included page references to the 1961 Random House edition. Where there is a change in the Gabler edition from the Random House edition, I have underlined the episode and line number.

3. Page references are to the Viking Critical Edition of *A Portrait of the Artist as a Young Man*, ed. Chester G. Anderson (New York: Viking, 1968). A capital 'P' will indicate future references to *Portrait*.

4. Richard Ellmann, *James Joyce* (New York: Oxford University Press, 1982; orig. edn 1959) p. 358.

5. Quoted in Richard Ellmann, *James Joyce*, p. 163; from *My Brother's Keeper*, ed. Richard Ellmann (New York: The Viking Press, 1958) pp. 103–4.

11

Reading Virginia Woolf: *Mrs. Dalloway* and *To The Lighthouse*

I

Reading Woolf's fiction means participating in the process of sorting out values, for she does not measure her characters by a set of moral principles as, say, Jane Austen does in *Emma*. On every page we experience Woolf's own quest for meaning, her puzzlement with life's riddles, her sense of wonder intermingled with her anxiety and doubt. In the voices of her narrators, we feel the presence of Woolf desperately trying to create meaning from the material within her narrative. This effort to create meaning mirrors the major subject of her novels: the quest of her characters to create meaning within a world in which time and mortality are the first principles and where order – divine or otherwise – is absent. Woolf is the subject of her fiction, and the form is the correlative to her search for personality, character, and meaning. But because her search is the act of desperation of a person living on the edge, we realize that she is willing to settle for something far more ephemeral for both herself and her characters: moments of apparent unity, temporary states of feeling which inevitably must pass; aesthetic insights that are undermined by the imperfection of art; resting places that are marked by the absence of turmoil rather than by the presence of anything vital except her language. In other words, her quest is for islands in which the soul's turmoil might rest before continuing on its excruciatingly painful mortal journey. Yet she knew that moments of visions, those intense and splendid oases of the soul when one could not separate the dancer from the dance, were always more real in their anticipation than their effects. Like Joyce, she felt the gap between word and world; but, even more than Joyce until *Finnegans Wake*, for her the word was often more real than the world. Writing for Woolf was not merely – as for the other writers in this study – an effort to define her past, but also a refuge and antidote for madness. Writing fiction enabled her to feel that her life had purpose and value: 'Now I'm writing fiction again I feel my force glow straight from me at its fullest' (*Diaries*, II, 19 June 1923).[1] Reading Woolf depends on discarding notions of the biographical fallacy or notions of pure textuality in favour of a willingness to respond to the poignant, intense, impulsive, caring presence whose voice speaks and performs the imagined world of the novel. Woolf's aesthetic programme enacts the *value* of feelings and emotions. While she sought in her work an escape from personality, what she actually does is redefine the concept of personality in terms which include moments of feeling. In an important 1920 diary entry she wrote:

> I figure that the approach will be entirely different this time: no scaffolding, scarcely a brick to be seen; all crepuscular, but the heart, the passion, humour, everything as bright as fire in the mist.... I suppose the danger is the damned egotistical self: which ruins Joyce and [Dorothy] Richardson to my mind: is one pliant & rich enough to provide a wall for the book from oneself without its becoming, as in Joyce and Richardson, narrow & restricting?
>
> (*Diaries*, II, 26 Jan. 1920)

For Woolf, realism meant, among other things, sincerity and depth of feeling: 'Am I writing *The Hours* [an earlier title for *Mrs. Dalloway*] from deep emotion? Of course the mad part tries me so much, makes my mind squint so badly that I can hardly face spending the next weeks at it' (*Diaries*, II, 19 June 1923). Yet she had a fear that she might misuse the precious avatar of language:

> One must write from deep feeling, said Dostoevsky. And do I? Or do I fabricate with words, loving them as I do? No I think not.... I daresay its true, however, that I haven't that 'reality' gift. I insubstantise, wilfully to some extent, distrusting reality – its cheapness. But to get further. Have I the power of conveying the true reality? Or do I write essays about myself?
>
> (*Diaries* II, 19 June 1923)

Yet, at times, what is most real to Woolf is the language she uses to create an alternative to the painful reality of the world in which she lives. Put another way, Woolf wanted to intrude into the space between the tick and the tock of passing time and create significant time, to, as she puts it in the passage I quoted in my first chapter, rescue life from 'waste, deadness, superfluity' by 'saturat[ing] every atom' with the significance of artistic understanding (*Diaries*, III, 28 Nov. 1928). (Not only Lily Briscoe, but in their own ways, Mrs. Dalloway and Mrs. Ramsay are trying to do the same.)

The search for verbal correlatives to non-verbal experience is a characteristic theme of British modernism; the search is a function of traditional British empiricism that believes in the power of the mind to control the world as well as a challenge to that empiricism. In Woolf's quest to discover the language for and to give artistic shape to the interior light of the mind, we should see a kinship with Lawrence's efforts to dramatize the unconscious experience and Joyce's efforts to penetrate beneath the levels of conscious behaviour. Woolf's web of multiple connections moves towards but never quite reaches unity for the reader, because the reader is always aware that Woolf is obsessively insisting on unity in a world which she knows at the deepest level lacks it. Thus the reader is aware that despite Woolf's desire to imitate unity, she is forced to create it. Because her rhetoric convinces her readers – male and female – that our world is her world, we too are the subjects of Woolf's fiction. The verbal connections become less a signifier of deeper spiritual unity than a substitute for it and, finally, a reminder of what can never be there in a Godless world.

On one hand, Woolf presents a humanism based on multiple subjectivity. On the other, she enacts a deconstruction of that humanism based on her anxiety that only the immediacy of the text could have any reality for her. Woolf understood and feared this paradox in her work:

> I think writing must be formal. The art must be respected.... If one lets the mind run loose, it becomes egotistic: personal, which I detest; like Robert Graves. At the same time the irregular fire must be there; & perhaps to loose it, one must begin by being chaotic, but not appear in public like that.
>
> (*Diaries* II, 18 Nov. 1924)

Like Joyce and Eliot, Woolf wanted to write about her experience when it represented the experience of others. To paraphrase what

Joyce in Ulysses has Stephen Dedalus say of Shakespeare, 'she wanted to find in the world without as actual what was in [her] world within as possible'.

The novel is, of course, a realistic genre whose central generic and canonical debate has revolved around what constitutes realism – what is real, real truth and how does one render it if one can locate it? Is 'reality' the details – the specifity – of the lives and conditions of the imagined world? Or is reality based on correlation to an *a priori* world? Are characters whose thoughts and feelings respond to the social and historical conditions in which they find themselves more real than characters whose minds are not historically defined? Is it the texture – the recognizable nouns, verbs, and adjectives – of the language used by an omniscient narrator that makes a novel real? Or is it the kinship between how we plot our own narrative actions: dreaming, scheming, planning? Or is the true realism – as Sterne implies in *Tristram Shandy* – the digressions from a narrative line, from consistent behaviour, and from literal language?

The point of departure of Woolf's reality is the Austen world of English country houses, rigid social customs, and understated feelings and attitudes. But her 'reality' focuses on the individual moments of heightened perceptions, although she does not neglect the physical details of daily life or the historical or economic teleology that Marxists believe shape human life. For her 'reality' does include a keen awareness of the World War, and the permanent change it wrought in England's social fabric.

Like Lily in *To the Lighthouse*, Woolf wishes to isolate events from their temporal dimension and give them pictorial shape. To be sure, the spatial arrangement of her novels owes much to impressionism's desire to displace the conventional idiom of perception with fresh, human perceptions of what the eye and mind actually experience and to cubism's insistence on seeing a figure or object on its spatial plane and from multiple perspectives. In *Mrs. Dalloway*, to emphasize how there is not one reality, she depicts London from the perspective of every character in terms of his or her individual interior space.

But the words are those of Woolf, who, like a cubist painter, tries to give space definition. To use terms she uses in a letter to Jacques Ravarat, she is one of the writers 'who are trying to catch and consolidate and consummate (whatever the word is for making literature) those splashes of yours' (*Letters*, II, 3 Oct. 1924).

In her fiction each life is a group of spaces defined by lines (of experience, of family, of social circumstances) but only partially filled with substance. According to Bell, Woolf 'is claiming for herself the ability, or at least the intention, to see events out of time, to apprehend processes of thought and feeling as though they were pictorial shapes'.[2] But she fully understands that this is a quest, not a reachable goal, and that such pictorial shapes belie the very processes they describe. Mrs. Dalloway, for example, needs rather more from Richard and her daughter than they provide, and is left with rather large gaps to fill with parties, diurnal activity, and, most importantly, memories. For Woolf knew that human memory – in its functions of imposing order and discovering significance – has a kinship with the more developed sensibility of the artist. The artist goes a step further and transforms memory into the formal design of a painting, a novel, a musical composition.

Woolf is trying to give shape to moments of experience without ordering them any more than is necessary. As do the characters within her novels, Woolf uses memory to draw lines that make sense of experience, but the artist goes one step further and embodies experience with artistic form. The reader is educated by the novels to understand the kinship between memory and artistic sensibility. Like the perceiver of cubist paintings, the reader must give the space definition in terms that she or he can understand. But Woolf understands that this search for the moment out of time is a quest, not a reachable goal, and any such pictorial shapes, including those achieved by her characters – Lily's, for example – or her herself inevitably belie the processes that they decribe. As she wrote in a 6 May 1935 diary entry, '[T]he more complex a vision ... the less it is able to sum up & make linear' (*Diaries* IV).

The unity of both novels – indeed, all Woolf novels except *Orlando* – depends on a web of connections woven by the narrator outside the mind of the characters. For Woolf, the novel is like a canvas, a material surface on which to place words, to recreate a new reality by verbal strokes of the brush and patches of colour. She is concerned with the formal and chromatic effect of the relationship among words and sentences apart from any anterior reality it imitates. Like Lily, she wants to discover a moment out of time, and to weave a texture that might unify the diverse temporal moments into something more. Because unity exists in the mind of the omniscient narrator as it exists in the eye of the painter, Lily's quest to complete her painting is in a metonymical relationship with the speaker's effort to discover unity in the texture of events she narrates. Thus Lily's thought, 'he must have reached it', echoes Mr. Ramsay's silent reflection: 'I have reached it' (p. 308). Completing the painting not only takes us back to Mrs. Ramsay's social choreography, it metonymically enacts for the reader the completion of the novel because it accomplishes the aesthetic goal defined from the first page; it enacts how, for those who belong to what we might call Woolf's Sensitive and Aesthetic Elect, 'any turn in the wheel of sensation has the power to crystallise and transfix the moment upon which its gloom or radiance rests' (p. 9). The intricate texture of images and echoes enables her to both overcome and evade the polarities and paradoxes implied by the story. Yet are we not aware that the resolution – depending on spatially arranged verbal relationships that transcend the quests of the characters and the traditional ironic view of the omniscient narrator – is akin to modern painting's resolution of multiple perspectives on a flat plane? The transpersonal moment of visions of epiphanic unity is in a tension with the traditional narrative perspective – in Woolf's case a narrative perspective that has a paratactic rather than a syntactic quality.

On one hand, in Woolf, the reader experiences a disembodied voice mediating between separate consciousness; on the other, the most physical aspect of a Woolf novel is the narrative voice. Of course, the disembodied voice is most and least a presence in the 'Time Passes' section: 'I cannot make ["Time passes"] out – here is the most difficult abstract piece of writing – I have to give an empty house, no people's characters, the passage of time, all eyeless and featureless with nothing to cling to.... Is it nonsense, is it brilliance? Why am I so flown with words, & apparently free to do exactly what I like? ... this is not made up; it is the literal fact' (*Diaries* III, 18 Apr. 1926). The voice is simultaneously more personal and more distant than the traditional omniscient narrator. It is more personal because we feel Woolf's compelling urgency; it is more objective because it at times takes a hawklike or Godlike perspective which actively focuses on the pattern at the expense of characters. In doing so, does not Woolf escape the imprisoning conditions of human life and the quest to define herself as artist on a different level of reality? And this has continuities with the iconoclastic aestheticism of the 1890s that was a source of modernism.

In Woolf's novels the narrator's withholding and deferral of significance are as much a part of the narrator's telling as the rendering of it. One might even say that the narrator mediates rather than renders the multiple points of view and that in the act of mediation the narrator eschews the traditional ironic perspective that is such a distinctive feature of omniscient narration in the English novel. Indeed, the quest for meaning is antithetical to conclusive meaning – a meaning which is at least partially aligned with Mr. Ramsay's autocratic positivism. To the extent that Lily's line carries closure, it, like any vision, has a trace of the certainty that Woolf both sought and wished to avoid. The moment of vision is, then, an intimation of both immortality and mortality, for its suspension of time coexists with its awareness of passing time and, as the vision is assigned to past time, the moment takes us another step toward what the voice of To the Lighthouse calls that 'fabled land where our brightest hopes are extinguished, our frail barks founder in darkness' (p. 11). If the ecstatic vision, the epiphanic moment, moves to stability and stasis, it must carry the trace of mortality.

Woolf is the paradigmatic text for the *aporia* of modern criticism. For she enacts the division between the quest for reality of humanistic formalism and the contention of deconstruction that language can never probe to the centre of reality. The diary entries quoted above enact that *aporia*. Woolf's voice enacts the position of an outsider within her imagined worlds. She has a sense of herself writing as a woman in a man's world (including a literary culture dominated by men), writing as a modernist but shaped by the Victorian world, and writing as someone whose beliefs are tentative formulations in a world which values certainty. Even as she seeks a centre, even as she strains for a deeper reality and psychology of character than that found in prior fiction, she creates a texture of language that at once seeks and eschews a dialogue with reality. Creating on its own plane a texture of impressions freed from anterior reality, Woolf's novels are a correlative to the flat surfaces of cubism that resolve foreground and background.

II

Mrs. Dalloway is a lyrical novel rather than a narrative one: while empathetic to the life of Clarissa, the voice transcends her individual perspective and places her in an historical and cultural context of which she is a part. The novel is poised between voice and character, life and death, war and peace, lyric and narrative; it is that poise, that balance, that gives it its magnificence. *Mrs. Dalloway* is autobiographical because it explores the similarities and differences between what we call madness and what we call sanity. For Woolf, no theme could be more urgent. The novel enables her to examine attitudes and states of mind that are crucial to her experience.

By choosing a day in Clarissa's life in which her past returns with a difference (Peter's and to a lesser extent Sally's return to her life), Woolf uses the reiterative possibilities of fiction to juxtapose past and present through memory and to cast a taut design that weaves a pattern of now and then. It is the linearity, the temporality of fiction that makes possible its spatiality. As we reread *Mrs. Dalloway*, does it not progress, pulsate outward in concentric circles from crucial memories rather than proceed in a linear movement through time? Within those circles are missed opportunities, disappointments, and parallels to other lives. The novel ironically fulfils the title character's wish that she might have her life to live over again, while it urges us to see that she would have made the same decisions if she had such an opportunity.

Mrs. Dalloway is Woolf's response to Joyce's *Ulysses*, a work she grudgingly admired, despite what she felt was its tediousness and coarseness. Is Miss Kilman's mackintosh coat an effort to evoke the enigmatic and marginal Man in the Macintosh in *Ulysses*? Depicting one day in the life of a middle-class woman, Woolf gives the title character no mythic identity. Like *Ulysses*, *Mrs. Dalloway* takes place in a large, impersonal city in the month of June; and Woolf chooses a crystallizing day because Peter and Sally return to her life from the past and her double, Septimus Smith, commits suicide. Clarissa is no more aware of the parallels to Septimus Smith than Bloom is aware of his mythic identity as the modern Odysseus or the putative Moses. But while the reader is urged to see Bloom as a humanistic hero whose values and strong sense of self might point the way to redeem Ireland – that is, to see Bloom as a representative figure whose signifying function is established by the novel – Mrs. Dalloway never emerges from her own analytic half-light and the narrator's ironic bathos which reduce her to a ghost or shadow; she 'had the oddest sense of being herself invisible; unseen; unknown' (p. 14). She regards her physical appearance with self-contempt: '[S]he had a narrow pea-stick figure; a ridiculous little face, beaked like a bird's' (p. 14).

Despite the apparently monologic or univocal voice, the complexity of Woolf's perceptions gives the novel's omniscient narrator a richly polyphonic or dialogic voice which renders the full complexity of Clarissa, Peter, and even Septimus. Opening *Mrs. Dalloway* takes us into an imagined world in which sensibility and feeling count for everything and where traditional manners and morality and their effects count for little. This latter world is presented as a vestige of Victorianism; it is epitomized by Hugh Whitbread who, as Peter said, 'had no heart, no brain, nothing but the manners and breeding of an English gentleman' (p. 8). In this melancholy world, love is not a passionate impulse, but a kind of habit. People in late middle age are conscious of approaching death. The central event is a suicide. There is little promise implied by the young people such as Elizabeth or Miss Kilman. The dawn of a clear June morning is the setting for the novel that is an elegy for Clarissa, Septimus Smith, and for the ineffectual society to which Clarissa belongs.

Virginia Woolf has captured the agony of Clarissa's loneliness, the results of her sexual repression and frigidity, and her capitulation to social convention. Clarissa's life is a function of a few crucial decisions made years ago. In a sense, her life is over because she has missed her chance for love with both Peter and Sally and settled for something less. Clarissa feared intimacy with Peter because 'everything had to be shared; everything gone into' (p. 10); she chooses the separateness that culminates in the room in the attic. Peter recalls that 'there was always something cold in Clarissa' (p. 73). Had she responded to her impulse to love a woman, she might have been fulfiilled. Repressed to the point of frigidity, she is both attracted to and frightened by the spontaneity of Peter and Sally. For her, giving parties provides the possibility of unity that her personal life lacks. She requires the admiration of others to complete her: 'How much she wanted it – that people should look pleased as she came in' (p. 13). The passivity of Clarissa, locked into her stereotypical social roles of ageing hostess, supportive political wife, and household managers, contrasts with Peter, who remains alive and open to possibilities; even as he confronts ageing, disappointment, and loneliness, he lives and speaks according to his feelings.

The novel's efficacy depends on its taut ironic tone and deft stylistic control. Notice how Woolf uses the image of Richard as a spider to urge the reader to see Clarissa as victim:

> And as a single spider's thread after wavering here and there attaches itself to the point of a leaf, so Richard's mind, recovering from its lethargy, set now on his wife, Clarissa, whom Peter Walsh had loved so passionately; and Richard had had a sudden vision of her there at luncheon.
>
> (pp. 172–3)

Woolf strikingly contrasts Richard and Peter, who is presented in lucid, straightforward syntax without metaphor as the person whom Mrs. Dalloway had *loved passionately* – as her missed alternative to Richard. Richard's use of words like 'vision' and 'miracle' are bathetic:

> He stopped at the crossing; and repeated – being simple by nature, and undebauched, because he had tramped, and shot; being pertinacious and dogged, having championed the downtrodden and followed his instincts in the House of Commons; being preserved in his simplicity yet at the same time grown rather speechless, rather stiff – he repeated that it was a miracle that he should have married Clarissa; a miracle – his life had been a miracle, he thought; hesitating to cross.
>
> (p. 175)

Does not the syntax mock Richard's egotism and conceit by deliberately imitating the pompousness and indecision of a man who is entrusted to be one of the nation's leaders? Does not the diction – 'preserved in his simplicity', 'grown rather speechless', 'stiff', 'hesitating to cross' – depict a man approaching senility and death?

Like Forster's Fielding, Peter values personal relationships and feels they add to the 'infinite richness, this life' (p. 248). Thus he is drawn to Clarissa's party in part because he shares her social values, but much more because he still is attracted to her like a moth to a flame. Yet he feels 'something arrogant; unimaginative, prudish' within her, and recalls a moment when her harsh attitude towards a woman who had a baby before marriage had made Peter feel 'the death of her soul' (p. 89). That day lives as part of the searing present for Peter because it was the day he and Clarissa had first seen Richard. Peter is a twentieth-century man who believes not in ultimate values, but in the value of experience for its own sake. But he also doubts himself because of his failure to win Clarissa. As much as Clarissa and Septimus, he is beset by self-doubt: '[H]e could not come up to the scratch, being always apt to see round things ... and to tire very easily of mute devotion and to want variety in love' (p. 241). Yet for all his failings, he has the capacity to love and to renew himself. In Peter's presence, Clarissa feels that she has made little of her life, even while Peter is feeling that he has much life left.

Peter's present life is composed of love affairs, work, and quarrels, as hers is not. When he weeps and she consoles him, she realizes that, 'If I had married him, this gaiety would have been mine all day!'; but she retreats from the impulse to say, 'Take me with you', retreats to the psychological enclosure she has built for herself (p. 70). Peter feels young in his passion for Daisy, just as Clarissa feels old for the lack of passionate love. Is not Woolf implying we are what we love? Peter, like Clarissa, savours his experience, but his, of course, is more recent; Peter thinks, 'the compensation of growing old ... was simply this; that the passions remain as strong as ever, but one has gained – at last! – the power which adds the supreme flavour to existence, – the power of taking hold of experience, of turning it round, slowly, in the light' (p. 119). Yet Peter thinks that the pleasure and meaning of life are much less personal than when he was young, but surely the experience of Septimus and Clarissa contradicts this. Peter's love for Daisy is easy for him because he will not suffer as Clarissa has made him suffer.

The 'solitary traveller' who 'by conviction' is 'an atheist perhaps' and who thinks 'Nothing exists outside us except a state of mind' is not only Peter but Woolf herself (p. 85). In his life Peter has rejected the possibility of surrender ('let me blow to nothingness with the rest'), but Septimus succumbs to this death wish and it has its appeal for Clarissa (p. 87). Peter can not forget Clarissa who, for all her faults, still captivates; like Jane Austen's Emma, he is an example of 'himself creating what he saw'. As the imaginative man, half-creating what he sees, Peter is an artist figure; indeed, as he fantasizes about a girl he follows, he reflects that 'the better part of life' is 'made up' (p. 81). His self-image as 'an adventurer, reckless, ... romantic buccaneer' sustains him (p. 80). Like Septimus and Clarissa, Peter gives meaning to the sky and branches and uses his imagination as a refuge from 'this fever of living' (p. 86). Yet his youthful 'revelations' about the death of her soul and his prediction that Clarissa will marry Richard become self-fulfilling prophecies that help create the reality that he now sees. Indeed, we feel that he may have lost Clarissa because he was unable to respond to her needs and Richard's challenge.

Like Stevens and Yeats, Woolf believes that there is continuity between artistic activity and imaginative activity that sustains all of us. But Mrs. Dalloway's belief that she is a refuge and a radiance is an ironic version of this belief. By an act of will she feels she can draw 'the parts [of herself] together' and become 'a radiancy no doubt in some dull lives, a refuge for the lonely to come to, perhaps' (p. 55). But except for Peter, who has a nostalgic feeling for his first love, does this radiance really matter? Isn't this forced radiance a substitute for passion and creativity? Woolf is examining a life which lacks the certainty of religion or authority, but, which unlike her own, does not have the compensation of art. It is as if she is doing research into the lives of those who do not have, like herself or Lily Briscoe, the artistic activity of creating worlds to sustain them.

The novel's prevailing tone is ironic bathos, a sense that life is far less than religious and literary texts have preached. By incongruous juxtaposition or inflated rhetoric, Woolf undermines the notion that human life yields sublime experience. According to Bell, 'she maintained an attitude sometimes of mild, sometimes of aggressive agnosticism'.[3] How, Woolf asks, do we create meaning in 'this late age of the world's experience' when airplanes deface the sky with advertisements and we poignantly seek to discover an equivalent for the sacraments and rituals of religion in the suspicion that a politically prominent figure occupies a chauffered motor car (p. 13)? Note the narrator's description of the clouds on which man has grotesquely written an advertisement for toffee: 'the clouds ... moved freely, as if destined to cross from West to East on a mission of the greatest importance which would never be revealed' (p. 30). Isn't Septimus a parody of romantic visionaries who read the signature of human things upon nature, who anthropomorphize nature, who see the expression of divine order in nature's disorder? Instead of Christ or instead of Joyce's great humanistic hero, Bloom, Woolf's London has for its 'prophet' a pathetic self-appointed scapegoat who commits suicide.

To the extent that the novels of 1890–1930 reflect that we no longer believe Christianity's promise of salvation, the anticipation of death – final, conclusive, insignificant death – becomes the determining factor of how humans live. As in Joyce's 'The Dead' and Forster's *Howards End*, the major character in *Mrs. Dalloway* (as in *To the Lighthouse*) is death. And death has a seductive attractiveness for Woolf as the mother of Beauty that makes it possible to wrench meaning by imposing form (or discourse) on the flux of life (or story). The process of reading *Mrs. Dalloway* shows us that death lurks in every crevice of the imagined world, just as emptiness and loneliness define every life. The novel's world is blighted and darkened by death. The novel is pervaded by constant reminders of the ravages of war, beginning with the early reference to Mrs. Foxcroft 'eating her heart out because that nice boy was killed' (p. 5). Septimus is, of course, a war victim. Mrs. Dalloway has had a bout of influenza which has affected her heart. She has been consigned to an attic room for recuperation, but this room leaves her separate from her family and desperately dependent on social ritual and memory to create meaning, even though she values this separation as independence. Death is never absent from the text for more than a few pages, nor is it absent from the thoughts of Mrs. Dalloway or Septimus Smith. Death is in the lines from *Cymbeline* that echo in her mind:

> Fear no more the heat o' the sun
> Nor the furious winter's rages.
>
> (p. 13)

It is in her opening premonition, fulfilled by Septimus Smith's suicide, 'standing there at the open window, that something awful was about to happen' (p. 3). The candle in her attic room, like the candle in Greta's and Gabriel's room in 'The Dead', suggests death. Does not Woolf expect us to think of Bronte's *Jane Eyre* where Rochester confined his wife in the attic?

Isn't Woolf playing on Clarissa's initials and implying that Clarissa's life is moving towards death – just as surely as Septimus's – and just as surely as in the recitation of the alphabet, C inevitably passes to D. When Clarissa learns that Richard will not return for lunch she feels 'shrivelled, aged, breastless' (p. 45). Her enemy is mortality of which she is acutely conscious: '[S]he feared time itself, and read on Lady Bruton's face, as if it had been a dial cut in impassive stone, the dwindling of life; how year by year her share was sliced' (p. 44). Mrs. Dalloway is the woman

Woolf feared that she might become. Ageing, lonely, living in the memories of the past, bothered by petty grievances, and regretful of the choices she has made ('Oh if she could have had her life over again!'), she sews as if she were sewing her own shroud (p. 14). Life is reduced to surfaces because she made the wrong choices.

Woolf uses verbal puns to imbue the reader's consciousness with a sense of imminent death. Clarissa 'stiffened a little; she would stand at the top of her stairs'. The recurring old women are reminiscent of the libidinous, often ageing figures that Aschenbach confronts in *Death in Venice*. The grey nurse knitting next to Peter, while he dreams, recalls the classical, Parcae knitting men's fate; Carrie Dempster (whose initials are the same as Clarissa's) suggests Clarissa's mortality. The influenza that may have affected her heart recalls the illness of Hans Castorp in *The Magic Mountain*; and the sterility and moral confusion that beset London in 1923, the bankruptcy of public figures and the absence of private values, recall Mann's vision of Europe. We should think of *Mrs. Dalloway*, along with *Women in Love*, as England's Weimar novels, novels of a world that has lost its moorings and in which its inhabitants desperately seek for values or at least sustaining illusions.

The scope of *Mrs. Dalloway* belies the view that it is a novel of manners. Its mention of Einstein and Mendel, its focus on the aeroplane and the limousine in the early pages, the prominence of the war and its effects, as well as the preparation for future battles implied by the young boys in uniform, make it an historical document about England in a period of cultural transformation. The inclusiveness of the novel also depends on historical backgound (the Roman presence in England), religious contexts (Christianity's origins and promises), and references to English literary culture – Shakespeare and the Romantics – which Woolf both wants to use as points of reference and to modify.

Although Peter conceives of himself as an heir to adventurers of the past, he is not motivated by ideals of service to Church or State: for he believes, 'Nothing exists outside us except a state of mind' (p. 85). Woolf implies that the social and historical context – with its inconclusiveness, its discontinuities and violence to the past – demands that her subject be the economics of sensibility: the give and take between memories and the present, between the self and other in personal relationships. One might say that Woolf's novels seek to be post-historical because history has ceased to provide sense-making patterns.

Mrs. Dalloway includes every social class. Woolf is very much aware of the schism between the haves and the have-nots. She shows the irony of London's poor people discovering value in the pageantry of the monarchy by thinking 'of the heavenly life divinely bestowed upon Kings' (p. 27). After his five years in India, Peter is struck by the change in London. Not only have the positions of the lower classes and the young changed, but social mores have become less rigid; Peter sees a 'shift in the whole pyramidal accumulation which in his youth had seemed immovable' (p. 246). Moreover, Clarissa's relation with her servants, and, in particular the vignette of Lucy about servants who had to leave a play in the middle lest they be late, shows how stratified England still is. But because Church and State are no longer a benign helpful force, military training deprives men of their uniqueness and turns them 'into a stiff yet staring corpse by discipline' (p. 77). Miss Kilman finds in religious fervour and piety an outlet for class resentment: 'She in touch with invisible presences! Heavy, ugly, commonplace, without kindness or grace, she know the meaning of life! Miss Kilman stood there ... (with the power and taciturnity of some prehistoric monster armoured for primeval warfare)' (p. 190). (Does the rhetoric of insult with which the voice dilutes Miss Kilman reveal something about the failure of Woolf's historical consciousness, particularly her lack of range in her class sympathy?)

Even more than the other novelists in this study, Woolf challenges nineteenth-century conceptions about a coherent self. Woolf depicts the ironic tension between, on the one hand, elaborate and often vestigial social rules in which people no longer quite believe, and on the other, the incoherence of personalities struggling for definition and meaning in life. To recall my quotation of 'An Ordinary Evening in New Haven' in my first chapter, for Woolf, character becomes 'the cry of the occasion' rather than a stable core of attitudes and values. Continuously, the self reassembles itself in different shapes – shapes that draw upon the range of possibilities stored in the psyche and shaped by prior experience. And the striking parallels between characters show that the possibilities of behaviour vary less from person to person than the reader might expect. In Woolf, the self one presents depends on one's most recent experiences. The self is something one creates and recreates; each experience brings temporary coherence to one's personality: 'That was her self when some effort, some call on her to be her self, drew the parts together, she alone knew how different, how incompatible and composed so for the world only into one centre, one diamond, one ... meeting-point' (p. 55). But temporary coherence is like the syntax of daily discourse, where the next sentence takes precedence over the blurring memory of the last. Clarissa's radical oscillation between depression and exaltation, between past and present, between regret and satisfaction, between longing for an alternative life and glorying in this one, and between nihilism and affirmation of life, does not give her a stable core. Her momentary triumphs must be seen in the context of her living a narrow, constrained existence in which social rituals have replaced values and in which the lack of self-confidence creates erratic lurches of feeling rather than a fully coherent self. Clarissa requires others to complete her, to give her meaning.

The form enacts the temptations to narcissism and solipsism as the central crises of the characters' lives. Woolf understands that Clarissa's curse is the artist's curse – to be detached from life, observing and recording it, but not fully living within it; Clarissa regrets that she has not made more of her life – that she has written a fragmented, disrupted narrative, and that she has scant hopes of writing a different life-narrative. Thus the present is displaced by the past. Clarissa's fear of becoming 'invisible; unseen; unknown' reflects Woolf's fear of immersing herself in her art to the point that she becomes remote from life as well as her concomitant fear that if one ceases to create, life is only emptiness and loneliness. 'That is all', the self-contained and reflexive phrase that at times seems to epitomize Clarissa's life, reflects these fears. In Woolf's novels, self-love is the antithesis of the affirmative value of making other people's lives more pleasurable and more meaningful by means of affection, understanding, and tolerance. The novel examines possible alternatives to emptiness, isolation, and disengagement, but offers only the poignant feeling of temporary community achieved by the ersatz social ritual of the concluding party.

To establish the continuity between life and art, Woolf stresses that reading is a mode of perceiving. No one can quite make out the apocalyptic message of the airplane. In every experience Septimus Smith reads confirmation of his own views, namely that 'The secret signal which one generation passes, under disguise, to the next is loathing, hatred, despair' (p. 134). That Septimus discovers confirmation of his views shows us that reading texts, like reading experience, is inevitably a subjective experience. But is he any more subjective a reader than Clarissa or Hugh Whitbread? Each character has trouble connecting with his own experience and understanding that of others. Each character perceives reflexively. To avoid nihilism, to discover meaning in one's life, one has to become actively aware of others and of the context of experience in which one is living. By showing the kinship between disparate people, the narrative presence transcends the parochialism of self-isolation and reaches beyond her own consciousness. For example, when the narrator renders Septimus's feelings in terms of Clarissa's quotation from *Cymbeline*, 'Fear no more, says the heart in the body; fear no more' (p. 211), the reader shares an ironic awareness of which the characters are oblivious. For we realize that this line – simultaneously urging passionate participation in life and submission to the sensual appeal of death – is not only Clarissa's but Woolf's. The urgency of the novel depends upon our realization that *Mrs. Dalloway* is exploring Septimus's insight that 'it might be possible that the world itself is without meaning', a view confirmed by Richard's momentary perception of 'the worthlessness of this life' (pp. 133, 172).

At the essence of *Mrs. Dalloway* is the relationship that never comes off between Peter and Clarissa. She is unable and unwilling to share completely her thoughts and feelings, to become the mutually empathetic other to another person which in the novels of the 1890–1930 period is the one compensation for a world without God. Yet she maintains her independence at a great cost. Isolated from social relations, waiting passively for events, including her husband's return, while keeping herself busy with trivial details, Clarissa's character fulfils Woolf's early paratactic description: 'She sliced like a knife through everything; at the same time was outside, looking on' (p. 11). At a crucial time that knife had cut the bond to Peter. Since then, Clarissa's life has narrowed to the kind of social entrapment in which we see her, but it is not the narrative she would have chosen for her life, had she the energy to give her life direction: 'Oh if she could have had her life over again! she thought, stepping on to the pavement, could have looked even differently!' (p. 14). In the reminiscence of Clarissa, the sterile present contrasts with the past of more hopeful days. Her sensibility seems too fastidious, too delicate for the life around her.

Her hatred – described as 'a brutal monster', a kind of dinosaur which inhabits her imagination, just as a threatening finny sea-monster lurked at the edge of Woolf's psyche, wanting to devour her rationality and sanity – for her daughter's friend, the ugly and religious Miss Kilman, undermines her very essence; it 'gave her physical pain, and made all pleasure in beauty, in friendship, in being well, in being loved and making her home delightful rock, quiver, and bend. . . .' (p. 17). It exposes her to the possibility – and for the reader it is a very real possibility enacted by the form of the novel – that 'the whole panoply of content [of her life] were nothing but self-love' (p. 17). Yet the hatred is a passionate feeling toward others, and the self-love on which the hatred is based triggers her creative energies, as when she delights in her life and feels 'one must pay back from this secret deposit of exquisite moments' (p. 43).

Because Clarissa lacks a central core, she is vulnerable to despair over the smallest occurrences. She realizes that she lacks something essential: 'It was not beauty; it was not mind. It was something central which permeated; something warm which broke up surfaces and rippled the cold contact of man and woman, or of women together' (p. 46). She is unresponsive to men, but capable of the pleasure – which she barely acknowledges – of being aroused by women. The constraints of respectability prevent her from following her sexual bent. Sally Seton represents the libidinous, forbidden, unacknowledged self. At other times in the presence of a woman, she felt 'some astonishing significance, some pressure of rapture . . . an illumination' (p. 47).

As in Eliot, Conrad, Lawrence, and Joyce, allusions suggest the fullness of the present in comparison to the emptiness of the past, as well as the inevitable passing of the present into the dead past. Woolf was influenced by Joyce's mythic and allusive method; but while he used past and present to question one another – after all, Bloom's humanity, pacifism, and eloquence are privileged over Odysseus's occasional disregard for life and bellicose behaviour – Woolf regards Clarissa Dalloway from an ironic perspective. For example, she implies a comic perspective when she shows Clarissa thinking of her party in terms that would be more appropriate to martyrdom or crises of the soul: 'Why seek pinnacles and stand drenched in fire? Might it consume her anyhow! Burn her to cinders! Better anything, better brandish one's torch and hurl it to earth than taper and dwindle away like some Ellie Henderson!' (p.

255). The party is described as if it were a religious ceremony or an epic battle: Ellie is 'weaponless' because she lacks financial means (p. 256). The occasion deprives her of her humanity, for she hyperbolically 'felt herself a stake driven in at the top of her stairs' (p. 259). Woolf understands that Clarissa not only lacks proportion but importance; for Clarissa expends emotional energies on a minor social occasion which would more appropriately be reserved for more important matters: 'Anything, any explosion, any horror was better than people wandering aimlessly, standing in a bunch at a corner like Ellie Henderson, not even caring to hold themselves upright' (p. 255). The Prime Minister's presence at this social ritual undermines his stature; '[H]oarding secrets he would die to defend, though it was only some little piece of tittle-tattle dropped by a court footman' he is in the same company as Hugh Whitbread (p. 262). If Septimus has fought in the war, Clarissa Dalloway has 'acquitted herself honourably in the field of [social] battle' where her parasol is 'a sacred weapon' (pp. 43–4). Despite the mock heroic mode, Woolf takes her very seriously as a sad, poignant figure: on one hand, Clarissa is a social anachronism in a world which no longer will sustain the hierarchies on which her way of life depends; on the other, for Woolf she is a product of a social system which is reluctant to give a place to women.

The imagined world of *Mrs. Dalloway* is seeped in death and without any promise of meaningful life. Woolf understands that the enemy of significance in art and in life is the relentless movement of time which – by presenting new experience so that man must prepare for what will happen next – refuses to allow the mind to think at length about significance. Art must struggle to locate significant time between the tick-tock of passing time. Yet the repetition of phrases (particularly the ones about death from *Othello* and *Cymbeline*) and episodes creates the possibility of significance. Repetition undermines the sense of continuous movement and progress by emphasizing that human life repeats itself rather than progresses. When we speak of stasis and spatiality in fiction, we are partly expressing our desire to arrest time and the opportunity to 'frame' or 'confine' action and words within our mental space. As we read *Mrs. Dalloway*, our experience has a spatial and temporal dimension.

Like a cubist painter Woolf wants to show different facets of the whole; thus by pulling together past and putative future into a single moment of the present – by rearranging spatial and temporal planes Woolf discovers order and significance. Her collage method has more in common with modern painting than with the Victorian novel, a form whose emphasis on story and nominalistic representation resembles nineteenth-century narrative painting. Indeed, Woolf's movement from character to character without authorial comment emphasizes the reader's role in discovering the inherent parallelism, and makes him a more active participant. It may be that the novel's major revelation is that disparate characters share common bonds: every character becomes a face of the other, and, the major figures – Clarissa Dalloway, Sally Seton, Peter Walsh, Septimus Smith, Elizabeth – are aspects of the voice who for a time shares their perspective.

The parallels within the text, by which each character comes to double the other, emphasize that figures like Septimus, Carrie Dempster and 'a seedy nondescript man' are different in degree but not kind from what we think of as a socially prominent, conventional upper middle-class matron. Another of Clarissa's doubles is the old lady who survives alone, but is inevitably approaching death in the room opposite her house; we realize that the rather infirm and prematurely ageing Clarissa in her attic room is moving inevitably in the same direction. Yet, paradoxically, as characters come to more and more resemble one another, we also become more conscious of their subtle differences. At times, Woolf creates seeming parallels only to draw important distinctions between them. Miss Kilman's probable sexual interest in Elizabeth recalls Clarissa's for Sally; but Woolf's judgement of Miss Kilman is clearly hostile: 'If she could grasp her, if she could clasp her, if she could make her hers absolutely and forever and then die; that was all she wanted' (pp. 199–200). Characteristically, Woolf establishes the possibility of parallels, only to step aside and question them. In fact, as her parentheses and qualifications indicate, if we could think of Woolf's temperament in terms of the syntax of a sentence, it would be in a mode that is appositional and interrogative.

The novel insists compulsively on the parallel between Septimus and Clarissa. Like Clarissa, Septimus is pale and beak-nosed (pp. 14, 20). Both are prey to their own imaginations. Clarissa must contend with the 'brutal monster' of hatred; for Septimus there is horror beneath which periodically comes 'almost to the surface' and threatens to 'burst into flames' (p. 21). Both intuitively sense that the world may be without meaning, may be, as Conrad puts it, 'a remorseless process'. Clarissa identifies with Septimus in his suicide: 'She felt somehow very like him – the young man who had killed himself. She felt glad that he had done it; thrown it away' (p. 283). She longs for death as a consummation:

> A thing there was that mattered; a thing, wreathed about with chatter, defaced, obscured in her own life, let drop every day in corruption, lies, chatter. This he had preserved. Death was defiance. Death was an attempt to communicate; people feeling the impossibility of reaching the centre which, mystically, evaded them; closeness drew apart; rapture faded, one was alone. There was an embrace in death.
>
> (pp. 280–1)

She seeks in death what she lacks in life. Put another way, isn't death to Clarissa what painting is to Lily in *To the Lighthouse* and what writing novels was to Woolf?

The parallel between the socially prominent Mrs. Dalloway and the insane outsider, Septimus Smith, is both a crucial aesthetic device and a deeply felt insight. It enacts Woolf's perception that a thin line divides sanity and madness, civilization and barbarism, love and hate, isolation and participation in the community, communication and incoherence, form and chaos. Reading *Mrs. Dalloway*, we feel that Woolf understands that placement on one side or the other of that line depends upon circumstances and who is doing the perceiving. In Septimus, Woolf depicts the loneliness, the pathos, the spasmodic energy and apathy of madness as only one who lives with its fear and knowledge can. She wrote in her diary: 'Wave crashes. I wish I were dead! I've only a few years to live, I hope. I cant face this horror any more' (*Diaries*, III, 15 Sept. 1926). Is not this passage recalled by Clarissa's perception of her movement into the drawing room in terms of the suspense of diving into the sea which after at first appearing to be threatening proves benign:

> She ... felt often as she stood hesitating one moment on the threshold of her drawing-room, an exquisite suspense, such as might stay a diver before plunging while the sea darkens and brightens beneath him, and the waves which threaten to break, but only gently split their surface, roll and conceal and encrust as they just turn over the weeds with pearl.
>
> (p. 44)

Both Septimus and Mrs. Dalloway, we realize, suffer from a kind of narcissism, and suffer from their lack of interest in things outside themselves. Septimus Smith has a homosexual fixation on Evans, a man who is 'undemonstrative in the company of women' (p. 130). Like Clarissa, who cannot come to terms with her attraction to Sally, he has trouble feeling; he became engaged to Lucrezia because 'the panic was on him – that he could not feel' (p. 131). Clarissa's husband consigning her to the attic room is not so different from the solution of Bradshaw – which Lucrezia resists – of sending Septimus to a home for the mentally disturbed. In *Mrs. Dalloway*, isn't Woolf implying that the social taboo against homosexuality helps create fragmented, unfulfilled lives? Within their stifled claustrophobic worlds, Clarissa and Septimus cannot open the doors and windows of their libido.

In an era which she sees as lacking accepted moral certainties and common political and religious beliefs, Woolf stresses the continuity between the artist's creative process and the necessary process by which each character – mad or sane – creates himself. The theme of imagination is present in the way each person creates his own story and the way characters seek public ceremonies to complete their lives. The surprising parallels between characters suggest a continuity between the order of art and the kind of ordering that is necessary for a coherent life in the modern world. We see each character as a kind of artist trying to discover the plot lines of the tale that each wants to tell themselves about themselves, even as each discards from his or her own stories those ingredients that he/she does not like. Thus, while the novel contradicts her view of herself, Mrs. Dalloway perceives herself as creating 'a meeting-point [of different selves], a radiancy no doubt in some dull lives, a refuge for the lonely to come to, perhaps' (p. 55). Such stories of reading selves become a metaphor both for the kinds of texts we each can create and for the knowledge that such stories are functions of our own needs and thus partly apocryphal. Like an artist Septimus hears the words no one speaks and seeks to convey his visions to others. In the tale he tells himself, Septimus sees himself as Christ, the scapegoat and eternal sufferer. Put another way, Septimus hears not the traditional nightingales of Greek myth, but rather hears sparrows which carry God's message that there is no death – a message ironically belied by the novel.

Septimus identifies with Christ's 'eternal suffering' which he equates with 'eternal loneliness'. But his terrifying sense of isolation is only a radical version of the loneliness felt by Clarissa, his wife, Peter, and even Richard. Peter's vision of death, in which the 'fever of living' will cease and he will 'blow to nothingness with the rest', establishes a parallel to Septimus; so does his imaginatively endowing the 'sky and branches' with images of womanhood (p. 87). 'This susceptibility to impressions [that] had been [Peter's] undoing' (p. 107) is even more true for Clarissa and Septimus. Septimus's oscillation between the imaginary world of his madness and the real world is different in degree but not kind from Mrs. Dalloway's oscillation between internal depression and her social encounters with other people. When Lucrezia is making a hat, she and Septimus share moments of intimacy that are as genuine as any between Peter and Clarissa or Richard and Clarissa. Isn't his message of 'universal' love as close as any to the meaning of the novel? And in their moments of intimacy, he feels that 'life is good. The sun was hot' affirming life in the very terms that Clarissa evokes. When she feels 'drenched in fire' at the party, we recall the passage in which Septimus experiences ecstasy in his relationship with Lucrezia: 'Miracles, revelations, agonies, loneliness, falling through the sea, down, down into the flames, all were burnt out ...' (p. 216). Even Richard Dalloway used the word 'miracle' to describe his relationship. The reader notices not only the extremity and desperation of Woolf's quest for meaning in terms of personal relationships – relationships that by their failure undermine that quest – but notices the apposition of flames with what for Woolf is the amorphous, threatening sea.

Septimus overcomes skepticism with his belief that he has discovered the solution, the divine message. And Clarissa, for all her skepticism also believed that the 'unseen might survive, be recovered somehow attached to this person or that, or even haunting certain places after death' (p. 232) – which is not too different from what Septimus believes about Evans. Clarissa's belief that she and Peter survive even death anticipates that of Septimus Smith, but it is a belief that is not really supported by the values of the novel:

> Somehow in the streets of London, on the ebb and flow of things, here, there, she survived, Peter survived, lived in each other, she being part, she was positive, of the trees at home; of the house there, ugly, rambling all to bits and pieces as it was; part of people she had never met; being laid out like a mist

between the people she knew best, who lifted her on their
branches as she had seen the trees lift the mist ...

(p. 12)

Does she not imagine Peter seeing her as dead in much the same
way as Septimus imagines Evans seeing him dead? We know from
Leonard Woolf's *Beginning Again: an Autobiography of the Years
1911–1918* about Virginia's hostile attitudes toward psychiatrists.
Dr. Holmes assures Septimus that 'there was nothing whatever
the matter with him' (p. 139). Rather than offer compassion, Sir
William Bradshaw, 'the ghostly helper, the priest of science',
proves to his patients that he 'was master of his own actions,
which the patient was not' (p. 153). Bradshaw is a surrogate for,
and a radical allegorization of, the values of Richard Dalloway and
Hugh Whitbread, a point emphasized by his presence at the
Dalloway party. But the doctor who counsels others on their
private lives is unable to organize his own life. In an interesting
sexual image that recalls the wealth of silver that divides the
Goulds in *Nostromo*, Lady Bradshaw thinks 'sometimes of the
patient, sometimes, excusably, of the wall of gold, mounting
minute by minute while she waited; the wall of gold that was
mounting between them and all shifts and anxieties (she had
borne them bravely) ...' (p. 143). Indeed, Lady Bradshaw, like
Lucrezia and Clarissa, has become subsumed by her husband's
life, and lost much of her independence. Sir William preaches a
credo of proportion, but Woolf emphasizes that proportion is
often accompanied by her sister, Conversion, who 'offers help,
but desires power; smites out of her way roughly the dissentient,
or dissatisfied; bestows her blessing on those who, looking
upward, catch submissively from her eyes the light of their own'
(p. 131). And we realize that in its demanding wilfulness the spirit
of Conversion threatens tolerance, love, and pluralism – and is
epitomized by Miss Kilman's religious zealotry.
    The ending establishes the validity of Sally's despairing, if not
nihilistic image of a human being as an isolated prisoner
scratching his life on the walls of cells which he or she alone
inhabits. The ending is pessimistic and undermines the ecstasy of
Peter because we see that people fail to respond to one another.
We know from that morning's meeting as well as Clarissa's and
Peter's reminiscences that any dialogue between them will end in
frustration for both. Peter and Sally do not understand one

another or the Dalloways. Sally Seton, the person with whom Clarissa had once connected, is 'despairing of human relationships' (p. 293). Sally's question 'what can one know even of the people one lives with every day?' emphasizes the difficulty of our understanding one another (p. 293). We see how people try to possess one another in order to confirm their own reality. Richard thinks of Elizabeth as *his* daughter as Clarissa had thought of Elizabeth as 'my Elizabeth'. And isn't that why Peter, desperate for confirmation of his decision to marry Daisy, feels 'terror' and 'ecstasy' at Clarissa's presence (p. 296)? The ecstasy Peter feels for a woman whom he knows is frigid, whom he knows had spoiled his life, is poignantly ironic. We know that nothing will happen between them. Has he, as he believes, really grown in understanding or depth of feeling? Given his fixation with Clarissa, can he make a commitment to Daisy or to anyone? Within the context of the whole novel, can Clarissa's arrival be more than momentarily significant for Peter? Will their ensuing moments not yield the same disappointment as their morning interview? Thus the final passage must be taken as ironic and reflexive because it will soon be followed by inevitable disappointment. Even though this is the kind of triumph she would welcome, we see the limitations of Clarissa's radiancy. And she herself has reflected that these momentary triumphs were no longer enough, 'though she loved it and felt it tingle and sting, still these semblances, these triumphs (dear old Peter, for example, thinking her so brilliant), had a hollowness; at arm's length they were, not in the heart; and it might be that she was growing old but they satisfied her no longer as they used' (p. 265). At the very height of her triumph, she realizes its hollowness and feels the delicious reality of her hatred for Miss Kilman: 'Elizabeth's seducer; the woman who had crept in to steal and defile' (p. 266). Pathetically, this is the most sustained emotion in her life: 'Kilman was her enemy. That was satisfying; that was real.... She hated her: she loved her' (pp. 265–66). Doesn't she 'love Miss Kilman' because Miss Kilman is the cause of making her feel hatred and anger?

It is *Walpurgisnacht*, the night the memories of her past come alive. The phrase that echoes through her mind is an anticipation of death ('Fear no more the heat of the sun', p. 283) and – because of her use of the phrase in the opening moments of the novel – emphasizes her lack of progress; yet it now appears without the ominous phrase 'nor the furious winter's rages' (p. 13). Her identification with Septimus ('She felt somehow very like him – the young man who had killed himself. She felt glad that he had done it; thrown it away', p. 283) shows how she is tempted by death and how thin the line is beween insider and outsider. His death makes her feel the 'beauty' and 'fun' of life, but is it a morbid beauty that realizes that the possibility of death is in every day and that we are always approaching death? Peter's image of the soul emerging from obscurity to take part in the surface of life effectively comments on the triviality of the party and the kinds of superficial needs it answers.

> For this is the truth about our soul, he thought, our self, who fish-like inhabits deep seas and plies among obscurities threading her way between the boles of giant weeds, over sun-flickered spaces and on and on into gloom, cold, deep, inscrutable; suddenly she shoots to the surface and sports on the wind-wrinkled waves; that is, has a positive need to brush, scrape, kindle herself, gossiping.
>
> (p. 244)

The image recalls the insidiously half-submerged Becky in *Vanity Fair* hiding her primitive instincts beneath the surface. We see the selfishness of Clarissa's sensibility, for she does not pity Septimus but emotionally feeds off his death to delight narcissistically in her party.

That she has Peter's admiration is hardly surprising. Away from India, Peter is adrift from his moorings, lonely, and nostalgic. For Peter, Clarissa has 'that gift still; to be; to exist; to sum it all up in the moment as she passed'; although she does have her husband's affection, *he* has consigned her to the attic (p. 264). She is the mirage, the dream-figure for the solitary traveller – who is not only Peter, but Richard and even Sally, and potentially the reader. The real meaning of the party is in the unexpected guests, Sally Seton and Peter Walsh, her two possibilities for passionate love, whom Woolf uses to show the reader what Clarissa has passed up. Both Peter and Sally feel that Clarissa lacks something and has sacrificed something in marrying Richard. Even Peter's belief that we understand more as we grow older is hollow in light of what we know of his continuing infatuation with Clarissa and Daisy.

Much has been made of Clarissa's final epiphany: 'No pleasure could equal, she thought, ... this having done with the triumphs of youth, lost herself in the process of living, to find it, with a shock of delight, as the sun rose, as the day sank' (p. 282). But most of the day she has been melancholy, and we should not take this spasm of happiness for the whole. The reader's epiphany is that Mrs. Dalloway has had an *ersatz epiphany*. For what did she make happen, what did she accomplish? She has simply gathered people together for what is primarily banal social conversation. The party is a social ritual that does not create meaningful feelings of community or opportunities for understanding. The pleasure she credits to Richard with bringing ('It was due to Richard', p. 282) is belied by the sterile and apparently sexless life she settles for. We should not be misled by her momentary happiness from contemplating the quality of life that she has been leading and will continue to lead. At the end we realize that Clarissa has fulfilled Peter's prediction that she will be the perfect hostess:

> Her severity, her prudery, her woodenness were all warmed through now, and she had about her as she said good-bye to the thick gold-laced man who was doing his best, and good luck to him, to look important, an inexpressible dignity; an exquisite cordiality; as if she wished the whole world well, and must now, being on the very verge and rim of things, take her leave.
>
> (pp. 264–5)

But the perfection she achieves contains within it the promise of approaching death. Are Septimus's views that charity, faith and kindness are in short supply really disproved by the ending? If his paranoid fantasy that human nature has condemned him to death is far from the mark, so is Clarissa's view that her party can provide meaning and significance to others.

III

To the Lighthouse is a companion novel, if not a sequel, to *Mrs. Dalloway*. It is another of Woolf's researches into the form of fiction. But it is also a research into her past, for Mr. Ramsay is based on her father, Leslie Stephen, and Mrs. Ramsay depends on her mother. As Poole writes:

> Virginia idolised her mother. Julia represented for her every-

thing that was beautiful, life-giving, spontaneous, intuitive, loving and natural. She watched her father impose upon her mother again and again, smiting mercilessly down at her again and again ... [O]n occasion Virginia hated her father in the same way as little James does in the novel which describes their family life together, *To the Lighthouse*. But also, of course, she loved him and admired him profoundly. This ambiguous swing between admiration for his immensely human and intellectual abilities, and contempt for his unmanly and despotic impositions upon his womenfolk, marked Virginia's view of her father to her dying day.[4]

Thus *To the Lighthouse* is a most personal novel in which Woolf is struggling to come to terms with her past. One feels her trying to do justice to her tyrannical, self-absorbed, but loving and impressive father.

To the Lighthouse enables Virginia Woolf to come to terms with the burden of her past, particularly her dominant father and her elusive but sensitive mother. In probing the needs and desires of the Ramsays and their guests, Woolf reminds us how the quirks and idiosyncracies of those who can channel their energies into socially acceptable directions (the masterful but insensitive Mr. Ramsay, in particular) are not so different from the fantasies and delusions of those whom society chooses to regard as mad pariahs, such as Septimus Smith. But most of all, *To the Lighthouse* enabled her to inquire into the relationship between art and life, and between memory and experience, and to show how artistic creation is related to the ordering and distorting qualities of memory. Do not memory and artistic creativity both depend upon the mind's ability to create meaning from the past and to inform the present with insights that such meaning can provide?

In Woolf's memory, it is her mother who provided the fecundity and energy, who attended to the children's needs, who made life bearable in a house in which an oppressive, larger-than-life, famous father dominated. In a dualism that recalls the dichotomy Lawrence draws between male and female qualities, Mrs. Ramsay represents the subjective – feelings, personal relationships, the possibility of discovering meaning and even unity if only temporarily. For the children, her husband, the young couple, Charles Tansley, William Bankes, and Lily, Mrs. Ramsay is not a god, but like a god. Thus she has the capacity to create rapture in Mr.

Bankes: '[T]he sight of her reading a fairy tale to her boy had upon him precisely the same effect as the solution of a scientific problem so that he rested in contemplation of it, and felt . . . that barbarity was tamed, the reign of chaos subdued' (p. 74). By contrast, Mr. Ramsay represents objective facts, recognition of life's difficulties, achievements, ambition, and enterprise. The Ramsays dramatize Woolf's view of the fundamental differences between the male and female minds. As Poole writes, the male is depicted as 'egocentric, rough, bruising, insensitive, hammering, dominant, "fact"-obsessed, cynical, reductive, ironical, contemptuous', while the female 'esteem[s]' insight, vision, beauty, harmony, colour'.[5] In her diary on 28 Nov. 1928, she writes: 'Father's birthday. He would have been, 1832, 96, yes, today; and could have been 96, like other people one has known; but mercifully was not. His life would have entirely ended mine. What would have happened? No writing, no books; – inconceivable' (*Diaries*, III). In *To the Lighthouse*, Woolf's version of *Sons and Lovers*, she gives the laurel of victory to Mrs. Ramsay, whose perspicacity dominates Part I; she has a window into the souls and feelings of others and single-handedly creates a feeling of community. Part III of *To the Lighthouse* is in part a not very successful effort to assuage the guilt and disloyalty to her father's memory which she feels for writing Part I.

To understand *To the Lighthouse*, one has to feel Woolf as a presence within the text. In a sense, the novel tests and discards a number of values – including intellectual prominence, knowledge, and power – before settling for a tentative affirmation of private values – family, self-knowledge, art for its own sake – even while never losing sight of their limitations. Or, put another way, it discards the male values associated with Mr. Ramsay and affirms the female values associated with Lily and Mrs. Ramsay. In particular, one hears the voice of a woman who feels her creative energies stifled and engulfed by a male world, who feels that female qualities have been depreciated at the expense of male ones, who feels that women writers are patronized and disregarded, and women's potential subordinated to male needs. Lily notes that Mrs. Ramsay 'pitied men always as if they lacked something – women never, as if they had something' (p. 129). Yet while she gives life to the men, Mrs. Ramsay neglects herself: 'she often felt she was nothing but a sponge sopped full of human emotions' (p. 51). In a sense she dies in sacrificial service to her husband, her family and others. She asks 'What have I done with my life?' and 'wonders' 'how she had ever felt any emotion or affection for him ' (p. 125).

Despite the perfection Mrs. Ramsay feels at the end of Part I, the set scene cannot displace our understanding of the cost to her of her *service* to a demanding wilful husband. That Mr. Ramsay loves but patronizes his wife informs Woolf's barely suppressed anger which we feel intermittently bursting through the book's surface: 'He liked to think that she was not clever, not book-learned at all' (p. 182). Yet he desperately requires her: 'She [looks] at the same time animated and alive as if all her energies were being fused into force, burning and illuminating ... and into this delicious fecundity, this fountain and spray of life, the fatal sterility of the male plunged itself, like a beak of brass, barren and bare' (p. 58). It is as if Mrs. Ramsay were the creative imagination fertilizing the sterile intellect – indeed the male pen(is). Doesn't Woolf want her novel to 'burn' and 'illuminate' for readers as Mrs. Ramsay does for Mr. Ramsay?

Mr. Ramsay has an eye for the extraordinary, not the ordinary, while Mrs. Ramsay has the reverse perspective. He is concerned with the cosmic perspective, she with the human (she needs to marry other people to validate her own life and seems obsessed with arranging matches). Isn't it the fusion of the qualities of Mr. and Mrs. Ramsay that makes the artist who writes *To the Lighthouse*? Mr. Ramsay is a wordmaker, while Mrs. Ramsay favours silence; yet it is she who takes words most seriously: 'All this phrase-making was a game, she thought, for if she had said half what he said, she would have blown her brains out by now' (p. 106). Mrs. Ramsay provides an island from this world: '[S]he had the whole of the other sex under her protection' (p. 13). Her beauty attracts people to her, but that beauty is a function of other qualities: 'her simplicity', 'her singleness of mind', and her spontaneity (p. 46). For her husband, Mrs. Ramsay is a refuge who temporarily offers stability, tranquility, meaning, and significance. She creates the possibility of community and relationship as well as moments of insight for others. That Mr. Ramsay relies upon his wife to renew him, to recreate him, to fertilize his soul is validated by the perception of others. Thus James feels Mrs. Ramsay 'rise in a rosy-flowered fruit tree laid with leaves and dancing boughs into which the beak of brass, the arid scimitar of his father, the egotistical man, plunged and smote, demanding sympathy' (p. 60).

To the Lighthouse enacts a dialogue between the quest to approach reality or truth or understanding and the possibility that such goals are illusions or mirages. As we have seen, reading major British novelists in the 1890–1930 period depends on responding to this dialogue. Lily Briscoe seeks truth from Mrs. Ramsay, truth in the form of an intimacy that Mrs. Ramsay can only occasionally give her. She desperately hopes that intimacy with Mrs. Ramsay will unlock 'some secret which Lily Briscoe believed people must have for the world to go on at all' (p. 78). She seeks in Mrs. Ramsay a secret sharer, an empathetic other to complete herself and 'teach [her] everything' (p. 79). Lily regards her as a source of sustenance; Lily 'knew knowledge and wisdom were stored up in Mrs. Ramsay's heart', but she does not quite know how to reach it (p. 79). Thinking of how she might reach Mrs. Ramsay, Lily describes the process of learning about people in terms of the metaphor of 'a bee, drawn by some sweetness or sharpness in the air intangible to touch or taste, one haunted the dome-shaped hive, ranged the wastes of the air over the countries of the world alone, and then haunted the hives with their murmurs and their stirrings; the hives, which were people' (p. 80). Lily is attracted to her for both sexual and spiritual reasons: 'Could loving, as people called it, make her and Mrs. Ramsay one? for it was not knowledge but unity that she desired, not inscription on tablets, nothing that could be written in any language known to men, but intimacy itself, which is knowledge, she had thought, leaning her head on Mrs. Ramsay's knee' (p. 79). As in *Mrs. Dalloway*, a central character is more attracted to women than men, but Lily, like Clarissa, reflects what Poole called Woolf's 'sexual anesthesia' – which he attributes quite convincingly to molestation by the Duckworths: 'She could not feel any normal sexual feeling, and sexual matters were attended in her mind with fantasies of horror and dread.'[6]

Woolf realized that personal relationships had to provide the order and meaning that religion, empire, and social hierarchies once provided. The personal is all the more important when religion and politics fail; thus the 'man of genius', the political leader for whom Bankes waits will never come (p. 142). Yet Woolf understood that human relationships always fall short, and require lies and evasions to sustain them; put another way, Mrs. Ramsay reflects her creator's perception that human relations are not only flawed and despicable, but self-seeking at their best.

To the Lighthouse is, among other things, a defensive effort to define meaning and value in a world where suffering, death, and poverty are dominant factors. The novel's centre of values, Mrs. Ramsay, sees life as 'terrible, hostile, and quick to pounce on you', as 'her old antagonist', and this view of the self as in conflict with the world it inhabits is Woolf's own (pp. 92, 120).

In *To the Lighthouse*, as in *Mrs. Dalloway* and Joyce's 'The Dead', death is the major determinant of form. The novel emphasizes the ephemeral quality of life, and the need for human beings to rescue significance and impose meaning. According to Leonard Woolf, 'Death, I think, was always very near the surface of Virginia's mind, the contemplation of death. It was part of the deep imbalance of her mind. She was "half in love with easeful Death".'[7] If death is the antagonist, the creative memory – the mind's ability to recapture and give shape to the past – is the hero and protagonist. Mrs. Ramsay feels the presence of death as a continual presence even in her Isle of Skye retreat. Marie's, the maid, father is dying of cancer. The pig's skull hanging in the children's room suggests the presence of death and mortality. But, more to the point, the *re-reader* knows that for all her vitality Mrs. Ramsay herself will soon be dead along with two of her children, and this casts a deep pall of sadness over the novel. Her death lends a special poignance to her need to arrange marriages and live her life through her children, for are not these activities futile efforts to impose order on life and thus to forestall death?

Mr. Ramsay himself lives with the feeling that 'withered old age' and death will forestall his efforts to plod forward in his intellectual quest (p. 55). When he looks from the mountain top he sees not, like Moses, the promised land but 'the long wastes of the ages' (p. 56). Is Ramsay not of the class of persons whom Sir Isaiah Berlin calls foxes – those whose thought is 'scattered and diffused' and who 'pursue many ends' – rather than those whom he calls hedgehogs – those gifted or inspired persons who 'relate everything to a single central vision ... a single, universal, organizing principle in terms of which all that they are and say has significance'?[8] Did not Woolf strive to be a hedgehog and unlike her father Leslie Stephen who is a Victorian fox more than a Victorian sage? Thus Ramsay is particularly vulnerable to time and mortality, because he needs time to work through toward his goal. Yet he has already done his best work, and undoubtedly knows it. He knows that his reputation will not last very long. Within the text, he becomes an objectification of Woolf's own aspirations and fears as a writer; his concern about how 'men will speak of him hereafter' is hers (p. 56).

To the Lighthouse is about the problem of creating meaning from the flux and inchoate form of life, and this problem is explored in terms of two kinds of experiences: 1. creating temporary unity within the present by arranging and organizing experience as much as possible; 2. imposing through memory an order upon the past. Woolf's novels are about the process of discovering and creating order and significance in the present from the bits and snips of the past. Woolf understands that we rely on memory and art to meet the challenge thrown down by the global questions of William Bankes: 'What does one live for? Why, one asked oneself, does one take all these pains for the human race to go on?' (p. 134).

'The Window', the title of Part One, represents the division between the outside world and the world created within the house – and the inevitable division within oneself. At the centre of 'The Window' is the rapport between the Ramsays which, like all human relationships, has its limitations. 'The Window' preserves the intimacy of the present, shuts people off temporarily from night (representing evil, death, and the unknown) and the sea (representing the amoral indifferent cosmos), and creates an oasis within: '[H]ere, inside the room, seemed to be order and dry land; there, outside, a reflection in which things wavered and vanished, waterily' (p. 147).

As in 'The Dead', a story to which Woolf may very well be alluding, a social gathering gives way to a middle-aged couple's moment of intimacy. But unlike the Conroys, the Ramsays do share a special intimacy which continually renews and recreates them. In To the Lighthouse, as in Mrs. Dalloway, reading is a mode of perceiving and suggests the parallel between reading texts and reading lives. Woolf stresses the value of reading as a catalyst to deeper feelings and intense moments that prepare the ground for richer human relationships. The reading of Grimm's fairy tale about the fisherman and his wife is testament to the importance of reading as a mode of perception; it is another way that Mrs. Ramsay is a lighthouse teaching her family and others how to see. Yet Woolf realizes that reading texts, like reading lives, is a quest towards permanence, understanding, and meaning – a quest that despite its occasional partial successes will always fall short of its goal. Reading Scott, Mr. Ramsay 'forgot himself completely' and enjoys 'the astonishing delight and feeling of vigour that it gave him' (p. 180). And reading Shakespeare's ninety-eighth sonnet, Mrs. Ramsay has a parallel experience:

> All the odds and ends of the day stuck to this magnet; her mind felt swept, felt clean. And then there it was, suddenly entire; she held it in her hands, beautiful and reasonable, clear and complete, the essence sucked out of life and held rounded here – the sonnet.
>
> (p. 181)

Mrs. Ramsey *wants* her husband's reproof for her pessimism about the Paul and Minta marriage, and he wants her 'to tell him that she loved him' (p. 184). Although 'she never could say what she felt' (p. 185), her smile and her acknowledging the truth of his prophecy have the effect of creating the moment of intimacy for both of them. The end of 'The Window' requires a double perspective. True, it ends with her thought, 'Nothing on earth can equal this happiness' (p. 186), and their mutual fulfilment. Yet we have seen from what precedes that her life has its limitations, and that her marriage has not only defined but confined her. The echo of 'The Dead' has an ironic resonance in view of her approaching death.

Mrs. Ramsay is the choreographer of the lives of others, and she is far more successful at it than Clarissa Dalloway; it is she who silently inspires Paul to propose to Minta. Moments after the party is over, she thinks,

> Yes, that was done then, accomplished; and as with all things done, became solemn. Now one thought of it, cleared of chatter and emotion, it seemed always to have been, only was shown now and so being shown, struck everything into stability. They would, she thought, going on again, however long they lived, come back to this night; this moon; this wind; this house; and to her too. It flattered her ... to think how, wound about in their hearts, however long they lived she would be woven.... All that would be revived again in the lives of Paul and Minta; 'the Rayleys' – she tried the new name over; and she felt, with her hand on the nursery door, that community of feeling with other people which emotion gives as if the walls of partition had become so thin that practically (the feeling was one of relief and happiness) it was all one stream, and chairs, tables, maps, were

hers, were theirs, it did not matter whose, and Paul and Minta would carry it on when she was dead.

(pp. 170–1)

In arranging the engagement of Paul and Minta, Mrs. Ramsay has created 'a community of feeling' in which the partitions that divide people have almost broken down. As surely as the artist, Mrs. Ramsay has created meaning that lives past her death and shapes the lives of others who in their turn shape the lives of others. That the most intense experience of daily life can have a value and a form is central to the novel's aesthetic: 'Here, she felt, putting the spoon down, was the still space that lies about the heart of things, where one could move or rest; could wait now (they were all helped) listening; could then, like a hawk which lapses suddenly from its high station, flaunt and sink on laughter easily ...' (pp. 158–9). Thus one's sensibility and one's actions have a kind of immortality. And we think of the impression she had made on Tansley as 'the most beautiful person he had ever seen ... [F]or the first time in his life Charles Tansley felt an extraordinary pride' – not in scholarship nor personal gain, but simply in accompanying Mrs. Ramsay (p. 25). And that scene, too, we know will live in his memory. But in the final part of *To The Lighthouse*, we learn that the Rayleys' marriage is hardly a success, and the immortality of which she dreams can hardly be said to occur. Mrs. Ramsay seeks the kind of unity in life that she admires in an arrangement of fruit, an arrangement such as Woolf might have seen depicted in a Cézanne painting. Mrs. Ramsay's feeling that reaching to take a pear will spoil the fruit arrangement embodies Woolf's regret that perfection is rarely if ever found in life.

For her part Mrs. Ramsay needs to mate Lily with William. Lily is divided in the face of romantic love; on the one hand she understands its beauty and exhilaration; but on the other she fears its 'degradation' and 'dilution'. While Mrs. Ramsay renews her husband and responds to Bankes and her children, even to Tansley, does she understand Lily who, in part at least, really does want to retain her independence as a single woman and live for her painting? But Lily, like Clarissa, seems asexual. Lily associates Paul with sexual love, but for her such passion has atavistic overtones:

It rose like a fire sent up in token of some celebration by savages on a distant beach ... [S]he felt again her own headlong desire to throw herself off the cliff and be drowned looking for a pearl brooch on a beach. And the roar and the crackle repelled her with fear and disgust, as if while she saw its splendour and power she saw too how it fed on the treasure of the house, greedily, disgustingly, and she loathed it.

(p. 261)

We think perhaps of how Aschenbach, another repressed adult past forty, associates his passion for Tadzio with primitive lands. Although Lily 'loved William Bankes' (p. 263), and 'his friendship had been one of the pleasures of her life', Woolf is insisting that love need not be the prelude to marriage, or even to sexual intimacy. The putative marital happiness that Mrs. Ramsay had created for the Rayleys is belied by their actual lives. She has not, after all, created something that is lasting. For Woolf, only the creative imagination fulfilled by artistic creation can do that.

That Mrs. Ramsay remembers a day twenty years ago as if it were yesterday stresses the importance of memory in giving shape to the very day that the characters are living (and the importance to the re-reader of his memory of his first reading of the pages of *To The Lighthouse*) (p. 132). She regrets that James 'will remember all his life' his father's prophecy about the weather on the day at age six when he planned to go to the lighthouse. In Part III, Lily, by making sense of her past experience at the Ramsay house, is trying to discover significance in her present life and art. As in Proust, memory triggers complex emotions about people. For William Bankes the dunes become an elegiac moment for the friendship he once had with Ramsay: '[T]here, like the body of a young man laid up in peat for a century, with the red fresh on his lips, was his friendship, in its acuteness and reality, laid up across the bay among the sandhills' (p. 35); the trace of mortality is always present in memory and in art. *To the Lighthouse* is an attempt to immortalize such moments and to unify them into one grand experience. That is why the book stresses memories of experience frozen in time by the mind and why the act of perception is the subject of memories and the narrative.

The entire novel revolves around a contest between death and life, order and flux, creative imagination and the 'scraps and fragment' of ordinary experience (p. 136). No sooner does Mrs. Ramsay or Lily experience unity than 'there was a sense of things having been blown apart, of space, of irresponsibility' (p. 111). *To the Lighthouse* is a novel which, like *Sons and Lovers*, is about the very processes of creating meaning from inchoate personal experience. The struggle for order and meaning within each of the characters' lives is not only the central action of the novel, but the activity that engaged Woolf herself. Does not her own art mime Lily's struggles to render what she sees rather than merely what convention dictates? 'It was in that moment's flight between the picture and her canvas that the demons set on her who often brought her to the verge of tears and made this passage from conception to work as dreadful as any down a dark passage for a child' (p. 32). Style and form enact and affirm the principles of order, sensibility, and discrimination that Mrs. Ramsay lives by. But the possibility of disorder, insensitivity, and personal failure are always threatening to intrude into the novel's imagined world. In 'her strange severity, her extreme courtesy', her refusal to 'regret her decision, evade difficulties, or slur over duties', Mrs. Ramsay not only represents a queenly presence in the social world, a presence that provides standards for others, but also a concept of order which has its correlative in the tight design of the book's structure and texture (p. 14). Yet the process by which the consciousness of characters even within a day, even an hour, oscillates between feelings of unity and disunity creates a tension between formal coherence and the possibility that life lacks meaning. Lily's or Mrs. Ramsay's despair at one moment is given meaning by the ecstasy of a subsequent one, and vice versa. Like Woolf herself, the characters often live at the edge of desperation, even madness.

Because for Woolf epiphanic moments which momentarily order ephemeral perceptions are in themselves values, the readers must not reduce the text to image patterns or mythic echoes; such an approach deprives the novel of its movement and leaves it cold and static.[9] In Woolf, the moments of intense experience take their meaning from the process of chronological experience dramatized within the narrative. Thus, at the centre of the novel is Lily, trying to create meaning out of the flux of life. For her,

suddenly the meaning which, for no reason at all, as perhaps [Mr. and Mrs. Ramsay] are stepping out of the Tube or ringing a doorbell, descends on people, making them symbolical, making them representative, came upon them, and made them in the dusk standing, looking, the symbols of marriage, husband and wife.

(pp. 110–11)

But such epiphanic and symbolic moments can only be temporary, even if they pretend to a permanence that eludes human perceptions; thus in the next instance Lily sees them simply as Mr. and Mrs. Ramsay watching their children play catch.

Woolf's fictions enact for the reader that the ephemeral quality of life is itself the subject; on one hand, her novels stress significant moments, moments when life coheres into unity and arrests the inevitable flux of time; on the other, these gaps in time undermine both the taut plot we expect of traditional fiction and the organic reading that imposes coherent order. Woolf's aesthetic stresses a dialogue between text and reader; the reader, by providing his or her own emotions, completes the novel and knits the strands of the novel together. Thus she wrote to Roger Fry:

> I meant *nothing* by *The Lighthouse*. One has to have a central line down the middle of the book to hold the design together. I saw that all sorts of feelings would accrue to this, but I refused to think them out, and trusted that people would make it the deposit for their own emotions – which they have done, one thinking it means one thing another another. I can't manage Symbolism except in this vague, generalised way. Whether it's right or wrong I don't know; but directly I'm told what a thing means, it becomes hateful to me.
>
> (*Letters*, III. 1764, 27 May 1927)

An artist who relies on her inner vision, rather than anterior reality, Lily Briscoe paints what she knows, not what she sees. If her concept of form requires it, she paints a tree or a line although it may exist only in the mind's eye: 'I shall put the tree further in the middle; then I shall avoid that awkward space' (p. 128). Yet her artistic epiphany is created by human emotions – a vision that, notwithstanding Mrs. Ramsay's pity for William Bankes, he 'is not in the least pitiable. He had his work, Lily said to herself. She remembered, all of a sudden as if she had found a treasure, that she had her work' (p. 128). Thus the ground for Lily's epiphanic moment of wholeness depends on her personal, independent critique of Mrs. Ramsay's pity for Bankes. By showing that Lily's art requires the impetus of human feeling, Woolf urges the reader to see that non-representational art is neither merely second-hand copying of the insights of others nor cold geometric forms. That Lily's formal non-realist's aesthetic depends on humanistic values helps us understand how we should read.

To the Lighthouse enacts a dialogue between feelings of emptiness and the search for compensating plenitudes – plenitudes provided by memories and – for the artist – the consolation of form. Lily feels, as Mrs. Ramsay had, the impotence of language to describe feeling: 'For how could one express in words these emotions of the body? express that emptiness there?' (p. 265). But, at a crucial moment – almost like the lines that define the shape of her painting – she recalls Mrs. Ramsay's presence so vividly that it defines her own present space and significance. For a moment – but only a moment – she believes that memory can renew Mrs. Ramsay and that the power of her feelings is enough to recreate the past. Yet the effect of the memory enables her to complete her picture.

For Lily Briscoe the post-Impressionist, 'the question [is] one of the relations of the masses, of lights and shadows', but art is much more than that (p. 82). Art for Lily – as for Woolf – is 'the deposit of each day's living mixed with something more secret than she had ever spoken or shown', and that deposit expresses her deepest feelings (p. 81). One might say that Mrs. Ramsay influences or educates Lily's aesthetic values, as Lily educates the reader to respond to those of the narrative presence of the novel.

Aren't things spoilt then, Mrs. Ramsay may have asked (it seemed to have happened so often, this silence by her side) by saying them? Aren't we more expressive thus? The moment at least seemed extraordinarily fertile. She rammed a little hole in the sand and covered it up, by way of burying in it the perfection of the moment. It was like a drop of silver in which one dipped and illumined the darkness of the past.

(p. 256)

Storing up the past serves as a metaphor for not only what Lily has done and is doing now, but what Woolf's narrator is doing as she writes of Lily's triumph. The view that saying too much can spoil things is not only Mrs. Ramsay's, but her creator's. Similarly, Woolf's presence shapes our reading.

Mrs. Ramsay is a kind of artist who not only has the ability to lose her personality in empathy with another, but to become something else: 'It was odd, she thought, how if one was alone, one leant to inanimate things; trees, streams, flowers; felt they expressed one; felt they became one; felt they knew one, in a sense were one; felt an irrational tenderness thus (she looked at that long steady light) as for oneself' (pp. 97–8). We recall Keats's negative capability or Coleridge's idea of the secondary imagination; Woolf's visionary moment links her to the Romantic tradition in which the imagination transforms and 'half creates' – to use Wordsworth's term in 'Tintern Abbey' (p. 106). The identification of Mrs. Ramsay and the lighthouse, of her ecstasy with the light it throws, is captured in the following passage in which the movement of Mrs. Ramsay's thought as she approaches an ecstatic moment is intermingled with the perception of light.

[S]he looked at the steady light, the pitiless, the remorseless, which was so much her, yet so little her, which had her at its beck and call, ... but for all that she thought, watching it with fascination, hypnotised, as if it were stroking with its silver fingers some sealed vessel in her brain whose bursting would flood her with delight, she had known happiness, ... and it silvered the rough waves a little more brightly as daylight faded, and the blue went out of the sea and it rolled in waves of pure lemon which curved and swelled and broke upon the beach and the ecstasy burst in her eyes and waves of pure delight raced over the floor of her mind and she felt, It is enough! It is enough!

(pp. 99–100)

When Mrs. Ramsay intermingles in the lives of others, she produces, if not ecstasies, moments of significance. More than his relentless pursuit of truth, she is Mr. Ramsay's lighthouse. For Lily, she is the catalyst for solving the problem in her painting. She is the lighthouse for Charles and Paul, whom 'she made ... believe that he could do whatever he wanted' and who notices the lighthouse when he returns from proposing (p. 119). Indeed, Paul identifies the Ramsay house as his lighthouse and associates Mrs. Ramsay with light: 'The house was all lit up, and the lights after the darkness made his eyes feel full, and he said to himself, childishly, as he walked up the drive, Lights, lights, lights, and

repeated in a dazed way, Lights, lights, lights . . .' (p. 119).
Woolf is embodied in Lily's quest for artistic values and Mrs.
Ramsay's quest for personal ones. The equation between Lily's
painting and Woolf's writing is crucial, but so is the equation
between Mrs. Ramsay's effects on people and the goals that Woolf
wants to achieve. Woolf establishes a relationship between Mrs.
Ramsay's quest to achieve wholeness and unity in personal
relationships and Lily's quest to complete her picture. Mrs.
Ramsay is expected and expects herself to create the unity which
will give the dinner meaning: 'And the whole of the effort of
merging and flowing and creating rested on her' (p. 126). And she
thinks of her task in terms of the crucial image of sailing a ship:

> [I]n pity for [William Bankes], life being now strong enough to
> bear her on again, she began all this business, as a sailor not
> without weariness sees the wind fill his sail and yet hardly
> wants to be off again and thinks how, had the ship sunk, he
> would have whirled round and round and found rest on the
> floor of the sea.
>
> (p. 127)

The image captures the continuing and finally futile quest to keep
one's bearings in a cosmos – represented by the sea – which is
indifferent towards both quest and goal.
The sailing image is fulfilled – a term I use to mean given its
significance in terms of the evolving pattern and the retrospective
spatial dimension – by Mrs. Ramsay's figuratively reaching the
lighthouse at the end of 'The Window' (and later, in Part III, the
sailing image is recalled by the successful, yet ironic, voyage of
Mr. Ramsay with which the novel concludes). As her party
coheres, Mrs. Ramsay experiences a moment of perfect rapture:

> Nothing need be said; nothing could be said. There it was, all
> round them. It partook, she felt, carefully helping Mr. Bankes to
> a specially tender piece, of eternity; as she had already felt about
> something different once before that afternoon; there is a
> coherence in things, a stability; something, she meant, is
> immune from change, and shines out (she glanced at the
> window with its ripple of reflected lights) in the face of the
> flowing, the fleeting, the spectral, like a ruby; so that again
> tonight she had the feeling she had had once today, already, of

peace, of rest. Of such moments, she thought, the thing is made
that endures.

(p. 158)

The stability that Mrs. Ramsay feels is very much what Lily seeks
in her painting and Woolf seeks in her fiction – the subduing of
diverse impressions to the unity of the whole. It is what Woolf is
trying to achieve for her reader, and it is imaged by the lighthouse,
pointedly evoked by the verb 'shines out'. Woolf's novels are both
a quest to define those moments and to achieve them within her
text, and an acknowledgement that such moments must be
ephemeral.

Yet these moments are inevitably transitory. As in Joyce we
should think of the quest for epiphany as more important than the
epiphanic moment. The epiphanic moment is always to occur
or has occurred. Here the unity is threatened by versions of male
insecurity: Mr. Ramsay's 'extreme anxiety about himself' (p. 162)
and Tansley's self-doubt; 'Am I saying the right thing? Am I
making a good impression?' (p. 163). As soon as the people leave
the room, the party is consigned to the past – the word with which
Section XVIII closes. In light of her own death and that of two of
her children a few pages later, Mrs. Ramsay's epiphany is
particularly ironic and shows the futility of forestalling time. Even
the great moment inevitably fades into the past. The very
conditions of mortality, Woolf implies, make the quest for these
moments of perfection, of coherence, of significance, all the more
important. Such moments are as close as life comes to art.

Does not Lily's final vision emphasize its transitoriness, its
consignment to the past? 'I have *had* my vision' (p. 310, my
emphasis). We know from the novel's narrative code – specifically,
no sooner do we read of Mrs. Ramsay's epiphany than we learn
both of her death and her failure to shape the relationship between
Paul and Minta – that visions cannot wrench themselves from
temporality. Since Mrs. Ramsay's triumphant vision had given
'The Window' a similar closure and since Lily had conceived the
resolving line at the end of that section, the narrative code warns
us not to be seduced by Lily's epiphany or even the voice's
visionary experience. Are not secular visions always ironized by
what is missing: the deeply felt passionate relationship with God in
which the seeker completes himself, or, in other terms, in which
the world and word become one? That Lily's final thoughts ('It was

done; it was finished') echo Christ's words on the cross ('*consummate est*') emphasizes Woolf's awareness of this irony. The verticals – Lily's parodic line, the lighthouse (a man-made substitution for God's creation of light), Mr. Carmichael standing – are equated with the quest to discover meaning in a world where God is no longer a factor. As with all the writers of this period, the concept of God is the absent signifier hovering over the text and the imagined world created by the text. We recall Mrs. Ramsay's religious scepticism, as she thinks, as her creator might of death and suffering: 'How could any Lord have made this world?' (p. 98). As in *Mrs. Dalloway*, the absence of Christian belief is a striking fact in the novel. But unlike Hardy, Lawrence, Joyce and Yeats, unbelief really does not struggle with belief. When Mrs. Ramsay hears herself muttering the conventional Victorian shibboleth, 'We are in the hands of the Lord', she dismisses it as a lie (p. 97): 'With her mind she had always seized the fact that there is no reason, order, justice: but suffering, death, the poor. There was no treachery too base for the world to commit; she knew that' (p. 98).

When she becomes like the artist surveying her creation, Mrs. Ramsay creates a kind of unity, a moment of *kairos*, of significance, of the kind that used to be associated with religion: 'She looked at the window in which the candle flames burnt brighter now that the panes were black, and looking at that outside the voices came to her very strangely, as if they were voices at a service in a cathedral, for she did not listen to the words' (pp. 165–6). But verticals and linearity are also equated with the masculine need to progress, dominate, and conquer – with Mr. Ramsay's need to move 'from start to finish' through the letters of the alphabet (p. 55) – in contrast to the novel's intense effort to render somehow the dynamic, evanescent, shifting interconnecting and intersecting planes and spheres of reality. Thus the equation of the journey to the lighthouse with the completion of the painting is itself an acknowledgement of the paradox that completing a work – fixing an impression in time – belies the flux and hence the possibilities of reality. As with Lawrence, to be complete or finished is equated with death, while the flux of the quest for values is itself a value aligned with being fully alive. It is the movement towards the goal that gives life significance – reaching towards the lighthouse, pressing on in the attempt to solve the problem of the painting, trying to pull together the novel. Put another way, as in the series with which I concluded the prior sentence, the verb takes precedence over its object. Ultimately, the verticals become ironized by temporality, by the inability of the characters or the narrator to close the gap between the signifier and the signified. Indeed, reaching the lighthouse and completing the painting, like Mrs. Ramsay's vision, is another poignant and very emphatic step towards death. Just as the second section, 'Time Passes', dramatizes how time preys on things human, the narrative shows us that not only Lily's painting but Woolf's writing is not immune to time. Yet, unlike a painting, the literary text if and when published can be repeated often enough so that it has the chance to survive time.

In Section V, Part III, 'The Lighthouse', Woolf specifically equates the act of memory with the act of Lily's artistic creation: 'And as she dipped into the blue paint, she dipped too into the past there. Now Mrs. Ramsay got up, she remembered' (p. 256). But memories of Mrs. Ramsay *are* the catalyst for Lily's intense experience. The powerful presence of the past in human lives is a Woolf theme. Lily half expects Mrs. Ramsay to return from the past to the present:

> For the whole world seemed to have dissolved in this early morning hour into a pool of thought, a deep basin of reality, and one could almost fancy that had Mr. Carmichael spoken, for instance, a little tear would have rent the surface pool. And then? Something would emerge. A hand would be shoved up, a blade would be flashed.
>
> (pp. 266–7)

Lily wants to believe in the immortaliy of art – 'How "you" and "I" and "she" pass and vanish; nothing stays; all changes; but not words, not paint' (p. 267) – but she fears that her paintings will be hung in attics and stored under a sofa. Dissolving into tears for Mrs. Ramsay, and for the immortality that she herself will never achieve and for her own realization that she too will die, she silently asks Mr. Carmichael, who by his presence had become objectified into the other she seeks now that Mrs. Ramsay and Bankes (we have no idea if he is living or dead) are not here:

> What was it then? What did it mean? Could things thrust their hands up and grip one; could the blade cut; the fist grasp? Was there no safety? No learning by heart of the ways of the world?

No guide, no shelter, but all was miracle, and leaping from the pinnacle of a tower into the air? Could it be, even for elderly people, that this was life – startling, unexpected, unknown?

(p. 268)

Is not this perception that the real significance of life is these moments which contain the 'startling', the 'unexpected', and the 'unknown' central to Woolf's aesthetic? The text enacts this in Lily's tears and her desperate insistence on meaning in a life 'so short' and 'so inexplicable'. In the pathos of Lily's quest, we feel Woolf's own:

For one moment she felt that if they both got up, here, now on the lawn and demanded an explanation, why was it so short, why was it so inexplicable, said it with violence, as two fully equipped human beings from whom nothing should be hid should speak, then, beauty would roll itself up; the space would fill; those empty flourishes would form into shape; if they shouted loud enough Mrs. Ramsay would return.

(p. 268)

The beauty of art confers meaning by the filling of empty spaces, by organizing unity among details, and by providing the coherence of epiphanic insight. But moments of order and beauty are temporary and not sufficient to provide plenitude.

We feel Woolf's identification with Lily when the latter thinks in literary rather than painterly terms: '[L]ike everything else this strange morning the words became symbols, wrote themselves all over the grey-green walls. If only she could put them together, she felt, write them out in some sentence, then she could have got at the truth of things' (p. 219). Lily's perceptions might be those of Woolf if we substitute writing for painting: 'It was a miserable machine, an inefficient machine, she thought, the human apparatus for painting or for feeling; it always broke down at the critical moment; heroically, one must force it on' (p. 287). Lily's creative imagination not only recalls Mrs. Ramsay from the past, but transforms her into a symbolic, if ambiguous figure in the present. As an artist she wants to achieve the kind of unity that Mrs. Ramsay achieves in life: 'One wanted, she thought, dipping her brush deliberately, to be on a level with ordinary experience, to feel simply that's a chair, that's a table, and yet at the same time,

It's a miracle, it's an ecstasy' (pp. 299–300). To inform ordinary experience with meaning is, as we have seen, a crucial goal of Woolf's art – a goal that can be approached but never reached.

Woolf depicts acts of memory as kinds of narratives. The prototype for the way memory both recaptures and permanently loses experience is Mrs. Ramsay's recollection of the Mannings: '[N]ow she went among them like a ghost; and it fascinated her, as if, while she had changed, that particular day, now become very still and beautiful, had remained there, all these years' (p. 132). This image describes not only the position of Lily, Mr. Ramsay, and his returning children in Part III, but also the position of Woolf as she returned to the memories of her parents' home and relationship. In a reversal which privileges reading over living, imagination over results, the experience of memory is specifically equated with reading a book. Mrs. Ramsay, during the dinner party, wants to

> return to that dream land, that unreal but fascinating place, the Mannings' drawing-room at Marlow twenty years ago; where one moved about without haste or anxiety, for there was no future to worry about. She knew what happened to them, what to her. It was like reading a good book again, for she knew the end of the story, since it happened twenty years ago, and life, which shot down even from this dining-room table in cascades, heaven knows where, was sealed up there, and lay, like a lake, placidly between its banks.
>
> (p. 140)

Yet, finally, Mrs. Ramsay censors the escapism of fantasy with the lesson of reason; she acknowledges that they have had a life beyond her consciousness and she had one beyond theirs, and finds the thought 'strange and distasteful' (p. 133).

In Part II, 'Time Passes', the perspective becomes impersonal, detached, hawklike. Death is an insistent presence. At first the 'airs' – Woolf's metaphor for indifferent, relentless time – have little effect on the house when it is inhabited, but, after the family fails to return, the 'airs' begin to reclaim the house as their own, and the house and its contents decay. Part II responds to Mrs. Ramsay's allegorical question – 'What was the value, the meaning of things?' – with an allegorical answer (p. 183). To the detached perspective, Mrs. Ramsay's death and the deaths of Prue and

Andrew are mere parentheses to the larger processes of life it records. The omniscient, distanced, and ironic voice is the antithesis of the personal, subjective presence which was something of a window into the consciousness of the characters, especially Mrs. Ramsay and Lily. But here the focus is on the house, from which human life is absent, and this is all the more moving and effective because of Part One.

At times in Part Two, one aspect of the polyphonic voice has a vatic tone. It does not speak of a benevolent order but of a nature that is indifferent to man's presence and aspiration and which depends on man to humanize it in terms to which he can respond:

> [I]t seemed as if the universe were battling and tumbling, in brute confusion and wanton lust aimlessly by itself ... [T]he stillness and the brightness of the day were as strange as the chaos and tumult of night, with the trees standing there, and the flowers standing there, looking before them, looking up, yet beholding nothing, eyeless, and so terrible.
>
> (p. 203)

Nature reclaims the house until the residents give word that they will return; then the house is described in terms suggesting rebirth: 'some rusty laborious birth seemed to be taking place' (p. 210). With man's return the setting is humanized and given its meaning; in man's absence nature is chaotic. Indeed, another aspect of the voice seeks to verbalize the responses of the non-verbal experience of 'the mystic, the visionary' who regrets his failure to compose order from fragments and to discover meaning in the night and is denied an answer to such basic questions as 'What am I, What is this?' (p. 198). In 'Time Passes' the world is presented as an unreadable hieroglyph that cannot be allegorized except as impenetrable signifiers: '[I]t seems impossible ... that we should ever compose from their fragments a perfect whole or read in the littered pieces the clear words of truth' (p. 193).

For Woolf is mocking the visionary romantic voice which proclaims with confidence that 'good triumphs, happiness prevails, order rules' (p. 199), or that declares that nature contains 'some absolute good' or has 'a knowledge of the sorrows of mankind' (p. 199) – and the reader who reads in search of conclusive interpretations of reality from her work. The war makes such a quest impossible. The war undermines the position that we live in a benign cosmos, for seekers on the beach would find

> something out of harmony with this jocundity and this serenity. There was the silent apparition of an ashen-coloured ship for instance, come, gone; there was a purplish stain upon the bland surface of the sea as if something had boiled and bled, invisibly, beneath.... It was difficult blandly to overlook them; to abolish their significance in the landscape; to continue, as one walked by the sea, to marvel how beauty outside mirrored beauty within.... That dream, of sharing, completing, of finding in solitude on the beach an answer, was then but a reflection in a mirror, and the mirror itself was but the surface glassiness which forms in quiescence when the nobler powers sleep beneath? Impatient, despairing yet loth to go (for beauty offers her lures, has her consolations), to pace the beach was impossible; contemplation was unendurable; the mirror was broken.
>
> (pp. 201–2)

For this reason man must create his own order in art (the painting of Lily) if he is to fulfil his dream of sharing and completing reality. Woolf is turning the traditional image of mirror held up to nature inside out and using it as an image of narcissism and solipsism. She is also implying that in the modern world – despoiled by war – a conception of a benevolent cosmos ordered by a 'divine goodness' (a phrase she uses ironically) is apocryphal (p. 192). Man seeks order, perhaps in a walk by the sea, but

> [N]o image with semblance of serving and divine promptitude comes readily to hand bringing the night to order and making the world reflect the compass of the soul.... Almost it would appear that it is useless in such confusion to ask the night those questions as to what, and why, and wherefore, which tempt the sleeper from his bed to seek an answer.
>
> (p. 193)

The pacers on the beach disappear at this point as nature reclaims the house; nevertheless, the continuation of life is both its own answer to cosmic questions and to such disruptions of human continuity as those created by the Great War.

In the final part, 'The Lighthouse', Lily has a strong feeling that this is a crucial day in her life, but she is frustrated with her painting. Mr. Ramsay stalks about muttering 'Perished. Alone' and Lily thinks of his picture which she had been working on ten years ago (p. 220). Mr. Ramsay turns to Lily as he had formerly turned to Mrs. Ramsay; but she is unresponsive to his need not only because she is inexperienced with the supplicating male, but because he is interfering with her work: 'She hated playing at painting. A brush, the one dependable thing in a world of strife, ruin, chaos – that one should not play with, knowingly even: she detested it' (p. 224). Ironically, praising his boots is enough to fulfil his need – his pathetic masculine need for admiration, although she does not feel sympathy: 'They had reached, she felt, a sunny island where peace dwelt, sanity reigned and the sun forever shone, the blessed islands of good boots' (p. 230). Until she praises his boots, she had, as his children will on the boat, resented his demands. Yet, masculinity triumphs in all its crassness and insensitivity. While earlier he had been described as 'the leader of the doomed expedition', he now leads a successful expedition which comes together as surely as did his wife's party ten years earlier (p. 57).

The memory of Mrs. Ramsay is a catalyst for Lily's personal growth. She recalls how Mrs. Ramsay's life had refuted and now refutes Lily's prejudice about 'the ineffectiveness of action, the supremacy of thought' (p. 292), and modified her grotesque idea of Charles Tansley: 'Half one's notions of other people were, after all, grotesque. They served private purposes of one's own' (p. 293). In Lily's mind, past and present merge; she imagines Mrs. Ramsay sitting in her house as she might have ten years ago, solicitous of the happiness of others but needing to affirm her own life by bringing others together in marriage: Paul and Minta, Lily and Bankes, Prue and a future lover. But Lily understands that time prevents Mrs. Ramsay from imposing order on life, as her death and the failure of the Rayleys' marriage makes clear.

As in Wordsworth, past memories affect current emotions and attitudes. Shaped by her memory of Mrs. Ramsay, Lily is – at least on this day – better able to relate to people and to get outside of herself and the protection of her art. She now takes part in the kind of meaningful silent speech that had been the basis of Mrs. Ramsay's ability to achieve empathy. She feels that Mr. Carmichael and she had not needed to speak. They had been thinking the same things and he had answered her without her asking him anything. He stood there as if he were spreading his hands over all the weakness and suffering of mankind; she thought he was surveying, tolerantly and compassionately, their final destiny.

(p. 309)

Hasn't Lily achieved a moment of community and sense of unity like those of Mrs. Ramsay? It is as if she were adopting Mrs. Ramsay's values at last. She has grown in tolerance, sympathy, understanding, and the ability to feel. She understands Mr. Ramsay as a human being rather than a symbol and feels the sympathy that he required that morning. In the last section this heightened emotional life informs her painting:

She looked at the steps; they were empty; she looked at her canvas; it was blurred. With a sudden intensity, as if she saw it clear for a second, she drew a line there, in the centre. It was done; it was finished. Yes, she thought, laying down her brush in extreme fatigue, I have had my vision.

(p. 310)

And it is as if the novel coheres; for isn't the complete painting the necessary metaphor for the art of writing the novel? The painting concludes a series of perceptions and fulfils a number of formal patterns: Mr. Ramsay's physical quest to take his son to the lighthouse and pay his penance to the memory of his wife; his quest to have his children; Lily's aesthetic and emotional maturation; James and Cam's passage from childhood to adulthood; the fulfilment of the symbol of the lighthouse – light, truth, immortality – as a counter to the flux and relativity of life and the writing of the novel.

The intermingling of the ordinary and the metaphorical is Woolf's characteristic way of telling. At times, however, she creates comparisons that urge a response that the literal level does not justify. Put another way, the intensity and energy of metaphors and allusions (discourse) do not merely complement the action (story), but violate the conventions of the novel of manners and morals. Such meaning unsupported by and even at odds with the action gives Woolf's novel its polyphonic character despite its frequently monologic voice.

Such a technique enables her to give individuality and complexity to a character's perception – to create a dialogic effect – without
fully surrendering her monologic voice. For example, to stress
James's anxiety, even paranoia, Woolf has James think of his father
as a wagon wheel crushing someone's foot:

> Suppose then that as a child sitting helpless in a perambulator,
> or on some one's knee, he had seen a waggon crush ignorantly
> and innocently, some one's foot? Suppose he had seen the foot
> first, in the grass, smooth, and whole; then the wheel; and the
> same foot, purple, crushed. But the wheel was innocent. So
> now, when his father came striding down the passage knocking
> them up early in the morning to go to the Lighthouse down it
> came over his foot, over Cam's foot, over anybody's foot.
>
> (p. 275)

But does Mr. Ramsay's conduct justify James's bizarre oedipal
fantasy of killing his father?

> [I]t was not him, that old man reading, whom he wanted to kill,
> but it was the thing that descended on him – without his
> knowing it perhaps: that fierce sudden black-winged harpy,
> with its talons and its beak all cold and hard, that struck and
> struck at you (he could feel the beak on his bare legs, where it
> had struck when he was a child), and then made off, and there
> he was again, an old man very sad, reading his book.
>
> (pp. 273–4)

Indeed, is not such a metaphor a sublimated version of the
violence which finally results in the World War? True, he recalls
his father's disturbing prophecy of rain years ago – the prophecy
that blasted his expectations of a perfect childhood day. Even if we
accept James's deep oedipal love for his mother ('she alone spoke
the truth; to her alone could he speak it' [p. 278]), the image of his
mother as a flowering tree fertilizing his father's sword – an image
that in Part III takes the form of the sword smiting through the tree
– is inappropriate to the responses of a young boy and not really
justified by the adolescent's felt experience as we see it: '[S]ome-
thing flourished up in the air, something arid and sharp
descended even there, like a blade, a scimitar, smiting through the
leaves and flowers even of that happy world and making it shrivel

and fall' (p. 276). By urging a metaphorical significance that action and characterization do not justify, Woolf sets up a tension between the language and the action that it comments upon, a tension that becomes central to our experience of reading her novels. (By contrast, metaphors in traditional novels such as *Emma* or *Tom Jones* do not create alternative effects, but reinforce the effects of action that is described.)

By having her narrator use questions and parentheses, Woolf qualifies the authority of her speaker's commentary and even her presentation of narrative vignettes, while suggesting the possibility of alternative commentary and episodes which would provide different perspectives. Reading lives, like reading texts, is an insuperable task. Thus Woolf's narrator, like her implied reader or narratee, is always marginal and always something of an outsider. Woolf is empathetic with those who, like all of us, are excluded from the plenitude of understanding, whether it be Bankes who feels nothing at dinner, Tansley who enters into the conversation without Lily's obvious deference to his masculine role, Lily who resents that she is patronized as a woman by Tansley and by Mrs. Ramsay as a single person – or the omniscient narrator, who is always at one remove from the imagined world she describes, and the reader, who is at a still further remove from the imagined world.

The lighthouse is an ordering principle within the sea; the sea suggests to Mrs. Ramsay (and Woolf as we know from *The Waves*) the process of the indifferent cosmos. But the amorphous, immeasurable sea also represents the resolution of death that Woolf both feared and sought:

> The monotonous fall of the waves on the beach ... remorselessly beat the measure of life, made one think of the destruction of the island and its engulfment in the sea, and warned her whose day had slipped past in one quick doing after another that it was all ephemeral as a rainbow – this sound which had been obscured and concealed under the other sounds suddenly thundered hollow in her ears and made her look up with an impulse of terror.
>
> (pp. 27–8)

As Poole notes, Rhoda in *The Waves* thinks of the waves in these terms: 'Rolling me over the waves will shoulder me under.

Everything falls in a tremendous shower, dissolving me.'[10] We recall the association of waves with destruction and madness in her diary: 'Let me watch the wave rise. I watch. Vanessa. Children. Failure. Yes; I detect that. Failure, failure. (the wave rises)' (*Diaries*, III, 15 Sept. 1926). And the wave promises to contain the dreaded sea monster – her 'vision of a fin rising on a wide blank sea' – that objectifies her fear of madness, of the unknown (*Diaries*, III, 4 Sept. 1927). Hadn't she written before that the 'old devil has once more got his spine through the waves'?[11] Within this interior sea, Woolf's lighthouse is the novel she is trying to write, a novel in which she proposes different ways of seeing and knowing.

Notes

1. I quote from *The Diaries of Virginia Woolf*, 4 vols, ed. Anne Oliver Bell (New York: Harcourt, Brace, Jovanovich, 1977–82) and *The Letters of Virginia Woolf*, 6 vols, ed. Nigel Nicholson (New York: Harcourt, Brace, Jovanovich, 1975–80).

   When I quote from the text of Woolf's novels, page numbers in parentheses refer to *Mrs. Dalloway* (New York: Harcourt, Brace & World, 1925), and *To the Lighthouse* (New York: Harcourt, Brace & World, 1927).

2. See Quentin Bell, *Virginia Woolf: a Biography*, 2 vols (New York: Harcourt, Brace, Jovanovich, 1972) II. 107.

3. Bell, II. 135–6.

4. Roger Poole, *The Unknown Virginia Woolf* (New York: Cambridge University Press, 1978) p. 14.

5. Poole, pp. 260–1.

6. Poole, p. 33.

7. Leonard Woolf, *The Journey Not The Arrival Matters*, p. 73; quoted in Poole, p. 23.

8. Berlin, Sir Isaiah, *The Hedgehog and the Fox: an Essay on Tolstoy's View of History* (New York: Simon Schuster, 1955) p. 1.

9. See, for example, Avrom Fleishman's discussion of *To the Lighthouse* in his *Virginia Woolf: a Critical Reading* (Baltimore: The Johns Hopkins University Press, 1975).

10. See Poole, p. 269.

11. See Bell, II. 109–10.

Selected Bibliography

I have included all the critical and scholarly studies cited in my notes plus a selection of works that are essential to the study of the early modern British novel and to understanding the current critical mindscape.

I GENERAL WORKS

Abrams, M. H., *The Mirror and the Lamp: Romantic Theory and the Critical Tradition* (New York: Oxford University Press, 1953).
_____, *Natural Supernaturalism: Tradition and Revolution in Romantic Literature* (New York: Norton, 1971).
_____, 'The Deconstructive Angel', *Critical Inquiry*, 4 (1977) pp. 425–38.
_____, 'How to Do Things with Texts', *Partisan Review*, 46 (1979) pp. 366–88.
Aristotle, *Poetics*, trans. Preston H. Epps (Chapel Hill: University of North Carolina Press, 1942; rpt. 1970).
Auerbach, Erich, *Mimesis: the Representation of Reality in Western Literature*, trans. Willard Trask (Princeton University Press, 1953).
Bakhtin, Mihkail, *Problems of Doestoevsky's Poetics*, ed. & trans. Caryl Emerson (Minneapolis: University of Minnesota Press, 1984).
_____, *The Dialogic Imagination*, ed. Michael Holquist, trans. Caryl Emerson and Michael Holquist (Austin: The University of Texas Press, 1981).
Barthes, Roland, 'Introduction to the Structural Analysis of Narrative' in *Image-Music-Text*, trans. Stephen Heath (New York: Hill & Wang, 1977) pp. 79–124.
_____, *The Pleasure of the Text* (New York: Hill & Wang, 1974).
_____, *S/Z* (New York: Hill & Wang, 1974).
Batchelor, John, *The Edwardian Novelists* (New York: St. Martin's Press, 1982).
Beach, Joseph Warren, *The Twentieth Century Novel: Studies in Technique* (New York: Appleton-Century, 1932).
Beja, Morris, *Epiphany in the Modern Novel* (Seattle: University of Washington Press, 1971).
Benjamin, Walter, *Illuminations* (trans. Harry Zohn, 1968. Rpt. New York: Schocken, 1969).
Berlin, Sir Isaiah, *The Hedgehog and the Fox: an Essay on Tolstoy's View of History* (New York: Simon Schuster, 1955).
Bloom, Harold, *The Anxiety of Influence: a Theory of Poetry* (New York: Oxford University Press, 1973).
_____, *A Map of Misreading* (New York: Oxford University Press, 1975).
_____, (ed.), *Romanticism and Consciousness* (New York: Norton, 1970).

Booth, Wayne, *The Rhetoric of Fiction* (University of Chicago Press, 1961; rev. edn 1983).
_____, 'Between Two Generations: the Heritage of the Chicago School' in *Profession 82* (1982) pp. 19–26.
_____, *Critical Understanding: the Powers and Limits of Pluralism* (University of Chicago Press, 1979).
_____, *Now Don't Try to Reason With Me: Essays and Ironies for a Credulous Age* (University of Chicago Press, 1970).
_____, 'The Rhetoric of Fiction and The Poetics of Fiction', *Novel*, 1:2 (winter 1968) pp. 105–13.
_____, *The Rhetoric of Irony* (University of Chicago Press, 1974).
Bradbury, Malcolm, *Possibilities: Essays on the State of the Novel* (New York: Oxford University Press, 1973).
Bradley, F. H., *Appearance and Reality* 2nd edn (London, 1908).
Brooks, Peter, *Reading For The Plot* (New York: Knopf, 1984).
Burke, Kenneth, *The Philosophy of Literary Form* (New York: Vintage, 1957).
Cain, William E., *The Crisis in Criticism: Theory, Literature, and Reform in English Studies* (Baltimore: Johns Hopkins University Press, 1984).
Calderwood, James L. and Toliver, Harold E., *Perspectives on Fiction* (New York: Oxford University Press, 1968).
Castillo, Debra A., *The Translated World* (Talahasee: Florida State University/University Press of Florida, 1985).
Chatman, Seymour Benjamin, *Story and Discourse: Narrative Structure in Fiction and Film* (Ithaca: Cornell University Press, 1978).
Crane, R. S., 'The Concept of Plot and the Plot of *Tom Jones*' in R. S. Crane (ed.), *Critics and Criticism* (University of Chicago Press, 1957).
Culler, Jonathan, *On Deconstruction: Theory and Criticism After Structuralism* (Ithaca: Cornell University Press, 1982).
_____, *The Pursuit of Signs: Semiotics, Literature, Deconstruction* (Ithaca: Cornell University Press, 1981).
_____, *Structuralist Poetics: Structuralism, Linguistics and the Study of Literature* (Ithaca: Cornell University Press, 1975).
De Man, Paul, *Allegories of Reading: Figural Language in Rousseau, Nietzsche and Proust* (New Haven, Conn.: Yale University Press, 1979).
_____, *Blindness and Insight: Essays in the Rhetoric of Contemporary Criticism* (New York: Oxford University Press, 1971).
Derrida, Jacques, *Writing and Difference* (University of Chicago Press, 1978).
Eagleton, Terry, *Literary Theory: an Introduction* (Minneapolis: University of Minnesota Press, 1983).
Eco, Umberto, *The Name of the Rose*, trans. William Weaver (New York: Warner Books, 1983).
Eliot, T. S., *Selected Essays*, new edn (New York: Harcourt, Brace & World, 1950).
Ellmann, Richard, *Eminent Domain* (New York: Oxford University Press, 1967).
Ellmann, Richard and Charles Feidelson, Jr, (eds), *The Modern Tradition: Backgrounds of Modern Literature* (New York: Oxford University Press, 1965).
Elsen, Albert E., *Rodin* (New York: Museum of Modern Art, 1963).

Fish, Stanley, *Is There a Text in the Class?* (Cambridge: Harvard University Press, 1980).

Forster, E. M., *Aspects of the Novel* (New York: Harcourt, Brace & World, 1954; orig. edn 1927).

Foucault, Michel, *Language, Counter-Memory, Practice: Selected Essays and Interviews*, trans. Donald F. Bouchard and Sherry Simon (Ithaca, N.Y.: Cornell University Press, 1977).

Frank, Joseph, 'Spatial Form in Modern Literature', *Sewanee Review*, 53 (1945) pp. 221–40, 435–56, 643–53.

_____, 'Spatial Form: an Answer to Critics', *Critical Inquiry*, 4 (winter 1977) pp. 231–52.

_____, *The Widening Gyre: Crisis and Mastery in Modern Literature* (New Brunswick, N.J.: Rutgers University Press, 1963).

Friedman, Alan, *The Turn of the Novel* (New York: Oxford University Press, 1966).

Frye, Northrop, *Anatomy of Criticism: Four Essays* (Princeton University Press, 1957).

Genette, Gerard, *Narrative Discourse: an Essay in Method*, trans. Jane E. Lewin (Ithaca, N.Y.: Cornell University Press, 1980).

Girard, Rene, *Deceit, Desire, and the Novel: Self and Other in Literary Structure*, trans. Yvonne Freccero (Baltimore: The Johns Hopkins University Press, 1965).

Glueck, Grace, 'A Lively Review of the Futurist Experience', *New York Times, Arts and Leisure* (1 May 1983).

_____, 'John Miro Exhibit, Sculpture and Ceramics', *New York Times* (4 May 1984) p. C24.

Gould, Stephen Jay, Review essay of Evelyn Fox Feller, *A Feeling for Organism: the Life and Work of Barbara McClintock*, *New York Review of Books*, 31:5 (20 Mar. 1984) pp. 3–6.

Graff, Gerald, *Literature Against Itself: Literary Ideas in Modern Society* (University of Chicago Press, 1979).

Harari, Josue (ed.), *Textual Strategies: Perspectives in Post-Structuralist Criticism* (Ithaca, N.Y.: Cornell University Press, 1979).

Hardy, Barbara Nathan, 'Toward a Poetics of Fiction: an Approach Through Narrative', *Novel*, 2:1 (autumn 1968) pp. 5–14.

Hartman, Geoffrey, *Criticism in the Wilderness* (New Haven, Conn.: Yale University Press, 1980).

_____, 'The Culture of Criticism', *PMLA*, 99:3 (May 1984).

_____, *Saving the Text: Literature, Derrida, Philosophy* (Baltimore: The Johns Hopkins University Press, 1981).

Harvey, W. J., *Character and the Novel* (Ithaca, N.Y.: Cornell University Press, 1965).

Hirsch, E. D., *The Aims of Interpretation* (University of Chicago Press, 1976).

_____, *Validity in Interpretation* (New Haven, Conn.: Yale University Press, 1967).

Hofstadter, Douglas, *Gödel, Escher, Bach: an Eternal Golden Braid* (New York: Basic Books, 1979).

Holland, Norman M., *The Dynamics of Literary Response* (New York: Oxford University Press, 1968).

Iser, Wolfgang, *The Implied Reader: Patterns of Communication in Prose Fiction from Bunyan to Beckett* (Baltimore: The Johns Hopkins University Press, 1974).

———, *The Act of Reading: a Theory of Aesthetic Response* (Baltimore: The Johns Hopkins University Press, 1978).

James, Henry, 'The Art of Fiction' (1884), in James E. Miller (ed.), *Theory of Fiction: Henry James* (Lincoln: University of Nebraska Press, 1972).

———, *The Art of the Novel: Critical Prefaces*, ed. R. P. Blackmur (New York: Charles Scribner's Sons, 1934).

———, *Notes on Novelists* (New York: Charles Scribner's Sons, 1914).

Kellman, Steven G., *Loving Reading: Erotics of the Text* (Hamden, Connecticut: Archon–The Shoe String Press, 1985).

Kenner, Hugh, *The Pound Era* (Berkeley and Los Angeles: University of California Press, 1971).

Kermode, Frank, *The Genesis of Secrecy: an Interpretation of Narrative* (Cambridge, Mass.: Harvard University Press, 1979).

———, *Romantic Image* (London: Routledge & Kegan Paul, 1957).

———, 'Secrets and Narrative Sequence', in Mitchell, W. J. T. (ed.), *On Narrative* (University of Chicago Press, 1981).

———, *The Sense of an Ending: Studies in the Theory of Fiction* (New York: Oxford University Press, 1966).

———, *The Art of Telling: Essays on Fiction* (Cambridge: Harvard University Press, 1983).

Kiely, Robert, *Beyond Egotism* (Cambridge: Harvard University Press, 1980).

Langbaum, Robert, *The Modern Spirit: Essays on the Continuity of Nineteenth and Twentieth Century Literature* (New York: Oxford University Press, 1970).

———, 'The Epiphanic Mode in Wordsworth and Modern Literature', *New Literary History*, 14:2 (winter 1983).

Leavis, F. R., *The Great Tradition: George Eliot, Henry James, Joseph Conrad* (London: Chatto & Windus, 1948).

Lentricchia, Frank, *After the New Criticism* (University of Chicago Press, 1980).

Levine, George, *The Realistic Imagination: English Fiction from Frankenstein to Lady Chatterley* (University of Chicago Press, 1981).

Lodge, David, *Language of Fiction: Essays in Criticism and Verbal Analysis of the English Novel* (New York: Columbia University Press, 1966).

———, *The Modes of Modern Writing: Metaphor, Metonymy, and the Typology of Modern Literature* (Ithaca, N.Y.: Cornell University Press, 1977).

———, *Working with Structuralism: Essays and Reviews on Nineteenth- and Twentieth-Century Literature* (London: Routledge & Kegan Paul, 1981).

Lubbock, Percy, *The Craft of Fiction* (New York: Viking, 1957, orig. edn 1921).

Lukacs, Georg, *Studies in the European Novel* (New York: Grossett & Dunlap, 1964).

Mack, Maynard and Ian Gregor (eds), *Imagined Worlds: Essays in Honour of John Butt* (London: Methuen, 1968).

Marcus, Steven, *The Other Victorians: a Study of Sexuality and Pornography in*

Mid-Nineteenth-Century England (New York: Basic Books, 1966).

Martz, Louis L. and Williams, Aubrey (eds), *The Author in His Work* (New Haven, Conn.: Yale University Press, 1978).

McKeon, Richard, *Thought, Action, and Passion* (University of Chicago Press, 1954).

Miller, D. A., *Narrative and its Discontents: Problems of Closure in the Traditional Novel* (Princeton University Press, 1981).

Miller, J. Hillis, *The Disappearance of God: Five Nineteenth-Century Writers* (Cambridge, Mass.: Harvard University Press, 1963).

———, *Fiction and Repetition: Seven English Novels* (Cambridge, Mass.: Harvard University Press, 1982).

———, *Poets of Reality: Six Twentieth Century Writers* (Cambridge: The Belknap Press of Harvard University Press, 1965).

———, *The Form of Victorian Fiction* (Notre Dame: University of Notre Dame Press, 1968).

Mitchell, W. J. T. (ed.), *On Narrative* (University of Chicago Press, 1981), repr. of articles from *Critical Inquiry*, 7:1 (autumn 1980) and 7:4 (summer 1981).

Norris, Margot, *Beasts of the Modern Imagination: Darwin, Nietzsche, Kafka, Ernst, and Lawrence* (Baltimore: The Johns Hopkins University Press, 1985).

Nuttal, A. D., *A New Mimesis: Shakespeare and the Representation of Reality* (New York: Methuen, 1983).

Plato, *Symposium*, trans. Walter Hamilton (New York: Penguin, 1951).

Poulet, Georges, 'Phenomenology of Reading', *New Literary History*, 1:1 (Oct. 1969) pp. 53–68.

———, 'Criticism and the Experience of Interiority,' in *The Structuralist Controversy: The Languages of Criticism and the Sciences of Man*, ed. Richard Macksey and Eugene Donato (Baltimore: Johns Hopkins University Press, 1970).

Pratt, Mary Louise, *Towards A Speech Act Theory of Literary Discourse* (Bloomington: Indiana University Press, 1977).

Price, Martin, *Forms of Life: Character and Moral Imagination in the Novel* (New Haven, Conn.: Yale University Press, 1983).

Riffaterre, Michael, 'Interpretative and Descriptive Poetry: a Reading of Wordsworth's "Yew-Trees"', *New Literary History*, 4 (winter 1973).

Rosenbaum, S. P. (ed.), *The Bloomsbury Group* (University of Toronto Press, 1975).

Sacks, Sheldon, *Fiction and the Shape of Belief* (Berkeley and Los Angeles: University of California Press, 1967).

———, (ed.), *On Metaphor* (University of Chicago Press, 1979).

Said, Edward, *Beginnings: Intention and Method* (New York: Basic Books, 1975).

Scholes, Robert (ed.), *Approaches to the Novel* (San Francisco: Chandler Publishing Co., 1961; rev. edn 1966).

Scholes, Robert and Robert Kellogg, *The Nature of Narrative* (New York: Oxford University Press, 1966).

Schorer, Mark *et. al.* (eds), *Criticism: the Foundation of Modern Literary Judgement*, rev. edn (New York: Harcourt, Brace, 1958).

————, *The World We Imagine* (New York: Farrar, Straus, Giroux, 1968).

————, 'Technique as Discovery', *Hudson Review* (1948), repr. in Calderwood, James L. and Toliver, Harold E., *Perspectives on Fiction* (New York: Oxford University Press, 1968).

Schwarz, Daniel R., *The Humanistic Heritage: Critical Theories of The English Novel From James to Hillis Miller* (London: Macmillan; Philadelphia: University of Pennsylvania Press, 1986).

Searle, John R., *Speech Acts: an Essay in the Philosophy of Language* (London: Cambridge University Press, 1969).

————, *Expression and Meaning: Studies in the Theory of Speech Acts* (Cambridge, England; New York: Cambridge University Press, 1979).

————, Review of *On Deconstruction*, by Jonathan Culler, *New York Review of Books*, 27 October 1983, 74–79.

————, Kiefer, Ferenc, & Bierwisch, Manfred, (eds), *Speech Act Theory and Pragmatics* (Dordrecht, Holland; Boston: D. Reidel, 1980).

Smith, Barbara Herrnstein, 'Narrative Versions, Narrative Theories', in Mitchell, W. J. T. (ed.), *On Narrative* (University of Chicago Press, 1981).

————, *Poetic Closure: a Study of How Poems End* (University of Chicago Press, 1968).

Sturrock, John, *Structuralism and Since: from Levi-Strauss to Derrida* (Oxford University Press, 1979).

Suleiman, Susan, and Crosman, Inge (eds), *The Reader in the Text: Essays on Audience and Interpretation* (Princeton University Press, 1980).

Thickstun, William, *Visionary Closure in the Modern Novel* (London: Macmillan, 1987).

Todorov, Tzvetan, 'Structural Analysis of Narrative', *Novel*, 3:1 (autumn 1969) pp. 70–6.

————, *The Poetics of Prose*, trans. Richard Howard (Ithaca, N.Y.: Cornell University Press, 1977).

Tompkins, Jane P. (ed.), *Reader Response Criticism* (Baltimore: The Johns Hopkins University Press, 1980).

Torgovnick, Marianna, *Closure in the Novel* (Princeton University Press, 1981).

Trilling, Lionel, *The Liberal Imagination* (New York: Viking Press, 1950).

————, *The Opposing Self: Nine Essays in Criticism* (New York: Viking Press, 1955).

Van Ghent, Dorothy, *The English Novel: Form and Function* (New York: Harper & Row, 1953).

Watt, Ian, *The Rise of the Novel* (Berkeley and Los Angeles: University of California Press, 1957).

Weinstein, Philip M., *The Semantics of Desire: Changing Models of Identity from Dickens to Joyce* (Princeton, N.J.: Princeton University Press, 1984).

White, Hayden, 'The Value of Narrativity in the Representation of Reality', in Mitchell, W. J. T. (ed.), *On Narrative* (University of Chicago Press, 1981).

Williams, Raymond, *The English Novel from Dickens to Lawrence* (New York: Oxford University Press, 1970).

————, *Politics and Letters* (London: New Left Books, 1979).

Wilson, Edmund, *Axel's Castle: a Study in the Imaginative Literature of 1870–*

1930 (New York: Charles Scribner's Sons, 1959).

Woolf, Virginia, 'Mr. Bennett and Mrs. Brown' (1924) in *The Captain's Death Bed* (New York: Harcourt, Brace & Co., 1950).

II HISTORICAL

Annan, Noel, 'The Intellectual Aristocracy', in *Studies in Social History. A Tribute to G. M. Trevelyan,* ed. J. H. Plumb (London & New York: Longmans, Green, 1955).

Cox, C. B. and Dyson, A. E. (eds), *The Twentieth-Century Mind,* 3 vols (London: Oxford University Press, 1972).

Dangerfield, George, *The Strange Death of Liberal England* (New York: Capricorn Books, 1935; repr. New York: Putnam, 1980).

Ford, Boris (ed.), *The Modern Age,* vol. 7 of *The Pelican Guide to English Literature,* 3rd edn (Baltimore: Penguin, 1973).

Fussell, Paul, *The Great War and Modern Memory* (New York: Oxford University Press, 1975).

Great Victorian Paintings (London: Arts Council Publication, 1968).

Houghton, Walter E., *The Victorian Frame of Mind* (New Haven, Conn.: Yale University Press, 1957).

Hynes, Samuel, *The Edwardian Turn of Mind* (Princeton University Press, 1968).

Lester, John A., Jr, *Journey Through Despair 1880–1914* (Princeton University Press, 1968).

III FEMINIST

Abel, Elizabeth (ed.), *Writing and Sexual Difference,* Special issue of *Critical Inquiry,* 8 (1981). See especially 'Editor's Introduction', pp. 173–8; and Elaine Showalter, 'Feminist Criticism in the Wilderness', pp. 179–205.

Felman, Shoshana (ed.), *Literature and Psychoanalysis* (Baltimore: The Johns Hopkins University Press, 1982).

Fetterley, Judith, *The Resisting Reader: a Feminist Approach to American Fiction* (Bloomington: Indiana University Press, 1978).

Frye, Joanne S., *Living Stories, Telling Lives: Women in the Novel* (Ann Arbor: University of Michigan Press, 1985).

Gallop, Jane, *The Daughter's Seduction: Feminism and Psychoanalysis* (Ithaca, N.Y.: Cornell University Press, 1982).

Gilbert, Sandra M. and Gubar, Susan, *The Madwoman in the Attic: The Woman Writer and the Nineteenth-Century Imagination* (New Haven, Conn.: Yale University Press, 1979).

Heilbrun, Carolyn and Higonnet, Margaret R. (eds), *The Representation of Women in Fiction* (Baltimore: Johns Hopkins University Press, 1983).

Jacobus, Mary, *Reading Woman: Essays in Feminist Criticism* (New York: Columbia University Press, 1986).

———, (ed.), *Women Writing and Writing About Women* (New York: Barnes & Noble, 1979).

Kolodny, Annette, 'Dancing Through the Minefield: Some Observations on the Theory, Practice and Politics of a Feminist Literary Criticism', *Feminist Studies*, 6 (1980) pp. 1–25.

Lacan, Jacques, *Feminine Sexuality*, eds. J. Mitchell and J. Rose (London: Macmillan, 1982).

Marks, Elaine and de Courtivron, Isabelle (eds), *New French Feminisms: an Anthology* (Amherst: University of Massachusetts Press, 1980).

McConnell-Ginet, Sally and Furman, Nelly (eds), *Women and Language in Literature and Society* (New York: Praeger, 1980).

Miller, Nancy K., 'Emphasis Added: Plots and Plausibilities in Women's Fiction', *PMLA*, 96 (1981) pp. 36–48.

Millett, Kate, *Sexual Politics* (New York: Doubleday, 1970).

Showalter, Elaine, *A Literature of Their Own: British Women Novelists from Brontë to Lessing* (Princeton University Press, 1977).

Woolf, Virginia, *A Room of One's Own* (New York: Harcourt, Brace & World, 1957; orig. edn 1929).

IV   MARXIST

Demetz, Peter, *Marx, Engels, and the Poets*, trans. Jeffrey L. Sammons (University of Chicago Press, 1967).

Eagleton, Terry, *Marxism and Literary Criticism* (London: Methuen, 1976).

———, *Criticism and Ideology* (London: NLB, 1976).

Jameson, Frederic, *Marxism and Form* (Princeton University Press, 1972).

———, *The Political Unconscious* (Ithaca, N.Y.: Cornell University Press, 1981).

Williams, Raymond, *Marxism and Literature* (Oxford University Press, 1977).

V   THOMAS HARDY

De Laura, David J., ' "The Ache of Modernism" in Hardy's Later Novels', *ELH*, XXII (1967) pp. 380–99.

Eliot, T. S., *After Strange Gods* (New York: Harcourt, Brace & Co., 1934).

Friedman, Alan, 'Thomas Hardy: "Weddings Be Funerals" ' in *The Turn of the Novel*, pp. 38–65 (New York: Harcourt, Brace & Co., 1966).

Gittings, Robert, *Young Thomas Hardy* (Boston: Little, Brown, 1975).

———, *Thomas Hardy's Later Years* (Boston: Little, Brown, 1978).

Gose, Elliot B., Jr., 'Psychic Evolution: Darwinism and Initiation in *Tess of the d'Urbervilles*', *NCF* 18 (1963).

Gregor, Ian, *The Great Web: The Form of Hardy's Major Fiction* (London: Faber & Faber, 1974).

———, 'What Kind of Fiction Did Hardy Write?', *Essays in Criticism*, 16 (1966) pp. 290–308.

Guerard, Albert J. (ed.), *Hardy: a Collection of Critical Essays* (Englewood Cliffs, N.J.: Prentice-Hall, 1973).

———, *Thomas Hardy: The Novels and Stories* (Cambridge, Mass.: Harvard University Press, 1949).

Hardy, Florence Emily, *The Early Life of Thomas Hardy* (New York: Macmillan, 1928).

———, *The Later Years of Thomas Hardy* (New York: Macmillan, 1930).

Howe, Irving, *Thomas Hardy* (New York: Macmillan, 1967).

Johnson, Bruce, *True Correspondence: a Phenomenology of Thomas Hardy's Novels* (Jacksonville: Florida State University Press, 1983).

Kramer, Dale (ed.), *Critical Approaches to the Fiction of Thomas Hardy* (London: Macmillan, 1979).

Miller, J. Hillis, *Thomas Hardy: Distance and Desire* (Cambridge, Mass: Harvard University Press, 1970).

Millgate, Michael, *Thomas Hardy: His Career as a Novelist* (New York: Random House, 1971).

———, *Thomas Hardy: a Biography* (New York: Random House, 1982).

Modern Fiction Studies, Thomas Hardy issue, VI (Fall 1960).

Pinion, F. B., *A Hardy Companion: a Guide to the Works of Thomas Hardy and Their Background* (New York: St. Martin's, 1968).

Southern Review, The, Thomas Hardy Centennial Issue, VI (summer 1940).

Squires, Michael, *The Pastoral Novel: Studies in George Eliot, Thomas Hardy, and D. H. Lawrence* (Charlottesville: University of Virginia Press, 1974).

Vigar, Penelope, *The Novels of Thomas Hardy: Illusion and Reality* (London: Athlone Press, 1974).

Webster, Harvey Curtis, *On a Darkling Plain: the Art and Thought of Thomas Hardy* (University of Chicago Press, 1947).

Woolf, Virginia, 'The Novels of Thomas Hardy', in *The Second Common Reader* (New York, 1932; first published in *The Times Literary Supplement*, 19 Jan. 1928).

VI   JOSEPH CONRAD

Baines, Jocelyn, *Joseph Conrad: a Critical Biography* (New York: McGraw-Hill, 1960).

Daleski, H. M., *Joseph Conrad: the Way of Dispossession* (New York: Holmes & Meier, 1976).

Fleishman, Avrom, *Conrad's Politics: Community and Anarchy in the Fiction of Joseph Conrad* (Baltimore: The Johns Hopkins University Press, 1967).

Guerard, Albert, *Conrad the Novelist* (Cambridge, Mass.: Harvard University Press, 1958).

Guetti, James, *The Limits of Metaphor: a Study of Melville, Conrad, and Faulkner* (Ithaca, N.Y.: Cornell University Press, 1967).

Hay, Eloise Knapp, *The Political Novels of Joseph Conrad* (University of Chicago Press, 1963).

Jean-Aubry, G. *Joseph Conrad: Life and Letters*, 2 vols (Garden City, N.Y.: Doubleday, Page & Co., 1927).

Johnson, Bruce, *Conrad's Models of Mind* (Minneapolis: University of Minnesota Press, 1971).

Karl, Frederick, *Joseph Conrad: the Three Lives* (New York: Farrar, Straus & Giroux, 1979).

Meyer, Bernard, *Joseph Conrad: a Psychoanalytic Biography* (Princeton, N.J.: Princeton University Press, 1967).

Moser, Thomas, *Joseph Conrad: Achievement and Decline* (Cambridge University Press, 1957).

Nadjer, Zdzislaw, *Conrad's Polish Background* (London: Oxford University Press, 1964).

———, *Joseph Conrad: a Chronicle* trans. Halina Carroll-Najder (New Brunswick, N.J.: Rutgers University Press, 1983).

Rosenfield, Claire, *Paradise of Snakes: an Archetypal Analysis of Conrad's Political Novels* (Chicago University Press, 1967).

Schwarz, Daniel, *Conrad: 'Almayer's Folly' Through 'Under Western Eyes'* (London: Macmillan Press; Ithaca, N.Y.: Cornell University Press, 1980).

———, *Conrad: the Later Fiction* (London: Macmillan Press; New York: The Humanities Press, 1982).

Van Ghent, Dorothy, 'Introduction to *Nostromo*. By Joseph Conrad' (New York: Holt, Rhinehart & Winston, 1961).

Watt, Ian, *Conrad in the Nineteenth Century* (Berkeley and Los Angeles: University of California Press, 1979).

Watts, C. T. (ed.), *Joseph Conrad's Letters to R. B. Cunninghame-Graham* (Cambridge University Press, 1969).

VII D. H. LAWRENCE

Balbert, Peter and Marcus, Phillip L. (eds), *D. H. Lawrence: a Centenary Consideration* (Ithaca, N.Y.: Cornell University Press, 1985).

Cavitch, David, *D. H. Lawrence and the New World* (New York and London: Oxford University Press, 1969).

Daleski, H. M., *The Forked Flame: a Study of D. H. Lawrence* (London: Faber & Faber, 1965).

Delavenay, Emile, *D. H. Lawrence, the Man and His Work: the Formative Years: 1885–1919*, trans. Katharine M. Delavenay (Carbondale: Southern Illinois University Press, 1972).

Gordon, David J., *D. H. Lawrence As A Literary Critic* (New Haven, Conn.: Yale University Press, 1960).

Hamalian, Leo, *D. H. Lawrence in Italy* (New York: Taplinger, 1982).

Herzinger, Kim, *D. H. Lawrence in His Time: 1908–1915* (Lewisberg, Pa.: Bucknell University Press, 1982).

Kermode, Frank, *D. H. Lawrence* (New York: Viking Press, 1973).

Kinkead-Weekes, Mark, 'The Marble and the Statue: The Exploratory Imagination of D. H. Lawrence', in Maynard Mack and Ian Gregor (eds), *Imagined Worlds: Essays on Some English Novels and Novelists in Honor of John Butt* (London: Methuen, 1968).

Lawrence, D. H., *Letters*, vol. I, ed. James T. Boulton (1979); vol. II, eds George J. Zytaruk and James T. Boulton (1981); vol. III, eds James T. Boulton and Andrew Robertson (New York: Cambridge University Press, 1984).

_____, *Letters*, ed. Aldous Huxley (New York: Viking Press, 1932).

_____, *The Collected Letters*, ed. Harry T. Moore (New York: Viking Press, 1962).

_____, *Apocalypse and the Writings on Revelation* (1932), ed. Mara Kalnins (New York: Cambridge University Press, 1980).

_____, *Fantasia of the Unconscious* (1922; repr. New York: Viking Press, 1960).

_____, *Phoenix II* (New York: The Viking Press, 1968).

_____, *Psychoanalysis and the Unconscious* (1921; repr. New York: Viking Press, 1960).

_____, *Study of Thomas Hardy and Other Essays*, ed. Bruce Steele (Cambridge University Press, 1984).

Martz, Louis, 'Portrait of Miriam: a Study in the Design of *Sons and Lovers*', in Maynard Mack and Ian Gregor (eds), *Imagined Worlds: Essays on Some English Novels and Novelists in Honor of John Butt* (London: Methuen, 1968).

Meyers, Jeffrey, *D. H. Lawrence and the Experience of Italy* (Philadelphia: University of Pennsylvania Press, 1982).

_____, (ed.) *D. H. Lawrence and Tradition* (Lambert: University of Massachusetts Press, 1985).

Moore, Harry T., *The Life and Works of D. H. Lawrence* (New York: Twayne, 1951).

_____, *The Priest of Love: a Life of D. H. Lawrence* (New York: Farrar, Straus & Giroux, 1974).

_____, (ed.), *A D. H. Lawrence Miscellany* (Carbondale: Southern Illinois University Press, 1959).

Moynahan, Julian, *The Deed of Life: the Novels and Tales of D. H. Lawrence* (Princeton University Press, 1963).

Parmenter, Ross, *Lawrence in Oaxaca: a Quest for the Novelist in Mexico* (Layton, Utah: Gibbs M. Smith, 1984).

Spilka, Mark, *The Love Ethic of D. H. Lawrence* (Bloomington: Indiana University Press, 1955).

_____, (ed.), *D. H. Lawrence: a Collection of Critical Essays* (Englewood Cliffs, N.J.: Prentice-Hall, 1963).

Tedlock, Ernest W., Jr, *D. H. Lawrence, Artist and Rebel: a Study of Lawrence's Fiction* (Albuquerque: University of New Mexico Press, 1963).

Woolf, Virginia, 'Notes on D. H. Lawrence', in *Collected Essays*, vol. I (London: The Hogarth Press, 1966).

Worthen, John, *D. H. Lawrence and the Idea of the Novel* (London: Macmillan Press, 1979).

VIII JAMES JOYCE

Blackmur, R. P., 'The Jew in Search of a Son', *Virginia Quarterly Review* XXIV (1948) pp. 109–112, repr. in *Eleven Essays on the European Novel* (New York: Harcourt, Brace & World, 1964).

Budgen, Frank, *James Joyce and the Making of Ulysses* orig. ed. 1934 (Bloomington: Indiana University Press, 1960).

Eliot, T. S., '*Ulysses*: Order and Myth', *The Dial* (Nov. 1923), repr. in *James Joyce: Two Decades of Criticism*, ed. Seon Givens (New York: Vanguard Press, 1948).

Ellmann, Richard, *James Joyce* (New York: Oxford University Press, rev. edn 1984).

———, *Ulysses on the Liffey* (New York: Oxford University Press, 1972).

———, *The Consciousness of Joyce* (New York: Oxford University Press, 1977).

———, 'The Big Word in "Ulysses" ', *The New York Review of Books*, 31:16 (25 Oct. 1984) pp. 31–2.

French, Marilyn, *The Book as World: James Joyce's Ulysses* (Cambridge, Mass.: Harvard University Press, 1976).

Gifford, Don and Seidman, Robert J., *Notes for Joyce: an Annotation of James Joyce's Ulysses* (New York: Sutton, 1974).

Gilbert, Stuart, *James Joyce's Ulysses* (New York: Random House, 1930; rev. edn 1952; rpt. 1955).

Goldberg, S. L., *The Classical Temper: a Study of James Joyce's Ulysses* (New York: Barnes & Noble, 1961).

Goldman, Arnold, *The Joyce Paradox: Form and Freedom in His Fiction* (London: Routledge & Kegan Paul, 1966).

Groden, Michael, *Ulysses in Progress* (Princeton University Press, 1977).

Hayman, David, *Ulysses: the Mechanics of Meaning* (Englewood Cliffs, N.J.: Prentice-Hall, 1970).

Herring, Phillip F. (ed.), *Joyce's Notes and Early Drafts for Ulysses* (Charlottesville: University of Virginia Press, 1977).

Joyce, James, *The Critical Writings*, eds Ellsworth Mason and Richard Ellmann (New York: Viking, 1959).

———, *Letters*, vol. I, ed. Stuart Gilbert (London: Faber & Faber, 1966).

———, *Dubliners: Text, Criticism, and Notes*, eds Robert Scholes and A. Walton Litz (New York: Viking Press, 1969).

———, *The James Joyce Archives: Ulysses* vols, ed. Michael Groden (New York: Garland Publishing, Inc., 1978).

———, *A Portrait of the Artist as Young Man* (1916; text corrected by Chester G. Anderson and edited by Richard Ellmann, New York: Viking Press, 1964).

———, *Selected Letters of James Joyce*, ed. Richard Ellmann (New York: Viking Press, 1975).

———, *Stephen Hero* (1944; rev. edn, ed. Theodore Spencer, New York: New Directions, 1963).

———, *Ulysses* (1922; rev. edn, New York: Modern Library – Random House, 1961).

_____, *Ulysses: a Critical and Synoptic Edition*, ed. Hans Gabler with Wolfhard Steppe and Claus Melchior (New York and London: Garland, 1984).

Joyce, Stanislaus, *My Brother's Keeper: James Joyce's 'Early Years'*, ed. Richard Ellmann (New York: Viking Press, 1958).

Kain, Richard, *Fabulous Voyager: a Study of James Joyce's Ulysses* (New York: Viking, 1947; repr. 1959).

Kenner, Hugh, *Joyce's Voices* (Berkeley: University of California Press, 1978).

_____, *Ulysses* (London: Allen & Unwin, 1980).

_____, *Dublin's Joyce* (1956; repr. Boston: Beacon Press, 1962).

Lawrence, Karen, *The Odyssey of Style in Ulysses* (Princeton University Press, 1981).

Rader, Ralph W., 'Exodus and Return: Joyce's *Ulysses* and the Fiction of the Actual', *University of Toronto Quarterly*, 48 (winter 1978/79) pp. 149–71.

Schwarz, Daniel R., *Reading Joyce's 'Ulysses'* (London: Macmillan; New York: St. Martin's Press, 1987).

Staley, Thomas F. (ed.), *Fifty Years: Ulysses* (Bloomington: Indiana University Press, 1974), repr. of *James Joyce Quarterly*, 10:1 (autumn 1972).

Stanford, W. B., *The Ulysses Theme* (Oxford: Blackwell, 1954).

Thornton, Weldon, *Allusions in Ulysses: a Line-by-Line Reference to Joyce's Complex Symbolism* (Chapel Hill: University of North Carolina Press, 1968; repr. New York: Simon & Schuster, 1973).

IX VIRGINIA WOOLF

Beja, Morris, 'Matches Struck in the Dark: Virginia Woolf's Moments of Vision', *Critical Quarterly*, IV (summer 1964), repr. in Morris Beja, ed. *Virginia Woolf, To the Lighthouse: a Casebook* (London: Macmillan, 1970).

Bell, Quentin, *Virginia Woolf: a Biography* (New York: Harcourt, Brace, Jovanovich, 1972).

DiBattista, Maria, *Virginia Woolf's Major Novels: the Fables of Anon* (New Haven, Conn.: Yale University Press, 1980).

Fleishman, Avrom, *Virginia Woolf: a Critical Reading* (Baltimore: The Johns Hopkins University Press, 1975).

Heilbrun, Carolyn, 'The Androgynous Vision in *To the Lighthouse*', in *Toward a Recognition of Androgyny* (New York: Alfred A. Knopf, 1968), repr. in Thomas S. W. Lewis, ed. *Virginia Woolf: a Collection of Criticism* (New York: McGraw-Hill, 1975).

Leaska, Mitchell, *The Novels of Virginia Woolf* (New York: John Jay Press, 1977).

Majundar, Robin and McLaurin, Allen (ed.), *Virginia Woolf: the Critical Heritage* (Boston: Routledge & Kegan Paul, 1975).

Marcus, Jane (ed.), *The Unknown Virginia Woolf: New Feminist Essays on Virginia Woolf* (Lincoln: University of Nebraska Press, 1981).

———, *Virginia Woolf: a Feminist Slant* (Lincoln: University of Nebraska Press, 1983).

McLaurin, Allen, *Virginia Woolf: the Echoes Enslaved* (Cambridge University Press, 1973).

Poole, Roger, *The Unknown Virginia Woolf* (New York: Cambridge University Press, 1978).

Richter, Harvena, *Virginia Woolf: the Inward Voyage* (Princeton University Press, 1970).

Rosenthal, Michael, *Virginia Woolf* (New York: Columbia University Press, 1979).

Silver, Brenda R., *Virginia Woolf's Reading Notebooks* (Princeton University Press, 1981).

Spilka, Mark, *Virginia Woolf's Quarrel With Grieving* (Lincoln: University of Nebraska Press, 1980).

Woolf, Leonard, *The Journey not the Arrival Matters: an Autobiography of the Years 1939–1969* (New York: Harcourt, Brace, Jovanovich, 1970).

Woolf, Virginia, *The Diaries of Virginia Woolf*, 4 vols, ed. Anne Oliver Bell (New York: Harcourt, Brace, Jovanovich, 1977–82).

———, *The Letters of Virginia Woolf*, 6 vols, ed. Nigel Nicholson (New York: Harcourt, Brace, Jovanovich, 1975–80).

X   E. M. FORSTER

Bradbury, Malcolm (ed.), *Forster: a Collection of Critical Essays* (Englewood Cliffs, N.J.: Prentice-Hall, 1966).

Colmer, John, *E. M. Forster: the Personal Voice* (London; Boston: Routledge & Kegan Paul, 1975).

Crews, Frederick C., *E. M. Forster: The Perils of Humanism* (Princeton University Press, 1962).

Das, G. K., *E. M. Forster's India* (London: Macmillan, 1977).

———, and John Beer (eds), *E. M. Forster: a Human Exploration* (New York University Press, 1969).

Forster, E. M., *Selected Letters of E. M. Forster*, eds Mary Lago, and P. N. Furbank (Cambridge: Harvard University Press, 1983).

Furbank, P. N., *E. M. Forster: a Life* (London: Secker & Warburg, 1977).

Herz, Judith Scherer and Robert K. Martin, *E. M. Forster: Centenary Revaluations* (University of Toronto Press, 1982).

Lewis, Robin Jared, *E. M. Forster's Passages to India* (New York: Columbia University Press, 1979).

Martin, Richard, *The Love That Failed: Ideal and Reality in the Writings of E. M. Forster* (The Hague: Mouton, 1974).

McConkey, James, *The Novels of E. M. Forster* (Ithaca, N.Y. Cornell University Press, 1957).

McDowell, Frederick P., *E. M. Forster* (New York: Twayne Publishers, 1969; rev. edn 1982).

Rosecrance, Barbara, *Forster's Narrative Vision* (Ithaca, N.Y.: Cornell University Press, 1982).

Schwarz, Daniel R., 'The Importance of E. M. Forster's *Aspects of the Novel*', *The South Atlantic Quarterly*, 82 (spring 1983) pp. 189–208.

Shahane, Vasant A. (ed.), *Approaches to E. M. Forster: a Centenary Volume* (New Delhi: Arnold-Heinemann, 1981).

Stone, Wilfred, *The Cave and the Mountain: a Study of E. M. Forster* (Stanford University Press, 1966).

Trilling, Lionel, *E. M. Forster* (New York: New Directions, 1964; orig. edn 1943).

Index